SUNDAY

MISSAL

2017–2018

✝ Living with Christ

LITURGICAL CALENDAR FOR YEAR B *(2017-2018)*

✝Living with Christ

SUNDAY MISSAL

2017-2018

with Prayers and Hymns

Approved for use in Canada

NOVALIS

©2017 Novalis Publishing Inc.

Novalis Publishing Inc.
10 Lower Spadina Ave., Suite 400
Toronto, ON M5V 2Z2
Canada

Telephone: 1-800-387-7164
Fax: 1-800-204-4140
Email: books@novalis.ca

www.novalis.ca

Since 1936 Novalis has dedicated itself to the development of pastoral
resources which assist the People of God in preparing for and participating
in the liturgy.

Please write, phone, or visit us for further information on our publications,
or visit our website at www.novalis.ca.

For more suggested intentions for the Prayer of the Faithful, please visit:
www.livingwithchrist.ca.

Editor-in-chief: Natalia Kononenko, email: LWC@novalis.ca

Associate editor: Nancy Keyes

Music: All credits accompany the music texts.

Cover design & layout: Jessica AuCoin

ISBN: 978-2-89688-488-9

ISSN: 0832-5324

Printed in Canada

All rights reserved. No part of this publication may be reproduced,
stored in a retrieval system, or transmitted in any form, or by any means,
electronic, mechanical, photocopying, recording, or otherwise, without the
express written permission of the publisher.

We acknowledge the support of the Government of Canada.

Contents

*Every consecrated host
is made to burn itself up
with love in a human heart.*

Saint John Mary Vianney

Introductory Rites

ENTRANCE CHANT
(or Entrance Antiphon — ▶ The appropriate day)

GREETING
In the name of the Father, and of the Son, and of the Holy Spirit. **Amen.**

1 The grace of our Lord Jesus Christ, and the love of God, and the communion of the Holy Spirit be with you all.

2 Grace to you and peace from God our Father and the Lord Jesus Christ.

3 The Lord be with you.

And with your spirit.

PENITENTIAL ACT
(or Rite for the Blessing and Sprinkling of Water, p. 7)

Brothers and sisters, let us acknowledge our sins, and so prepare ourselves to celebrate the sacred mysteries. *(Pause)*

1 **I confess to almighty God**
   and to you, my brothers and sisters,
   that I have greatly sinned,
   in my thoughts and in my words,
   in what I have done and in what I have
      failed to do,
   through my fault, through my fault,
   through my most grievous fault;

therefore I ask blessed Mary ever-Virgin,
all the Angels and Saints,
and you, my brothers and sisters,
to pray for me to the Lord our God.

May almighty God have mercy on us, forgive us
our sins, and bring us to everlasting life. **Amen.**

Lord, have mercy.	**Lord, have mercy.**
or Kyrie, eleison.	**Kyrie, eleison.**
Christ, have mercy.	**Christ, have mercy.**
or Christe, eleison.	**Christe, eleison.**
Lord, have mercy.	**Lord, have mercy.**
or Kyrie, eleison.	**Kyrie, eleison.**

2   Have mercy on us, O Lord.
For we have sinned against you.

Show us, O Lord, your mercy.
And grant us your salvation.

May almighty God have mercy on us, forgive us
our sins, and bring us to everlasting life. **Amen.**

Lord, have mercy.	**Lord, have mercy.**
or Kyrie, eleison.	**Kyrie, eleison.**
Christ, have mercy.	**Christ, have mercy.**
or Christe, eleison.	**Christe, eleison.**
Lord, have mercy.	**Lord, have mercy.**
or Kyrie, eleison.	**Kyrie, eleison.**

3 You were sent to heal the contrite of heart:

Lord, have mercy.	**Lord, have mercy.**
or Kyrie, eleison.	**Kyrie, eleison.**

You came to call sinners:

Christ, have mercy.	**Christ, have mercy.**
or Christe, eleison.	**Christe, eleison.**

You are seated at the right hand of the Father to intercede for us:

Lord, have mercy.	**Lord, have mercy.**
or Kyrie, eleison.	**Kyrie, eleison.**

May almighty God have mercy on us, forgive us our sins, and bring us to everlasting life. **Amen.**

(▶ Glory to God, p. 10)

RITE FOR THE BLESSING AND SPRINKLING OF WATER

Dear brothers and sisters, let us humbly beseech the Lord our God to bless this water he has created, which will be sprinkled on us as a memorial of our Baptism. May he help us by his grace to remain faithful to the Spirit we have received. *(Pause)*

1 Almighty ever-living God, who willed that through water, the fountain of life and the source of purification, even souls should be cleansed and receive the gift of eternal life; be pleased, we pray, to bless this water, by which we seek protection on this your day, O Lord. Renew the living spring of your grace within us and grant that by

this water we may be defended from all ills of spirit and body, and so approach you with hearts made clean and worthily receive your salvation. Through Christ our Lord. **Amen.**

2 Almighty Lord and God, who are the source and origin of all life, whether of body or soul, we ask you to bless this water, which we use in confidence to implore forgiveness for our sins and to obtain the protection of your grace against all illness and every snare of the enemy. Grant, O Lord, in your mercy, that living waters may always spring up for our salvation, and so may we approach you with a pure heart and avoid all danger to body and soul. Through Christ our Lord. **Amen.**

3 *During Easter Time:*
Lord our God, in your mercy be present to your people's prayers, and, for us who recall the wondrous work of our creation and the still greater work of our redemption, graciously bless this water. For you created water to make the fields fruitful and to refresh and cleanse our bodies. You also made water the instrument of your mercy: for through water you freed your people from slavery and quenched their thirst in the desert; through water the Prophets proclaimed the new covenant you were to enter upon with the human race; and last of all, through water, which Christ made holy in the Jordan, you have renewed our corrupted nature in the bath of regeneration. Therefore, may this water be for us a memorial of the Baptism we

have received, and grant that we may share in the gladness of our brothers and sisters who at Easter have received their Baptism. Through Christ our Lord. **Amen.**

Where it is customary to bless salt also, add:

We humbly ask you, almighty God: be pleased in your faithful love to bless this salt you have created, for it was you who commanded the prophet Elisha to cast salt into water, that impure water might be purified. Grant, O Lord, we pray, that, wherever this mixture of salt and water is sprinkled, every attack of the enemy may be repulsed and your Holy Spirit may be present to keep us safe at all times. Through Christ our Lord. **Amen.**

During the sprinkling, an appropriate song may be sung.

May almighty God cleanse us of our sins, and through the celebration of this Eucharist make us worthy to share at the table of his Kingdom. **Amen.**

GLORY TO GOD
Omitted during Advent and Lent.

Glory to God in the highest,
and on earth peace to people of good will.

We praise you,
we bless you,
we adore you,
we glorify you,
we give you thanks for your great glory,
Lord God, heavenly King,
O God, almighty Father.

Lord Jesus Christ, Only Begotten Son,
Lord God, Lamb of God, Son of the Father,
you take away the sins of the world,
    have mercy on us;
you take away the sins of the world,
    receive our prayer;
you are seated at the right hand of the Father,
    have mercy on us.

For you alone are the Holy One,
you alone are the Lord,
you alone are the Most High,
Jesus Christ,
with the Holy Spirit,
in the glory of God the Father.
Amen.

COLLECT (▶ *The appropriate day*)

Liturgy of the Word

READINGS (▶ *The appropriate day*)

HOMILY

PROFESSION OF FAITH

1 **Nicene Creed**
All bow at the words in italics.

I believe in one God,
the Father almighty,
maker of heaven and earth,
of all things visible and invisible.

I believe in one Lord Jesus Christ,
the Only Begotten Son of God,
born of the Father before all ages.
God from God, Light from Light,
true God from true God,
begotten, not made,
consubstantial with the Father;
through him all things were made.
For us men and for our salvation
he came down from heaven,
and by the Holy Spirit was incarnate
of the Virgin Mary,
and became man.
For our sake he was crucified under
Pontius Pilate,
he suffered death and was buried,
and rose again on the third day
in accordance with the Scriptures.

He ascended into heaven
and is seated at the right hand of the Father.
He will come again in glory
to judge the living and the dead
and his kingdom will have no end.

I believe in the Holy Spirit, the Lord,
    the giver of life,
who proceeds from the Father and the Son,
who with the Father and the Son is adored
    and glorified,
who has spoken through the prophets.

I believe in one, holy, catholic and
    apostolic Church.
I confess one Baptism for the forgiveness
    of sins
and I look forward to the resurrection of
    the dead
and the life of the world to come. Amen.

2 Apostles' Creed
All bow at the words in italics.

I believe in God,
the Father almighty,
Creator of heaven and earth,
and in Jesus Christ, his only Son, our Lord,
who was conceived by the Holy Spirit,
born of the Virgin Mary,
suffered under Pontius Pilate,
was crucified, died and was buried;
he descended into hell;
on the third day he rose again from the dead;
he ascended into heaven,
and is seated at the right hand of God
    the Father almighty;
from there he will come to judge
    the living and the dead.

I believe in the Holy Spirit,
the holy catholic Church,
the communion of saints,
the forgiveness of sins,
the resurrection of the body,
and life everlasting. Amen.

PRAYER OF THE FAITHFUL (▶ *The appropriate day*)

Liturgy of the Eucharist

PREPARATION OF THE GIFTS

Blessed are you, Lord God of all creation, for through your goodness we have received the bread we offer you: fruit of the earth and work of human hands, it will become for us the bread of life. **Blessed be God for ever.**

> By the mystery of this water and wine may we come to share in the divinity of Christ who humbled himself to share in our humanity.

Blessed are you, Lord God of all creation, for through your goodness we have received the wine we offer you: fruit of the vine and work of human hands, it will become our spiritual drink. **Blessed be God for ever.**

> With humble spirit and contrite heart may we be accepted by you, O Lord, and may our sacrifice in your sight this day be pleasing to you, Lord God.

> Wash me, O Lord, from my iniquity and cleanse me from my sin.

Pray, brothers and sisters, that my sacrifice and yours may be acceptable to God, the almighty Father.

May the Lord accept the sacrifice at your hands for the praise and glory of his name, for our good and the good of all his holy Church.

PRAYER OVER THE OFFERINGS
(The appropriate day)

THE EUCHARISTIC PRAYER

The Lord be with you. **And with your spirit.**
Lift up your hearts. **We lift them up to the Lord.**
Let us give thanks to the Lord our God.
It is right and just.

The Priest selects an appropriate Preface, which concludes with the Holy, Holy.

PREFACE I OF ADVENT

It is truly right and just, our duty and our salvation, always and everywhere to give you thanks, Lord, holy Father, almighty and eternal God, through Christ our Lord.

For he assumed at his first coming the lowliness of human flesh, and so fulfilled the design you formed long ago, and opened for us the way to eternal salvation, that, when he comes again in glory and majesty and all is at last made manifest, we who watch for that day may inherit the great promise in which now we dare to hope.

And so, with Angels and Archangels, with Thrones and Dominions, and with all the hosts and Powers of heaven, we sing the hymn of your glory, as without end we acclaim: **Holy, Holy** *(p. 38)*

PREFACE II OF ADVENT

It is truly right and just, our duty and our salvation, always and everywhere to give you thanks, Lord, holy Father, almighty and eternal God, through Christ our Lord.

For all the oracles of the prophets foretold him, the Virgin Mother longed for him with love beyond all telling, John the Baptist sang of his coming and proclaimed his presence when he came.

It is by his gift that already we rejoice at the mystery of his Nativity, so that he may find us watchful in prayer and exultant in his praise.

And so, with Angels and Archangels, with Thrones and Dominions, and with all the hosts and Powers of heaven, we sing the hymn of your glory, as without end we acclaim: **Holy, Holy** *(p. 38)*

PREFACE I OF THE NATIVITY OF THE LORD

It is truly right and just, our duty and our salvation, always and everywhere to give you thanks, Lord, holy Father, almighty and eternal God.

For in the mystery of the Word made flesh a new light of your glory has shone upon the eyes of our mind, so that, as we recognize in him God made visible, we may be caught up through him in love of things invisible.

And so, with Angels and Archangels, with Thrones and Dominions, and with all the hosts and Powers of heaven, we sing the hymn of your glory, as without end we acclaim: **Holy, Holy** *(p. 38)*

PREFACE II OF THE NATIVITY OF THE LORD

It is truly right and just, our duty and our salvation, always and everywhere to give you thanks, Lord, holy Father, almighty and eternal God, through Christ our Lord.

For on the feast of this awe-filled mystery, though invisible in his own divine nature, he has appeared visibly in ours; and begotten before all ages, he has begun to exist in time; so that, raising up in himself all that was cast down, he might restore unity to all creation and call straying humanity back to the heavenly Kingdom.

And so, with all the Angels, we praise you, as in joyful celebration we acclaim: **Holy, Holy** *(p. 38)*

PREFACE III OF THE NATIVITY OF THE LORD

It is truly right and just, our duty and our salvation, always and everywhere to give you thanks, Lord, holy Father, almighty and eternal God, through Christ our Lord.

For through him the holy exchange that restores our life has shone forth today in splendour: when our frailty is assumed by your Word not only does human mortality receive unending honour but by this wondrous union we, too, are made eternal.

And so, in company with the choirs of Angels, we praise you, and with joy we proclaim: **Holy, Holy** *(p. 38)*

PREFACE I OF THE BLESSED VIRGIN MARY

It is truly right and just, our duty and our salvation, always and everywhere to give you thanks, Lord, holy Father, almighty and eternal God, and to praise, bless, and glorify your name on the Solemnity of the Motherhood of the Blessed ever-Virgin Mary.

For by the overshadowing of the Holy Spirit she conceived your Only Begotten Son, and without losing the glory of virginity, brought forth into the world the eternal Light, Jesus Christ our Lord.

Through him the Angels praise your majesty, Dominions adore and Powers tremble before you. Heaven and the Virtues of heaven and the blessed Seraphim worship together with exultation. May our voices, we pray, join with theirs in humble praise, as we acclaim: **Holy, Holy** *(p. 38)*

PREFACE OF THE EPIPHANY OF THE LORD

It is truly right and just, our duty and our salvation, always and everywhere to give you thanks, Lord, holy Father, almighty and eternal God.

For today you have revealed the mystery of our salvation in Christ as a light for the nations, and, when he appeared in our mortal nature, you made us new by the glory of his immortal nature.

And so, with Angels and Archangels, with Thrones and Dominions, and with all the hosts and Powers of heaven, we sing the hymn of your glory, as without end we acclaim: **Holy, Holy** *(p. 38)*

PREFACE I OF LENT

It is truly right and just, our duty and our salvation, always and everywhere to give you thanks, Lord, holy Father, almighty and eternal God, through Christ our Lord.

For by your gracious gift each year your faithful await the sacred paschal feasts with the joy of minds made pure, so that, more eagerly intent on prayer and on the works of charity, and participating in the mysteries by which they have been reborn, they may be led to the fullness of grace that you bestow on your sons and daughters.

And so, with Angels and Archangels, with Thrones and Dominions, and with all the hosts and Powers of heaven, we sing the hymn of your glory, as without end we acclaim: **Holy, Holy** *(p. 38)*

PREFACE II OF LENT

It is truly right and just, our duty and our salvation, always and everywhere to give you thanks, Lord, holy Father, almighty and eternal God.

For you have given your children a sacred time for the renewing and purifying of their hearts, that, freed from disordered affections, they may so deal with the things of this passing world as to hold rather to the things that eternally endure.

And so, with all the Angels and Saints, we praise you, as without end we acclaim: **Holy, Holy** *(p. 38)*

PREFACE III OF LENT

It is truly right and just, our duty and our salvation, always and everywhere to give you thanks, Lord, holy Father, almighty and eternal God.

For you will that our self-denial should give you thanks, humble our sinful pride, contribute to the feeding of the poor, and so help us imitate you in your kindness.

And so we glorify you with countless Angels, as with one voice of praise we acclaim: **Holy, Holy** *(p. 38)*

PREFACE IV OF LENT

It is truly right and just, our duty and our salvation, always and everywhere to give you thanks, Lord, holy Father, almighty and eternal God.

For through bodily fasting you restrain our faults, raise up our minds, and bestow both virtue and its rewards, through Christ our Lord.

Through him the Angels praise your majesty, Dominions adore and Powers tremble before you. Heaven and the Virtues of heaven and the blessed Seraphim worship together with exultation. May our voices, we pray, join with theirs in humble praise, as we acclaim: **Holy, Holy** *(p. 38)*

PREFACE OF 1ST SUNDAY OF LENT

It is truly right and just, our duty and our salvation, always and everywhere to give you thanks, Lord, holy Father, almighty and eternal God, through Christ our Lord.

By abstaining forty long days from earthly food, he consecrated through his fast the pattern of our Lenten observance and, by overturning all the snares of the ancient serpent, taught us to cast out the leaven of malice, so that, celebrating worthily the Paschal Mystery, we might pass over at last to the eternal paschal feast.

And so, with the company of Angels and Saints, we sing the hymn of your praise, as without end we acclaim: **Holy, Holy** *(p. 38)*

PREFACE OF 2ND SUNDAY OF LENT

It is truly right and just, our duty and our salvation, always and everywhere to give you thanks, Lord, holy Father, almighty and eternal God, through Christ our Lord.

For after he had told the disciples of his coming Death, on the holy mountain he manifested to them his glory, to show, even by the testimony of the law and the prophets, that the Passion leads to the glory of the Resurrection.

And so, with the Powers of heaven, we worship you constantly on earth, and before your majesty without end we acclaim: **Holy, Holy** *(p. 38)*

PREFACE OF 3RD SUNDAY OF LENT

It is truly right and just, our duty and our salvation, always and everywhere to give you thanks, Lord, holy Father, almighty and eternal God, through Christ our Lord.

For when he asked the Samaritan woman for water to drink, he had already created the gift of faith within her and so ardently did he thirst for her faith, that he kindled in her the fire of divine love.

And so we, too, give you thanks and with the Angels praise your mighty deeds, as we acclaim: **Holy, Holy** *(p. 38)*

PREFACE OF 4TH SUNDAY OF LENT

It is truly right and just, our duty and our salvation, always and everywhere to give you thanks, Lord, holy Father, almighty and eternal God, through Christ our Lord.

By the mystery of the Incarnation, he has led the human race that walked in darkness into the radiance of the faith and has brought those born in slavery to ancient sin through the waters of regeneration to make them your adopted children.

Therefore, all creatures of heaven and earth sing a new song in adoration, and we, with all the host of Angels, cry out, and without end acclaim: **Holy, Holy** (p. 38)

PREFACE OF 5TH SUNDAY OF LENT

It is truly right and just, our duty and our salvations, always and everywhere to give you thanks, Lord, holy Father, almighty and eternal God, through Christ our Lord.

For as true man he wept for Lazarus his friend and as eternal God raised him from the tomb, just as, taking pity on the human race, he leads us by sacred mysteries to new life.

Through him the host of Angels adores your majesty and rejoices in your presence for ever. May our voices, we pray, join with theirs in one chorus of exultant praise, as we acclaim: **Holy, Holy** (p. 38)

PREFACE OF THE PASSION OF THE LORD

(Palm Sunday)

It is truly right and just, our duty and our salvation, always and everywhere to give you thanks, Lord, holy Father, almighty and eternal God, through Christ our Lord.

For, though innocent, he suffered willingly for sinners and accepted unjust condemnation to save the guilty. His Death has washed away our sins, and his Resurrection has purchased our justification.

And so, with all the Angels, we praise you, as in joyful celebration we acclaim: **Holy, Holy** *(p. 38)*

PREFACE I OF EASTER

It is truly right and just, our duty and our salvation, at all times to acclaim you, O Lord, but

> *Easter Vigil:* on this night
> *Easter Sunday and Octave:* on this day
> *rest of Easter Time:* in this time

above all to laud you yet more gloriously, when Christ our Passover has been sacrificed.

For he is the true Lamb who has taken away the sins of the world; by dying he has destroyed our death, and by rising, restored our life.

Therefore, overcome with paschal joy, every land, every people exults in your praise and even the heavenly Powers, with the angelic hosts, sing together the unending hymn of your glory, as they acclaim: **Holy, Holy** *(p. 38)*

PREFACE II OF EASTER

It is truly right and just, our duty and our salvation, at all times to acclaim you, O Lord, but in this time above all to laud you yet more gloriously, when Christ our Passover has been sacrificed.

Through him the children of light rise to eternal life and the halls of the heavenly Kingdom are thrown open to the faithful; for his Death is our ransom from death, and in his rising the life of all has risen.

Therefore, overcome with paschal joy, every land, every people exults in your praise and even the heavenly Powers, with the angelic hosts, sing together the unending hymn of your glory, as they acclaim: **Holy, Holy** *(p. 38)*

PREFACE III OF EASTER

It is truly right and just, our duty and our salvation, at all times to acclaim you, O Lord, but in this time above all to laud you yet more gloriously, when Christ our Passover has been sacrificed.

He never ceases to offer himself for us but defends us and ever pleads our cause before you: he is the sacrificial Victim who dies no more, the Lamb, once slain, who lives for ever.

Therefore, overcome with paschal joy, every land, every people exults in your praise and even the heavenly Powers, with the angelic hosts, sing together the unending hymn of your glory, as they acclaim: **Holy, Holy** *(p. 38)*

PREFACE IV OF EASTER

It is truly right and just, our duty and our salvation, at all times to acclaim you, O Lord, but in this time above all to laud you yet more gloriously, when Christ our Passover has been sacrificed.

For, with the old order destroyed, a universe cast down is renewed, and integrity of life is restored to us in Christ.

Therefore, overcome with paschal joy, every land, every people exults in your praise and even the heavenly Powers, with the angelic hosts, sing together the unending hymn of your glory, as they acclaim: **Holy, Holy** *(p. 38)*

PREFACE V OF EASTER

It is truly right and just, our duty and our salvation, at all times to acclaim you, O Lord, but in this time above all to laud you yet more gloriously, when Christ our Passover has been sacrificed.

By the oblation of his Body, he brought the sacrifices of old to fulfillment in the reality of the Cross and, by commending himself to you for our salvation, showed himself the Priest, the Altar, and the Lamb of sacrifice.

Therefore, overcome with paschal joy, every land, every people exults in your praise and even the heavenly Powers, with the angelic hosts, sing together the unending hymn of your glory, as they acclaim: **Holy, Holy** *(p. 38)*

PREFACE I OF THE ASCENSION OF THE LORD

It is truly right and just, our duty and our salvation, always and everywhere to give you thanks, Lord, holy Father, almighty and eternal God.

For the Lord Jesus, the King of glory, conqueror of sin and death, ascended (today) to the highest heavens, as the Angels gazed in wonder.

Mediator between God and man, judge of the world and Lord of hosts, he ascended, not to distance himself from our lowly state but that we, his members, might be confident of following where he, our Head and Founder, has gone before.

Therefore, overcome with paschal joy, every land, every people exults in your praise and even the heavenly Powers, with the angelic hosts, sing together the unending hymn of your glory, as they acclaim: **Holy, Holy** (p. 38)

PREFACE II OF THE ASCENSION OF THE LORD

It is truly right and just, our duty and our salvation, always and everywhere to give you thanks, Lord, holy Father, almighty and eternal God, through Christ our Lord.

For after his Resurrection he plainly appeared to all his disciples and was taken up to heaven in their sight, that he might make us sharers in his divinity.

Therefore, overcome with paschal joy, every land, every people exults in your praise and even the heavenly Powers, with the angelic hosts, sing together the unending hymn of your glory, as they acclaim: **Holy, Holy** (p. 38)

PREFACE OF PENTECOST

It is truly right and just, our duty and our salvation, always and everywhere to give you thanks, Lord, holy Father, almighty and eternal God.

For, bringing your Paschal Mystery to completion, you bestowed the Holy Spirit today on those you made your adopted children by uniting them to your Only Begotten Son.

This same Spirit, as the Church came to birth, opened to all peoples the knowledge of God and brought together the many languages of the earth in profession of the one faith.

Therefore, overcome with paschal joy, every land, every people exults in your praise and even the heavenly Powers, with the angelic hosts, sing together the unending hymn of your glory, as they acclaim: **Holy, Holy** *(p. 38)*

PREFACE OF HOLY TRINITY

It is truly right and just, our duty and our salvation, always and everywhere to give you thanks, Lord, holy Father, almighty and eternal God.

For with your Only Begotten Son and the Holy Spirit you are one God, one Lord: not in the unity of a single person, but in a Trinity of one substance.

For what you have revealed to us of your glory we believe equally of your Son and of the Holy Spirit, so that, in the confessing of the true and eternal Godhead, you might be adored in what is proper to each Person, their unity in substance, and their equality in majesty.

For this is praised by Angels and Archangels, Cherubim, too, and Seraphim, who never cease to cry out each day, as with one voice they acclaim: **Holy, Holy** *(p. 38)*

PREFACE I OF THE MOST HOLY EUCHARIST

It is truly right and just, our duty and our salvation, always and everywhere to give you thanks, Lord, holy Father, almighty and eternal God, through Christ our Lord.

For he is the true and eternal Priest, who instituted the pattern of an everlasting sacrifice and was the first to offer himself as the saving Victim, commanding us to make this offering as his memorial.

As we eat his flesh that was sacrificed for us, we are made strong, and, as we drink his Blood that was poured out for us, we are washed clean.

And so, with Angels and Archangels, with Thrones and Dominions, and with all the hosts and Powers of heaven, we sing the hymn of your glory, as without end we acclaim: **Holy, Holy** *(p. 38)*

PREFACE II OF THE MOST HOLY EUCHARIST

It is truly right and just, our duty and our salvation, always and everywhere to give you thanks, Lord, holy Father, almighty and eternal God, through Christ our Lord.

For at the Last Supper with his Apostles, establishing for the ages to come the saving memorial of the Cross, he offered himself to you as the unblemished Lamb, the acceptable gift of perfect praise.

Nourishing your faithful by this sacred mystery, you make them holy, so that the human race, bounded by one world, may be enlightened by one faith and united by one bond of charity.

And so, we approach the table of this wondrous Sacrament, so that, bathed in the sweetness of your grace, we may pass over to the heavenly realities here foreshadowed.

Therefore, all creatures of heaven and earth sing a new song in adoration, and we, with all the host of

Angels, cry out, and without end we acclaim: **Holy, Holy** *(p. 38)*

PREFACE OF JOHN THE BAPTIST

It is truly right and just, our duty and our salvation, always and everywhere to give you thanks, Lord, holy Father, almighty and eternal God, through Christ our Lord.

In his Precursor, Saint John the Baptist, we praise your great glory, for you consecrated him for a singular honour among those born of women.

His birth brought great rejoicing; even in the womb he leapt for joy at the coming of human salvation. He alone of all the prophets pointed out the Lamb of redemption.

And to make holy the flowing waters, he baptized the very author of Baptism and was privileged to bear him supreme witness by the shedding of his blood.

And so, with the Powers of heaven, we worship you constantly on earth, and before your majesty without end we acclaim: **Holy, Holy** *(p. 38)*

PREFACE I OF SUNDAYS IN ORDINARY TIME

It is truly right and just, our duty and our salvation, always and everywhere to give you thanks, Lord, holy Father, almighty and eternal God, through Christ our Lord.

For through his Paschal Mystery, he accomplished the marvellous deed, by which he has freed us from the yoke of sin and death, summoning us to the glory of being now called a chosen race, a royal priesthood, a holy nation, a people for your own possession, to proclaim everywhere your mighty works, for you have called us out of darkness into your own wonderful light.

And so, with Angels and Archangels, with Thrones and Dominions, and with all the hosts and Powers of heaven, we sing the hymn of your glory, as without end we acclaim: **Holy, Holy** *(p. 38)*

PREFACE II OF SUNDAYS IN ORDINARY TIME

It is truly right and just, our duty and our salvation, always and everywhere to give you thanks, Lord, holy Father, almighty and eternal God, through Christ our Lord.

For out of compassion for the waywardness that is ours, he humbled himself and was born of the Virgin; by the passion of the Cross he freed us from unending death, and by rising from the dead he gave us life eternal.

And so, with Angels and Archangels, with Thrones and Dominions, and with all the hosts and Powers of heaven, we sing the hymn of your glory, as without end we acclaim: **Holy, Holy** *(p. 38)*

PREFACE III OF SUNDAYS IN ORDINARY TIME

It is truly right and just, our duty and our salvation, always and everywhere to give you thanks, Lord, holy Father, almighty and eternal God.

For we know it belongs to your boundless glory, that you came to the aid of mortal beings with your divinity and even fashioned for us a remedy out of mortality itself, that the cause of our downfall might become the means of our salvation, through Christ our Lord.

Through him the host of Angels adores your majesty and rejoices in your presence for ever. May our voices, we pray, join with theirs in one chorus of exultant praise, as we acclaim: **Holy, Holy** *(p. 38)*

PREFACE IV OF SUNDAYS IN ORDINARY TIME

It is truly right and just, our duty and our salvation, always and everywhere to give you thanks, Lord, holy Father, almighty and eternal God, through Christ our Lord.

For by his birth he brought renewal to humanity's fallen state, and by his suffering, cancelled out our sins; by his rising from the dead he has opened the way to eternal life, and by ascending to you, O Father, he has unlocked the gates of heaven.

And so, with the company of Angels and Saints, we sing the hymn of your praise, as without end we acclaim: **Holy, Holy** *(p. 38)*

PREFACE V OF SUNDAYS IN ORDINARY TIME

It is truly right and just, our duty and our salvation, always and everywhere to give you thanks, Lord, holy Father, almighty and eternal God.

For you laid the foundations of the world and have arranged the changing of times and seasons; you formed man in your own image and set humanity over the whole world in all its wonder, to rule in your name over all you have made and for ever praise you in your mighty works, through Christ our Lord.

And so, with all the Angels, we praise you, as in joyful celebration we acclaim: **Holy, Holy** *(p. 38)*

PREFACE VI OF SUNDAYS IN ORDINARY TIME

It is truly right and just, our duty and our salvation, always and everywhere to give you thanks, Lord, holy Father, almighty and eternal God.

For in you we live and move and have our being, and while in this body we not only experience the daily effects of your care, but even now possess the pledge of life eternal.

For, having received the first fruits of the Spirit, through whom you raised up Jesus from the dead, we hope for an everlasting share in the Paschal Mystery.

And so, with all the Angels, we praise you, as in joyful celebration we acclaim: **Holy, Holy** *(p. 38)*

PREFACE VII OF SUNDAYS IN ORDINARY TIME

It is truly right and just, our duty and our salvation, always and everywhere to give you thanks, Lord, holy Father, almighty and eternal God.

For you so loved the world that in your mercy you sent us the Redeemer, to live like us in all things but sin, so that you might love in us what you loved in your Son, by whose obedience we have been restored to those gifts of yours that, by sinning, we had lost in disobedience.

And so, Lord, with all the Angels and Saints, we, too, give you thanks, as in exultation we acclaim: **Holy, Holy** *(p. 38)*

PREFACE VIII OF SUNDAYS IN ORDINARY TIME

It is truly right and just, our duty and our salvation, always and everywhere to give you thanks, Lord, holy Father, almighty and eternal God.

For, when your children were scattered afar by sin, through the Blood of your Son and the power of the Spirit, you gathered them again to yourself, that a people, formed as one by the unity of the Trinity, made the body of Christ and the temple of the Holy Spirit, might, to the praise of your manifold wisdom, be manifest as the Church.

And so, in company with the choirs of Angels, we praise you, and with joy we proclaim: **Holy, Holy** (p. 38)

PREFACE OF OUR LORD JESUS CHRIST, KING OF THE UNIVERSE

It is truly right and just, our duty and our salvation, always and everywhere to give you thanks, Lord, holy Father, almighty and eternal God.

For you anointed your Only Begotten Son, our Lord Jesus Christ, with the oil of gladness as eternal Priest and King of all creation, so that, by offering himself on the altar of the Cross as a spotless sacrifice to bring us peace, he might accomplish the mysteries of human redemption and, making all created things subject to his rule, he might present to the immensity of your majesty an eternal and universal kingdom, a kingdom of truth and life, a kingdom of holiness and grace, a kingdom of justice, love and peace.

And so, with Angels and Archangels, with Thrones and Dominions, and with all the hosts and

Powers of heaven, we sing the hymn of your glory, as without end we acclaim: **Holy, Holy** *(p. 38)*

PREFACE OF RECONCILIATION I

It is truly right and just that we should always give you thanks, Lord, holy Father, almighty and eternal God.

For you do not cease to spur us on to possess a more abundant life and, being rich in mercy, you constantly offer pardon and call on sinners to trust in your forgiveness alone.

Never did you turn away from us, and, though time and again we have broken your covenant, you have bound the human family to yourself through Jesus your Son, our Redeemer, with a new bond of love so tight that it can never be undone.

Even now you set before your people a time of grace and reconciliation, and, as they turn back to you in spirit, you grant them hope in Christ Jesus and a desire to be of service to all, while they entrust themselves more fully to the Holy Spirit.

And so, filled with wonder, we extol the power of your love, and, proclaiming our joy at the salvation that comes from you, we join in the heavenly hymn of countless hosts, as without end we acclaim: **Holy, Holy** *(p. 38)*

PREFACE OF RECONCILIATION II

It is truly right and just that we should give you thanks and praise, O God, almighty Father, for all you do in this world, through our Lord Jesus Christ.

For though the human race is divided by dissension and discord, yet we know that by testing us you change our hearts to prepare them for reconciliation.

Even more, by your Spirit you move human hearts that enemies may speak to each other again, adversaries join hands, and peoples seek to meet together.

By the working of your power it comes about, O Lord, that hatred is overcome by love, revenge gives way to forgiveness, and discord is changed to mutual respect.

Therefore, as we give you ceaseless thanks with the choirs of heaven, we cry out to your majesty on earth, and without end we acclaim: **Holy, Holy** *(p. 38)*

PREFACE OF VARIOUS NEEDS I

It is truly right and just to give you thanks and raise to you a hymn of glory and praise, O Lord, Father of infinite goodness.

For by the word of your Son's Gospel you have brought together one Church from every people, tongue, and nation, and, having filled her with life by the power of your Spirit, you never cease through her to gather the whole human race into one.

Manifesting the covenant of your love, she dispenses without ceasing the blessed hope of your Kingdom and shines bright as the sign of your faithfulness, which in Christ Jesus our Lord you promised would last for eternity.

And so, with all the Powers of heaven, we worship you constantly on earth, while, with all the Church, as one voice we acclaim: **Holy, Holy** *(p. 38)*

PREFACE OF VARIOUS NEEDS II

It is truly right and just, our duty and our salvation, always and everywhere to give you thanks, Lord, holy Father, creator of the world and source of all life.

For you never forsake the works of your wisdom, but by your providence are even now at work in our midst. With mighty hand and outstretched arm you led your people Israel through the desert. Now, as your Church makes her pilgrim journey in the world, you always accompany her by the power of the Holy Spirit and lead her along the paths of time to the eternal joy of your Kingdom, through Christ our Lord.

And so, with the Angels and Saints, we, too, sing the hymn of your glory, as without end we acclaim: **Holy, Holy** *(p. 38)*

PREFACE OF VARIOUS NEEDS III

It is truly right and just, our duty and our salvation, always and everywhere to give you thanks, holy Father, Lord of heaven and earth, through Christ our Lord.

For by your Word you created the world and you govern all things in harmony. You gave us the same Word made flesh as Mediator, and he has spoken your words to us and called us to follow him. He is the way that leads us to you, the truth that sets us free, the life that fills us with gladness.

Through your Son you gather men and women, whom you made for the glory of your name, into one family, redeemed by the Blood of his Cross and signed with the seal of the Spirit.

Therefore, now and for ages unending, with all the Angels, we proclaim your glory, as in joyful celebration we acclaim: **Holy, Holy** *(p. 38)*

PREFACE OF VARIOUS NEEDS IV

It is truly right and just, our duty and our salvation, always and everywhere to give you thanks, Father of mercies and faithful God.

For you have given us Jesus Christ, your Son, as our Lord and Redeemer.

He always showed compassion for children and for the poor, for the sick and for sinners, and he became a neighbour to the oppressed and the afflicted.

By word and deed he announced to the world that you are our Father and that you care for all your sons and daughters.

And so, with all the Angels and Saints, we exalt and bless your name and sing the hymn of your glory, as without end we acclaim: **Holy, Holy** *(p. 38)*

PREFACE OF EUCHARISTIC PRAYER II

It is truly right and just, our duty and our salvation, always and everywhere to give you thanks, Father most holy, through your beloved Son, Jesus Christ, your Word through whom you made all things, whom you sent as our Saviour and Redeemer, incarnate by the Holy Spirit and born of the Virgin.

Fulfilling your will and gaining for you a holy people, he stretched out his hands as he endured his Passion, so as to break the bonds of death and manifest the resurrection.

And so, with the Angels and all the Saints we declare your glory, as with one voice we acclaim: **Holy, Holy** *(below)*

PREFACE OF EUCHARISTIC PRAYER IV
It is truly right to give you thanks, truly just to give you glory, Father most holy, for you are the one God living and true, existing before all ages and abiding for all eternity, dwelling in unapproachable light; yet you, who alone are good, the source of life, have made all that is, so that you might fill your creatures with blessings and bring joy to many of them by the glory of your light.

And so, in your presence are countless hosts of Angels, who serve you day and night and, gazing upon the glory of your face, glorify you without ceasing.

With them we, too, confess your name in exultation, giving voice to every creature under heaven, as we acclaim:

HOLY, HOLY
Holy, Holy, Holy Lord God of hosts.
Heaven and earth are full of your glory.
Hosanna in the highest.
Blessed is he who comes in the name of the Lord.
Hosanna in the highest.

The Eucharistic Prayer continues:

EUCHARISTIC PRAYER I

To you, therefore, most merciful Father, we make humble prayer and petition through Jesus Christ, your Son, our Lord: that you accept and bless these gifts, these offerings, these holy and unblemished sacrifices, which we offer you firstly for your holy catholic Church. Be pleased to grant her peace, to guard, unite and govern her throughout the whole world, together with your servant N. our Pope and N. our Bishop, and all those who, holding to the truth, hand on the catholic and apostolic faith.

Remember, Lord, your servants

Christian Initiation (Scrutinies):
who are to present your chosen ones for the holy grace of your Baptism,

N. and N. and all gathered here, whose faith and devotion are known to you. For them, we offer you this sacrifice of praise or they offer it for themselves and all who are dear to them: for the redemption of their souls, in hope of health and well-being, and paying their homage to you, the eternal God, living and true.

Nativity of the Lord and Octave of the Nativity:
Celebrating the most sacred night (day) on which blessed Mary the immaculate Virgin brought forth the Saviour for this world, and

Epiphany of the Lord:
Celebrating the most sacred day on which your Only Begotten Son, eternal with you in your glory, appeared in a human body, truly sharing our flesh, and

Holy Thursday:
Celebrating the most sacred day on which our Lord Jesus Christ was handed over for our sake, and

Easter Vigil to Second Sunday of Easter:
Celebrating the most sacred night (day) of the Resurrection of our Lord Jesus Christ in the flesh, and

Ascension of the Lord:
Celebrating the most sacred day on which your Only Begotten Son, our Lord, placed at the right hand of your glory our weak human nature, which he had united to himself, and

Pentecost Sunday:
Celebrating the most sacred day of Pentecost, on which the Holy Spirit appeared to the Apostles in tongues of fire, and

In communion with those whose memory we venerate, especially the glorious ever-Virgin Mary, Mother of our God and Lord, Jesus Christ, and blessed Joseph, her Spouse, your blessed Apostles and Martyrs, Peter and Paul, Andrew,

James, John, Thomas, James, Philip, Bartholomew, Matthew, Simon and Jude; Linus, Cletus, Clement, Sixtus, Cornelius, Cyprian, Lawrence, Chrysogonus, John and Paul, Cosmas and Damian

and all your Saints; we ask that through their merits and prayers, in all things we may be defended by your protecting help. (Through Christ our Lord. Amen.)

Therefore, Lord, we pray: graciously accept this oblation of our service, that of your whole family;

Christian Initiation (Scrutinies):
which we make to you for your servants, whom you have been pleased to enroll, choose and call for eternal life and for the blessed gift of your grace. (Through Christ our Lord. Amen.)

Holy Thursday:
which we make to you as we observe the day on which our Lord Jesus Christ handed on the mysteries of his Body and Blood for his disciples to celebrate;

Easter Vigil to Second Sunday of Easter:
which we make to you also for those to whom you have been pleased to give the new birth of water and the Holy Spirit, granting them forgiveness of all their sins;

order our days in your peace, and command that we be delivered from eternal damnation and counted among the flock of those you have chosen. (Through Christ our Lord. Amen.)

Be pleased, O God, we pray, to bless, acknowledge, and approve this offering in every respect; make it spiritual and acceptable, so that it may become for us the Body and Blood of your most beloved Son, our Lord Jesus Christ.

On the day before he was to suffer,

Holy Thursday:
for our salvation and the salvation of all, that is today,

he took bread in his holy and venerable hands, and with eyes raised to heaven to you, O God, his almighty Father, giving you thanks, he said the blessing, broke the bread and gave it to his disciples, saying:

Take this, all of you, and eat of it,
for this is my Body
which will be given up for you.

In a similar way, when supper was ended, he took this precious chalice in his holy and venerable hands, and once more giving you thanks, he said the blessing and gave the chalice to his disciples, saying:

Take this, all of you, and drink from it,
for this is the chalice of my Blood,
the Blood of the new and eternal covenant,
which will be poured out for you and for many
for the forgiveness of sins.
Do this in memory of me.

The mystery of faith.

1 **We proclaim your Death, O Lord, and profess your Resurrection until you come again.**

2 **When we eat this Bread and drink this Cup, we proclaim your Death, O Lord, until you come again.**

3 **Save us, Saviour of the world, for by your Cross and Resurrection you have set us free.**

Therefore, O Lord, as we celebrate the memorial of the blessed Passion, the Resurrection from the dead, and the glorious Ascension into heaven of Christ, your Son, our Lord, we, your servants and your holy people, offer to your glorious majesty from the gifts that you have given us, this pure victim, this holy victim, this spotless victim, the holy Bread of eternal life and the Chalice of everlasting salvation.

Be pleased to look upon these offerings with a serene and kindly countenance, and to accept them, as once you were pleased to accept the gifts of your servant Abel the just, the sacrifice of Abraham, our father in faith, and the offering of your high priest Melchizedek, a holy sacrifice, a spotless victim.

In humble prayer we ask you, almighty God: command that these gifts be borne by the hands of your holy Angel to your altar on high in the sight of your divine majesty, so that all of us, who through this participation at the altar receive the most holy Body and Blood of your Son, may be filled with every grace and heavenly blessing. (Through Christ our Lord. Amen.)

Remember also, Lord, your servants N. and N., who have gone before us with the sign of faith and rest in the sleep of peace. *(Pause)* Grant them, O Lord, we pray, and all who sleep in Christ, a place of refreshment, light and peace. (Through Christ our Lord. Amen.)

To us, also, your servants, who, though sinners, hope in your abundant mercies, graciously grant some share and fellowship with your holy Apostles and Martyrs: with John the Baptist, Stephen, Matthias, Barnabas,

Ignatius, Alexander, Marcellinus, Peter, Felicity, Perpetua, Agatha, Lucy, Agnes, Cecilia, Anastasia

and all your Saints; admit us, we beseech you, into their company, not weighing our merits, but granting us your pardon, through Christ our Lord.

Through whom you continue to make all these good things, O Lord; you sanctify them, fill them with life, bless them, and bestow them upon us.

Through him, and with him, and in him, O God, almighty Father, in the unity of the Holy Spirit, all glory and honour is yours, for ever and ever. **Amen.**

(▶ Communion Rite, p. 69)

EUCHARISTIC PRAYER II

You are indeed Holy, O Lord, the fount of all holiness. Make holy, therefore, these gifts, we pray, by sending down your Spirit upon them like the dewfall, so that they may become for us the Body and Blood of our Lord Jesus Christ.

At the time he was betrayed and entered willingly into his Passion, he took bread and, giving thanks, broke it, and gave it to his disciples, saying:

Take this, all of you, and eat of it,
for this is my Body
which will be given up for you.

In a similar way, when supper was ended, he took the chalice and, once more giving thanks, he gave it to his disciples, saying:

Take this, all of you, and drink from it,
for this is the chalice of my Blood,
the Blood of the new and eternal covenant,
which will be poured out for you and for many
for the forgiveness of sins.
Do this in memory of me.

The mystery of faith.

1 **We proclaim your Death, O Lord, and profess your Resurrection until you come again.**

2 **When we eat this Bread and drink this Cup, we proclaim your Death, O Lord, until you come again.**

3 **Save us, Saviour of the world, for by your Cross and Resurrection you have set us free.**

Therefore, as we celebrate the memorial of his Death and Resurrection, we offer you, Lord, the Bread of life and the Chalice of salvation, giving thanks that you have held us worthy to be in your presence and minister to you.

Humbly we pray that, partaking of the Body and Blood of Christ, we may be gathered into one by the Holy Spirit.

Remember, Lord, your Church, spread throughout the world, and bring her to the fullness of charity, together with N. our Pope and N. our Bishop and all the clergy.

Christian Initiation (Scrutinies):
Remember also, Lord, your servants who are to present these chosen ones at the font of rebirth.

Remember also our brothers and sisters who have fallen asleep in the hope of the resurrection, and all who have died in your mercy: welcome them into the light of your face. Have mercy on us all, we pray, that with the Blessed Virgin Mary, Mother of God, with blessed Joseph, her Spouse, with the blessed Apostles, and all the Saints who have pleased you throughout the ages, we may merit to be co-heirs to eternal life, and may praise and glorify you through your Son, Jesus Christ.

Through him, and with him, and in him, O God, almighty Father, in the unity of the Holy Spirit, all glory and honour is yours, for ever and ever. **Amen.**

(▶ *Communion Rite, p. 69*)

EUCHARISTIC PRAYER III

You are indeed Holy, O Lord, and all you have created rightly gives you praise, for through your Son our Lord Jesus Christ, by the power and working of the Holy Spirit, you give life to all things and make them holy, and you never cease to gather a people to yourself, so that from the rising of the sun to its setting a pure sacrifice may be offered to your name.

Therefore, O Lord, we humbly implore you: by the same Spirit graciously make holy these gifts we have brought to you for consecration, that they may become the Body and Blood of your Son our Lord Jesus Christ, at whose command we celebrate these mysteries.

For on the night he was betrayed he himself took bread, and, giving you thanks, he said the blessing, broke the bread and gave it to his disciples, saying:

Take this, all of you, and eat of it,
for this is my Body
which will be given up for you.

In a similar way, when supper was ended, he took the chalice, and, giving you thanks, he said the blessing, and gave the chalice to his disciples, saying:

Take this, all of you, and drink from it,
for this is the chalice of my Blood,
the Blood of the new and eternal covenant,
which will be poured out for you and for many
for the forgiveness of sins.
Do this in memory of me.

The mystery of faith.

1 **We proclaim your Death, O Lord, and profess
your Resurrection until you come again.**

2 **When we eat this Bread and drink this Cup, we
proclaim your Death, O Lord, until you come
again.**

3 **Save us, Saviour of the world, for by your Cross
and Resurrection you have set us free.**

Therefore, O Lord, as we celebrate the memorial
of the saving Passion of your Son, his wondrous
Resurrection and Ascension into heaven, and as we
look forward to his second coming, we offer you in
thanksgiving this holy and living sacrifice.

Look, we pray, upon the oblation of your Church
and, recognizing the sacrificial Victim by whose
death you willed to reconcile us to yourself, grant
that we, who are nourished by the Body and Blood of
your Son and filled with his Holy Spirit, may become
one body, one spirit in Christ.

May he make of us an eternal offering to you,
so that we may obtain an inheritance with your
elect, especially with the most Blessed Virgin Mary,
Mother of God, with blessed Joseph, her Spouse,
with your blessed Apostles and glorious Martyrs,

(with Saint N.) and with all the Saints, on whose constant intercession in your presence we rely for unfailing help.

May this Sacrifice of our reconciliation, we pray, O Lord, advance the peace and salvation of all the world. Be pleased to confirm in faith and charity your pilgrim Church on earth, with your servant N. our Pope and N. our Bishop, the Order of Bishops, all the clergy, and the entire people you have gained for your own.

Christian Initiation (Scrutinies):
Assist your servants with your grace, O Lord, we pray, that they may lead these chosen ones by word and example to new life in Christ, our Lord.

Listen graciously to the prayers of this family, whom you have summoned before you: in your compassion, O merciful Father, gather to yourself all your children scattered throughout the world. To our departed brothers and sisters and to all who were pleasing to you at their passing from this life, give kind admittance to your kingdom. There we hope to enjoy for ever the fullness of your glory through Christ our Lord, through whom you bestow on the world all that is good.

Through him, and with him, and in him, O God, almighty Father, in the unity of the Holy Spirit, all glory and honour is yours, for ever and ever. **Amen.**

(▶ *Communion Rite, p. 69*)

EUCHARISTIC PRAYER IV

We give you praise, Father most holy, for you are great and you have fashioned all your works in wisdom and in love. You formed man in your own image and entrusted the whole world to his care, so that in serving you alone, the Creator, he might have dominion over all creatures. And when through disobedience he had lost your friendship, you did not abandon him to the domain of death. For you came in mercy to the aid of all, so that those who seek might find you. Time and again you offered them covenants and through the prophets taught them to look forward to salvation.

And you so loved the world, Father most holy, that in the fullness of time you sent your Only Begotten Son to be our Saviour. Made incarnate by the Holy Spirit and born of the Virgin Mary, he shared our human nature in all things but sin. To the poor he proclaimed the good news of salvation, to prisoners, freedom, and to the sorrowful of heart, joy. To accomplish your plan, he gave himself up to death, and, rising from the dead, he destroyed death and restored life.

And that we might live no longer for ourselves but for him who died and rose again for us, he sent the Holy Spirit from you, Father, as the first fruits for those who believe, so that, bringing to perfection his work in the world, he might sanctify creation to the full.

Therefore, O Lord, we pray: may this same Holy Spirit graciously sanctify these offerings, that they may become the Body and Blood of our Lord Jesus Christ for the celebration of this great mystery, which he himself left us as an eternal covenant.

For when the hour had come for him to be glorified by you, Father most holy, having loved his own who were in the world, he loved them to the end: and while they were at supper, he took bread, blessed and broke it, and gave it to his disciples, saying:

Take this, all of you, and eat of it,
for this is my Body
which will be given up for you.

In a similar way, taking the chalice filled with the fruit of the vine, he gave thanks, and gave the chalice to his disciples, saying:

Take this, all of you, and drink from it,
for this is the chalice of my Blood,
the Blood of the new and eternal covenant,
which will be poured out for you and for many
for the forgiveness of sins.
Do this in memory of me.

The mystery of faith.

1 **We proclaim your Death, O Lord, and profess your Resurrection until you come again.**

2 **When we eat this Bread and drink this Cup, we proclaim your Death, O Lord, until you come again.**

3 **Save us, Saviour of the world, for by your Cross and Resurrection you have set us free.**

Therefore, O Lord, as we now celebrate the memorial of our redemption, we remember Christ's Death and his descent to the realm of the dead, we proclaim his Resurrection and his Ascension to your right hand, and, as we await his coming in glory, we offer you his Body and Blood, the sacrifice acceptable to you which brings salvation to the whole world.

Look, O Lord, upon the Sacrifice which you yourself have provided for your Church, and grant in your loving kindness to all who partake of this one Bread and one Chalice that, gathered into one body by the Holy Spirit, they may truly become a living sacrifice in Christ to the praise of your glory.

Therefore, Lord, remember now all for whom we offer this sacrifice: especially your servant N. our Pope, N. our Bishop, and the whole Order of Bishops, all the clergy, those who take part in this offering, those gathered here before you, your entire people, and all who seek you with a sincere heart.

Remember also those who have died in the peace of your Christ and all the dead, whose faith you alone have known.

To all of us, your children, grant, O merciful Father, that we may enter into a heavenly inheritance with the Blessed Virgin Mary, Mother of God, with blessed Joseph, her Spouse, and with your Apostles and Saints in your kingdom. There, with the whole of creation, freed from the corruption of sin and death, may we glorify you through Christ our Lord, through whom you bestow on the world all that is good.

Through him, and with him, and in him, O God, almighty Father, in the unity of the Holy Spirit, all glory and honour is yours, for ever and ever. **Amen.**

(▶ *Communion Rite, p. 69*)

EUCHARISTIC PRAYER
FOR RECONCILIATION I

You are indeed Holy, O Lord, and from the world's beginning are ceaselessly at work, so that the human race may become holy, just as you yourself are holy.

Look, we pray, upon your people's offerings and pour out on them the power of your Spirit, that they may become the Body and Blood of your beloved Son, Jesus Christ, in whom we, too, are your sons and daughters. Indeed, though we once were lost and could not approach you, you loved us with the greatest love: for your Son, who alone is just, handed himself over to death, and did not disdain to be nailed for our sake to the wood of the Cross.

But before his arms were outstretched between heaven and earth, to become the lasting sign of your covenant, he desired to celebrate the Passover with his disciples.

As he ate with them, he took bread and, giving you thanks, he said the blessing, broke the bread and gave it to them, saying:

Take this, all of you, and eat of it,
for this is my Body
which will be given up for you.

In a similar way, when supper was ended, knowing that he was about to reconcile all things in himself through his Blood to be shed on the Cross, he took the chalice, filled with the fruit of the vine, and once more giving you thanks, handed the chalice to his disciples, saying:

Take this, all of you, and drink from it,
for this is the chalice of my Blood,
the Blood of the new and eternal covenant,
which will be poured out for you and for many
for the forgiveness of sins.
Do this in memory of me.

The mystery of faith.

1 **We proclaim your Death, O Lord, and profess your Resurrection until you come again.**

2 **When we eat this Bread and drink this Cup, we proclaim your Death, O Lord, until you come again.**

3 **Save us, Saviour of the world, for by your Cross and Resurrection you have set us free.**

Therefore, as we celebrate the memorial of your Son Jesus Christ, who is our Passover and our surest peace, we celebrate his Death and Resurrection from the dead, and looking forward to his blessed Coming, we offer you, who are our faithful and merciful God, this sacrificial Victim who reconciles to you the human race.

Look kindly, most compassionate Father, on those you unite to yourself by the Sacrifice of your Son, and grant that, by the power of the Holy Spirit, as they partake of this one Bread and one Chalice, they may be gathered into one Body in Christ, who heals every division.

Be pleased to keep us always in communion of mind and heart, together with N. our Pope and N. our Bishop. Help us to work together for the coming of your Kingdom, until the hour when we stand before you, Saints among the Saints in the halls of heaven, with the Blessed Virgin Mary, Mother of God, the blessed Apostles and all the Saints, and with our deceased brothers and sisters, whom we humbly commend to your mercy.

Then, freed at last from the wound of corruption and made fully into a new creation, we shall sing to you with gladness the thanksgiving of Christ, who lives for all eternity.

Through him, and with him, and in him, O God, almighty Father, in the unity of the Holy Spirit, all glory and honour is yours, for ever and ever. **Amen.**

(▶ *Communion Rite, p. 69*)

EUCHARISTIC PRAYER FOR RECONCILIATION II

You, therefore, almighty Father, we bless through Jesus Christ your Son, who comes in your name. He himself is the Word that brings salvation, the hand you extend to sinners, the way by which your peace is offered to us. When we ourselves had turned away from you on account of our sins, you brought us back to be reconciled, O Lord, so that, converted at last to you, we might love one another through your Son, whom for our sake you handed over to death.

And now, celebrating the reconciliation Christ has brought us, we entreat you: sanctify these gifts by the outpouring of your Spirit, that they may become the Body and Blood of your Son, whose command we fulfill when we celebrate these mysteries.

For when about to give his life to set us free, as he reclined at supper, he himself took bread into his hands, and, giving you thanks, he said the blessing, broke the bread and gave it to his disciples, saying:

> Take this, all of you, and eat of it,
> for this is my Body
> which will be given up for you.

In a similar way, on that same evening, he took the chalice of blessing in his hands, confessing your mercy, and gave the chalice to his disciples, saying:

> Take this, all of you, and drink from it,
> for this is the chalice of my Blood,
> the Blood of the new and eternal covenant,
> which will be poured out for you and for many
> for the forgiveness of sins.
> Do this in memory of me.

The mystery of faith.

1 **We proclaim your Death, O Lord, and profess your Resurrection until you come again.**

2 **When we eat this Bread and drink this Cup, we proclaim your Death, O Lord, until you come again.**

**3 Save us, Saviour of the world, for by your Cross
and Resurrection you have set us free.**

Celebrating, therefore, the memorial of the Death
and Resurrection of your Son, who left us this pledge
of his love, we offer you what you have bestowed on
us, the Sacrifice of perfect reconciliation.

Holy Father, we humbly beseech you to accept
us also, together with your Son, and in this saving
banquet graciously to endow us with his very Spirit,
who takes away everything that estranges us from
one another.

May he make your Church a sign of unity and an
instrument of your peace among all people and may
he keep us in communion with N. our Pope and
N. our Bishop and all the Bishops and your entire
people.

Just as you have gathered us now at the table of
your Son, so also bring us together, with the glorious Virgin Mary, Mother of God, with your blessed
Apostles and all the Saints, with our brothers and
sisters and those of every race and tongue who have
died in your friendship. Bring us to share with them
the unending banquet of unity in a new heaven and
a new earth, where the fullness of your peace will
shine forth in Christ Jesus our Lord.

Through him, and with him, and in him, O God,
almighty Father, in the unity of the Holy Spirit, all
glory and honour is yours, for ever and ever. **Amen.**

(▶ *Communion Rite, p. 69*)

EUCHARISTIC PRAYER FOR MASS FOR VARIOUS NEEDS I

The Church on the Path of Unity

You are indeed Holy and to be glorified, O God, who love the human race and who always walk with us on the journey of life. Blessed indeed is your Son, present in our midst when we are gathered by his love, and when, as once for the disciples, so now for us, he opens the Scriptures and breaks the bread.

Therefore, Father most merciful, we ask that you send forth your Holy Spirit to sanctify these gifts of bread and wine, that they may become for us the Body and Blood of our Lord Jesus Christ.

On the day before he was to suffer, on the night of the Last Supper, he took bread and said the blessing, broke the bread and gave it to his disciples, saying:

Take this, all of you, and eat of it,
for this is my Body
which will be given up for you.

In a similar way, when supper was ended, he took the chalice, gave you thanks and gave the chalice to his disciples, saying:

Take this, all of you, and drink from it,
for this is the chalice of my Blood,
the Blood of the new and eternal covenant,
which will be poured out for you and for many
for the forgiveness of sins.
Do this in memory of me.

The mystery of faith.

1 **We proclaim your Death, O Lord, and profess your Resurrection until you come again.**

2 **When we eat this Bread and drink this Cup, we proclaim your Death, O Lord, until you come again.**

3 **Save us, Saviour of the world, for by your Cross and Resurrection you have set us free.**

Therefore, holy Father, as we celebrate the memorial of Christ your Son, our Saviour, whom you led through his Passion and Death on the Cross to the glory of the Resurrection, and whom you have seated at your right hand, we proclaim the work of your love until he comes again and we offer you the Bread of life and the Chalice of blessing.

Look with favour on the oblation of your Church, in which we show forth the paschal Sacrifice of Christ that has been handed on to us, and grant that, by the power of the Spirit of your love, we may be counted now and until the day of eternity among the members of your Son, in whose Body and Blood we have communion.

Lord, renew your Church (which is in N.) by the light of the Gospel. Strengthen the bond of unity between the faithful and the pastors of your people, together with N. our Pope, N. our Bishop, and the whole Order of Bishops, that in a world torn by strife your people may shine forth as a prophetic sign of unity and concord.

Remember our brothers and sisters (N. and N.), who have fallen asleep in the peace of your Christ, and all the dead, whose faith you alone have known. Admit them to rejoice in the light of your face, and in the resurrection give them the fullness of life.

Grant also to us, when our earthly pilgrimage is done, that we may come to an eternal dwelling place and live with you for ever; there, in communion with the Blessed Virgin Mary, Mother of God, with the Apostles and Martyrs, (with Saint N.) and with all the Saints, we shall praise and exalt you through Jesus Christ, your Son.

Through him, and with him, and in him, O God, almighty Father, in the unity of the Holy Spirit, all glory and honour is yours, for ever and ever. **Amen.**

(▶ Communion Rite, p. 69)

EUCHARISTIC PRAYER FOR MASS FOR VARIOUS NEEDS II
God Guides His Church along the Way of Salvation

You are indeed Holy and to be glorified, O God, who love the human race and who always walk with us on the journey of life. Blessed indeed is your Son, present in our midst when we are gathered by his love and when, as once for the disciples, so now for us, he opens the Scriptures and breaks the bread.

Therefore, Father most merciful, we ask that you send forth your Holy Spirit to sanctify these gifts of bread and wine, that they may become for us the Body and Blood of our Lord Jesus Christ.

On the day before he was to suffer, on the night of the Last Supper, he took bread and said the blessing, broke the bread and gave it to his disciples, saying:

Take this, all of you, and eat of it,
for this is my Body
which will be given up for you.

In a similar way, when supper was ended, he took the chalice, gave you thanks and gave the chalice to his disciples, saying:

Take this, all of you, and drink from it,
for this is the chalice of my Blood,
the Blood of the new and eternal covenant,
which will be poured out for you and for many
for the forgiveness of sins.
Do this in memory of me.

The mystery of faith.

1 **We proclaim your Death, O Lord, and profess your Resurrection until you come again.**

2 **When we eat this Bread and drink this Cup, we proclaim your Death, O Lord, until you come again.**

3 **Save us, Saviour of the world, for by your Cross and Resurrection you have set us free.**

Therefore, holy Father, as we celebrate the memorial of Christ your Son, our Saviour, whom you led through his Passion and Death on the Cross to the glory of the Resurrection, and whom you have seated at your right hand, we proclaim the work of your love until he comes again and we offer you the Bread of life and the Chalice of blessing.

Look with favour on the oblation of your Church, in which we show forth the paschal Sacrifice of Christ that has been handed on to us, and grant that, by the power of the Spirit of your love, we may be counted now and until the day of eternity among the members of your Son, in whose Body and Blood we have communion.

And so, having called us to your table, Lord, confirm us in unity, so that, together with N. our Pope and N. our Bishop, with all Bishops, Priests and Deacons, and your entire people, as we walk your ways with faith and hope, we may strive to bring joy and trust into the world.

Remember our brothers and sisters (N. and N.), who have fallen asleep in the peace of your Christ, and all the dead, whose faith you alone have known. Admit them to rejoice in the light of your face, and in the resurrection give them the fullness of life.

Grant also to us, when our earthly pilgrimage is done, that we may come to an eternal dwelling place and live with you for ever; there, in communion with the Blessed Virgin Mary, Mother of God, with the Apostles and Martyrs, (with Saint N.) and with all the Saints, we shall praise and exalt you through Jesus Christ, your Son.

Through him, and with him, and in him, O God, almighty Father, in the unity of the Holy Spirit, all glory and honour is yours, for ever and ever. **Amen.**

(▶ Communion Rite, p. 69)

EUCHARISTIC PRAYER FOR MASS FOR VARIOUS NEEDS III

Jesus, the Way to the Father

You are indeed Holy and to be glorified, O God, who love the human race and who always walk with us on the journey of life. Blessed indeed is your Son, present in our midst when we are gathered by his love and when, as once for the disciples, so now for us, he opens the Scriptures and breaks the bread.

Therefore, Father most merciful, we ask that you send forth your Holy Spirit to sanctify these gifts of bread and wine, that they may become for us the Body and Blood of our Lord Jesus Christ.

On the day before he was to suffer, on the night of the Last Supper, he took bread and said the blessing, broke the bread and gave it to his disciples, saying:

Take this, all of you, and eat of it,
for this is my Body
which will be given up for you.

In a similar way, when supper was ended, he took the chalice, gave you thanks and gave the chalice to his disciples, saying:

Take this, all of you, and drink from it,
for this is the chalice of my Blood,
the Blood of the new and eternal covenant,
which will be poured out for you and for many
for the forgiveness of sins.
Do this in memory of me.

The mystery of faith.

1 **We proclaim your Death, O Lord, and profess your Resurrection until you come again.**

2 **When we eat this Bread and drink this Cup, we proclaim your Death, O Lord, until you come again.**

3 **Save us, Saviour of the world, for by your Cross and Resurrection you have set us free.**

Therefore, holy Father, as we celebrate the memorial of Christ your Son, our Saviour, whom you led through his Passion and Death on the Cross to the glory of the Resurrection, and whom you have seated at your right hand, we proclaim the work of your love until he comes again and we offer you the Bread of life and the Chalice of blessing.

Look with favour on the oblation of your Church, in which we show forth the paschal Sacrifice of Christ that has been handed on to us, and grant that, by the power of the Spirit of your love, we may be counted now and until the day of eternity among the members of your Son, in whose Body and Blood we have communion.

By our partaking of this mystery, almighty Father, give us life through your Spirit, grant that we may be conformed to the image of your Son, and confirm us in the bond of communion, together with N. our Pope and N. our Bishop, with all other Bishops, with Priests and Deacons, and with your entire people.

Grant that all the faithful of the Church, looking into the signs of the times by the light of faith, may constantly devote themselves to the service of the Gospel.

Keep us attentive to the needs of all that, sharing their grief and pain, their joy and hope, we may faithfully bring them the good news of salvation and go forward with them along the way of your Kingdom.

Remember our brothers and sisters (N. and N.), who have fallen asleep in the peace of your Christ, and all the dead, whose faith you alone have known. Admit them to rejoice in the light of your face, and in the resurrection give them the fullness of life.

Grant also to us, when our earthly pilgrimage is done, that we may come to an eternal dwelling place and live with you for ever; there, in communion with the Blessed Virgin Mary, Mother of God, with the Apostles and Martyrs, (with Saint N.) and with all the Saints, we shall praise and exalt you through Jesus Christ, your Son.

Through him, and with him, and in him, O God, almighty Father, in the unity of the Holy Spirit, all glory and honour is yours, for ever and ever. **Amen.**

(▶ *Communion Rite, p. 69*)

EUCHARISTIC PRAYER FOR MASS FOR VARIOUS NEEDS IV

Jesus, Who Went About Doing Good

You are indeed Holy and to be glorified, O God, who love the human race and who always walk with us on the journey of life. Blessed indeed is your Son, present in our midst when we are gathered by his love and when, as once for the disciples, so now for us, he opens the Scriptures and breaks the bread.

Therefore, Father most merciful, we ask that you send forth your Holy Spirit to sanctify these gifts of bread and wine, that they may become for us the Body and Blood of our Lord Jesus Christ.

On the day before he was to suffer, on the night of the Last Supper, he took bread and said the blessing, broke the bread and gave it to his disciples, saying:

Take this, all of you, and eat of it,
for this is my Body
which will be given up for you.

In a similar way, when supper was ended, he took the chalice, gave you thanks and gave the chalice to his disciples, saying:

Take this, all of you, and drink from it,
for this is the chalice of my Blood,
the Blood of the new and eternal covenant,
which will be poured out for you and for many
for the forgiveness of sins.
Do this in memory of me.

The mystery of faith.

1 **We proclaim your Death, O Lord, and profess your Resurrection until you come again.**

2 **When we eat this Bread and drink this Cup, we proclaim your Death, O Lord, until you come again.**

3 **Save us, Saviour of the world, for by your Cross and Resurrection you have set us free.**

Therefore, holy Father, as we celebrate the memorial of Christ your Son, our Saviour, whom you led through his Passion and Death on the Cross to the glory of the Resurrection, and whom you have seated at your right hand, we proclaim the work of your love until he comes again and we offer you the Bread of life and the Chalice of blessing.

Look with favour on the oblation of your Church, in which we show forth the paschal Sacrifice of Christ that has been handed on to us, and grant that, by the power of the Spirit of your love, we may be counted now and until the day of eternity among the members of your Son, in whose Body and Blood we have communion.

Bring your Church, O Lord, to perfect faith and charity, together with N. our Pope and N. our Bishop, with all Bishops, Priests and Deacons, and the entire people you have made your own.

Open our eyes to the needs of our brothers and sisters; inspire in us words and actions to comfort those who labour and are burdened. Make us serve them truly, after the example of Christ and at his command. And may your Church stand as a living witness to truth and freedom, to peace and justice, that all people may be raised up to a new hope.

Remember our brothers and sisters (N. and N.), who have fallen asleep in the peace of your Christ, and all the dead, whose faith you alone have known. Admit them to rejoice in the light of your face, and in the resurrection give them the fullness of life.

Grant also to us, when our earthly pilgrimage is done, that we may come to an eternal dwelling place and live with you for ever; there, in communion with the Blessed Virgin Mary, Mother of God, with the Apostles and Martyrs, (with Saint N.) and with all the Saints, we shall praise and exalt you through Jesus Christ, your Son.

Through him, and with him, and in him, O God, almighty Father, in the unity of the Holy Spirit, all glory and honour is yours, for ever and ever. **Amen.**

The Communion Rite

At the Saviour's command and formed by divine teaching, we dare to say:

Our Father, who art in heaven,
hallowed be thy name;
thy kingdom come,
thy will be done
on earth as it is in heaven.
Give us this day our daily bread,
and forgive us our trespasses,
as we forgive those who trespass against us;
and lead us not into temptation,
but deliver us from evil.

Deliver us, Lord, we pray, from every evil, graciously grant peace in our days, that, by the help of your mercy, we may be always free from sin and safe from all distress, as we await the blessed hope and the coming of our Saviour, Jesus Christ.

For the kingdom,
the power and the glory are yours
now and for ever.

Lord Jesus Christ, who said to your Apostles: Peace I leave you, my peace I give you, look not on our sins, but on the faith of your Church, and graciously grant her peace and unity in accordance with your will. Who live and reign for ever and ever. **Amen.**

The peace of the Lord be with you always.
And with your spirit.

Let us offer each other the sign of peace.

May this mingling of the Body and Blood of our Lord Jesus Christ bring eternal life to us who receive it.

Lamb of God, you take away the sins of the world, have mercy on us.

Lamb of God, you take away the sins of the world, have mercy on us.

Lamb of God, you take away the sins of the world, grant us peace.

1 Lord Jesus Christ, Son of the living God, who, by the will of the Father and the work of the Holy Spirit, through your Death gave life to the world, free me by this, your most holy Body and Blood, from all my sins and from every evil; keep me always faithful to your commandments, and never let me be parted from you.

2 May the receiving of your Body and Blood, Lord Jesus Christ, not bring me to judgment and condemnation, but through your loving mercy be for me protection in mind and body and a healing remedy.

Behold the Lamb of God, behold him who takes away the sins of the world. Blessed are those called to the supper of the Lamb.

Lord, I am not worthy that you should enter under my roof, but only say the word and my soul shall be healed.

May the Body (Blood) of Christ keep me safe for eternal life.

COMMUNION CHANT
(or Communion Antiphon — ▶ The appropriate day)

> What has passed our lips as food, O Lord, may we possess in purity of heart, that what has been given to us in time may be our healing for eternity.

PRAYER AFTER COMMUNION
(▶ The appropriate day)

Concluding Rites

ANNOUNCEMENTS *(Optional)*

BLESSING *(or Solemn Blessing — Optional)*

The Lord be with you.
And with your spirit.
May almighty God bless you,
the Father, and the Son, and the Holy Spirit.
Amen.

DISMISSAL
During Easter Octave, add the double alleluia.

1 Go forth, the Mass is ended.

2 Go and announce the Gospel of the Lord.

3 Go in peace, glorifying the Lord by your life.

4 Go in peace.

Thanks be to God.

December Saints' Days

The following saints are traditionally remembered in December in Canada.

3   Saint Francis Xavier

4   Saint John Damascene

6   Saint Nicholas

7   Saint Ambrose

9   Saint Juan Diego Cuauhtlatoatzin

11 Saint Damasus I

12 Our Lady of Guadalupe,
    Patroness of the Americas

13 Saint Lucy

14 Saint John of the Cross

21 Saint Peter Canisius

23 Saint John of Kanty

26 Saint Stephen

27 Saint John

28 The Holy Innocents

29 Saint Thomas Becket

31 Saint Sylvester I

December 3
1st Sunday of Advent

On the first Sunday of Advent, we as a Church enter a precious period of in-betweenness. It is a time of expectancy and longing, bated breath and watchful waiting. It is a time that calls us to explicitly reflect on the peculiarity of our position: our Lord has already come and we wait for him to come again. We return to the stories leading up to his birth each year, knowing that we are living in a kind of "already/not yet." We know our beloved and still we yearn to see his face.

In the Gospel today we are called to be watchful: "You do not know when the time will come"; "Beware, keep alert"; "Keep awake." These insistent passages call us to be attentive in our every moment. When we are alert, we become attuned to the vibrancy of all that surrounds us; any movement could signal the arrival of the Lord. It's a delightful kind of anticipation. The 18th-century Jesuit writer Jean Pierre de Caussade invites us, in our anticipation, into what he calls "the sacramentality of the present moment." What if every moment were one in which we might meet our God? What might we notice? How might we act? Let us pray for the grace to be receptive to God in every moment.

Kate McGee
Toronto, ON

ENTRANCE ANTIPHON *(Cf. Psalm 24.1-3)*
To you, I lift up my soul, O my God. In you, I have trusted; let me not be put to shame. Nor let my enemies exult over me; and let none who hope in you be put to shame.

INTRODUCTORY RITES *(p. 5)*

COLLECT
Grant your faithful, we pray, almighty God, the resolve to run forth to meet your Christ with righteous deeds at his coming, so that, gathered at his right hand, they may be worthy to possess the heavenly Kingdom. Through our Lord Jesus Christ, your Son, who lives and reigns with you in the unity of the Holy Spirit, one God, for ever and ever. **Amen.**

FIRST READING *(Isaiah 63.16b-17; 64.1, 3-8)*
You, O Lord, are our father;
"Our Redeemer from of old" is your name.
Why, O Lord, do you make us stray from your ways
and harden our heart, so that we do not fear you?
Turn back for the sake of your servants,
for the sake of the tribes that are your heritage.

O that you would tear open the heavens and come
    down,
so that the mountains would quake at your presence.
When you did awesome deeds that we did not
    expect,
you came down, the mountains quaked at your
    presence.
From ages past no one has heard,

no ear has perceived,
no eye has seen any God besides you,
who works for those who wait for him.

You meet those who gladly do right,
those who remember you in your ways.

But you were angry, and we sinned;
because you hid yourself we transgressed.
We have all become like one who is unclean,
and all our righteous deeds are like a filthy cloth.
We all fade like a leaf,
and our iniquities, like the wind, take us away.
There is no one who calls on your name,
or attempts to take hold of you;
for you have hidden your face from us,
and have delivered us into the hand of our iniquity.

Yet, O Lord, you are our Father;
we are the clay, and you are our potter;
we are all the work of your hand.

The word of the Lord. **Thanks be to God.**

RESPONSORIAL PSALM *(Psalm 80)*

Re - store us, O God; let your face shine, that we may be saved.

R̸. **Restore us, O God;
let your face shine, that we may be saved.**

Give ear, O Shepherd · of Israel,
you who are enthroned upon the cherubim,
    shine · **forth.**
Stir up your · **might,**
and come to · **save_us.** R̸.

Turn again, O God · of hosts;
look down from heaven, and · **see;**
have regard for this · **vine,**
the stock that your right hand has · **planted.** R̸.

But let your hand be upon the man at · **your** right,
the son of man you have made strong for
    your·-**self.**
Then we will never turn · **back_from_you;**
give us life, and we will call on your · **name.** R̸.

©2009 Gordon Johnston/Novalis

To hear the Sunday Psalms, visit www.livingwithchrist.ca.

SECOND READING *(1 Corinthians 1.3-9)*
Brothers and sisters: Grace to you and peace from
God our Father and the Lord Jesus Christ.

I give thanks to my God always for you because of
the grace of God that has been given you in Christ Jesus, for in every way you have been enriched in him,
in speech and knowledge of every kind — just as the
testimony of Christ has been strengthened among
you — so that you are not lacking in any spiritual gift
as you wait for the revealing of our Lord Jesus Christ.

He will also strengthen you to the end, so that
you may be blameless on the day of our Lord Jesus
Christ. God is faithful; by him you were called into
fellowship with his Son, Jesus Christ our Lord.

The word of the Lord. **Thanks be to God.**

GOSPEL ACCLAMATION *(Psalm 85.7)*
Alleluia. Alleluia. Show us your steadfast love, O
Lord, and grant us your salvation. **Alleluia.**

GOSPEL *(Mark 13.33-37)*
The Lord be with you. **And with your spirit.**
A reading from the holy Gospel according to Mark.
Glory to you, O Lord.

Jesus said to his disciples: "Beware, keep alert; for
you do not know when the time will come.

"It is like a man going on a journey, when he
leaves home and puts his slaves in charge, each with
a particular task, and commands the doorkeeper to
be on the watch. Therefore, keep awake — for you
do not know when the master of the house will
come, in the evening, or at midnight, or at cockcrow,

or at dawn, or else he may find you asleep when he comes suddenly.

"And what I say to you I say to all: Keep awake."

The Gospel of the Lord. **Praise to you, Lord Jesus Christ.**

PROFESSION OF FAITH (p. 11)

PRAYER OF THE FAITHFUL

The following intentions are suggestions only. There are more suggestions at www.livingwithchrist.ca

R. **Lord, hear our prayer.**

For the Church, eagerly awaiting the fulfillment of the children of God, we pray to the Lord: R.

For the world, longing for its promised salvation, we pray to the Lord: R.

For the sorrowing and despairing, the suffering and alienated, the forgotten and overlooked, we pray to the Lord: R.

For our parish and our diocese, working together as we await the Lord's return in glory, we pray to the Lord: R.

PREPARATION OF THE GIFTS (p. 14)

PRAYER OVER THE OFFERINGS

Accept, we pray, O Lord, these offerings we make, gathered from among your gifts to us, and may what you grant us to celebrate devoutly here below gain for us the prize of eternal redemption. Through Christ our Lord. **Amen.**

PREFACE (Advent I, p. 15)

COMMUNION ANTIPHON (Psalm 84.13)
The Lord will bestow his bounty, and our earth shall yield its increase.

PRAYER AFTER COMMUNION
May these mysteries, O Lord, in which we have participated, profit us, we pray, for even now, as we walk amid passing things, you teach us by them to love the things of heaven and hold fast to what endures. Through Christ our Lord. **Amen.**

SOLEMN BLESSING — ADVENT (Optional)
Bow down for the blessing.

May the almighty and merciful God, by whose grace you have placed your faith in the First Coming of his Only Begotten Son and yearn for his coming again, sanctify you by the radiance of Christ's Advent and enrich you with his blessing. **Amen.**

As you run the race of this present life, may he make you firm in faith, joyful in hope and active in charity. **Amen.**

So that, rejoicing now with devotion at the Redeemer's coming in the flesh, you may be endowed with the rich reward of eternal life when he comes again in majesty. **Amen.**

And may the blessing of almighty God, the Father, and the Son, and the Holy Spirit, come down on you and remain with you for ever. **Amen.**

DISMISSAL (p. 71)

December 10
2nd Sunday of Advent

Remember the scene in *How the Grinch Stole Christmas* when the Grinch is picturing Christmas morning in Whoville, "That's one thing I hate! All the noise, noise, noise, NOISE!" Sometimes the lead-up to Christmas is like that: overtired, screaming toddlers in the mall; non-stop Christmas music everywhere; or the incessant commercials on TV can all bring out the Grinch in the best of us.

So I am especially grateful for the calming voices in today's readings that encourage us to focus on what's *really* important during these weeks before Christmas. Both Isaiah and John the Baptist remind us that this season of Advent is about preparing the way for the Lord. It's about clearing some space, making room for Jesus and welcoming him into our lives in an ever deeper way.

For some of us, that might mean committing more time for prayer each day, even in the midst of the December hustle and bustle. Perhaps for others it means giving the gift of presence to someone who is lonely or housebound in this festive season. Maybe it is even something as simple as making a conscious effort to treat the harried cashier with courtesy and respect.

In today's celebration, prophetic voices reach out to us across the centuries. As we continue our Advent journey, may we have ears to hear their words and hearts to heed their call.

Teresa Whalen Lux
Regina, SK

ENTRANCE ANTIPHON *(Cf. Isaiah 30.19, 30)*
O people of Sion, behold, the Lord will come to save
the nations, and the Lord will make the glory of his
voice heard in the joy of your heart.

INTRODUCTORY RITES *(p. 5)*

COLLECT
Almighty and merciful God, may no earthly undertaking hinder those who set out in haste to meet your
Son, but may our learning of heavenly wisdom gain
us admittance to his company. Who lives and reigns
with you in the unity of the Holy Spirit, one God, for
ever and ever. **Amen.**

FIRST READING *(Isaiah 40.1-5, 9-11)*
Comfort, O comfort my people,
says your God.
Speak tenderly to Jerusalem,
and cry to her
that she has served her term,
that her penalty is paid,
that she has received from the Lord's hand
double for all her sins.

A voice cries out:
"In the wilderness prepare the way of the Lord,
make straight in the desert a highway for our God.
Every valley shall be lifted up,
and every mountain and hill be made low;
the uneven ground shall become level,
and the rough places a plain.
Then the glory of the Lord shall be revealed,

and all people shall see it together,
for the mouth of the Lord has spoken."

Get you up to a high mountain,
O Zion, herald of good tidings;
lift up your voice with strength,
O Jerusalem, herald of good tidings,
lift it up, do not fear;
say to the cities of Judah,
"Here is your God!"

See, the Lord God comes with might,
and his arm rules for him;
his reward is with him,
and his recompense before him.
He will feed his flock like a shepherd;
he will gather the lambs in his arms,
and carry them in his bosom,
and gently lead the mother sheep.

The word of the Lord. **Thanks be to God.**

RESPONSORIAL PSALM *(Psalm 85)*

Show us your stead-fast love, O Lord,
and grant us your sal-va-tion.

R. **Show us your steadfast love, O Lord,
and grant us your salvation.**

Let me hear what God the Lord will · **speak,**
for he will speak peace to his · **people.**
Surely his salvation is at hand for those who ·
fear_him,
that his glory may dwell · **in_our** land. R.

Steadfast love and faithfulness will · **meet;**
righteousness and peace will · **kiss_each_other.**
Faithfulness will spring up from the · **ground,**
and righteousness will look down · **from_the**
sky. R.

The Lord will give what is · **good,**
and our land will yield its · **increase.**
Righteousness will go be-·**fore_him,**
and will make a path · **for_his** steps. R.

©2009 Gordon Johnston/Novalis

To hear the Sunday Psalms, visit www.livingwithchrist.ca.

SECOND READING *(2 Peter 3.8-14)*
Do not ignore this one fact, beloved, that with the Lord one day is like a thousand years, and a thousand years are like one day. The Lord is not slow about his promise, as some think of slowness, but is patient with you, not wanting any to perish, but all to come to repentance.

But the day of the Lord will come like a thief, and then the heavens will pass away with a loud noise, and the elements will be dissolved with fire, and the earth and everything that is done on it will be disclosed.

Since all these things are to be dissolved in this way, what sort of persons ought you to be in leading lives of holiness and godliness, waiting for and hastening the coming of the day of God, because of which the heavens will be set ablaze and dissolved, and the elements will melt with fire? But, in accordance with his promise, we wait for new heavens and a new earth, where righteousness is at home.

Therefore, beloved, while you are waiting for these things, strive to be found by him at peace.

The word of the Lord. **Thanks be to God.**

GOSPEL ACCLAMATION *(Luke 3.4, 6)*
Alleluia. Alleluia. Prepare the way of the Lord, make straight his paths: all people shall see the salvation of God. **Alleluia.**

GOSPEL *(Mark 1.1-8)*
The Lord be with you. **And with your spirit.**
A reading from the holy Gospel according to Mark. **Glory to you, O Lord.**

The beginning of the good news of Jesus Christ, the Son of God.

As it is written in the Prophet Isaiah, "See, I am sending my messenger ahead of you, who will prepare your way; the voice of one crying out in the wilderness: 'Prepare the way of the Lord, make his paths straight,'" John the Baptist appeared in the wilderness, proclaiming a baptism of repentance for the forgiveness of sins. And people from the whole Judean countryside and all the people of Jerusalem were going out to him, and were baptized by him in the river Jordan, confessing their sins. Now John was clothed with camel's hair, with a leather belt around his waist, and he ate locusts and wild honey. He proclaimed, "The one who is more powerful than I is coming after me; I am not worthy to stoop down and untie the thong of his sandals. I have baptized you with water; but he will baptize you with the Holy Spirit."

The Gospel of the Lord. **Praise to you, Lord Jesus Christ.**

PROFESSION OF FAITH (p. 11)

PRAYER OF THE FAITHFUL

The following intentions are suggestions only. There are more suggestions at www.livingwithchrist.ca

R̥ **Lord, hear our prayer.**

For the Church, courageously open to inner and outer transformation by the Holy Spirit, we pray to the Lord: R̥

For the leaders of nations and communities, striving to build a society of righteousness, peace and justice, we pray to the Lord: ℟

For the poor, the weak and the helpless, we pray to the Lord: ℟

For this community, open to conversion and forgiveness, we pray to the Lord: ℟

PREPARATION OF THE GIFTS *(p. 14)*

PRAYER OVER THE OFFERINGS
Be pleased, O Lord, with our humble prayers and offerings, and, since we have no merits to plead our cause, come, we pray, to our rescue with the protection of your mercy. Through Christ our Lord. **Amen.**

PREFACE *(Advent I, p. 15)*

COMMUNION ANTIPHON *(Baruch 5.5; 4.36)*
Jerusalem, arise and stand upon the heights, and behold the joy which comes to you from God.

PRAYER AFTER COMMUNION
Replenished by the food of spiritual nourishment, we humbly beseech you, O Lord, that, through our partaking in this mystery, you may teach us to judge wisely the things of earth and hold firm to the things of heaven. Through Christ our Lord. **Amen.**

SOLEMN BLESSING AND DISMISSAL *(p. 79)*

December 17
3rd Sunday of Advent

As Christians, we recognize the season of Advent as a time of great anticipation in which we prepare for the coming of the Lord. In today's Gospel John the Baptist calls us to "Make straight the way of the Lord." This call to action is not easy in an ever-growing secular world.

Although it should be the very opposite, the season of Advent is perhaps the most difficult time of year to rise and to meet John's call. More often than not, today's reality is one where the season of Advent is inundated with commercialism and anything but Christ. To remain focused while we await the coming of the Lord is increasingly difficult and requires humility, discipline and patience. These qualities require a great deal of practice and prayer. Seemingly enough, the reverse is true as practice and prayer require a great deal of humility, discipline and patience.

If we are to lead a virtuous Christian life then we must follow John's example displaying humility, discipline and patience when responding to those who questioned him. Despite the heavy commercialization of Advent, let us as Christians persevere through prayer and practice as we celebrate and share the coming of the Lord with everyone that we encounter during this blessed season.

Dana Kenny
Charlottetown, PE

ENTRANCE ANTIPHON *(Philippians 4.4-5)*
Rejoice in the Lord always; again I say, rejoice. Indeed, the Lord is near.

INTRODUCTORY RITES *(p. 5)*

COLLECT
O God, who see how your people faithfully await the feast of the Lord's Nativity, enable us, we pray, to attain the joys of so great a salvation and to celebrate them always with solemn worship and glad rejoicing. Through our Lord Jesus Christ, your Son, who lives and reigns with you in the unity of the Holy Spirit, one God, for ever and ever. **Amen.**

FIRST READING *(Isaiah 61.1-2a, 10-11)*
The spirit of the Lord God is upon me,
because the Lord has anointed me;
he has sent me to bring good news to the oppressed,
to bind up the brokenhearted,
to proclaim liberty to the captives,
and release to the prisoners;
to proclaim the year of the Lord's favour.

I will greatly rejoice in the Lord,
my soul shall exult in my God;
for he has clothed me with the garments of salvation,
he has covered me with the robe of righteousness,
as a bridegroom decks himself with a garland,
and as a bride adorns herself with her jewels.

For as the earth brings forth its shoots,
and as a garden causes what is sown in it to
    spring up,

so the Lord God will cause righteousness and praise to spring up before all the nations.

The word of the Lord. **Thanks be to God.**

RESPONSORIAL PSALM *(Luke 1)*

R. **My soul shall exult in my God.**

My soul magnifies the · **Lord**
and my spirit rejoices in God · **my** Saviour,
for he has looked with favour on the lowliness
  of his · **servant.**
Surely, from now on all generations will · **call_
me** blessed. R.

For the Mighty One has done great things for · **me,**
and holy is · **his** name.
His mercy is for those who · **fear_him**
from generation to · **gener**-ation. R.

The Lord has filled the hungry with · **good_things**
and sent the rich a--**way** empty.
He has helped his servant · **Israel,**
in remembrance · **of_his** mercy. R.

©2009 Gordon Johnston/Novalis

To hear the Sunday Psalms, visit www.livingwithchrist.ca.

SECOND READING (1 Thessalonians 5.16-24)

Brothers and sisters, rejoice always, pray without ceasing, give thanks in all circumstances; for this is the will of God in Christ Jesus for you.

Do not quench the Spirit. Do not despise the words of Prophets, but test everything; hold fast to what is good; abstain from every form of evil.

May the God of peace himself sanctify you entirely; and may your spirit and soul and body be kept sound and blameless at the coming of our Lord Jesus Christ. The one who calls you is faithful, and he will do this.

The word of the Lord. **Thanks be to God.**

GOSPEL ACCLAMATION (Luke 4.18 [Isaiah 61.1])

Alleluia. Alleluia. The Spirit of the Lord is upon me; he has sent me to bring good news to the poor. **Alleluia.**

GOSPEL (John 1.6-8, 19-28)

The Lord be with you. **And with your spirit.**
A reading from the holy Gospel according to John.
Glory to you, O Lord.

There was a man sent from God, whose name was John. He came as a witness to testify to the light, so that all might believe through him. He himself was not the light, but he came to testify to the light.

This is the testimony given by John when the Jews sent priests and Levites from Jerusalem to ask him, "Who are you?" He confessed and did not deny it, but confessed, "I am not the Messiah." And they asked him, "What then? Are you Elijah?" He said, "I am not." "Are you the Prophet?" He answered, "No."

Then they said to him, "Who are you? Let us have an answer for those who sent us. What do you say about yourself?" He said, "I am the voice of one crying out in the wilderness, 'Make straight the way of the Lord,'" as the Prophet Isaiah said.

Now they had been sent from the Pharisees. They asked him, "Why then are you baptizing if you are neither the Messiah, nor Elijah, nor the Prophet?" John answered them, "I baptize with water. Among you stands one whom you do not know, the one who is coming after me; I am not worthy to untie the thong of his sandal." This took place in Bethany across the Jordan where John was baptizing.

The Gospel of the Lord. **Praise to you, Lord Jesus Christ.**

PROFESSION OF FAITH (p. 11)

PRAYER OF THE FAITHFUL

The following intentions are suggestions only. There are more suggestions at www.livingwithchrist.ca

R. **Lord, hear our prayer.**

For the Church, called to lead humanity to the light of Christ, we pray to the Lord: R.

For civil authorities fulfilling their responsibilities to guide people to a deeper appreciation of all the stages of life, we pray to the Lord: R.

For all who are facing the coming year without hope, we pray to the Lord: R.

For each of us, in our vocation to live the Good News, we pray to the Lord: R.

PREPARATION OF THE GIFTS (p. 14)

PRAYER OVER THE OFFERINGS

May the sacrifice of our worship, Lord, we pray, be offered to you unceasingly, to complete what was begun in sacred mystery and powerfully accomplish for us your saving work. Through Christ our Lord. **Amen.**

PREFACE (Advent II, p. 15)

COMMUNION ANTIPHON (Cf. Isaiah 35.4)
Say to the faint of heart: Be strong and do not fear. Behold, our God will come, and he will save us.

PRAYER AFTER COMMUNION

We implore your mercy, Lord, that this divine sustenance may cleanse us of our faults and prepare us for the coming feasts. Through Christ our Lord. **Amen.**

SOLEMN BLESSING AND DISMISSAL (p. 79)

December 24
4th Sunday of Advent

"The Lord is with you." One can only imagine how Mary felt receiving this knowledge. Despite her lowliness, she was chosen to give birth to the Son of God. She was perplexed and moved by what she heard, yet Mary accepted the tremendous responsibility and proclaimed a joyful "yes." Mary's faithful response to God's call carried her through life when, years later, she watched her son be put to death. Even then she drew on God for strength.

Just as Mary felt perplexed by the angels greeting, we too can feel overwhelmed by the intense love of God. In a few hours time, we will gather at the crèche and celebrate that the Word of God took on human form to be present with us. And then, after dying for our sins on the cross, Jesus remains with us through the Eucharist. The Lord is always with us.

It is astonishing to think that, regardless of our failings, we are not alone. As Advent comes to a close may we allow ourselves to find peace in the knowledge that God has a plan for each one of us and that the love of God will not lead us astray. God is with us every hour of the day, and we need only ask for the strength and hope that will allow us to overcome our challenges.

Elizabeth Chesley-Jewell
Toronto, ON

ENTRANCE ANTIPHON *(Cf. Isaiah 45.8)*
Drop down dew from above, you heavens, and let the clouds rain down the Just One; let the earth be opened and bring forth a Saviour.

INTRODUCTORY RITES *(p. 5)*

COLLECT
Pour forth, we beseech you, O Lord, your grace into our hearts, that we, to whom the Incarnation of Christ your Son was made known by the message of an Angel, may by his Passion and Cross be brought to the glory of his Resurrection. Who lives and reigns with you in the unity of the Holy Spirit, one God, for ever and ever. **Amen.**

FIRST READING *(2 Samuel 7.1-5, 8b-12, 14a, 16)*
Now when David, the king, was settled in his house, and the Lord had given him rest from all his enemies around him, the king said to the Prophet Nathan, "See now, I am living in a house of cedar, but the ark of God stays in a tent." Nathan said to the king, "Go, do all that you have in mind, for the Lord is with you."

But that same night the word of the Lord came to Nathan: "Go and tell my servant David: 'Thus says the Lord: Are you the one to build me a house to live in? I took you from the pasture, from following the sheep to be prince over my people Israel: and I have been with you wherever you went, and have cut off all your enemies from before you; and I will make for you a great name, like the name of the great ones of the earth.

"And I will appoint a place for my people Israel and will plant them, so that they may live in their own place, and be disturbed no more; and evildoers shall afflict them no more, as formerly, from the time that I appointed judges over my people Israel; and I will give you rest from all your enemies.

"Moreover the Lord declares to you, David, that the Lord will make you a house. When your days are fulfilled and you lie down with your ancestors, I will raise up your offspring after you, who shall come forth from your body, and I will establish his kingdom.

"I will be a father to him, and he shall be a son to me. Your house and your kingdom shall be made sure forever before me; your throne, David, shall be established forever.'"

The word of the Lord. **Thanks be to God.**

RESPONSORIAL PSALM *(Psalm 89)*

For - ev - er I will sing of your stead - fast love, O Lord.

R. **Forever I will sing of your steadfast love,
O Lord.**

I will sing of your steadfast love, O Lord,
    for-**ever**;
with my mouth I will proclaim your faithfulness
    to all gener-**ations.**
I declare that your steadfast love is established
    for-**ever**;
your faithfulness is as firm · **as_the** heavens. R.

You said, "I have made a covenant with my ·
    chosen_one,
I have sworn to my servant · **David:**
I will establish your descendants for-**ever,**
and build your throne for all · **gener**-ations." R.

He shall cry to me, "You are my · **Father,**
my God, and the Rock of my sal-**vation!"**
Forever I will keep my steadfast · **love_for_him,**
and my covenant with him will · **stand** firm. R.

©2009 Gordon Johnston/Novalis

To hear the Sunday Psalms, visit www.livingwithchrist.ca.

SECOND READING *(Romans 16.25-27)*

Brothers and sisters: To the One who is able to strengthen you according to my Gospel and the proclamation of Jesus Christ, according to the revelation of the mystery that was kept secret for long ages but is now disclosed, and through the prophetic writings is made known to all the Gentiles, according to the command of the eternal God, to bring about the obedience of faith — to the only wise God, through Jesus Christ, to whom be the glory forever! Amen.

The word of the Lord. **Thanks be to God.**

GOSPEL ACCLAMATION *(Luke 1.38)*

Alleluia. Alleluia. Here am I, the servant of the Lord: let it be done to me according to your word. **Alleluia.**

GOSPEL *(Luke 1.26-38)*

The Lord be with you. **And with your spirit.** A reading from the holy Gospel according to Luke. **Glory to you, O Lord.**

The Angel Gabriel was sent by God to a town in Galilee called Nazareth, to a virgin engaged to a man whose name was Joseph, of the house of David. The virgin's name was Mary.

And he came to her and said, "Hail, full of grace! The Lord is with you." But she was much perplexed by his words and pondered what sort of greeting this might be.

The Angel said to her, "Do not be afraid, Mary, for you have found favour with God. And now, you will conceive in your womb and bear a son, and you will name him Jesus.

"He will be great, and will be called the Son of the Most High, and the Lord God will give to him the throne of his father David. He will reign over the house of Jacob forever, and of his kingdom there will be no end."

Mary said to the Angel, "How can this be, since I am a virgin?" The Angel said to her, "The Holy Spirit will come upon you, and the power of the Most High will overshadow you; therefore the child to be born will be holy; he will be called Son of God.

"And now, your relative Elizabeth in her old age has also conceived a son; and this is the sixth month for her who was said to be barren. For nothing will be impossible with God." Then Mary said, "Here am I, the servant of the Lord; let it be done to me according to your word." Then the Angel departed from her.

The Gospel of the Lord. **Praise to you, Lord Jesus Christ.**

PROFESSION OF FAITH *(p. 11)*

PRAYER OF THE FAITHFUL

The following intentions are suggestions only. There are more suggestions at www.livingwithchrist.ca

℟. **Lord, hear our prayer.**

For leaders of the Church, entrusted to be good shepherds of God's people on earth, we pray to the Lord: ℟.

For those in positions of authority, called to act responsibly, we pray to the Lord: ℟.

For Christians everywhere, as they prepare to celebrate the birth of Christ, we pray to the Lord: R̶

For our community, as we work to heal our relationships with God and with one another, we pray to the Lord: R̶

PREPARATION OF THE GIFTS (p. 14)

PRAYER OVER THE OFFERINGS
May the Holy Spirit, O Lord, sanctify these gifts laid upon your altar, just as he filled with his power the womb of the Blessed Virgin Mary. Through Christ our Lord. **Amen.**

PREFACE (Advent II, p. 15)

COMMUNION ANTIPHON (Isaiah 7.14)
Behold, a Virgin shall conceive and bear a son; and his name will be called Emmanuel.

PRAYER AFTER COMMUNION
Having received this pledge of eternal redemption, we pray, almighty God, that, as the feast day of our salvation draws ever nearer, so we may press forward all the more eagerly to the worthy celebration of the mystery of your Son's Nativity. Who lives and reigns for ever and ever. **Amen.**

SOLEMN BLESSING AND DISMISSAL (p. 79)

December 25
Nativity of the Lord

It happened in the third year before his death. The year was 1223. The place: Greccio, Italy. Francis of Assisi wanted to awaken the faith and devotion of the people. He desired to celebrate with the greatest solemnity the memory of the birth of the Child Jesus and have the people experience the stable at Bethlehem.

He had a crib prepared with hay, an ox and a donkey. The Friars gathered and the people of Greccio came with candles and lanterns, lighting up the night and singing as they arrived at the crib. The man of God stood before the crib, filled with affection and overflowing with joy.

Mass was celebrated. Francis, as deacon, read the Gospel and preached with fervour about the humility of the poor King, who he called the Child of Bethlehem. Francis spoke with such tenderness and power that it was clearly evident it was not he, but the Spirit of God who was speaking.

It is said that Francis of Assisi went over to the crib, picked up the figure of the child Jesus and it seemed to wake from sleep. Francis' re-enactment of the birth of Jesus still awakens a love for the Child Jesus in the hearts of people.

"And the Word became flesh and lived among us."

Friar Ed Debono, OFM Conv
Kingston, ON

MASS DURING THE NIGHT

ENTRANCE ANTIPHON *(Psalm 2.7)*
The Lord said to me: You are my Son. It is I who have begotten you this day.
   or
Let us all rejoice in the Lord, for our Saviour has been born in the world. Today true peace has come down to us from heaven.

INTRODUCTORY RITES *(p.5)*

COLLECT
O God, who have made this most sacred night radiant with the splendour of the true light, grant, we pray, that we, who have known the mysteries of his light on earth, may also delight in his gladness in heaven. Who lives and reigns with you in the unity of the Holy Spirit, one God, for ever and ever. **Amen.**

FIRST READING *(Isaiah 9.2-4, 6-7)*
The people who walked in darkness have seen
   a great light;
those who lived in a land of deep darkness —
on them light has shone.
You have multiplied the nation,
you have increased its joy;
they rejoice before you
as with joy at the harvest,
as people exult when dividing plunder.

For the yoke of their burden,
and the bar across their shoulders,
the rod of their oppressor,
you have broken as on the day of Midian.

For a child has been born for us,
a son given to us;
authority rests upon his shoulders;
and he is named
Wonderful Counsellor, Mighty God,
Everlasting Father, Prince of Peace.

His authority shall grow continually,
and there shall be endless peace
for the throne of David and his kingdom.
He will establish and uphold it
with justice and with righteousness
from this time onward and forevermore.
The zeal of the Lord of hosts will do this.

The word of the Lord. **Thanks be to God.**

RESPONSORIAL PSALM *(Psalm 96)*

To-day is born our Sav-iour,— Christ— the Lord.

R. **Today is born our Saviour, Christ the Lord.**

O sing to the Lord a · **new** song;
sing to the Lord, · **all_the** earth.
Sing to the Lord, · **bless_his** name;
tell of his salvation from day · **to** day. R.

Declare his glory among · **the** nations,
his marvellous works among all · **the** peoples.
For great is the Lord, and greatly · **to_be** praised;
he is to be revered above · **all** gods. R.

Let the heavens be glad, and let the earth
 · **re**-joice;
let the sea roar, and all · **that** fills_it;
let the field exult, and every··**thing** in_it.
Then shall all the trees of the forest sing
 · **for** joy. R.

Rejoice before the Lord; for · **he_is** coming,
for he is coming to judge · **the** earth.
He will judge the world · **with** righteousness,
and the peoples · **with_his** truth. R.

©2009 Gordon Johnston/Novalis

SECOND READING *(Titus 2.11-14)*

Beloved: The grace of God has appeared, bringing salvation to all, training us to renounce impiety and worldly passions, and in the present age to live lives that are self-controlled, upright, and godly, while we wait for the blessed hope and the manifestation of the glory of our great God and Saviour, Jesus Christ.

He it is who gave himself for us that he might redeem us from all iniquity and purify for himself a people of his own who are zealous for good deeds.

The word of the Lord. **Thanks be to God.**

GOSPEL ACCLAMATION *(Luke 2.10-11)*

Alleluia. Alleluia. Good news and great joy to all the world: today is born our Saviour, Christ the Lord. **Alleluia.**

GOSPEL *(Luke 2.1-16)*

The Lord be with you. **And with your spirit.**
A reading from the holy Gospel according to Luke. **Glory to you, O Lord.**

In those days a decree went out from Caesar Augustus that all the world should be registered. This was the first registration and was taken while Quirinius was governor of Syria. All went to their own towns to be registered. Joseph also went from the town of Nazareth in Galilee to Judea, to the city of David called Bethlehem, because he was descended from the house and family of David. He went to be registered with Mary, to whom he was engaged and who was expecting a child.

While they were there, the time came for her to deliver her child. And she gave birth to her firstborn son and wrapped him in swaddling clothes, and laid him in a manger, because there was no place for them in the inn.

In that region there were shepherds living in the fields, keeping watch over their flock by night. Then an Angel of the Lord stood before them, and the glory of the Lord shone around them, and they were terrified. But the Angel said to them, "Do not be afraid; for see — I am bringing you good news of great joy for all the people: to you is born this day in the city of David a Saviour, who is the Christ, the Lord. This will be a sign for you: you will find a child wrapped in swaddling clothes and lying in a manger."

And suddenly there was with the Angel a multitude of the heavenly host, praising God and saying, "Glory to God in the highest heaven, and on earth peace among those whom he favours!"

When the Angels had left them and gone into heaven, the shepherds said to one another, "Let us go now to Bethlehem and see this thing that has taken place, which the Lord has made known to us." So they went with haste and found Mary and Joseph, and the child lying in the manger.

The Gospel of the Lord. **Praise to you, Lord Jesus Christ.**

PROFESSION OF FAITH (p.11. All kneel at the words "and by the Holy Spirit was incarnate.")

PRAYER OF THE FAITHFUL

The following intentions are suggestions only. There are more suggestions at www.livingwithchrist.ca

R. **Lord, hear our prayer.**

For the whole People of God, whose faithful witness brings Jesus into the world each day, we pray to the Lord: R.

For the land where Jesus was born and lived; for reconciliation and mutual respect of the peoples living there, we pray to the Lord: R.

For all whose joy this Christmas is diminished by suffering in mind or body, we pray to the Lord: R.

For ourselves, celebrating the joy of Christmas; and for those around us who, on this very night and day of Christmas, are lonely, we pray to the Lord: R.

PREPARATION OF THE GIFTS *(p. 14)*

PRAYER OVER THE OFFERINGS

May the oblation of this day's feast be pleasing to you, O Lord, we pray, that through this most holy exchange we may be found in the likeness of Christ, in whom our nature is united to you. Who lives and reigns for ever and ever. **Amen.**

PREFACE *(Nativity, p. 16)*

COMMUNION ANTIPHON *(John 1.14)*
The Word became flesh, and we have seen his glory.

PRAYER AFTER COMMUNION

Grant us, we pray, O Lord our God, that we, who are gladdened by participation in the feast of our Redeemer's Nativity, may through an honourable way of life become worthy of union with him. Who lives and reigns for ever and ever. **Amen.**

SOLEMN BLESSING — NATIVITY (Optional)

Bow down for the blessing.

May the God of infinite goodness, who by the Incarnation of his Son has driven darkness from the world and by that glorious Birth has illumined this most holy night (day), drive far from you the darkness of vice and illumine your hearts with the light of virtue. **Amen.**

May God, who willed that the great joy of his Son's saving Birth be announced to shepherds by the Angel, fill your minds with the gladness he gives and make you heralds of his Gospel. **Amen.**

And may God, who by the Incarnation brought together the earthly and heavenly realm, fill you with the gift of his peace and favour and make you sharers with the Church in heaven. **Amen.**

And may the blessing of almighty God, the Father, and the Son, and the Holy Spirit, come down on you and remain with you for ever. **Amen.**

DISMISSAL (p. 71)

MASS AT DAWN

ENTRANCE ANTIPHON *(Cf. Isaiah 9.1, 5; Luke 1.33)*
Today a light will shine upon us, for the Lord is born for us; and he will be called Wondrous God, Prince of peace, Father of future ages: and his reign will be without end.

INTRODUCTORY RITES *(p. 5)*

COLLECT
Grant, we pray, almighty God, that, as we are bathed in the new radiance of your incarnate Word, the light of faith, which illumines our minds, may also shine through in our deeds. Through our Lord Jesus Christ, your Son, who lives and reigns with you in the unity of the Holy Spirit, one God, for ever and ever. **Amen.**

FIRST READING *(Isaiah 62.11-12)*
The Lord has proclaimed to the end of the earth:
"Say to daughter Zion,
See, your salvation comes;
his reward is with him,
and his recompense before him.

"They shall be called 'The Holy People,'
'The Redeemed of the Lord';
and you shall be called 'Sought Out,'
'A City Not Forsaken.'"

The word of the Lord. **Thanks be to God.**

RESPONSORIAL PSALM *(Psalm 97)*

A light will shine on us this day:
The Lord is born for us.

℟. **A light will shine on us this day:**
The Lord is born for us.

The Lord is king! Let the earth re·-**joice;**
let the many coastlands be · **glad!**
Clouds and thick darkness are all a·-**round_him;**
righteousness and justice are the foundation
     of his · **throne.** ℟.

The mountains melt like wax before the · **Lord,**
before the Lord of all the · **earth.**
The heavens proclaim his · **righteousness;**
and all the peoples behold his · **glory.** ℟.

Light dawns for the · **righteous,**
and joy for the upright in · **heart.**
Rejoice in the Lord, O you · **righteous,**
and give thanks to his holy · **name!** ℟.

©2009 Gordon Johnston/Novalis

To hear the Sunday Psalms, visit www.livingwithchrist.ca.

SECOND READING *(Titus 3.4-7)*

When the goodness and loving kindness of God our Saviour appeared, he saved us, not because of any works of righteousness that we had done, but according to his mercy, through the water of rebirth and renewal by the Holy Spirit. This Spirit he poured out on us richly through Jesus Christ our Saviour, so that, having been justified by his grace, we might become heirs according to the hope of eternal life.

The word of the Lord. **Thanks be to God.**

GOSPEL ACCLAMATION *(Luke 2.14)*

Alleluia. Alleluia. Glory to God in the highest heaven; peace on earth to people of good will. **Alleluia.**

GOSPEL *(Luke 2.15-20)*

The Lord be with you. **And with your spirit.** A reading from the holy Gospel according to Luke. **Glory to you, O Lord.**

When the Angels had left them and gone into heaven, the shepherds said to one another, "Let us go now to Bethlehem and see this thing that has taken place, which the Lord has made known to us."

So they went with haste and found Mary and Joseph, and the child lying in the manger. When they saw this, they made known what had been told them about this child; and all who heard it were amazed at what the shepherds told them.

But Mary treasured all these words and pondered them in her heart. The shepherds returned, glorifying and praising God for all they had heard and seen, as it had been told them.

The Gospel of the Lord. **Praise to you, Lord Jesus Christ.**

PROFESSION OF FAITH *(p. 11. All kneel at the words "and by the Holy Spirit was incarnate.")*

PRAYER OF THE FAITHFUL *(p.106)*

PREPARATION OF THE GIFTS *(p. 14)*

PRAYER OVER THE OFFERINGS
May our offerings be worthy, we pray, O Lord, of the mysteries of the Nativity this day, that, just as Christ was born a man and also shone forth as God, so these earthly gifts may confer on us what is divine. Through Christ our Lord. **Amen.**

PREFACE *(Nativity, p. 16)*

COMMUNION ANTIPHON *(Cf. Zechariah 9.9)*
Rejoice, O Daughter Sion; lift up praise, Daughter Jerusalem: Behold, your King will come, the Holy One and Saviour of the world.

PRAYER AFTER COMMUNION
Grant us, Lord, as we honour with joyful devotion the Nativity of your Son, that we may come to know with fullness of faith the hidden depths of this mystery and to love them ever more and more. Through Christ our Lord. **Amen.**

SOLEMN BLESSING AND DISMISSAL *(p. 107)*

MASS DURING THE DAY

ENTRANCE ANTIPHON *(Cf. Isaiah 9.5)*
A child is born for us, and a son is given to us; his sceptre of power rests upon his shoulder, and his name will be called Messenger of great counsel.

INTRODUCTORY RITES *(p. 5)*

COLLECT
O God, who wonderfully created the dignity of human nature and still more wonderfully restored it, grant, we pray, that we may share in the divinity of Christ, who humbled himself to share in our humanity. Who lives and reigns with you in the unity of the Holy Spirit, one God, for ever and ever. **Amen.**

FIRST READING *(Isaiah 52.7-10)*
How beautiful upon the mountains are the feet of the messenger who announces peace, who brings good news, who announces salvation, who says to Zion, "Your God reigns."

Listen! Your watchmen lift up their voices, together they sing for joy; for in plain sight they see the return of the Lord to Zion.

Break forth together into singing, you ruins of Jerusalem; for the Lord has comforted his people, he has redeemed Jerusalem. The Lord has bared his holy arm before the eyes of all the nations; and all the ends of the earth shall see the salvation of our God.

The word of the Lord. **Thanks be to God.**

RESPONSORIAL PSALM *(Psalm 98)*

All the ends of the earth have seen the vic - t'ry of our God.

R. **All the ends of the earth have seen
the victory of our God.**

O sing to the Lord a · **new** song,
for he has done · **marvellous** things.
His right hand and his holy · **arm**
have brought · **him** victory. R.

The Lord has made known · **his** victory;
he has revealed his vindication in the sight
of · **the** nations.
He has remembered his steadfast love and
· **faithfulness**
to the house · **of** Israel. R.

All the ends of the earth · **have** seen
the victory of · **our** God.
Make a joyful noise to the Lord, all the · **earth;**
break forth into joyous song and · **sing**
praises. R.

Sing praises to the Lord with · **the** lyre,
with the lyre and the sound · **of** melody.
With trumpets and the sound of the · **horn**
make a joyful noise before the King,
  · **the** Lord. R.

©2009 Gordon Johnston/Novalis

To hear the Sunday Psalms, visit www.livingwithchrist.ca.

SECOND READING *(Hebrews 1.1-6)*

Long ago God spoke to our ancestors in many and various ways by the Prophets, but in these last days he has spoken to us by the Son, whom he appointed heir of all things, through whom he also created the ages.

He is the reflection of God's glory and the exact imprint of God's very being, and he sustains all things by his powerful word. When he had made purification for sins, he sat down at the right hand of the Majesty on high, having become as much superior to Angels as the name he has inherited is more excellent than theirs.

For to which of the Angels did God ever say, "You are my Son; today I have begotten you"? Or again, "I will be his Father, and he will be my Son"? And again, when he brings the firstborn into the world, he says, "Let all God's Angels worship him."

The word of the Lord. **Thanks be to God.**

GOSPEL ACCLAMATION

Alleluia. Alleluia. A holy day has dawned upon us. Come you nations and adore the Lord. Today a great light has come down upon the earth. **Alleluia.**

GOSPEL *(John 1.1-18)*

For the shorter version, omit the indented parts.

The Lord be with you. **And with your spirit.**
A reading from the holy Gospel according to John.
Glory to you, O Lord.

In the beginning was the Word, and the Word was with God, and the Word was God. He was in the beginning with God. All things came into being through him, and without him not one thing came into being. What has come into being in him was life, and the life was the light of the human race.

The light shines in the darkness, and the darkness did not overcome it.

> There was a man sent from God, whose name was John. He came as a witness to testify to the light, so that all might believe through him. He himself was not the light, but he came to testify to the light.

The true light, which enlightens everyone, was coming into the world. He was in the world, and the world came into being through him; yet the world did not know him. He came to what was his own, and his own people did not accept him. But to all who received him, who believed in his name, he gave power to become children of God, who were born, not of blood or of the will of the flesh or of the will of man, but of God.

And the Word became flesh and lived among us, and we have seen his glory, the glory as of a father's only-begotten son, full of grace and truth.

> John testified to him and cried out, "This was he of whom I said, 'He who comes after me ranks ahead of me because he was before me.'" From his fullness we have all received, grace upon grace. The law

indeed was given through Moses; grace and truth came through Jesus Christ. No one has ever seen God. It is God the only-begotten Son, who is close to the Father's heart, who has made him known. The Gospel of the Lord. **Praise to you, Lord Jesus Christ.**

PROFESSION OF FAITH (p. 11. All kneel at the words "and by the Holy Spirit was incarnate.")

PRAYER OF THE FAITHFUL (p.106)

PREPARATION OF THE GIFTS (p. 14)

PRAYER OVER THE OFFERINGS

Make acceptable, O Lord, our oblation on this solemn day, when you manifested the reconciliation that makes us wholly pleasing in your sight and inaugurated for us the fullness of divine worship. Through Christ our Lord. **Amen.**

PREFACE (Nativity, p. 16)

COMMUNION ANTIPHON (Cf. Psalm 97.3)

All the ends of the earth have seen the salvation of our God.

PRAYER AFTER COMMUNION

Grant, O merciful God, that, just as the Saviour of the world, born this day, is the author of divine generation for us, so he may be the giver even of immortality. Who lives and reigns for ever and ever. **Amen.**

SOLEMN BLESSING AND DISMISSAL (p. 107)

December 31
Holy Family of Jesus, Mary and Joseph

I have read all the recommended 'what-to-expect' books. Yet nothing prepared me for how utterly unprepared I felt as our family-of-now-three walked out of the maternity hospital. I figured they would stop us at the door. Surely, they had seen my pathetic attempts at diapering and feeding.

They did send us home and, even more surprisingly, I did eventually figure it out. However, I never felt ready as a parent. I was not ready for the feeling of the rush of love at my son's first smile, the gripping fear I experienced at the wake of fevers and late night hospital visits, or the overwhelming emotion washing over me as I saw him climb onto the yellow bus on his first day of school. That's the funny thing about parenting. Once you think you have figured it out, the kids are already onto the next stage: crawling, walking, running, dating, driving.

Only now, 22 years later, I realize one checklist matters. We find it at the conclusion to today's Gospel, where Jesus' formative years are summed up in seventeen words: "The child grew and became strong, filled with wisdom; and the favour of God was upon him."

Reflect today on what helps you and your loved ones grow strong in character, rich in wisdom and eager for God's favour. Know that whatever role or task God doles out, because of him we are more than prepared.

Caroline Pignat
Kanata, ON

ENTRANCE ANTIPHON *(Luke 2.16)*
The shepherds went in haste, and found Mary and Joseph and the Infant lying in a manger.

INTRODUCTORY RITES *(p. 5)*

COLLECT
O God, who were pleased to give us the shining example of the Holy Family, graciously grant that we may imitate them in practising the virtues of family life and in the bonds of charity, and so, in the joy of your house, delight one day in eternal rewards. Through our Lord Jesus Christ, your Son, who lives and reigns with you in the unity of the Holy Spirit, one God, for ever and ever. **Amen.**

Alternate readings can be found on p. 123.

FIRST READING *(Genesis 15.1-6; 17.3b-5, 15-16; 21.1-7)*
The word of the Lord came to Abram in a vision, "Do not be afraid, Abram, I am your shield; your reward shall be very great." But Abram said, "O Lord God, what will you give me, for I continue childless, and the heir of my house is Eliezer of Damascus?" And Abram said, "You have given me no offspring, and so a slave born in my house is to be my heir." But the word of the Lord came to him, "This man shall not be your heir; no one but your very own issue shall be your heir."

The Lord brought him outside and said, "Look toward heaven and count the stars, if you are able to count them." Then he said to him, "So shall your descendants be." And he believed the Lord; and the Lord reckoned it to him as righteousness.

God said to him, "As for me, this is my covenant with you: You shall be the father of a multitude of nations. No longer shall your name be Abram, but your name shall be Abraham; for I have made you the father of a multitude of nations."

God said to Abraham, "As for Sarah your wife, you shall not call her Sarai, but Sarah shall be her name. I will bless her, and moreover I will give you a son by her. I will bless her, and she shall give rise to nations; kings of peoples shall come from her."

The Lord dealt with Sarah as he had said, and the Lord did for Sarah as he had promised. Sarah conceived and bore Abraham a son in his old age, at the time of which God had spoken to him. Abraham gave the name Isaac to his son whom Sarah bore him. And Abraham circumcised his son Isaac when he was eight days old, as God had commanded him. Abraham was a hundred years old when his son Isaac was born to him. Now Sarah said, "God has brought laughter for me; everyone who hears will laugh with me." And she said, "Who would ever have said to Abraham that Sarah would nurse children? Yet I have borne him a son in his old age."

The word of the Lord. **Thanks be to God.**

RESPONSORIAL PSALM *(Psalm 105)*

The Lord is our God, mind - ful — of his cov - e - nant for - ev - er.

R̰. **The Lord is our God,
mindful of his covenant forever.**

O give thanks to the Lord, call · **on_his** name,
make known his deeds a--**mong_the** peoples.
Sing to him, sing · **praises** to him;
tell of all his · **wonderful** works. R̰.

Glory in his ho--**ly** name;
let the hearts of those who seek the Lord · **re**-joice.
Seek the Lord · **and** his strength;
seek his presence · **con**-tinually. R̰.

Remember the wonderful works he · **has** done,
his miracles, and the judgments · **he** uttered,
O offspring of his · **ser**-vant Abraham,
children of Jacob, · **his** chosen_ones. R̰.

He is mindful of his covenant · **for**-ever,
of the word that he commanded, for a thousand
     · **gener**-ations,
the covenant that he · **made** with Abraham,
his sworn promise · **to** Isaac. R̰.

©2009 Gordon Johnston/Novalis

SECOND READING *(Hebrews 11.8, 11-12, 17-19)*
By faith Abraham obeyed when he was called to set out for a place that he was to receive as an inheritance; and he set out, not knowing where he was going. By faith Sarah herself, though barren, received power to conceive, even when she was too old, because she considered him faithful who had promised.

Therefore from one person, and this one as good as dead, descendants were born, "as many as the stars of heaven and as the innumerable grains of sand by the seashore."

By faith Abraham, when put to the test, offered up Isaac. He who had received the promises was ready to offer up his only-begotten son, of whom he had been told, "It is through Isaac that descendants shall be named for you." Abraham considered the fact that God is able even to raise someone from the dead — and figuratively speaking, he did receive him back.

The word of the Lord. **Thanks be to God.**

GOSPEL ACCLAMATION *(Hebrews 1.1-2)*
Alleluia. Alleluia. Long ago God spoke to our ancestors by the Prophets; in these last days he has spoken to us by the Son. **Alleluia.**

GOSPEL *(Luke 2.22-40)*
For the shorter version, omit the indented parts.
The Lord be with you. **And with your spirit.**
A reading from the holy Gospel according to Luke.
Glory to you, O Lord.

When the time came for their purification according to the law of Moses, Mary and Joseph brought the child Jesus up to Jerusalem to present him to the Lord.

(as it is written in the law of the Lord, "Every firstborn male shall be designated as holy to the Lord"), and they offered a sacrifice according to what is stated in the law of the Lord, "a pair of turtledoves or two young pigeons."

Now there was a man in Jerusalem whose name was Simeon; this man was righteous and devout, looking forward to the consolation of Israel, and the Holy Spirit rested on him. It had been revealed to him by the Holy Spirit that he would not see death before he had seen the Christ of the Lord. Guided by the Spirit, Simeon came into the temple; and when the parents brought in the child Jesus, to do for him what was customary under the law,

Simeon took him in his arms and praised God, saying, "Master, now you are dismissing your servant in peace, according to your word; for my eyes have seen your salvation, which you have prepared in the presence of all peoples, a light for revelation to the Gentiles and for glory to your people Israel."

And the child's father and mother were amazed at what was being said about him. Then Simeon blessed them and said to his mother Mary, "This child is destined for the falling and the rising of many in Israel, and to be a sign that will be opposed so that the inner thoughts of many will be revealed — and a sword will pierce your own soul too."

There was also a Prophet, Anna the daughter of Phanuel, of the tribe of Asher. She was of a great age, having lived with her husband seven years after her marriage, then as a widow to the age of eighty-four. She never left the temple but worshipped there with fasting and prayer night and day. At that moment she came, and began to praise God and to speak about the child to all who were looking for the redemption of Jerusalem.

When Mary and Joseph had finished everything required by the law of the Lord, they returned to Galilee, to their own town of Nazareth. The child grew and became strong, filled with wisdom; and the favour of God was upon him.

The Gospel of the Lord. **Praise to you, Lord Jesus Christ.**

Mass resumes on p. 126.

Alternate readings:

FIRST READING *(Sirach 3.2-6, 12-14)*

The Lord honours a father above his children,
and he confirms a mother's rights over her sons.
Whoever honours their father atones for sins
and gains preservation from them;
when they pray, they will be heard.
Whoever respects their mother
is like one who lays up treasure.
The person who honours their father
will have joy in their own children,
and when they pray they will be heard.
Whoever respects their father will have a long life,
and whoever honours their mother obeys the Lord.

My child, help your father in his old age,
and do not grieve him as long as he lives.
Even if his mind fails, be patient with him;
because you have all your faculties,
do not despise him all the days of his life.
For kindness to your father will not be forgotten,
and will be credited to you against your sins —
a house raised in justice for you.

The word of the Lord. **Thanks be to God.**

RESPONSORIAL PSALM *(Psalm 128)*

Bless - ed   is   ev - ery - one   who fears   the   Lord,   who   walks   in   his   ways.

R. **Blessed is everyone who fears the Lord.**
or **Blessed is everyone who fears the Lord,**
   who walks in his ways.

Blessed is everyone who fears · **the** Lord,
who walks in · **his** ways.
You shall eat the fruit of the labour of · **your** hands;
you shall be happy, and it shall go well · **with**
   you. R.

Your wife will be like a fruit--**ful** vine
within · **your** house;
your children will be · **like** olive_shoots
around · **your** table. R.

Thus shall the man be blessed who fears · **the** Lord.
The Lord bless you · **from** Zion.
May you see the prosperity of · **Je**-rusalem
all the days of · **your** life. R.

©2009 Gordon Johnston/Novalis

To hear the Sunday Psalms, visit www.livingwithchrist.ca.

SECOND READING *(Colossians 3.12-21)*

The shorter reading ends at the asterisks.

Brothers and sisters: As God's chosen ones, holy
and beloved, clothe yourselves with compassion,
kindness, humility, meekness, and patience. Bear
with one another and, if anyone has a complaint
against another, forgive each other; just as the Lord
has forgiven you, so you also must forgive. Above all,
clothe yourselves with love, which binds everything
together in perfect harmony. And let the peace of
Christ rule in your hearts, to which indeed you were
called in the one body. And be thankful.

Let the word of Christ dwell in you richly; teach
and admonish one another in all wisdom; and with
gratitude in your hearts sing Psalms, hymns, and
spiritual songs to God. And whatever you do, in
word or deed, do everything in the name of the Lord
Jesus, giving thanks to God the Father through him.

* * *

Wives, be subject to your husbands, as is fitting in the Lord. Husbands, love your wives and never treat them harshly. Children, obey your parents in everything, for this is your acceptable duty in the Lord. Fathers, do not provoke your children, or they may lose heart.

The word of the Lord. **Thanks be to God.**

For the Gospel, see p. 121.

PROFESSION OF FAITH *(p. 11)*

PRAYER OF THE FAITHFUL

The following intentions are suggestions only. There are more suggestions at www.livingwithchrist.ca

R. **Lord, hear our prayer.**

For the Church, beacon of light to the family of nations, we pray to the Lord: R.

For governments throughout the world, in search of peace and understanding among the human family, we pray to the Lord: R.

For peace of mind for all who suffer, we pray to the Lord: R.

For our parish, example of family to all, we pray to the Lord: R.

PREPARATION OF THE GIFTS *(p. 14)*

PRAYER OVER THE OFFERINGS

We offer you, Lord, the sacrifice of conciliation, humbly asking that, through the intercession of the Virgin Mother of God and Saint Joseph, you may establish our families firmly in your grace and your peace. Through Christ our Lord. **Amen.**

PREFACE *(Nativity, p. 16)*

COMMUNION ANTIPHON *(Baruch 3.38)*
Our God has appeared on the earth, and lived among us.

PRAYER AFTER COMMUNION
Bring those you refresh with this heavenly Sacrament, most merciful Father, to imitate constantly the example of the Holy Family, so that, after the trials of this world, we may share their company for ever. Through Christ our Lord. **Amen.**

BLESSING AND DISMISSAL *(p. 71)*

January Saints' Days

The following saints are traditionally remembered in January in Canada.

1 Solemnity of Mary, the Holy Mother of God

2 Saints Basil the Great and Gregory Nazianzen

7 Saint André Bessette

8 Saint Raymond of Penyafort

12 Saint Marguerite Bourgeoys

13 Saint Hilary

17 Saint Anthony

20 Saint Fabian
Saint Sebastian

21 Saint Agnes

22 Saint Vincent

24 Saint Francis de Sales

26 Saints Timothy and Titus

27 Saint Angela Merici

28 Saint Thomas Aquinas

31 Saint John Bosco

January 1
Mary, the Holy Mother of God
World Day of Peace

Mary, the Mother of God, is honoured on this day as well as on many others. Joseph is her spouse, protector, provider and foster father to the Son of God. How was it that in spite of all of God's graces poured upon them, all details of God's plan was not known to them?

Our culture fosters a fierce autonomy. It has led to pride, to an independence from God our Father. The way back is difficult because it is frightening for us to live without being in complete control. But who on earth should have been more aware of the Father's plan than Mary and Joseph? They lived in the fullness of the Spirit and, yet, not in the fullness of knowledge. When Mary and Joseph heard news of God's revelation to the shepherds, rather than the other way around, they did not consider God had held out on them. Rather, Mary humbly "treasured all these words and pondered them in her heart" and continued to live a life totally trusting in God.

God became man so that we could enter into his love through his humility. The Eucharist exemplifies his humility and his love. Can we live lives of such profound humility? Profound dependence? Can we honour God our Father and Jesus our Lord, by remembering the grace of God is alive within us most fully, when we live like Mary?

Johanne Brownrigg
Orleans, ON

ENTRANCE ANTIPHON

Hail, Holy Mother, who gave birth to the King who rules heaven and earth for ever.

or (Cf. Isaiah 9.1, 5; Luke 1.33)

Today a light will shine upon us, for the Lord is born for us; and he will be called Wondrous God, Prince of peace, Father of future ages: and his reign will be without end.

INTRODUCTORY RITES *(p. 5)*

COLLECT

O God, who through the fruitful virginity of Blessed Mary bestowed on the human race the grace of eternal salvation, grant, we pray, that we may experience the intercession of her, through whom we were found worthy to receive the author of life, our Lord Jesus Christ, your Son. Who lives and reigns with you in the unity of the Holy Spirit, one God, for ever and ever. **Amen.**

FIRST READING *(Numbers 6.22-27)*

The Lord spoke to Moses: Speak to Aaron and his sons, saying, Thus you shall bless the children of Israel: You shall say to them,

The Lord bless you and keep you;
the Lord make his face to shine upon you,
and be gracious to you;
the Lord lift up his countenance upon you,
and give you peace.

So they shall put my name on the children of Israel, and I will bless them.

The word of the Lord. **Thanks be to God.**

RESPONSORIAL PSALM *(Psalm 67)*

May God be gra-cious to us and bless us.

R. **May God be gracious to us and bless us.**

May God be gracious to us · **and** bless_us
and make his face to shine · **up**-on_us,
that your way may be known up-·**on** earth,
your saving power a-·**mong** all nations. R.

Let the nations be glad and sing · **for** joy,
for you judge the peoples with equity and guide
    the nations up-·**on** earth.
Let the peoples praise you, · **O** God;
let all the · **peo**-ples praise_you. R.

The earth has yielded · **its** increase;
God, our God, · **has** blessed_us.
May God continue · **to** bless_us;
let all the ends of the · **earth** re-vere_him. R.

©2009 Gordon Johnston/Novalis

To hear the Sunday Psalms, visit www.livingwithchrist.ca.

SECOND READING *(Galatians 4.4-7)*
Brothers and sisters: When the fullness of time had
come, God sent his Son, born of a woman, born under
the law, in order to redeem those who were under the
law, so that we might receive adoption to sonship.

And because you are sons and daughters, God has sent the Spirit of his Son into our hearts, crying, "Abba! Father!" So you are no longer slave but son, and if son then also heir, through God.

The word of the Lord. **Thanks be to God.**

GOSPEL ACCLAMATION *(Hebrews 1.1-2)*
Alleluia. Alleluia. Long ago God spoke to our ancestors by the Prophets; in these last days he has spoken to us by the Son. **Alleluia.**

GOSPEL *(Luke 2.16-21)*
The Lord be with you. **And with your spirit.**
A reading from the holy Gospel according to Luke.
Glory to you, O Lord.

The shepherds went with haste to Bethlehem and found Mary and Joseph, and the child lying in the manger. When they saw this, they made known what had been told them about this child; and all who heard it were amazed at what the shepherds told them.

But Mary treasured all these words and pondered them in her heart.

The shepherds returned, glorifying and praising God for all they had heard and seen, as it had been told them.

After eight days had passed, it was time to circumcise the child; and he was called Jesus, the name given by the Angel before he was conceived in the womb.

The Gospel of the Lord. **Praise to you, Lord Jesus Christ.**

PROFESSION OF FAITH *(p. 11)*

PRAYER OF THE FAITHFUL
The following intentions are suggestions only. There are more suggestions at www.livingwithchrist.ca

R. **Lord, hear our prayer.**

For the Church, called to celebrate God's peace in the world, we pray to the Lord: R.

For all nations longing for God's kingdom of peace, we pray to the Lord: R.

For the Spirit of peace wherever there is fear, anxiety or anger, we pray to the Lord: R.

For this eucharistic community gathered around God's table of peace, we pray to the Lord: R.

PREPARATION OF THE GIFTS *(p. 14)*

PRAYER OVER THE OFFERINGS
O God, who in your kindness begin all good things and bring them to fulfillment, grant to us, who find joy in the Solemnity of the holy Mother of God, that, just as we glory in the beginnings of your grace, so one day we may rejoice in its completion. Through Christ our Lord. **Amen.**

PREFACE *(BVM, p. 17)*

COMMUNION ANTIPHON *(Hebrews 13.8)*
Jesus Christ is the same yesterday, today, and for ever.

PRAYER AFTER COMMUNION

We have received this heavenly Sacrament with joy, O Lord: grant, we pray, that it may lead us to eternal life, for we rejoice to proclaim the blessed ever-Virgin Mary Mother of your Son and Mother of the Church. Through Christ our Lord. **Amen.**

SOLEMN BLESSING — NEW YEAR (Optional)

Bow down for the blessing.

May God, the source and origin of all blessing, grant you grace, pour out his blessing in abundance, and keep you safe from harm throughout the year. **Amen.**

May he give you integrity in the faith, endurance in hope, and perseverance in charity with holy patience to the end. **Amen.**

May he order your days and your deeds in his peace, grant your prayers in this and in every place, and lead you happily to eternal life. **Amen.**

And may the blessing of almighty God, the Father, and the Son, and the Holy Spirit, come down on you and remain with you for ever. **Amen.**

DISMISSAL (p. 71)

January 7
Epiphany of the Lord

"Arise, shine, for your light has come," Isaiah says. He calls us to know God's presence, God's light on us, around us, and commands us to spread that light.

Isaiah tells the people of Israel that the light of God's blessing shines on them and beyond them. He sees nations streaming to them, attracted by God's light. Some Israelites thought God's favour was exclusively theirs. But God's light can be shared without diminishing it.

Every year at Easter the paschal candle, the Light of Christ, comes into a dark church and light is shared so the whole church glows. We proclaim light divided but never dimmed.

Epiphany celebrates God's light being revealed to all nations. The gospel, Paul says, has spread to the Gentiles. They have seen and received the light of Christ. Matthew tells of even earlier Gentile observers of that light, the Magi: "We observed his star at its rising, and have come to pay him homage."

The light that shone on the Magi shines on us. Jesus shares his light with us, and asks us to spread it. The light of our faith may seem fragile, but a small light can set the world on fire! Sharing the light of God's love, God's blessing does not diminish it – it grows in strength as it is shared. Let's keep it burning brightly!

Dinah Simmons
Halifax, NS

ENTRANCE ANTIPHON
(Cf. Malachi 3.1; 1 Chronicles 29.12)

Behold, the Lord, the Mighty One, has come; and kingship is in his grasp, and power and dominion.

INTRODUCTORY RITES *(p. 5)*

COLLECT

O God, who on this day revealed your Only Begotten Son to the nations by the guidance of a star, grant in your mercy that we, who know you already by faith, may be brought to behold the beauty of your sublime glory. Through our Lord Jesus Christ, your Son, who lives and reigns with you in the unity of the Holy Spirit, one God, for ever and ever. **Amen.**

FIRST READING *(Isaiah 60.1-6)*

Arise, shine, for your light has come,
and the glory of the Lord has risen upon you!
For darkness shall cover the earth,
and thick darkness the peoples;
but the Lord will arise upon you,
and his glory will appear over you.
Nations shall come to your light,
and kings to the brightness of your dawn.
Lift up your eyes and look around;
they all gather together, they come to you;
your sons shall come from far away,
and your daughters shall be carried on their
    nurses' arms.

Then you shall see and be radiant;
your heart shall thrill and rejoice,

because the abundance of the sea shall be brought
   to you,
the wealth of the nations shall come to you.
A multitude of camels shall cover you,
the young camels of Midian and Ephah;
all those from Sheba shall come.
They shall bring gold and frankincense,
and shall proclaim the praise of the Lord.

The word of the Lord. **Thanks be to God.**

RESPONSORIAL PSALM *(Psalm 72)*

Lord, eve-ry na-tion on earth will a-dore you.

℟. **Lord, every nation on earth will adore you.**

Give the king your justice, O · **God,**
and your righteousness to a king's · **son.**
May he judge your · **people** with righteousness,
and your · **poor** with justice. ℟.

In his days may righteousness · **flourish**
and peace abound, until the moon is no · **more.**
May he have dominion from · **sea** to sea,
and from the River to the · **ends_of** the earth. ℟.

May the kings of Tarshish and of the isles render
   him · **tribute,**
may the kings of Sheba and Seba bring · **gifts.**
May all kings fall · **down** be-fore_him,
all nations · **give** him service. ℟.

For he delivers the needy one who · **calls,**
the poor and the one who has no · **helper.**
He has pity on the · **weak_and** the needy,
and saves the · **lives_of** the needy. R.

©2009 Gordon Johnston/Novalis

To hear the Sunday Psalms, visit www.livingwithchrist.ca.

SECOND READING *(Ephesians 3.2-3a, 5-6)*

Brothers and sisters: Surely you have already heard of the commission of God's grace that was given me for you, and how the mystery was made known to me by revelation.

In former generations this mystery was not made known to humankind as it has now been revealed to his holy Apostles and Prophets by the Spirit: that is, the Gentiles have become fellow heirs, members of the same body, and sharers in the promise in Christ Jesus through the Gospel.

The word of the Lord. **Thanks be to God.**

GOSPEL ACCLAMATION *(See Matthew 2.2)*

Alleluia. Alleluia. We observed his star at its rising, and have come to pay homage to the Lord. **Alleluia.**

GOSPEL *(Matthew 2.1-12)*

The Lord be with you. **And with your spirit.** A reading from the holy Gospel according to Matthew. **Glory to you, O Lord.**

In the time of King Herod, after Jesus was born in Bethlehem of Judea, wise men from the East came to Jerusalem, asking, "Where is the child who has been born king of the Jews? For we observed his star at its rising, and have come to pay him homage."

When King Herod heard this, he was frightened, and all Jerusalem with him; and calling together all the chief priests and scribes of the people, he inquired of them where the Messiah was to be born. They told him, "In Bethlehem of Judea; for so it has been written by the Prophet: 'And you, Bethlehem, in the land of Judah, are by no means least among the rulers of Judah; for from you shall come a ruler who is to shepherd my people Israel.'"

Then Herod secretly called for the wise men and learned from them the exact time when the star had appeared. Then he sent them to Bethlehem, saying, "Go and search diligently for the child; and when you have found him, bring me word so that I may also go and pay him homage."

When they had heard the king, they set out; and there, ahead of them, went the star that they had seen at its rising, until it stopped over the place where the child was. When they saw that the star had stopped, they were overwhelmed with joy.

On entering the house, they saw the child with Mary his mother; and they knelt down and paid him homage. Then, opening their treasure chests, they offered him gifts of gold, frankincense, and myrrh.

And having been warned in a dream not to return to Herod, they left for their own country by another road.

The Gospel of the Lord. **Praise to you, Lord Jesus Christ.**

PROFESSION OF FAITH *(p. 11)*

PRAYER OF THE FAITHFUL

The following intentions are suggestions only. There are more suggestions at www.livingwithchrist.ca

R. **Lord, hear our prayer.**

For the Church, light of the nations, witness to the gospel of Christ Jesus, we pray to the Lord: R.

For the members of all faith communities working in mutual respect and acceptance, we pray to the Lord: R.

For those who seek food at our table and a place in our community, we pray to the Lord: R.

For ourselves, God's people, yearning to follow the Light of Christ, we pray to the Lord: R.

PREPARATION OF THE GIFTS *(p. 14)*

PRAYER OVER THE OFFERINGS

Look with favour, Lord, we pray, on these gifts of your Church, in which are offered now not gold or frankincense or myrrh, but he who by them is proclaimed, sacrificed and received, Jesus Christ. Who lives and reigns for ever and ever. **Amen.**

PREFACE *(Epiphany, p. 18)*

COMMUNION ANTIPHON *(Cf. Matthew 2.2)*
We have seen his star in the East, and have come with gifts to adore the Lord.

PRAYER AFTER COMMUNION

Go before us with heavenly light, O Lord, always and everywhere, that we may perceive with clear sight and revere with true affection the mystery in which you have willed us to participate. Through Christ our Lord. **Amen.**

SOLEMN BLESSING — EPIPHANY *(Optional)*

Bow down for the blessing.

May God, who has called you out of darkness into his wonderful light, pour out in kindness his blessing upon you and make your hearts firm in faith, hope and charity. **Amen.**

And since in all confidence you follow Christ, who today appeared in the world as a light shining in darkness, may God make you, too, a light for your brothers and sisters. **Amen.**

And so when your pilgrimage is ended, may you come to him whom the Magi sought as they followed the star and whom they found with great joy, the Light from Light, who is Christ the Lord. **Amen.**

And may the blessing of almighty God, the Father, and the Son, and the Holy Spirit, come down on you and remain with you for ever. **Amen.**

DISMISSAL *(p. 71)*

January 14
2nd Sunday in Ordinary Time
World Day of Migrants and Refugees

John knew immediately that Jesus was the Lamb of God, the one who takes away our sins, the Promised One of God. In John's heart there was no hesitation or doubt, rather I imagine joy and delight! When the two disciples run up to Jesus, he asks them, "What are you looking for?" They reply, "Rabbi," which means 'Teacher.' I believe Jesus asks the same question of you and me. How do we answer him? Maybe we can't answer that question, unless we face a deeper question: "What is God asking of me?" Am I truly *letting* that question shape me? Are you and I ready, like Samuel, to say: "Speak Lord, for your servant is listening?" Can we accept his invitation to 'discipleship,' to love and serve God with generosity and mercy?

World Day of Migrants and Refugees invites us to 'come and see' the faithful and courageous works of so many volunteers, organizations and parishes serving migrants and refugees. As strong advocates with a commitment to care for others, these 'disciples' put the gospel into action. They show us, and those they serve, the working hands, feet, and heart of our merciful and loving Messiah. Will you and I, along with Samuel, John and the first disciples, 'come and see,' trusting in the Lord's love and saving power – given to us and through us for others?

Julie Cachia
Toronto, ON

ENTRANCE ANTIPHON *(Psalm 65.4)*
**All the earth shall bow down before you, O God,
and shall sing to you, shall sing to your name, O
Most High!**

INTRODUCTORY RITES *(p. 5)*

COLLECT
Almighty ever-living God, who govern all things,
both in heaven and on earth, mercifully hear the
pleading of your people and bestow your peace on
our times. Through our Lord Jesus Christ, your Son,
who lives and reigns with you in the unity of the
Holy Spirit, one God, for ever and ever. **Amen.**

FIRST READING *(1 Samuel 3.3b-10, 19)*
Samuel was lying down in the temple of the Lord,
where the ark of God was. Then the Lord called,
"Samuel! Samuel!" and he said, "Here I am!" Samuel
ran to Eli, and said, "Here I am, for you called me."
But Eli said, "I did not call; lie down again." So he
went and lay down.

The Lord called again, "Samuel!" Samuel got up
and went to Eli, and said, "Here I am, for you called
me." But he said, "I did not call, my son; lie down
again." Now Samuel did not yet know the Lord, and
the word of the Lord had not yet been revealed to him.

The Lord called Samuel again, a third time. And
he got up and went to Eli, and said, "Here I am, for
you called me." Then Eli perceived that the Lord was
calling the boy. Therefore Eli said to Samuel, "Go,
lie down; and if he calls you, you shall say, 'Speak,

Lord, for your servant is listening.'" So Samuel went and lay down in his place.

Now the Lord came and stood there, calling as before, "Samuel! Samuel!" And Samuel said, "Speak, for your servant is listening."

As Samuel grew up, the Lord was with him and let none of his words fall to the ground.

The word of the Lord. **Thanks be to God.**

RESPONSORIAL PSALM *(Psalm 40)*

R. **Here I am, Lord; I come to do your will.**

I waited patiently for the · **Lord;**
he inclined to me and · **heard** my cry.
He put a new song in · **my** mouth,
a song of praise · **to** our God. R.

Sacrifice and offering you do not de-·**sire,**
but you have given me an · **o**-pen ear.
Burnt offering · **and** sin_offering
you have · **not** re-quired. R.

Then I said, "Here I · **am;**
In the scroll of the book it is · **written** of me.
I delight to do your will, O · **my** God;
your law is with-·**in** my heart." R.

I have told the glad news of de·-**liverance**
in the great · **con**-gre-gation;
see, I have not restrained · **my** lips,
as you · **know,** O Lord. R.

©2009 Gordon Johnston/Novalis

To hear the Sunday Psalms, visit www.livingwithchrist.ca.

SECOND READING *(1 Corinthians 6.13c-15a, 17-20)*

Brothers and sisters: The body is meant not for for-nication but for the Lord, and the Lord for the body. And God raised the Lord and will also raise us by his power.

Do you not know that your bodies are members of Christ? But anyone united to the Lord becomes one spirit with him. Shun fornication! Every sin that a person commits is outside the body; but the fornica-tor sins against the body itself.

Or do you not know that your body is a temple of the Holy Spirit within you, which you have from God, and that you are not your own? For you were bought with a price; therefore glorify God in your body.

The word of the Lord. **Thanks be to God.**

GOSPEL ACCLAMATION *(See John 1.41, 17)*

Alleluia. Alleluia. We have found the Messiah: Jesus Christ, who brings us grace and truth. **Alleluia.**

GOSPEL *(John 1.35-42)*

The Lord be with you. **And with your spirit.**
A reading from the holy Gospel according to John.
Glory to you, O Lord.

John was standing with two of his disciples, and as he watched Jesus walk by, he exclaimed, "Look, here is the Lamb of God!" The two disciples heard him say this, and they followed Jesus.

When Jesus turned and saw them following, he said to them, "What are you looking for?" They said to him, "Rabbi" (which translated means Teacher), "where are you staying?" He said to them, "Come and see." They came and saw where he was staying, and they remained with him that day. It was about four o'clock in the afternoon.

One of the two who heard John speak and followed him was Andrew, Simon Peter's brother. He first found his brother Simon and said to him, "We have found the Messiah" (which is translated the Christ). He brought Simon to Jesus, who looked at him and said, "You are Simon son of John. You are to be called Cephas" (which is translated Peter).

The Gospel of the Lord. **Praise to you, Lord Jesus Christ.**

PROFESSION OF FAITH (p. 11)

PRAYER OF THE FAITHFUL

The following intentions are suggestions only. There are more suggestions at www.livingwithchrist.ca

R. **Lord, hear our prayer.**

For the Church, hearing and proclaiming God's call to holiness, we pray to the Lord: R.

For world leaders, working for a lasting peace, we pray to the Lord: R.

For those who hunger for food, for understanding and for companionship, we pray to the Lord: ℟

For all refugees, searching for welcome, peace and security in their new homeland, we pray to the Lord: ℟

For ourselves, gathered to share the gifts of faith, hope and love, we pray to the Lord: ℟

PREPARATION OF THE GIFTS (p. 14)

PRAYER OVER THE OFFERINGS
Grant us, O Lord, we pray, that we may participate worthily in these mysteries, for whenever the memorial of this sacrifice is celebrated the work of our redemption is accomplished. Through Christ our Lord. **Amen.**

PREFACE (Sundays in Ordinary Time, p. 29)

COMMUNION ANTIPHON (Cf. Psalm 22.5)
You have prepared a table before me, and how precious is the chalice that quenches my thirst.
   or (1 John 4.16)
We have come to know and to believe in the love that God has for us.

PRAYER AFTER COMMUNION
Pour on us, O Lord, the Spirit of your love, and in your kindness make those you have nourished by this one heavenly Bread one in mind and heart. Through Christ our Lord. **Amen.**

BLESSING AND DISMISSAL (p. 71)

January 21
3rd Sunday in Ordinary Time
Week of Prayer for Christian Unity
"Your right hand, O Lord, glorious in power"

The Ninevites' conversion is quite astounding. Such an immediate and all-encompassing turning away from sin in this wicked and non-Israelite city (even down to its animals) towards a faith in God akin to Abraham's or that of Moses was a testament to God's power and a telling criticism of Israel's infidelity.

The God whose very way of being is the source and reason for such salvation is described in today's psalm: God is true, merciful, steadfast in love, good, and upright. This is the God we know in Jesus of Nazareth who dwelt among us and who offers us fullness of life. Today's readings encourage us to follow the example of those in the past who have given to this God of love a complete and unreserved response of faith.

The first disciples demonstrate such readiness and resolve: leaving behind their thriving business ventures, family and employees, they follow Jesus regardless of the cost. Their actions are not a counsel to shirk life's responsibilities, but to make God the priority. Saint Paul also advises living with this detached perspective, always ready to follow and to make Jesus' way our own. May such unity in willing discipleship be a gift for us and for the entire Christian family.

Christine Mader
Waverley, NS

ENTRANCE ANTIPHON (*Cf. Psalm 95.1, 6*)

O sing a new song to the Lord; sing to the Lord, all the earth. In his presence are majesty and splendour, strength and honour in his holy place.

INTRODUCTORY RITES (*p. 5*)

COLLECT

Almighty ever-living God, direct our actions according to your good pleasure, that in the name of your beloved Son we may abound in good works. Through our Lord Jesus Christ, your Son, who lives and reigns with you in the unity of the Holy Spirit, one God, for ever and ever. **Amen.**

FIRST READING (*Jonah 3.1-5, 10*)

The word of the Lord came to Jonah, saying, "Get up, go to Nineveh, that great city, and proclaim to it the message that I tell you." So Jonah set out and went to Nineveh, according to the word of the Lord.

Now Nineveh was an exceedingly large city, a three days' walk across. Jonah began to go into the city, going a day's walk. And he cried out, "Forty days more, and Nineveh shall be overthrown!"

And the people of Nineveh believed God; they proclaimed a fast, and everyone, great and small, put on sackcloth.

When God saw what they did, how they turned from their evil ways, God changed his mind about the calamity that he had said he would bring upon them; and he did not do it.

The word of the Lord. **Thanks be to God.**

RESPONSORIAL PSALM (Psalm 25)

Lord, make me know your ways.

R. **Lord, make me know your ways.**

Make me to know your ways, O · **Lord;**
teach me · **your** paths.
Lead me in your truth, and · **teach_me,**
for you are the God of my · **sal**-vation. R.

Be mindful of your mercy, O Lord, and of your
     steadfast · **love,**
for they have been from · **of** old.
According to your steadfast love re-·**member_me,**
for the sake of your goodness, · **O** Lord! R.

Good and upright is the · **Lord;**
therefore he instructs sinners in · **the** way.
He leads the humble in what is · **right,**
and teaches the humble · **his** way. R.

©2009 Gordon Johnston/Novalis

To hear the Sunday Psalms, visit www.livingwithchrist.ca.

SECOND READING (1 Corinthians 7.29-31)
Brothers and sisters, the appointed time has grown
short; from now on, let even those who have wives
be as though they had none, and those who mourn
as though they were not mourning, and those who
rejoice as though they were not rejoicing, and those

who buy as though they had no possessions, and those who deal with the world as though they had no dealings with it. For the present form of this world is passing away.

The word of the Lord. **Thanks be to God.**

GOSPEL ACCLAMATION *(Mark 1.15)*
Alleluia. Alleluia. The kingdom of God has come near: repent and believe the good news! **Alleluia.**

GOSPEL *(Mark 1.14-20)*
The Lord be with you. **And with your spirit.**
A reading from the holy Gospel according to Mark. **Glory to you, O Lord.**

After John was arrested, Jesus came to Galilee, proclaiming the good news of God, and saying, "The time is fulfilled, and the kingdom of God has come near; repent, and believe in the good news."

As Jesus passed along the Sea of Galilee, he saw Simon and his brother Andrew casting a net into the sea — for they were fishermen. And Jesus said to them, "Come follow me and I will make you fishers of people." And immediately they left their nets and followed him.

As Jesus went a little farther, he saw James son of Zebedee and his brother John, who were in their boat mending the nets. Immediately he called them; and they left their father Zebedee in the boat with the hired men, and followed him.

The Gospel of the Lord. **Praise to you, Lord Jesus Christ.**

PROFESSION OF FAITH *(p. 11)*

PRAYER OF THE FAITHFUL

The following intentions are suggestions only. There are more suggestions at www.livingwithchrist.ca

R̪. **Lord, hear our prayer.**

For unity among Christians across the country and around the world, we pray to the Lord: R̪.

For peace in our world, our churches, our schools and our families, we pray to the Lord: R̪.

For all who are lonely, isolated or grieving, we pray to the Lord: R̪.

For ourselves gathered here, messengers of the Good News of Jesus Christ, we pray to the Lord: R̪.

PREPARATION OF THE GIFTS *(p. 14)*

PRAYER OVER THE OFFERINGS

Accept our offerings, O Lord, we pray, and in sanctifying them grant that they may profit us for salvation. Through Christ our Lord. **Amen.**

PREFACE *(Sundays in Ordinary Time, p. 29)*

COMMUNION ANTIPHON *(Cf. Psalm 33.6)*
Look toward the Lord and be radiant; let your faces not be abashed.
   or (John 8.12)
I am the light of the world, says the Lord; whoever follows me will not walk in darkness, but will have the light of life.

PRAYER AFTER COMMUNION

Grant, we pray, almighty God, that, receiving the grace by which you bring us to new life, we may always glory in your gift. Through Christ our Lord. **Amen.**

BLESSING AND DISMISSAL *(p. 71)*

January 28
4th Sunday in Ordinary Time

"Be silent, and come out of him!" Jesus teaches us today. How often do we wish these words could be spoken to an anxiety that we are experiencing? Part of the gift Jesus gives us each day is the ability to say 'enough' to a source of suffering in our lives.

Silence becomes a method of approaching the source of our troubles. Often in silence we gain the gift of insight into our immediate concerns. Psychologists may offer an explanation that illustrates the benefits of taking the time to allow our minds to obtain a second or third opinion on a matter before us. On the other hand, Jesus offers us a few words to use as a guide. In silence we are allowed to create a time and space for inspiration and perspective. These become a sort of modern day "words of the prophets" for us – speaking to our particular time and circumstance.

The gift of prophecy works in many ways – in good times and bad – to reassure us that all will be well as we have the faithful assurance from the rock of our salvation. Consider the flow of water and its enormous power, especially when experienced in silence. Surely the creator of the water must possess even more impressive powers. So let us say a prayer of thanksgiving today for the gift of this teaching.

John O'Brien
Oakville, ON

ENTRANCE ANTIPHON *(Psalm 105.47)*
Save us, O Lord our God! And gather us from the nations, to give thanks to your holy name, and make it our glory to praise you.

INTRODUCTORY RITES *(p. 5)*

COLLECT
Grant us, Lord our God, that we may honour you with all our mind, and love everyone in truth of heart. Through our Lord Jesus Christ, your Son, who lives and reigns with you in the unity of the Holy Spirit, one God, for ever and ever. **Amen.**

FIRST READING *(Deuteronomy 18.15-20)*
Moses spoke to the people; he said: "The Lord your God will raise up for you a Prophet like me from among your own kin; you shall heed such a Prophet. This is what you requested of the Lord your God at Horeb on the day of the assembly when you said: 'Let me not hear the voice of the Lord my God any more, or ever again see this great fire, lest I die.'

"Then the Lord replied to me: 'They are right in what they have said. I will raise up for them a Prophet like you from among their own kin; I will put my words in his mouth, and he shall speak to them everything that I command him.

"'Anyone who does not heed the words that he shall speak in my name, I myself will hold him accountable. But any Prophet who speaks in the name of other gods, or who presumes to speak in my name a word that I have not commanded him to speak — that Prophet shall die.'"

The word of the Lord. **Thanks be to God.**

RESPONSORIAL PSALM *(Psalm 95)*

O that to-day you would lis-ten to the voice of the Lord. Do not hard-en your hearts!

R. **O that today you would listen to the voice of the Lord. Do not harden your hearts!**

O come, let us sing to · **the** Lord.
Let us make a joyful noise to the rock of our ·
sal-vation!
Let us come into his presence with · **thanks**-giving;
let us make a joyful noise to him with songs · **of**
praise! R.

O come, let us worship and · **bow** down,
let us kneel before the Lord, · **our** Maker!
For he is our God, and we are the people of ·
his pasture,
and the sheep of · his hand. R.

O that today you would listen to · **his** voice!
Do not harden your hearts, as at Meribah, as on
the day at Massah in · **the** wilderness,
when your ancestors tested me, and put me to ·
the proof,
though they had seen · **my** work. R.

©2009 Gordon Johnston/Novalis

SECOND READING *(1 Corinthians 7.32-35)*

Brothers and sisters, I want you to be free from anxieties. The unmarried man is anxious about the affairs of the Lord, how to please the Lord; but the married man is anxious about the affairs of the world, how to please his wife, and his interests are divided.

The unmarried woman and the virgin are concerned about the affairs of the Lord, so that they may be holy in body and spirit; but the married woman is concerned about the affairs of the world, how to please her husband.

I say this for your own benefit, not to put any restraint upon you, but to promote good order and unhindered devotion to the Lord.

The word of the Lord. **Thanks be to God.**

GOSPEL ACCLAMATION *(Matthew 4.16)*

Alleluia. Alleluia. The people who sat in darkness have seen a great light, and for those who sat in the region and shadow of death, light has dawned. **Alleluia.**

GOSPEL *(Mark 1.21-28)*

The Lord be with you. **And with your spirit.**
A reading from the holy Gospel according to Mark. **Glory to you, O Lord.**

The disciples went to Capernaum; and when the Sabbath came, Jesus entered the synagogue and taught. They were astounded at his teaching, for he taught them as one having authority, and not as the scribes. Just then there was in their synagogue a man with an unclean spirit, and he cried out, "What have you to do with us, Jesus of Nazareth? Have you come to destroy us? I know who you are, the Holy One of God."

But Jesus rebuked him, saying, "Be silent, and come out of him!" And the unclean spirit, convulsing the man and crying with a loud voice, came out of him. They were all amazed, and they kept on asking one another, "What is this? A new teaching — with authority! He commands even the unclean spirits, and they obey him."

At once Jesus' fame began to spread throughout the surrounding region of Galilee.

The Gospel of the Lord. **Praise to you, Lord Jesus Christ.**

PROFESSION OF FAITH (p. 11)

PRAYER OF THE FAITHFUL

The following intentions are suggestions only. There are more suggestions at www.livingwithchrist.ca

R. **Lord, hear our prayer.**

For the Church, speaking with God's loving authority, we pray to the Lord: R.

For world leaders to act with integrity, we pray to the Lord. R.

For all who face the future with fear or uncertainty, we pray to the Lord: R.

For ourselves, gathered to hear and put into action God's healing love, we pray to the Lord: R.

PREPARATION OF THE GIFTS *(p. 14)*

PRAYER OVER THE OFFERINGS
O Lord, we bring to your altar these offerings of our service: be pleased to receive them, we pray, and transform them into the Sacrament of our redemption. Through Christ our Lord. **Amen.**

PREFACE *(Sundays in Ordinary Time, p. 29)*

COMMUNION ANTIPHON *(Cf. Psalm 30.17-18)*
Let your face shine on your servant. Save me in your merciful love. O Lord, let me never be put to shame, for I call on you.

or (Matthew 5.3-4)

Blessed are the poor in spirit, for theirs is the Kingdom of Heaven. Blessed are the meek, for they shall possess the land.

PRAYER AFTER COMMUNION
Nourished by these redeeming gifts, we pray, O Lord, that through this help to eternal salvation true faith may ever increase. Through Christ our Lord. **Amen.**

BLESSING AND DISMISSAL *(p. 71)*

February Saints' Days

The following saints are traditionally remembered in February in Canada.

3   Saint Blaise
     Saint Ansgar

5   Saint Agatha

6   Saint Paul Miki and Companions

8   Saint Jerome Emiliani
     Saint Josephine Bakhita

10 Saint Scholastica

11 Our Lady of Lourdes

14 Saints Cyril and Methodius

17 The Seven Holy Founders of
      the Servite Order

21 Saint Peter Damian

23 Saint Polycarp

February 4
5th Sunday in Ordinary Time

This year we listen to the Evangelist Mark. His is the shortest of the four Gospels. In today's few verses, Mark reveals the intensity and urgency of Jesus.

Jesus was compelled to share the Good News as deeply and broadly as possible. Look at the work he accomplishes in one day. First, he teaches in the synagogue and frees a man from an unclean spirit. Then, in Simon's home, he heals Simon's mother-in-law of a serious fever. And then, he spends the evening healing the sick and casting out demons. Mark tells us that the whole city was gathered at the door.

After all that intense effort, Jesus is up the next morning before sunrise and goes away to pray alone. His energy is renewed in prayer with his Father and then he sets out again, moving from one town to the next, proclaiming the loving mercy of God. Let us remember, he walked everywhere he went.

Jesus knew his mission. He had no time to waste.

Do we dare ask for that grace of urgency? We can try. Start each day in prayer, deliberately treat everyone we meet as brothers and sisters of Jesus Christ, and stay alert for God's invitations to live ever more deeply in his love and mercy.

Marilyn Sweet
Falmouth, NS

ENTRANCE ANTIPHON *(Psalm 94.6-7)*
O come, let us worship God and bow low before the God who made us, for he is the Lord our God.

INTRODUCTORY RITES *(p. 5)*

COLLECT
Keep your family safe, O Lord, with unfailing care, that, relying solely on the hope of heavenly grace, they may be defended always by your protection. Through our Lord Jesus Christ, your Son, who lives and reigns with you in the unity of the Holy Spirit, one God, for ever and ever. **Amen.**

FIRST READING *(Job 7.1-4, 6-7)*
Job spoke to his friends: "Does not the human being have a hard service on earth, and are not their days like the days of a labourer? Like a slave who longs for the shadow, and like a labourer who looks for their wages, so I am allotted months of emptiness, and nights of misery are apportioned to me.

"When I lie down I say, 'When shall I rise?' But the night is long, and I am full of tossing until dawn.

"My days are swifter than a weaver's shuttle, and come to their end without hope. Remember that my life is a breath; my eye will never again see good."

The word of the Lord. **Thanks be to God.**

RESPONSORIAL PSALM *(Psalm 147)*

Sing prais-es to the Lord___who heals the bro-ken heart-ed.

R. **Sing praises to the Lord**
who heals the broken hearted.
or **Alleluia!**

How good it is to sing praises · **to** our God;
for he is gracious, and a song of · **praise** is fitting.
The Lord builds · **up** Je-rusalem;
he gathers the · **outcasts** of Israel. R.

The Lord heals the · **bro**-ken-hearted,
and binds · **up** their wounds.
He determines the · **number** of the stars;
he gives to all of · **them** their names. R.

Great is our Lord, and a-**bundant** in power;
his understanding · **is_be**-yond measure.
The Lord lifts · **up** the downtrodden;
he casts the wicked · **to** the ground. R.

©2009 Gordon Johnston/Novalis

To hear the Sunday Psalms, visit www.livingwithchrist.ca.

SECOND READING *(1 Corinthians 9.16-19, 22-23)*
Brothers and sisters: If I proclaim the Gospel, this gives me no ground for boasting, for an obligation is laid on me, and woe to me if I do not proclaim the Gospel! For if I do this of my own will, I have a reward; but if not of my own will, I am entrusted with a commission. What then is my reward? Just this: that in my proclamation I may make the Gospel free of charge, so as not to make full use of my rights in the Gospel.

For though I am free with respect to all, I have made myself a slave to all, so that I might win more of them.

To the weak I became weak, so that I might win the weak. I have become all things to all people, that I might by all means save some. I do it all for the sake of the Gospel, so that I may share in its blessings.

The word of the Lord. **Thanks be to God.**

GOSPEL ACCLAMATION *(Matthew 8.17)*
Alleluia. Alleluia. Christ took our infirmities, and bore our diseases. **Alleluia.**

GOSPEL *(Mark 1.29-39)*
The Lord be with you. **And with your spirit.**
A reading from the holy Gospel according to Mark.
Glory to you, O Lord.

As soon as Jesus and his disciples left the synagogue, they entered the house of Simon and Andrew, with James and John. Now Simon's mother-in-law was in bed with a fever, and they told Jesus about her at once. He came and took her by the hand and lifted her up. Then the fever left her, and she began to serve them.

That evening, at sunset, they brought to Jesus all who were sick or possessed with demons. And the whole city was gathered around the door. And he cured many who were sick with various diseases, and cast out many demons; and he would not permit the demons to speak, because they knew him.

In the morning, while it was still very dark, Jesus got up and went out to a deserted place, and there he prayed. And Simon and his companions hunted for him. When they found him, they said to him, "Everyone is searching for you."

He answered, "Let us go on to the neighbouring towns, so that I may proclaim the message there also; for that is what I came out to do." And Jesus went throughout Galilee, proclaiming the message in their synagogues and casting out demons.

The Gospel of the Lord. **Praise to you, Lord Jesus Christ.**

PROFESSION OF FAITH (p. 11)

PRAYER OF THE FAITHFUL

The following intentions are suggestions only. There are more suggestions at www.livingwithchrist.ca

R. **Lord, hear our prayer.**

For all witnesses to the Gospel, called to proclaim the Good News of God's love, we pray to the Lord: R.

For leaders of nations, called to respond to suffering in our world, we pray to the Lord: R.

For all who work in healing professions, called to alleviate suffering, we pray to the Lord: R.

For ourselves, the People of God, called to follow Christ in service, prayer and witness, we pray to the Lord: R⁄

PREPARATION OF THE GIFTS (p. 14)

PRAYER OVER THE OFFERINGS
O Lord our God, who once established these created things to sustain us in our frailty, grant, we pray, that they may become for us now the Sacrament of eternal life. Through Christ our Lord. **Amen.**

PREFACE (Sundays in Ordinary Time, p. 29)

COMMUNION ANTIPHON (Cf. Psalm 106.8-9)
Let them thank the Lord for his mercy, his wonders for the children of men, for he satisfies the thirsty soul, and the hungry he fills with good things.
   or (Matthew 5.5-6)
Blessed are those who mourn, for they shall be consoled. Blessed are those who hunger and thirst for righteousness, for they shall have their fill.

PRAYER AFTER COMMUNION
O God, who have willed that we be partakers in the one Bread and the one Chalice, grant us, we pray, so to live that, made one in Christ, we may joyfully bear fruit for the salvation of the world. Through Christ our Lord. **Amen.**

BLESSING AND DISMISSAL (p. 71)

February 11
6th Sunday in Ordinary Time
World Day of the Sick

The leper in today's Gospel violated the religious rules laid out in the Book of Leviticus – he broke the Law by approaching a clean man. Even then, Jesus did not send the leper away.

Rather, Our Lord was so moved with pity that he touched the leper (yet another religious violation). Jesus also insisted that the man present himself to the priests, as an example of his obedience to the law and recognizing this as a helpful, necessary step in order for the man to be fully reintegrated into the community.

The lesson is: we must constantly opt to serve our brothers and sisters in need. Also, we must respect laws that are truly designed to serve the common good. Sometimes social and economic problems seem too big and complex for us to handle. Oftentimes, it is just plain easier to settle for inaction.

But Jesus shows us the best response: "I do choose. Be made clean."

I wonder if in this story leprosy is really meant to be a metaphor of brokenness. Can we recognize that we, as well as our society, suffer from various sorts of brokenness? Might we also need to kneel before Jesus requesting the deepest healing for which humanity yearns? Is today a new opportunity for each of us to choose to accept Jesus' challenge to fully love our neighbour?

Joe Gunn
Ottawa, ON

ENTRANCE ANTIPHON *(Cf. Psalm 30.3-4)*
Be my protector, O God, a mighty stronghold to save
me. For you are my rock, my stronghold! Lead me,
guide me, for the sake of your name.

INTRODUCTORY RITES *(p. 5)*

COLLECT
O God, who teach us that you abide in hearts that are
just and true, grant that we may be so fashioned by
your grace as to become a dwelling pleasing to you.
Through our Lord Jesus Christ, your Son, who lives
and reigns with you in the unity of the Holy Spirit,
one God, for ever and ever. **Amen.**

FIRST READING *(Leviticus 13.1-2, 45-46)*
The Lord spoke to Moses and Aaron, saying: "When
someone has on the skin of their body a swelling
or an eruption or a spot, and it turns into a leprous
disease on the skin of their body, that person shall
be brought to Aaron the priest or to one of his sons
the priests.

"Anyone who has the leprous disease shall wear
torn clothes and let the hair of their head be dishev-
elled and shall cover their upper lip and cry out, 'Unclean, unclean.' That person shall remain unclean as
long as the disease persists; and being unclean, such
a one shall live alone with their dwelling outside
the camp."

The word of the Lord. **Thanks be to God.**

RESPONSORIAL PSALM *(Psalm 32)*

You are my ref-uge, Lord; with de-liv-er-ance you sur-round me.

R. **You are my refuge, Lord;**
with deliverance you surround me.

Blessed is the one whose transgression is
for-**given,**
whose sin is · **covered.**
Blessed is the one to whom the Lord imputes no
in-**iquity,**
and in whose spirit there is no de-**ceit.** R.

I acknowledged my sin to · **you,**
and I did not hide my in-**iquity;**
I said, "I will confess my transgressions to the ·
Lord,"
and you forgave the guilt of my · **sin.** R.

1 - Be glad in the Lord and rejoice, O · **righteous,**
4 - and shout for joy, all you upright in · **heart.** R.

©2009 Gordon Johnston/Novalis

To hear the Sunday Psalms, visit www.livingwithchrist.ca.

SECOND READING *(1 Corinthians 10.31 – 11.1)*
Brothers and sisters: Whether you eat or drink, or whatever you do, do everything for the glory of God. Give no offence to Jews or to Greeks or to the Church of God, just as I try to please everyone in everything I do, not seeking my own advantage, but that of many, so that they may be saved. Be imitators of me, as I am of Christ.

The word of the Lord. **Thanks be to God.**

GOSPEL ACCLAMATION *(Luke 7.16)*
Alleluia. Alleluia. A great Prophet has risen among us; God has looked favourably on his people. **Alleluia.**

GOSPEL *(Mark 1.40-45)*
The Lord be with you. **And with your spirit.**
A reading from the holy Gospel according to Mark. **Glory to you, O Lord.**

A man with leprosy came to Jesus begging him, and kneeling said to Jesus, "If you choose, you can make me clean." Moved with pity, Jesus stretched out his hand and touched him, and said to him, "I do choose. Be made clean!" Immediately the leprosy left him, and he was made clean.

After sternly warning him Jesus sent him away at once, saying to him, "See that you say nothing to anyone; but go, show yourself to the priest, and offer for your cleansing what Moses commanded, as a testimony to them."

But the man went out and began to proclaim it freely, and to spread the word, so that Jesus could no longer go into a town openly, but stayed out in the country; and people came to Jesus from every quarter.

The Gospel of the Lord. **Praise to you, Lord Jesus Christ.**

PROFESSION OF FAITH *(p. 11)*

PRAYER OF THE FAITHFUL

The following intentions are suggestions only. There are more suggestions at www.livingwithchrist.ca

R. **Lord, hear our prayer.**

For the Church, communicating Jesus' healing presence to the world, we pray to the Lord: R.

For world leaders, called to lead all nations in harmony, we pray to the Lord: R.

For the sick and those who minister to them, we pray to the Lord: R.

For us here today, united in faith and love, we pray to the Lord: R.

PREPARATION OF THE GIFTS *(p. 14)*

PRAYER OVER THE OFFERINGS

May this oblation, O Lord, we pray, cleanse and renew us and may it become for those who do your will the source of eternal reward. Through Christ our Lord. **Amen.**

PREFACE *(Sundays in Ordinary Time, p. 29)*

COMMUNION ANTIPHON *(Cf. Psalm 77.29-30)*

They ate and had their fill, and what they craved the Lord gave them; they were not disappointed in what they craved.

or (John 3.16)

God so loved the world that he gave his Only Begotten Son, so that all who believe in him may not perish, but may have eternal life.

PRAYER AFTER COMMUNION

Having fed upon these heavenly delights, we pray, O Lord, that we may always long for that food by which we truly live. Through Christ our Lord. **Amen.**

BLESSING AND DISMISSAL *(p. 71)*

February 14
Ash Wednesday

The opening of today's first reading and the end of the second both contain a small but resonant word that can easily be overlooked. The word is "now." This little word, I think, captures both the hope and the urgency of the opportunity offered to us in Lent.

"Even now, says the Lord, return to me with all your heart." My interpretation is that it is never too late for repentance and conversion. Even in the face of the baggage from the past that may be weighing us down – our bad choices, our failures, our sinfulness – "even now" God gently but insistently invites us back.

In the letter to the Corinthians, Paul is even more insistent: "See, now is the acceptable time." Lent calls us to examine and renew our relationship with God and with one another here, now, not at some vague future date, when I might have more time or when my life is more organized. We could learn much from our Buddhist brothers and sisters about living in the present moment!

As we enter into our Lenten observance this year, let us take to heart God's call to repentance, prayer, integrity and wholeness. May neither regret nor procrastination prevent us from responding to that call – *now!*

Krystyna Higgins
Guelph, ON

ENTRANCE ANTIPHON *(Wisdom 11.24, 25, 27)*
You are merciful to all, O Lord, and despise nothing that you have made. You overlook people's sins, to bring them to repentance, and you spare them, for you are the Lord our God.

GREETING *(p. 5)*
The Penitential Act *and the* Glory to God *are omitted today.*

COLLECT
Grant, O Lord, that we may begin with holy fasting this campaign of Christian service, so that, as we take up battle against spiritual evils, we may be armed with weapons of self-restraint. Through our Lord Jesus Christ, your Son, who lives and reigns with you in the unity of the Holy Spirit, one God, for ever and ever. **Amen.**

FIRST READING *(Joel 2.12-18)*
Even now, says the Lord, return to me with all your heart, with fasting, with weeping, and with mourning; rend your hearts and not your clothing.

Return to the Lord, your God, for he is gracious and merciful, slow to anger, and abounding in steadfast love, and relents from punishing.

Who knows whether the Lord will not turn and relent, and leave a blessing behind him: a grain offering and a drink offering to be presented to the Lord, your God?

Blow the trumpet in Zion; sanctify a fast; call a solemn assembly; gather the people. Sanctify the congregation; assemble the aged; gather the children, even infants at the breast. Let the bridegroom leave his room, and the bride her canopy.

Between the vestibule and the altar let the priests, the ministers of the Lord, weep. Let them say, "Spare your people, O Lord, and do not make your heritage a mockery, a byword among the nations. Why should it be said among the peoples, 'Where is their God?'"

Then the Lord became jealous for his land, and had pity on his people.

The word of the Lord. **Thanks be to God.**

RESPONSORIAL PSALM *(Psalm 51)*

Have mer - cy, O Lord, for we have sinned.

R. **Have mercy, O Lord, for we have sinned.**

Have mercy on me, O God, according
    to your steadfast · **love;**
according to your abundant mercy blot out
    my trans-·**gressions.**
Wash me thoroughly from my in-·**iquity,**
and cleanse me from my · **sin.** R.

For I know my trans-·**gressions,**
and my sin is ever be-·**fore_me.**
Against you, you alone, have I · **sinned,**
and done what is evil in your · **sight.** R.

Create in me a clean heart, O · **God,**
and put a new and right spirit with--**in_me.**
Do not cast me away from your · **presence,**
and do not take your holy spirit from · **me.** R.

Restore to me the joy of your sal--**vation,**
and sustain in me a willing · **spirit.**
O Lord, open my · **lips,**
and my mouth will declare your · **praise.** R.

©2009 Gordon Johnston/Novalis

To hear the Sunday Psalms, visit www.livingwithchrist.ca.

SECOND READING *(2 Corinthians 5.20 – 6.2)*
Brothers and sisters: We are ambassadors for Christ,
since God is making his appeal through us; we entreat you on behalf of Christ, be reconciled to God.
For our sake God made Christ to be sin who knew no
sin, so that in Christ we might become the righteousness of God. As we work together with him, we urge
you also not to accept the grace of God in vain. For
the Lord says, "At an acceptable time I have listened
to you, and on a day of salvation I have helped you."
See, now is the acceptable time; see, now is the day
of salvation!

The word of the Lord. **Thanks be to God.**

GOSPEL ACCLAMATION *(Psalm 95.7-8)*
Praise and honour to you, Lord Jesus Christ! Today,
do not harden your hearts, but listen to the voice
of the Lord. **Praise and honour to you, Lord Jesus
Christ!**

GOSPEL *(Matthew 6.1-6, 16-18)*

The Lord be with you. **And with your spirit.**
A reading from the holy Gospel according to Matthew. **Glory to you, O Lord.**

Jesus said to the disciples: "Beware of practising your piety before people in order to be seen by them; for then you have no reward from your Father in heaven.

"So whenever you give alms, do not sound a trumpet before you, as the hypocrites do in the synagogues and in the streets, so that they may be praised by others. Truly I tell you, they have received their reward. But when you give alms, do not let your left hand know what your right hand is doing, so that your alms may be done in secret; and your Father who sees in secret will reward you.

"And whenever you pray, do not be like the hypocrites; for they love to stand and pray in the synagogues and at the street corners, so that they may be seen by others. Truly I tell you, they have received their reward. But whenever you pray, go into your room and shut the door and pray to your Father who is in secret; and your Father who sees in secret will reward you.

"And whenever you fast, do not look dismal, like the hypocrites, for they disfigure their faces so as to show others that they are fasting. Truly I tell you, they have received their reward. But when you fast, put oil on your head and wash your face, so that your fasting may be seen not by others but by your Father who is in secret; and your Father who sees in secret will reward you."

The Gospel of the Lord. **Praise to you, Lord Jesus Christ.**

BLESSING AND DISTRIBUTION OF ASHES

Dear brothers and sisters, let us humbly ask God our Father that he be pleased to bless with the abundance of his grace these ashes, which we will put on our heads in penitence. *(Pause)*

1 O God, who are moved by acts of humility and respond with forgiveness to works of penance, lend your merciful ear to our prayers and in your kindness pour out the grace of your blessing on your servants who are marked with these ashes, that, as they follow the Lenten observances, they may be worthy to come with minds made pure to celebrate the Paschal Mystery of your Son. Through Christ our Lord. **Amen.**

2 O God, who desire not the death of sinners, but their conversion, mercifully hear our prayers and in your kindness be pleased to bless these ashes, which we intend to receive upon our heads, that we, who acknowledge we are but ashes and shall return to dust, may, through a steadfast observance of Lent, gain pardon for sins and newness of life after the likeness of your Risen Son. Who lives and reigns for ever and ever. **Amen.**

While the faithful come forward to receive ashes, an appropriate song may be sung.

1 Repent, and believe in the Gospel.
2 Remember that you are dust, and to dust you shall return.

PRAYER OF THE FAITHFUL

The following intentions are suggestions only. More suggestions are available at www.livingwithchrist.ca

R. **Lord, hear our prayer.**

For the Church, proclaiming renewal in the ashes both distributed and received, we pray to the Lord: R.

For leaders in the world community, called to creative action towards life beyond the ashes of violence and war, we pray to the Lord: R.

For all who taste dust and ashes in their own personal experience, we pray to the Lord: R.

For the members of this assembly, accepting Lenten ashes as an invitation to fullness of life, we pray to the Lord: R.

* Ash Wednesday Service: When ashes are blessed outside Mass, the ceremony concludes with the Prayer over the People *and the* Blessing *(p. 180).*

PREPARATION OF THE GIFTS *(p. 14)*

PRAYER OVER THE OFFERINGS

As we solemnly offer the annual sacrifice for the beginning of Lent, we entreat you, O Lord, that, through works of penance and charity, we may turn away from harmful pleasures and, cleansed from our sins, may become worthy to celebrate devoutly the Passion of your Son. Who lives and reigns for ever and ever. **Amen.**

PREFACE *(Lent III-IV, p. 19)*

COMMUNION ANTIPHON *(Cf. Psalm 1.2-3)*
**He who ponders the law of the Lord day and night
will yield fruit in due season.**

PRAYER AFTER COMMUNION
May the Sacrament we have received sustain us, O
Lord, that our Lenten fast may be pleasing to you
and be for us a healing remedy. Through Christ our
Lord. **Amen.**

PRAYER OVER THE PEOPLE
Pour out a spirit of compunction, O God, on those
who bow before your majesty, and by your mercy
may they merit the rewards you promise to those
who do penance. Through Christ our Lord. **Amen.**

BLESSING AND DISMISSAL *(p. 71)*

February 18
1st Sunday of Lent

The more pain and sacrifice you experience on your journey, the more satisfying your arrival at your destination.

Athletes who train excessively will say that the victory, the medal is well worth the extra work. Students who hit the books instead of going to a movie or to a party will always have as their reward the satisfaction of knowing that they have achieved the best grade possible.

Jesus was thrust into the wilderness for 40 long days and was constantly tempted by Satan. We know, of course, that he did not succumb to any temptation and he was provided divine, angelic support in his struggle.

The athlete and the student who choose to sacrifice have a specific goal in mind. Their self-oblation is driven by the long-range reward of achieving a medal or a diploma. When they see their friends or classmates enjoying the things that they deny themselves, they are sustained by thoughts of the final victory.

Like Jesus, we are expected to endure our 40-day fast as an unconditional offering to God, not because of the promise of reward when the summit is finally reached. Still, when the time of our sacrifice and commitment is fulfilled, the inherent bounty is that the kingdom of God is nearer.

Frank Campbell
Enfield, NS

Parishes engaged in the Rite of Christian Initiation of Adults (RCIA) *may celebrate the* Rite of Election *today.*

ENTRANCE ANTIPHON *(Cf. Psalm 90.15-16)*
When he calls on me, I will answer him; I will deliver him and give him glory, I will grant him length of days.

Rite of Election (Cf. Ps 104.3-4):
Let the hearts that seek the Lord rejoice; turn to the Lord and his strength; constantly seek his face.

INTRODUCTORY RITES *(p. 5)*

COLLECT
Grant, almighty God, through the yearly observances of holy Lent, that we may grow in understanding of the riches hidden in Christ and by worthy conduct pursue their effects. Through our Lord Jesus Christ, your Son, who lives and reigns with you in the unity of the Holy Spirit, one God, for ever and ever. **Amen.**

Rite of Election:
O God, who though you are ever the cause of the salvation of the human race now gladden your people with grace in still greater measure, look mercifully, we pray, upon your chosen ones, that your compassionate and protecting help may defend both those yet to be born anew and those already reborn. Through our Lord Jesus Christ, your Son, who lives and reigns with you in the unity of the Holy Spirit, one God, for ever and ever. **Amen.**

FIRST READING *(Genesis 9.8-15)*

God said to Noah and to his sons with him, "As for me, I am establishing my covenant with you and your descendants after you, and with every living creature that is with you, the birds, the domestic animals, and every animal of the earth with you, as many as came out of the ark. I establish my covenant with you, that never again shall all flesh be cut off by the waters of a flood, and never again shall there be a flood to destroy the earth."

God said, "This is the sign of the covenant that I make between me and you and every living creature that is with you, for all future generations: I have set my bow in the clouds, and it shall be a sign of the covenant between me and the earth. When I bring clouds over the earth and the bow is seen in the clouds, I will remember my covenant that is between me and you and every living creature of all flesh; and the waters shall never again become a flood to destroy all flesh."

The word of the Lord. **Thanks be to God.**

RESPONSORIAL PSALM *(Psalm 25)*

Your paths, Lord, are love and faith-ful-ness

for those who keep your cov-e-nant.

R. **Your paths, Lord, are love and faithfulness
for those who keep your covenant.**

Make me to know your ways, · **O** Lord;
teach · **me** your paths.
Lead me in your · **truth,** and teach_me,
for you are the God of · **my** sal-vation. R.

Be mindful of your mercy, O Lord, and of your
    stead-**fast** love,
for they have been · **from** of old.
According to your steadfast · **love** re-member_me,
for the sake of your · **goodness,** O Lord! R.

Good and upright · **is_the** Lord;
therefore he instructs sinners · **in** the way.
He leads the humble in · **what** is right,
and teaches the · **humble** his way. R.

©2009 Gordon Johnston/Novalis

To hear the Sunday Psalms, visit www.livingwithchrist.ca.

SECOND READING *(1 Peter 3.18-22)*
Beloved: Christ suffered for sins once for all, the righteous for the unrighteous, in order to bring you to God. He was put to death in the flesh, but made alive in the spirit, in which also he went and made a proclamation to the spirits in prison. In former times these did not obey, when God waited patiently in the days of Noah, during the building of the ark, in which a few, that is, eight persons, were saved through water.

Baptism, which this prefigured, now saves you — not as a removal of dirt from the body, but as an appeal to God for a good conscience through the resurrection of Jesus Christ, who has gone into heaven and is at the right hand of God, with Angels, Authorities, and Powers made subject to him.

The word of the Lord. **Thanks be to God.**

GOSPEL ACCLAMATION *(Matthew 4.4)*
Praise and honour to you, Lord Jesus Christ! Man does not live by bread alone, but by every word that comes from the mouth of God. **Praise and honour to you, Lord Jesus Christ!**

GOSPEL *(Mark 1.12-15)*
The Lord be with you. **And with your spirit.**
A reading from the holy Gospel according to Mark. **Glory to you, O Lord.**

After Jesus was baptized, the Spirit drove him out into the wilderness. He was in the wilderness forty days, tempted by Satan; and he was with the wild beasts; and the Angels waited on him.

Now after John was arrested, Jesus came to Galilee, proclaiming the good news of God, and saying, "The time is fulfilled, and the kingdom of God has come near; repent, and believe in the good news."

The Gospel of the Lord. **Praise to you, Lord Jesus Christ.**

For parishes engaged in the RCIA, *the* Rite of Election *takes place now.*

PROFESSION OF FAITH *(p. 11)*

PRAYER OF THE FAITHFUL

The following intentions are suggestions only. More suggestions are available at www.livingwithchrist.ca

R. **Lord, hear our prayer.**

For the Church, called to transformation in the spirit of Lent, we pray to the Lord: R.

For all who exercise authority over others, we pray to the Lord: R.

For all who dwell in the darkness of poverty, injustice, war or disease, we pray to the Lord: R.

For this community, called to be Good News for all we encounter, we pray to the Lord: R.

PREPARATION OF THE GIFTS *(p. 14)*

PRAYER OVER THE OFFERINGS

Give us the right dispositions, O Lord, we pray, to make these offerings, for with them we celebrate the beginning of this venerable and sacred time. Through Christ our Lord. **Amen.**

Rite of Election:

Almighty ever-living God, who restore us by the Sacrament of Baptism to eternal life as we confess your name, receive, we beseech you, the offerings and prayers of your servants and command that those who hope in you may have their desires fulfilled and their sins cancelled out. Through Christ our Lord. **Amen.**

PREFACE *(1st Sunday of Lent, p. 20)*

COMMUNION ANTIPHON *(Matthew 4.4)*
One does not live by bread alone, but by every word that comes forth from the mouth of God.
or (Cf. Psalm 90.4)
The Lord will conceal you with his pinions, and under his wings you will trust.
Rite of Election (Ephesians 1.7):
In Christ, we have redemption by his Blood and forgiveness of our sins, in accord with the riches of his grace.

PRAYER AFTER COMMUNION
Renewed now with heavenly bread, by which faith is nourished, hope increased, and charity strengthened, we pray, O Lord, that we may learn to hunger for Christ, the true and living Bread, and strive to live by every word which proceeds from your mouth. Through Christ our Lord. **Amen.**

Rite of Election:
May this Sacrament we have received purify us, we pray, O Lord, and grant your servants freedom from all blame, that those bound by a guilty

conscience may glory in the fullness of heavenly remedy. Through Christ our Lord. **Amen.**

PRAYER OVER THE PEOPLE

May bountiful blessing, O Lord, we pray, come down upon your people, that hope may grow in tribulation, virtue be strengthened in temptation, and eternal redemption be assured. Through Christ our Lord. **Amen.**

BLESSING AND DISMISSAL *(p. 71)*

February 25
2nd Sunday of Lent

A central focus of our Lent journey is dealing with the tension between life and death. Like the disciples at the Transfiguration, we too try to reconcile death with the glory of God. We often ask what this 'rising from death' means.

Occasionally we have a dramatic 'rising from death' experience when we, like Isaac in our first reading, walk away from a near-to-death experience.

More commonly, though, it means rising above the despair, hardships and poverties that Saint Paul lists in his letter to the Romans. After weighing the troubles of life against the glory of God, Paul concludes: "In all these things we are more than conquerors through him who loved us."

But eventually for Jesus and for each one of us as baptized Christians, 'rising from death' means passing from this life to the next, to eternal joy in the nearer presence of God. It is this dying and rising again that we celebrate at every baptism, each confession, and every time we gather around the altar to receive Christ at Mass.

Like the Transfiguration, Holy Eucharist draws us into the Paschal Mystery. As we receive anew the blessed and broken body of Christ, let us resolve to live into this mystery of the mercy of God.

Beverly Illauq
Kemptville, ON

ENTRANCE ANTIPHON *(Cf. Psalm 26.8-9)*
Of you my heart has spoken: Seek his face. It is your
face, O Lord, that I seek; hide not your face from me.
   or (Cf. Psalm 24.6, 2, 22)
Remember your compassion, O Lord, and your
merciful love, for they are from of old. Let not our
enemies exult over us. Redeem us, O God of Israel,
from all our distress.

INTRODUCTORY RITES *(p. 5)*

COLLECT
O God, who have commanded us to listen to your
beloved Son, be pleased, we pray, to nourish us in-
wardly by your word, that, with spiritual sight made
pure, we may rejoice to behold your glory. Through
our Lord Jesus Christ, your Son, who lives and reigns
with you in the unity of the Holy Spirit, one God, for
ever and ever. **Amen.**

FIRST READING *(Genesis 22.1-2, 9-13, 15-18)*
God tested Abraham. He said to him, "Abraham!"
And Abraham said, "Here I am."
   God said, "Take your son, your only son Isaac,
whom you love, and go to the land of Moriah, and
offer him there as a burnt offering on one of the
mountains that I shall show you."
   When Abraham and Isaac came to the place that
God had shown him, Abraham built an altar there
and laid the wood in order. He bound his son Isaac,
and laid him on the altar, on top of the wood. Then
Abraham reached out his hand and took the knife
to kill his son.

But the Angel of the Lord called to him from heaven, and said, "Abraham, Abraham!" And he said, "Here I am." The Angel said, "Do not lay your hand on the boy or do anything to him; for now I know that you fear God, since you have not withheld your son, your only son, from me."

Abraham looked up and saw a ram, caught in a thicket by its horns. Abraham went and took the ram and offered it up as a burnt offering instead of his son.

The Angel of the Lord called to Abraham a second time from heaven, and said, "By myself I have sworn, says the Lord: Because you have done this, and have not withheld your son, your only son, I will indeed bless you, and I will make your offspring as numerous as the stars of heaven and as the sand that is on the seashore. And your offspring shall possess the gate of their enemies, and by your offspring shall all the nations of the earth gain blessing for themselves, because you have obeyed my voice."

The word of the Lord. **Thanks be to God.**

RESPONSORIAL PSALM *(Psalm 116)*

I will walk be-fore the Lord, in the land of the liv-ing.

R. **I will walk before the Lord,**
in the land of the living.

I kept my faith, even when I · **said,**
"I am greatly · **af**-flicted."
Precious in the sight of the · **Lord**
is the death of · **his** faithful_ones. R.

O Lord, I am your · **servant.**
You have loosed · **my** bonds.
I will offer to you a thanksgiving · **sacrifice**
and call on the name of · **the** Lord. R.

I will pay my vows to the · **Lord**
in the presence of all · **his** people,
in the courts of the house of the · **Lord,**
in your midst, O · **Je**-rusalem. R.

©2009 Gordon Johnston/Novalis

To hear the Sunday Psalms, visit www.livingwithchrist.ca.

SECOND READING *(Romans 8.31b-35, 37)*
Brothers and sisters: If God is for us, who is against us? He who did not withhold his own Son, but gave him up for all of us, will he not with him also give us everything else?

Who will bring any charge against God's elect? It is God who justifies. Who is to condemn?

It is Christ Jesus, who died, yes, who was raised, who is at the right hand of God, who indeed intercedes for us.

Who will separate us from the love of Christ? Will hardship, or distress, or persecution, or famine, or nakedness, or peril, or sword?

No, in all these things we are more than conquerors through him who loved us.

The word of the Lord. **Thanks be to God.**

GOSPEL ACCLAMATION *(See Luke 9.35)*
Praise and honour to you, Lord Jesus Christ! From the bright cloud the Father's voice is heard: This is my Son, the Beloved, listen to him. **Praise and honour to you, Lord Jesus Christ!**

GOSPEL *(Mark 9.2-10)*
The Lord be with you. **And with your spirit.** A reading from the holy Gospel according to Mark. **Glory to you, O Lord.**

Jesus took with him Peter and James and John, and led them up a high mountain apart, by themselves. And he was transfigured before them, and his clothes became dazzling white, such as no one on earth could bleach them.

And there appeared to them Elijah and Moses, who were talking with Jesus. Then Peter said to Jesus, "Rabbi, it is good for us to be here; let us make three dwellings, one for you, one for Moses, and one for Elijah." Peter did not know what to say, for they were terrified.

Then a cloud overshadowed them, and from the cloud there came a voice, "This is my Son, the Beloved; listen to him!" Suddenly when they looked around, they saw no one with them any more, but only Jesus.

As they were coming down the mountain, he ordered them to tell no one about what they had seen, until after the Son of Man had risen from the dead. So they kept the matter to themselves, questioning what this rising from the dead could mean.

The Gospel of the Lord. **Praise to you, Lord Jesus Christ.**

PROFESSION OF FAITH *(p. 11)*

PRAYER OF THE FAITHFUL

The following intentions are suggestions only. More suggestions are available at www.livingwithchrist.ca

R. **Lord, hear our prayer.**

For the family of God, faithful to Jesus' call to repent and believe the Good News, we pray to the Lord: R.

For world leaders, called to govern with justice and compassion, we pray to the Lord: R.

For all who suffer illness, discomfort and pain, we pray to the Lord: R.

For our community, ever striving to be true followers of Jesus, we pray to the Lord: R.

PREPARATION OF THE GIFTS (p. 14)

PRAYER OVER THE OFFERINGS

May this sacrifice, O Lord, we pray, cleanse us of our faults and sanctify your faithful in body and mind for the celebration of the paschal festivities. Through Christ our Lord. **Amen.**

PREFACE (2nd Sunday of Lent, p. 21)

COMMUNION ANTIPHON (Matthew 17.5)

This is my beloved Son, with whom I am well pleased; listen to him.

PRAYER AFTER COMMUNION

As we receive these glorious mysteries, we make thanksgiving to you, O Lord, for allowing us while still on earth to be partakers even now of the things of heaven. Through Christ our Lord. **Amen.**

PRAYER OVER THE PEOPLE

Bless your faithful, we pray, O Lord, with a blessing that endures for ever, and keep them faithful to the Gospel of your Only Begotten Son, so that they may always desire and at last attain that glory whose beauty he showed in his own Body, to the amazement of his Apostles. Through Christ our Lord. **Amen.**

BLESSING AND DISMISSAL (p. 71)

March Saints' Days

The following saints are traditionally remembered in March in Canada.

4   Saint Casimir

7   Saints Perpetua and Felicity

8   Saint John of God

9   Saint Frances of Rome

17   Saint Patrick

18   Saint Cyril of Jerusalem

19   Saint Joseph, Principal Patron of Canada

23   Saint Turibius of Mogrovejo

March 4
3rd Sunday of Lent

Our Lenten journey is well underway. Is the enthusiasm with which we welcomed Ash Wednesday, at the start of a season of inner growth, flourishing? Or has it dimmed? Lent is a time to deepen our relationship with God. Has our progress been a source of delight to God? If not, it's never too late to begin!

Today's first reading reviews the Ten Commandments. God has expectations of us. Jesus later summarized the lot into two all-encompassing commandments: love God and love your neighbour. Are our relationships with others life-giving?

Today in John's Gospel, we see Jesus in the temple as Passover approaches. He is outraged that his "Father's house" is being used as a trading centre. He cleanses it and restores it to a prayerful state. Are we striving for wholeness or are our souls in need of spring-cleaning?

We might ask ourselves today: what cobwebs might we wipe away before we celebrate Easter? Does pride distance us from God or others? Are we self-centred, unforgiving or un-giving? Do we judge, criticize or fail to recognize the needs of others? In the silence of our hearts, do we hear God whispering, "Come back to me"? We are temples of the Spirit, called to holiness and to the joy of eternal life. How blessed are we!

Barbara d'Artois
Pierrefonds, QC

Parishes engaged in the Rite of Christian Initiation of Adults (RCIA) *may celebrate the* 1st Scrutiny *today (p. 205).*

ENTRANCE ANTIPHON *(Cf. Psalm 24.15-16)*

My eyes are always on the Lord, for he rescues my feet from the snare. Turn to me and have mercy on me, for I am alone and poor.

or (Cf. Ezekiel 36.23-26)

When I prove my holiness among you, I will gather you from all the foreign lands; and I will pour clean water upon you and cleanse you from all your impurities, and I will give you a new spirit, says the Lord.

INTRODUCTORY RITES *(p. 5)*

COLLECT

O God, author of every mercy and of all goodness, who in fasting, prayer and almsgiving have shown us a remedy for sin, look graciously on this confession of our lowliness, that we, who are bowed down by our conscience, may always be lifted up by your mercy. Through our Lord Jesus Christ, your Son, who lives and reigns with you in the unity of the Holy Spirit, one God, for ever and ever. **Amen.**

FIRST READING *(Exodus 20.1-17)*

For the shorter version, omit the indented parts.

God spoke all these words: I am the Lord your God, who brought you out of the land of Egypt, out of the house of slavery; you shall have no other gods before me.

You shall not make for yourself an idol, whether in the form of anything that is in heaven above, or that is on the earth beneath, or that is in the water under the earth. You shall not bow down to them or worship them; for I the Lord your God am a jealous God, punishing children for the iniquity of parents, to the third and the fourth generation of those who reject me, but showing steadfast love to the thousandth generation of those who love me and keep my commandments.

You shall not make wrongful use of the name of the Lord your God, for the Lord will not acquit anyone who misuses his name.

Remember the Sabbath day, and keep it holy. Six days you shall labour and do all your work. But the seventh day is a Sabbath to the Lord your God; you shall not do any work — you, your son or your daughter, your male or female slave, your livestock, or the alien resident in your towns. For in six days the Lord made heaven and earth, the sea, and all that is in them, but rested the seventh day; therefore the Lord blessed the Sabbath day and consecrated it.

Honour your father and your mother, so that your days may be long in the land that the Lord your God is giving you.

You shall not murder. You shall not commit adultery. You shall not steal. You shall not bear false witness against your neighbour. You shall not covet your neighbour's house; you shall not covet your neighbour's wife, or male or female slave, or ox, or donkey, or anything that belongs to your neighbour.

The word of the Lord. **Thanks be to God.**

RESPONSORIAL PSALM *(Psalm 19)*

Lord, you have the words of e-ter-nal life.

R. **Lord, you have the words of eternal life.**

The law of the Lord is · **perfect,**
reviving the · **soul;**
the decrees of the Lord are · **sure,**
making · **wise** the simple. R.

The precepts of the Lord are · **right,**
rejoicing the · **heart;**
the commandment of the Lord is · **clear,**
en--**lightening** the eyes. R.

The fear of the Lord is · **pure,**
enduring for--**ever;**
the ordinances of the Lord are · **true**
and righteous · **al**-to-gether. R.

More to be desired are they than · **gold,**
even much fine · **gold;**
sweeter also than · **honey,**
and drippings · **of** the honeycomb. R.

©2009 Gordon Johnston/Novalis

To hear the Sunday Psalms, visit www.livingwithchrist.ca.

SECOND READING *(1 Corinthians 1.18, 22-25)*
Brothers and sisters: The message about the Cross is foolishness to those who are perishing, but to us who are being saved it is the power of God.

For Jews demand signs and Greeks desire wisdom, but we proclaim Christ crucified, a stumbling block to Jews and foolishness to Gentiles, but to those who are the called, both Jews and Greeks, Christ the power of God and the wisdom of God.

For God's foolishness is wiser than human wisdom, and God's weakness is stronger than human strength.

The word of the Lord. **Thanks be to God.**

GOSPEL ACCLAMATION *(John 3.16)*
Praise and honour to you, Lord Jesus Christ! God so loved the world that he gave his only Son, that everyone who believes in him may have eternal life. **Praise and honour to you, Lord Jesus Christ!**

GOSPEL *(John 2.13-25)*
The Lord be with you. **And with your spirit.**
A reading from the holy Gospel according to John. **Glory to you, O Lord.**

The Passover of the Jews was near, and Jesus went up to Jerusalem. In the temple he found people selling cattle, sheep, and doves, and the money changers seated at their tables. Making a whip of cords, he drove all of them out of the temple, both the sheep and the cattle. He also poured out the coins of the money changers and overturned their tables. He told those who were selling the doves, "Take these things out of here! Stop making my Father's house a marketplace!"

His disciples remembered that it was written, "Zeal for your house will consume me."

The Jews then said to him, "What sign can you show us for doing this?" Jesus answered them, "Destroy this temple, and in three days I will raise it up." They then said, "This temple has been under construction for forty-six years, and will you raise it up in three days?" But Jesus was speaking of the temple of his body.

After he was raised from the dead, his disciples remembered that he had said this; and they believed the Scripture and the word that Jesus had spoken.

When he was in Jerusalem during the Passover festival, many believed in his name because they saw the signs that he was doing. But Jesus on his part would not entrust himself to them, because he knew all people and needed no one to testify about human nature, for he himself knew what was within the human person.

The Gospel of the Lord. **Praise to you, Lord Jesus Christ.**

PROFESSION OF FAITH (p. 11)

PRAYER OF THE FAITHFUL

The following intentions are suggestions only. More suggestions are available at www.livingwithchrist.ca

R. **Lord, hear our prayer.**

For Church leaders who teach with the wisdom, courage and zeal that come from the Holy Spirit, we pray to the Lord: R.

For peaceful discernment in the hearts of those called to positions of leadership, we pray to the Lord: R.

For all who desire freedom from oppression in their lives, we pray to the Lord: R.

For ourselves, called to live the message of Jesus, we pray to the Lord: R.

PREPARATION OF THE GIFTS (p. 14)

PRAYER OVER THE OFFERINGS
Be pleased, O Lord, with these sacrificial offerings, and grant that we who beseech pardon for our own sins may take care to forgive our neighbour. Through Christ our Lord. **Amen.**

PREFACE (Lent I-II, p. 18)

COMMUNION ANTIPHON (Cf. Psalm 83.4-5)
The sparrow finds a home, and the swallow a nest for her young: by your altars, O Lord of hosts, my King and my God. Blessed are they who dwell in your house, for ever singing your praise.

PRAYER AFTER COMMUNION
As we receive the pledge of things yet hidden in heaven and are nourished while still on earth with the Bread that comes from on high, we humbly entreat you, O Lord, that what is being brought about in us in mystery may come to true completion. Through Christ our Lord. **Amen.**

PRAYER OVER THE PEOPLE

Direct, O Lord, we pray, the hearts of your faithful, and in your kindness grant your servants this grace: that, abiding in the love of you and their neighbour, they may fulfill the whole of your commands. Through Christ our Lord. **Amen.**

BLESSING AND DISMISSAL *(p. 71)*

CHRISTIAN INITIATION: 1ST SCRUTINY

ENTRANCE ANTIPHON *(Ezekiel 36.23-26)*
When I prove my holiness among you, I will gather you from all the foreign lands and I will pour clean water upon you and cleanse you from all your impurities, and I will give you a new spirit, says the Lord.

or (Cf. Isaiah 55.1)
Come to the waters, you who are thirsty, says the Lord; you who have no money, come and drink joyfully.

INTRODUCTORY RITES *(p. 5)*

COLLECT
Grant, we pray, O Lord, that these chosen ones may come worthily and wisely to the confession of your praise, so that in accordance with that first dignity which they lost by original sin they may be fashioned anew through your glory. Through our Lord Jesus Christ, your Son, who lives and reigns with you in the unity of the Holy Spirit, one God, for ever and ever. **Amen.**

FIRST READING *(Exodus 17.3-7)*
In the wilderness the people thirsted for water; and the people complained against Moses and said, "Why did you bring us out of Egypt, to kill us and our children and livestock with thirst?" So Moses cried out to the Lord, "What shall I do with this people? They are almost ready to stone me."

The Lord said to Moses, "Go on ahead of the people, and take some of the elders of Israel with you; take in your hand the staff with which you struck the Nile, and go. I will be standing there in front of you on the rock at Horeb. Strike the rock, and water will come out of it, so that the people may drink." Moses did so, in the sight of the elders of Israel.

He called the place Massah and Meribah, because the children of Israel quarrelled and tested the Lord, saying, "Is the Lord among us or not?"

The word of the Lord. **Thanks be to God.**

RESPONSORIAL PSALM *(Psalm 95)*

R. **O that today you would listen to the voice of the Lord. Do not harden your hearts!**

O come, let us sing to · **the** Lord;
let us make a joyful noise to the rock of our ·
sal-vation!
Let us come into his presence with · **thanks**-giving;
let us make a joyful noise to him with songs · **of**
praise! R.

O come, let us worship and · **bow** down,
let us kneel before the Lord, · **our** Maker!
For he is our God, and we are the people of ·
his pasture,
and the sheep of · **his** hand. R̶

O that today you would listen to · **his** voice!
Do not harden your hearts, as at Meribah, as on
the day at Massah in · **the** wilderness,
when your ancestors tested me, and put me to ·
the proof,
though they had seen · **my** work. R̶

©2009 Gordon Johnston/Novalis

To hear the Sunday Psalms, visit www.livingwithchrist.ca.

SECOND READING *(Romans 5.1-2, 5-8)*
Brothers and sisters: Since we are justified by faith,
we have peace with God through our Lord Jesus
Christ, through whom we have obtained access to
this grace in which we stand; and we boast in our
hope of sharing the glory of God.

And hope does not disappoint us, because God's
love has been poured into our hearts through the
Holy Spirit that has been given to us. For while we
were still weak, at the right time Christ died for the
ungodly. Indeed, rarely will anyone die for a righteous person — though perhaps for a good person
someone might actually dare to die. But God proves
his love for us in that while we still were sinners
Christ died for us.

The word of the Lord. **Thanks be to God.**

GOSPEL ACCLAMATION *(John 4.42, 15)*

Praise and honour to you, Lord Jesus Christ! Lord, you are truly the Saviour of the world; give me living water, that I may never be thirsty. **Praise and honour to you, Lord Jesus Christ!**

GOSPEL *(John 4.5-42)*

For the shorter reading, omit the indented parts.

The Lord be with you. **And with your spirit.** A reading from the holy Gospel according to John. **Glory to you, O Lord.**

Jesus came to a Samaritan city called Sychar, near the plot of ground that Jacob had given to his son Joseph. Jacob's well was there, and Jesus, tired out by his journey, was sitting by the well. It was about noon.

A Samaritan woman came to draw water, and Jesus said to her, "Give me a drink." (His disciples had gone to the city to buy food.)

The Samaritan woman said to him, "How is it that you, a Jew, ask a drink of me, a woman of Samaria?" (Jews do not share things in common with Samaritans.) Jesus answered her, "If you knew the gift of God, and who it is that is saying to you, 'Give me a drink,' you would have asked him, and he would have given you living water."

The woman said to him, "Sir, you have no bucket, and the well is deep. Where do you get that living water? Are you greater than our father Jacob, who gave us the well, and with his children and his flocks drank from it?" Jesus said to her, "Everyone who drinks of this water will be thirsty again, but the one who drinks of the water that I will give will never be thirsty. The water that I will give him will become in him a spring of water gushing up to eternal life." The woman said to him, "Sir, give me this water, so that I may never be thirsty or have to keep coming here to draw water."

Jesus said to her, "Go, call your husband, and come back." The woman answered him, "I have no husband." Jesus said to her, "You are right in saying, 'I have no husband'; for you have had five husbands, and the one you have now is not your husband. What you have said is true!" The woman said to him, "Sir,

"I see that you are a Prophet. Our ancestors worshipped on this mountain, but you say that the place where people must worship is in Jerusalem."

Jesus said to her, "Woman, believe me, the hour is coming when you will worship the Father neither on this mountain nor in Jerusalem. You worship what you do not know; we worship what we know, for salvation is from the Jews. But the hour is coming, and is now here, when the true worshippers will worship the Father in spirit and truth, for the Father seeks such as these to worship him. God is spirit, and those who worship him must worship in spirit and truth."

The woman said to him, "I know that the Messiah is coming" (who is called the Christ). "When he comes, he will proclaim all things to us." Jesus said to her, "I am he, the one who is speaking to you."

Just then his disciples came. They were astonished that he was speaking with a woman, but no one said, "What do you want?" or, "Why are you speaking with her?" Then the woman left her water jar and went back to the city. She said to the people, "Come and see a man who told me everything I have ever done! He cannot be the Messiah, can he?" They left the city and were on their way to him. Meanwhile the disciples were urging him, "Rabbi, eat something." But he said to them, "I have food to eat that you do not know about." So the disciples said to one another, "Surely no one has brought him something to eat?"

Jesus said to them, "My food is to do the will of him who sent me and to complete his work. Do you not say, 'Four months more, then comes the harvest'? But I tell you, look around you, and see how the fields are ripe for harvesting. The reaper is already receiving wages and is gathering fruit for eternal life, so that sower and reaper may rejoice together. For here the saying holds true, 'One sows and another reaps.' I sent you to reap that for which you did not labour. Others have laboured, and you have entered into their labour."

Many Samaritans from that city believed in Jesus. because of the woman's testimony, "He told me everything I have ever done."

So when they [the Samaritans] came to him, they asked him to stay with them; and he stayed there two days. And many more believed because of his word. They said to the woman, "It is no longer because of what you said that we believe, for we have heard for ourselves, and we know that this is truly the Saviour of the world."

The Gospel of the Lord. **Praise to you, Lord Jesus Christ.**

PROFESSION OF FAITH *(p. 11)*

PRAYER OF THE FAITHFUL *(p. 202)*

PREPARATION OF THE GIFTS *(p. 14)*

PRAYER OVER THE OFFERINGS
May your merciful grace prepare your servants, O Lord, for the worthy celebration of these mysteries and lead them to it by a devout way of life. Through Christ our Lord. **Amen.**

PREFACE *(3rd Sunday of Lent, p. 21)*

COMMUNION ANTIPHON *(Cf. John 4.14)*
For anyone who drinks it, says the Lord, the water I shall give will become in him a spring welling up to eternal life.

PRAYER AFTER COMMUNION
Give help, O Lord, we pray, by the grace of your redemption and be pleased to protect and prepare those you are to initiate through the Sacraments of eternal life. Through Christ our Lord. **Amen.**

PRAYER OVER THE PEOPLE
Direct, O Lord, we pray, the hearts of your faithful, and in your kindness grant your servants this grace: that, abiding in the love of you and their neighbour, they may fulfill the whole of your commands. Through Christ our Lord. **Amen.**

BLESSING AND DISMISSAL *(p. 71)*

March 11
4th Sunday of Lent

While it may seem odd, I look forward to Lent all year because it permits me the luxury of meditating on the rich tradition of lament that is often forgotten or ignored altogether. Lament is the action of truly mourning the incompleteness of our lives, our society and our world in the sight of God. There is a wealth of emotions bubbling in the reading from Chronicles as the destruction of Jerusalem and the Temple has effectively terminated the sacred worship space of the Jewish people. Psalm 137 reiterates the destruction and we are drawn into the devastation through the psalmist's plaintive words.

John's Gospel shows a way out of the lament and devastation: "God so loved the world that he gave his only-begotten Son." Love is the path out of lament and devastation. Through this ultimate sacrifice on our behalf, we become people of the light forever abandoning the darkness that threatens to overshadow hope.

In a few days, we will set our faces to Jerusalem, to liturgically journey with Jesus during his passion, death and resurrection. Today, we witness the second Scrutiny for the Catechumens. The scrutinies are rites for spiritual self-searching. We as church support the elect with our prayers as they journey toward the Cross.

Marilyn-Ann Elphick
Mississauga, ON

Parishes engaged in the Rite of Christian Initiation of Adults (RCIA) *may celebrate the* 2nd Scrutiny *today (p. 219).*

ENTRANCE ANTIPHON *(Cf. Isaiah 66.10-11)*
Rejoice, Jerusalem, and all who love her. Be joyful, all who were in mourning; exult and be satisfied at her consoling breast.

INTRODUCTORY RITES *(p. 5)*

COLLECT
O God, who through your Word reconcile the human race to yourself in a wonderful way, grant, we pray, that with prompt devotion and eager faith the Christian people may hasten toward the solemn celebrations to come. Through our Lord Jesus Christ, your Son, who lives and reigns with you in the unity of the Holy Spirit, one God, for ever and ever. **Amen.**

FIRST READING *(2 Chronicles 36.14-17a, 19-23)*
All the leading priests and the people were exceedingly unfaithful, following all the abominations of the nations; and they polluted the house of the Lord that he had consecrated in Jerusalem.

The Lord, the God of their ancestors, persistently sent his messengers to them, because he had compassion on his people and on his dwelling place; but they kept mocking the messengers of God, despising his words, and scoffing at his Prophets, until the wrath of the Lord against his people became so great that there was no remedy.

Therefore the Lord brought up against them the king of the Chaldeans, who burned the house of God, broke down the wall of Jerusalem, burned all its palaces with fire, and destroyed all its precious vessels. The king took into exile in Babylon those who had escaped from the sword, and they became servants to him and to his sons until the establishment of the kingdom of Persia, to fulfill the word of the Lord by the mouth of Jeremiah, until the land had made up for its Sabbaths. All the days that it lay desolate it kept Sabbath, to fulfill seventy years.

In the first year of King Cyrus of Persia, in fulfillment of the word of the Lord spoken by Jeremiah, the Lord stirred up the spirit of King Cyrus of Persia so that he sent a herald throughout all his kingdom and also declared in a written edict: "Thus says King Cyrus of Persia: The Lord, the God of heaven, has given me all the kingdoms of the earth, and he has charged me to build him a house at Jerusalem, which is in Judah. Whoever is among you of all his people, may the Lord his God be with him! Let him go up."

The word of the Lord. **Thanks be to God.**

RESPONSORIAL PSALM *(Psalm 137)*

Let my tongue cling to my mouth if   I   do not re-

mem-ber you!_

R. **Let my tongue cling to my mouth
if I do not remember you!**

By the rivers of · **Babylon** —
there we sat down and there · **we** wept
when we remembered · **Zion.**
On the willows there we hung up · **our** harps. R.

For there our · **captors**
asked us · **for** songs,
and our tormentors asked for · **mirth,_saying,**
"Sing us one of the songs · **of** Zion!" R.

How could we sing the Lord's · **song**
in a for--**eign** land?
If I forget you, O Je--**rusalem,**
let my right · **hand** wither! R.

Let my tongue cling to the roof of my · **mouth,**
if I do not · **re**-member_you,
if I do not set Je--**rusalem**
above my high--**est** joy. R.

©2009 Gordon Johnston/Novalis

To hear the Sunday Psalms, visit www.livingwithchrist.ca.

SECOND READING *(Ephesians 2.4-10)*

God, who is rich in mercy, out of the great love with which he loved us even when we were dead through our trespasses, made us alive together with Christ — for it is by grace you have been saved.

And God raised us up with Christ and seated us with him in the heavenly places in Christ Jesus, so that in the ages to come God might show the immeasurable riches of his grace in kindness toward us in Christ Jesus.

For by grace you have been saved through faith, and this is not your own doing; it is the gift of God. This is not the result of works, so that no one may boast. For we are what he has made us, created in Christ Jesus for good works, which God prepared beforehand to be our way of life.

The word of the Lord. **Thanks be to God.**

GOSPEL ACCLAMATION *(John 3.16)*

Praise and honour to you, Lord Jesus Christ! God so loved the world that he gave his only Son, that everyone who believes in him may have eternal life. **Praise and honour to you, Lord Jesus Christ!**

GOSPEL *(John 3.14-21)*

The Lord be with you. **And with your spirit.** A reading from the holy Gospel according to John. **Glory to you, O Lord.**

Jesus said to Nicodemus: "Just as Moses lifted up the serpent in the wilderness, so must the Son of Man be lifted up, that whoever believes in him may have eternal life. For God so loved the world that he gave his only-begotten Son, so that everyone who believes in him may not perish but may have eternal life.

"Indeed, God did not send the Son into the world to condemn the world, but in order that the world might be saved through him. The one who believes in him is not condemned; but the one who does not believe is condemned already, for not having believed in the name of the only-begotten Son of God.

"And this is the judgment, that the light has come into the world, and people loved darkness rather than light because their deeds were evil. For all who do evil hate the light and do not come to the light, so that their deeds may not be exposed. But those who do what is true come to the light, so that it may be clearly seen that their deeds have been done in God."

The Gospel of the Lord. **Praise to you, Lord Jesus Christ.**

PROFESSION OF FAITH *(p. 11)*

PRAYER OF THE FAITHFUL

The following intentions are suggestions only. There are more suggestions at www.livingwithchrist.ca

R. **Lord, hear our prayer.**

For the Church, called to submit humbly to the searching light of Christ, we pray to the Lord: R.

For leaders with courage, wisdom and compassion, we pray to the Lord: R.

For people weighed down by poverty, despair or infirmity, we pray to the Lord: R.

In thanksgiving for the witness of all catechumens, we pray to the Lord: **R.**

PREPARATION OF THE GIFTS (p. 14)

PRAYER OVER THE OFFERINGS
We place before you with joy these offerings, which bring eternal remedy, O Lord, praying that we may both faithfully revere them and present them to you, as is fitting, for the salvation of all the world. Through Christ our Lord. **Amen.**

PREFACE (Lent I-II, p. 18)

COMMUNION ANTIPHON (Cf. Psalm 121.3-4)
Jerusalem is built as a city bonded as one together. It is there that the tribes go up, the tribes of the Lord, to praise the name of the Lord.

PRAYER AFTER COMMUNION
O God, who enlighten everyone who comes into this world, illuminate our hearts, we pray, with the splendour of your grace, that we may always ponder what is worthy and pleasing to your majesty and love you in all sincerity. Through Christ our Lord. **Amen.**

PRAYER OVER THE PEOPLE
Look upon those who call to you, O Lord, and sustain the weak; give life by your unfailing light to those who walk in the shadow of death, and bring those rescued by your mercy from every evil to reach the highest good. Through Christ our Lord. **Amen.**

BLESSING AND DISMISSAL (p. 71)

CHRISTIAN INITIATION: 2ND SCRUTINY

ENTRANCE ANTIPHON (Cf. Psalm 24.15-16)
My eyes are always on the Lord, for he rescues my feet from the snare. Turn to me and have mercy on me, for I am alone and poor.

INTRODUCTORY RITES (p. 5)

COLLECT
Almighty ever-living God, give to your Church an increase in spiritual joy, so that those once born of earth may be reborn as citizens of heaven. Through our Lord Jesus Christ, your Son, who lives and reigns with you in the unity of the Holy Spirit, one God, for ever and ever. **Amen.**

FIRST READING (1 Samuel 16.1b, 6-7, 10-13)
The Lord said to Samuel, "Fill your horn with oil and set out; I will send you to Jesse of Bethlehem, for I have provided for myself a king among his sons."

When the sons of Jesse came, Samuel looked on Eliab and thought, "Surely the Lord's anointed is now before the Lord." But the Lord said to Samuel, "Do not look on his appearance or on the height of his stature, because I have rejected him; for the Lord does not see as the human sees; the human looks on the outward appearance, but the Lord looks on the heart."

Jesse made seven of his sons pass before Samuel, and Samuel said to Jesse, "The Lord has not chosen any of these." Samuel said to Jesse, "Are all your sons here?" And he said, "There remains yet the youngest, but he is keeping the sheep." And Samuel said to Jesse, "Send and bring him; for we will not sit down until he comes here." Jesse sent and brought David in. Now he was ruddy, and had beautiful eyes, and was handsome. The Lord said, "Rise and anoint him; for this is the one."

Then Samuel took the horn of oil, and anointed him in the presence of his brothers; and the spirit of the Lord came mightily upon David from that day forward.

The word of the Lord. **Thanks be to God.**

RESPONSORIAL PSALM *(Psalm 23)*

R⃮ **The Lord is my shepherd; I shall not want.**

The Lord is my shepherd, I shall · **not** want.
He makes me lie down in · **green** pastures;
he leads me be-·**side** still waters;
he re-·**stores** my soul. R⃮

He leads me in right paths for his · **name's** sake.
Even though I walk through the darkest valley,
　I fear · **no** evil;
for · **you** are with_me;
your rod and your · **staff** — they comfort_me. R⃮

You prepare a table · **be**-fore_me
in the presence · **of_my** enemies;
you anoint my · **head** with oil;
my · **cup** over-flows. R⃮

Surely goodness and mercy · **shall** follow_me
all the days of · **my** life,
and I shall dwell in the · **house_of** the Lord
my · **whole** life long. R.

©2009 Gordon Johnston/Novalis

To hear the Sunday Psalms, visit www.livingwithchrist.ca.

SECOND READING *(Ephesians 5.8-14)*

Brothers and sisters: Once you were darkness, but now in the Lord you are light. Live as children of light — for the fruit of the light is found in all that is good and right and true.

Try to find out what is pleasing to the Lord. Take no part in the unfruitful works of darkness, but instead expose them. For it is shameful even to mention what such people do secretly; but everything exposed by the light becomes visible, for everything that becomes visible is light. Therefore it is said, "Sleeper, awake! Rise from the dead, and Christ will shine on you."

The word of the Lord. **Thanks be to God.**

GOSPEL ACCLAMATION *(John 8.12)*

Praise and honour to you, Lord Jesus Christ! I am the light of the world, says the Lord; whoever follows me will have the light of life. **Praise and honour to you, Lord Jesus Christ!**

GOSPEL *(John 9.1-41)*

For the shorter version, omit the indented parts.

The Lord be with you. **And with your spirit.**
A reading from the holy Gospel according to John.
Glory to you, O Lord.

As Jesus walked along, he saw a man blind from birth.

His disciples asked him, "Rabbi, who sinned, this man or his parents, that he was born blind?"

Jesus answered, "Neither this man nor his parents sinned; he was born blind so that God's works might be revealed in him. We must work the works of him who sent me while it is day; night is coming when no one can work. As long as I am in the world, I am the light of the world." When he had said this,

He spat on the ground and made mud with the saliva and spread the mud on the man's eyes, saying to him, "Go, wash in the pool of Siloam" (which means Sent).

Then the man who was blind went and washed, and came back able to see. The neighbours and those who had seen him before as a beggar began to ask, "Is this not the man who used to sit and beg?" Some were saying, "It is he." Others were saying, "No, but it is someone like him." He kept saying, "I am the man."

But they kept asking him, "Then how were your eyes opened?" He answered, "The man called Jesus made mud, spread it on my eyes, and said to me, 'Go to Siloam and wash.' Then I went and washed and received my sight." They said to him, "Where is he?" He said, "I do not know."

They brought to the Pharisees the man who had formerly been blind. Now it was a Sabbath day when Jesus made the mud and opened his eyes. Then the Pharisees also began to ask him how he had received his sight. He said to them, "He put mud on my eyes. Then I washed, and now I see." Some of the Pharisees said, "This man is not from God, for he does not observe the Sabbath." But others said, "How can a man who is a sinner perform such signs?" And they were divided. So they said again to the blind man, "What do you say about him? It was your eyes he opened." He said, "He is a Prophet."

They did not believe that he had been blind and had received his sight until they called the parents of the man who had received his sight and asked them, "Is this your son, who you say was born blind? How then does he now see?" His parents answered, "We know that this is our son, and that he was born blind; but we do not know how it is that now he sees, nor do we know who opened his eyes. Ask him; he is of age. He will speak for himself." His parents said this because they were afraid of the Jewish authorities, who had already agreed that anyone who confessed Jesus to be the Messiah would be put out of the synagogue. Therefore his parents said, "He is of age; ask him."

So for the second time they called the man who had been blind, and they said to him, "Give glory to God! We know that this man is a sinner." He answered, "I do not know whether he is a sinner. One thing I do know, that though I was blind, now I see." They said to him, "What did he do to you? How did he open your eyes?" He answered them, "I have told you already, and you would not listen. Why do you want to hear it again? Do you also want to become his disciples?" Then they reviled him, saying, "You are his disciple, but we are disciples of Moses. We know that God has spoken to Moses, but as for this man, we do not know where he comes from."

The man answered, "Here is an astonishing thing! You do not know where he comes from, and yet he opened my eyes. We know that God does not listen to sinners, but he does listen to one who worships him and obeys his will. Never since the world began has it been heard that anyone opened the eyes of a person born blind. If this man were not from God, he could do nothing." They answered him, "You were born entirely in sins, and are you trying to teach us?" And they drove him out.

Jesus heard that they had driven him out, and when he found him, he said, "Do you believe in the Son of Man?" He answered, "And who is he, sir? Tell me, so that I may believe in him." Jesus said to him, "You have seen him, and the one speaking with you is he." He said, "Lord, I believe." And he worshipped him.

Jesus said, "I came into this world for judgment so that those who do not see may see, and those who do see may become blind." Some of the Pharisees near him heard this and said to him, "Surely we are not blind, are we?" Jesus said to them, "If you were blind, you would have no sin. But now that you say, 'We see,' your sin remains." The Gospel of the Lord. **Praise to you, Lord Jesus Christ.**

PROFESSION OF FAITH *(p. 11)*

PRAYER OF THE FAITHFUL *(p. 217)*

PREPARATION OF THE GIFTS *(p. 14)*

PRAYER OVER THE OFFERINGS

We place before you with joy these offerings, which bring eternal remedy, O Lord, praying that we may both faithfully revere them and present them to you, as is fitting, for those who seek salvation. Through Christ our Lord. **Amen.**

PREFACE *(4th Sunday of Lent, p. 21)*

COMMUNION ANTIPHON *(Cf. John 9.11, 38)*
The Lord anointed my eyes; I went, I washed, I saw and I believed in God.

PRAYER AFTER COMMUNION

Sustain your family always in your kindness, O Lord, we pray, correct them, set them in order, graciously protect them under your rule, and in your unfailing goodness direct them along the way of salvation. Through Christ our Lord. **Amen.**

PRAYER OVER THE PEOPLE

Look upon those who call to you, O Lord, and sustain the weak; give life by your unfailing light to those who walk in the shadow of death, and bring those rescued by your mercy from every evil to reach the highest good. Through Christ our Lord. **Amen.**

BLESSING AND DISMISSAL *(p. 71)*

March 18
5th Sunday of Lent

Jeremiah believed that God was fully aware of sin in human history, and so God had come up with a new strategy for addressing the problem: a new covenant that would make it possible for human beings to be faithful. In this loving plan, a lasting and intimate bond between God and God's people would be formed when the law was written directly on people's hearts (minds and wills), and past sins would be forgiven and forgotten.

Although the author of the letter to the Hebrews knows Jesus was Son and sinless, he insists the Son did not go through life without feeling the temptations and sufferings we all do. Faced with his imminent death, Jesus experienced his own agony. Indeed, Jesus could become the source of eternal salvation in large part because he shared our humanity.

Jesus' death is the moment in which the divine love for human beings – and the new covenant in his blood – is most powerfully revealed. It is the means by which a new and intimate communion between God and believers, facilitated by God's Holy Spirit, is inaugurated. Happily, then, we ask for clean hearts and blotted-out transgressions so that our solidarity with Christ can shine forth fully for others' sake.

Christine Mader
Waverley, NS

National Collection for Development & Peace

Parishes engaged in the Rite of Christian Initiation of Adults (RCIA) *may celebrate the* 3rd Scrutiny *today (p. 233).*

ENTRANCE ANTIPHON *(Cf. Psalm 42.1-2)*

Give me justice, O God, and plead my cause against a nation that is faithless. From the deceitful and cunning rescue me, for you, O God, are my strength.

INTRODUCTORY RITES *(p. 5)*

COLLECT

By your help, we beseech you, Lord our God, may we walk eagerly in that same charity with which, out of love for the world, your Son handed himself over to death. Through our Lord Jesus Christ, your Son, who lives and reigns with you in the unity of the Holy Spirit, one God, for ever and ever. **Amen.**

FIRST READING *(Jeremiah 31.31-34)*

The days are surely coming, says the Lord,
when I will make a new covenant
with the house of Israel and the house of Judah.
It will not be like the covenant that I made with
    their fathers
when I took them by the hand
to bring them out of the land of Egypt —
a covenant that they broke,
though I was their husband,
says the Lord.

But this is the covenant
that I will make with the house of Israel after
    those days,
says the Lord:

I will put my law within them,
and I will write it on their hearts;
and I will be their God, and they shall be my people.
No longer shall they teach one another, or say to
     each other,
"Know the Lord,"
for they shall all know me,
from the least of them to the greatest, says the Lord;
for I will forgive their iniquity,
and remember their sin no more.

The word of the Lord. **Thanks be to God.**

RESPONSORIAL PSALM *(Psalm 51)*

Cre-ate in me   a clean heart,_   O   God.

R. **Create in me a clean heart, O God.**

Have mercy on me, O God, according to your
     stead--**fast** love;
according to your abundant mercy blot out my ·
     trans-gressions.
Wash me thoroughly from my · **in**-iquity,
and cleanse me · **from** my sin. R.

Create in me a clean heart, · **O** God,
and put a new and right spirit · **with**-in_me.
Do not cast me away from · **your** presence,
and do not take your holy · **spirit** from me. R.

Restore to me the joy of your · **sal**-vation,
and sustain in me a will-**ing** spirit.
Then I will teach transgressors · **your** ways,
and sinners will re-**turn** to you. R.

©2009 Gordon Johnston/Novalis

To hear the Sunday Psalms, visit www.livingwithchrist.ca.

SECOND READING *(Hebrews 5.7-9)*

In the days of his flesh, Jesus offered up prayers and
supplications, with loud cries and tears, to the one
who was able to save him from death, and he was
heard because of his reverent submission. Although
he was a Son, he learned obedience through what he
suffered; and having been made perfect, he became
the source of eternal salvation for all who obey him.

The word of the Lord. **Thanks be to God.**

GOSPEL ACCLAMATION *(John 12.26)*

Praise and honour to you, Lord Jesus Christ! Whoever serves me must follow me, says the Lord; where
I am, there will my servant be also. **Praise and honour to you, Lord Jesus Christ!**

GOSPEL *(John 12.20-33)*

The Lord be with you. **And with your spirit.**
A reading from the holy Gospel according to John.
Glory to you, O Lord.

Among those who went up to worship at the festival were some Greeks. They came to Philip, who
was from Bethsaida in Galilee, and said to him, "Sir,
we wish to see Jesus." Philip went and told Andrew;
then Andrew and Philip went and told Jesus. Jesus

answered them, "The hour has come for the Son of Man to be glorified. Very truly, I tell you, unless a grain of wheat falls into the earth and dies, it remains just a single grain; but if it dies, it bears much fruit. The person who loves their life loses it, and the person who hates their life in this world will keep it for eternal life.

"Whoever serves me must follow me, and where I am, there will my servant be also. Whoever serves me, the Father will honour.

"Now my soul is troubled. And what should I say — 'Father, save me from this hour'? No, it is for this reason that I have come to this hour. Father, glorify your name."

Then a voice came from heaven, "I have glorified it, and I will glorify it again."

The crowd standing there heard it and said that it was thunder. Others said, "An Angel has spoken to him." Jesus answered, "This voice has come for your sake, not for mine. Now is the judgment of this world; now the ruler of this world will be driven out. And I, when I am lifted up from the earth, will draw all people to myself."

Jesus said this to indicate the kind of death he was to die.

The Gospel of the Lord. **Praise to you, Lord Jesus Christ.**

PROFESSION OF FAITH *(p. 11)*

PRAYER OF THE FAITHFUL

The following intentions are suggestions only. There are more suggestions at www.livingwithchrist.ca

R. **Lord, hear our prayer.**

For the Church, as we reflect and act upon the words of Jesus today, we pray to the Lord: R.

For governments, responsible for ensuring a life of dignity for all, we pray to the Lord: R.

For the women, men and children throughout the world who struggle through each day, we pray to the Lord: R.

For our community, thirsting for justice and the courage to express our solidarity with the poor this Lent, we pray to the Lord: R.

PREPARATION OF THE GIFTS *(p. 14)*

PRAYER OVER THE OFFERINGS

Hear us, almighty God, and, having instilled in your servants the teachings of the Christian faith, graciously purify them by the working of this sacrifice. Through Christ our Lord. **Amen.**

PREFACE *(Lent I-II, p. 18)*

COMMUNION ANTIPHON *(John 12.24)*

Amen, Amen I say to you: Unless a grain of wheat falls to the ground and dies, it remains a single grain. But if it dies, it bears much fruit.

PRAYER AFTER COMMUNION

We pray, almighty God, that we may always be counted among the members of Christ, in whose Body and Blood we have communion. Who lives and reigns for ever and ever. **Amen.**

PRAYER OVER THE PEOPLE

Bless, O Lord, your people, who long for the gift of your mercy, and grant that what, at your prompting, they desire they may receive by your generous gift. Through Christ our Lord. **Amen.**

BLESSING AND DISMISSAL *(p. 71)*

CHRISTIAN INITIATION: 3RD SCRUTINY

ENTRANCE ANTIPHON *(Cf. Psalm 17.5-7)*

The waves of death rose about me; the pains of the netherworld surrounded me. In my anguish I called to the Lord; and from his holy temple he heard my voice.

INTRODUCTORY RITES *(p. 5)*

COLLECT

Grant, O Lord, to these chosen ones that, instructed in the holy mysteries, they may receive new life at the font of Baptism and be numbered among the members of your Church. Through our Lord Jesus Christ, your Son, who lives and reigns with you in the unity of the Holy Spirit, one God, for ever and ever. **Amen.**

FIRST READING *(Ezekiel 37.12-14)*

Thus says the Lord God: "I am going to open your graves, and bring you up from your graves, O my people; and I will bring you back to the land of Israel. And you shall know that I am the Lord, when I open your graves, and bring you up from your graves, O my people.

"I will put my spirit within you, and you shall live, and I will place you on your own soil; then you shall know that I, the Lord, have spoken and will act," says the Lord.

The word of the Lord. **Thanks be to God.**

RESPONSORIAL PSALM *(Psalm 130)*

With the Lord there is stead - fast love and great pow'r to re - deem.

R. **With the Lord there is steadfast love
and great power to redeem.**

Out of the depths I cry to you, O · **Lord.**
Lord, hear · **my** voice!
Let your ears be at-**tentive**
to the voice of my sup-**pli**-cations! R.

If you, O Lord, should mark in-**iquities,**
Lord, who · **could** stand?
But there is forgiveness with · **you,**
so that you may be · **re**-vered. R.

I wait for the · **Lord,**
my soul waits, and in his word · **I** hope;
my soul waits for the · **Lord**
more than watchmen for · **the** morning. R.

For with the Lord there is steadfast · **love,**
and with him is great power to · **re**-deem.
It is he who will redeem · **Israel**
from all its · **in**-iquities. R.

©2009 Gordon Johnston/Novalis

SECOND READING *(Romans 8.8-11)*
Brothers and sisters: Those who are in the flesh cannot please God. But you are not in the flesh; you are in the Spirit, since the Spirit of God dwells in you. Anyone who does not have the Spirit of Christ does not belong to him.

But if Christ is in you, though the body is dead because of sin, the Spirit is life because of righteousness.

If the Spirit of God who raised Jesus from the dead dwells in you, he who raised Christ from the dead will give life to your mortal bodies also through his Spirit that dwells in you.

The word of the Lord. **Thanks be to God.**

GOSPEL ACCLAMATION *(John 11.25, 26)*
Praise and honour to you, Lord Jesus Christ! I am the resurrection and the life, says the Lord; whoever believes in me will never die. **Praise and honour to you, Lord Jesus Christ!**

GOSPEL *(John 11.1-45)*
For the shorter version, omit the indented parts.
The Lord be with you. **And with your spirit.**
A reading from the holy Gospel according to John.
Glory to you, O Lord.

> Now a certain man, Lazarus, was ill. He was from Bethany, the village of Mary and her sister Martha. Mary was the one who anointed the Lord with perfume and wiped his feet with her hair; her brother Lazarus was ill. So

The sisters [of Lazarus] sent a message to Jesus, "Lord, he whom you love is ill." But when Jesus heard this, he said, "This illness does not lead to death; rather it is for God's glory, so that the Son of God may be glorified through it." Accordingly, though Jesus loved Martha and her sister and Lazarus, after having heard that Lazarus was ill, he stayed two days longer in the place where he was. Then after this he said to the disciples, "Let us go to Judea again."

The disciples said to him, "Rabbi, the people there were just now trying to stone you, and are you going there again?" Jesus answered, "Are there not twelve hours of daylight? Those who walk during the day do not stumble, because they see the light of this world. But those who walk at night stumble, because the light is not in them."

After saying this, he told them, "Our friend Lazarus has fallen asleep, but I am going there to awaken him." The disciples said to him, "Lord, if he has fallen asleep, he will be all right." Jesus, however, had been speaking about his death, but they thought that he was referring merely to sleep. Then Jesus told them plainly, "Lazarus is dead. For your sake I am glad I was not there, so that you may believe. But let us go to him." Thomas, who was called the Twin, said to his fellow disciples, "Let us also go, that we may die with him."

When Jesus arrived, he found that Lazarus had already been in the tomb four days.

Now Bethany was near Jerusalem, some two miles away, and many Jews had come to Martha and Mary to console them about their brother.

When Martha heard that Jesus was coming, she went and met him, while Mary stayed at home. Martha said to Jesus, "Lord, if you had been here, my brother would not have died. But even now I know that God will give you whatever you ask of him." Jesus said to her, "Your brother will rise again." Martha said to him, "I know that he will rise again in the resurrection on the last day." Jesus said to her, "I am the resurrection and the life. Whoever believes in me, even though they die, will live, and everyone who lives and believes in me will never die. Do you believe this?" She said to him, "Yes, Lord, I believe that you are the Christ, the Son of God, the one coming into the world."

When she had said this, she went back and called her sister Mary, and told her privately, "The Teacher is here and is calling for you." And when Mary heard it, she got up quickly and went to him. Now Jesus had not yet come to the village, but was still at the place where Martha had met him. The Jews who were with her in the house, consoling her, saw Mary get up quickly and go out. They followed her because they thought that she was going to the tomb to weep there.

When Mary came where Jesus was and saw him, she knelt at his feet and said to him, "Lord, if you had been here, my brother would not have died." When Jesus saw her weeping, and the Jews who came with her also weeping, he [Jesus] was greatly disturbed in spirit and deeply moved. He said, "Where have you laid him?" They said to him, "Lord, come and see." Jesus began to weep. So the Jews said, "See how he loved him!" But some of them said, "Could not he who opened the eyes of the blind man have kept this man from dying?"

Then Jesus, again greatly disturbed, came to the tomb. It was a cave, and a stone was lying against it. Jesus said, "Take away the stone." Martha, the sister of the dead man, said to him, "Lord, already there is a stench because he has been dead four days." Jesus said to her, "Did I not tell you that if you believed, you would see the glory of God?" So they took away the stone. And Jesus looked upward and said, "Father, I thank you for having heard me. I knew that you always hear me, but I have said this for the sake of the crowd standing here, so that they may believe that you sent me."

When he had said this, he cried with a loud voice, "Lazarus, come out!" The dead man came out, his hands and feet bound with strips of cloth, and his face wrapped in a cloth. Jesus said to them, "Unbind him, and let him go."

Many of the Jews therefore, who had come with Mary and had seen what Jesus did, believed in him.

The Gospel of the Lord. **Praise to you, Lord Jesus Christ.**

PROFESSION OF FAITH (p. 11)

PRAYER OF THE FAITHFUL (p. 231)

PREPARATION OF THE GIFTS (p. 14)

PRAYER OVER THE OFFERINGS

Hear us, almighty God, and, having instilled in your servants the first fruits of the Christian faith, graciously purify them by the working of this sacrifice. Through Christ our Lord. **Amen.**

PREFACE *(5th Sunday of Lent, p. 22)*

COMMUNION ANTIPHON *(Cf. John 11.26)*

Everyone who lives and believes in me will not die for ever, says the Lord.

PRAYER AFTER COMMUNION

May your people be at one, O Lord, we pray, and in wholehearted submission to you may they obtain this grace: that, safe from all distress, they may readily live out their joy at being saved and remember in loving prayer those to be reborn. Through Christ our Lord. **Amen.**

PRAYER OVER THE PEOPLE

Bless, O Lord, your people, who long for the gift of your mercy, and grant that what, at your prompting, they desire they may receive by your generous gift. Through Christ our Lord. **Amen.**

BLESSING AND DISMISSAL *(p. 71)*

March 25
Passion (Palm Sunday)
World Day of Youth

"Turn the other cheek." Many people identify this as a central teaching from Jesus, but it only appears in the Gospels of Matthew and Luke. Nevertheless, Mark's narrative of Jesus' passion and death illustrates what this saying means.

Jesus does not resist when they arrest him, nor does he defend himself at trial. He simply acknowledges his true identity, then submits to mockery, crucifixion and death. But this confirms who he really was: when the centurion saw *how* Jesus died he said, "Truly this man was God's Son!"

The Old Testament tells us about individuals suffering for the sake of their faith. Second Isaiah presents God's servant who submitted to physical attacks knowing that God was with him, and in Psalm 22 an individual describes his persecution and suffering but in the end is confident that God will deliver him. However, Paul tells us that Jesus sacrificed even more, emptying himself of his divinity to become one of us in order to die on the cross for us.

This is the paschal mystery we celebrate at every Eucharist. Jesus gave his body and blood over to death so that we can have life. As we share the bread and wine, we remember that sacrifice and celebrate its effect in our lives today.

John L. McLaughlin
Toronto, ON

Commemoration of the Lord's Entrance into Jerusalem

FIRST FORM: The Procession

INTRODUCTION

The people, carrying palm branches, gather in a suitable place distinct from the church to which the procession will move. The assembly may sing Hosanna! *or another suitable hymn.*

Ho - san - na, ho - san - na, ho - san - na in the high - est. Ho - san - na, ho - san - na, ho - san - na in the high - est.

© *Michel Guimont*

GREETING *(p. 5)*

Dear brothers and sisters, since the beginning of Lent until now we have prepared our hearts by penance and charitable works. Today we gather together to herald with the whole Church the beginning of the celebration of our Lord's Paschal Mystery, that is to say, of his Passion and Resurrection. For it was to accomplish this mystery that he entered his own city of Jerusalem. Therefore, with all faith and devotion, let us commemorate the Lord's entry into the city for our salvation, following in his footsteps, so that, being made by his grace partakers of the Cross, we may have a share also in his Resurrection and in his life.

Let us pray.

1 Almighty ever-living God, sanctify these branches with your blessing, that we, who follow Christ the King in exultation, may reach the eternal Jerusalem through him. Who lives and reigns for ever and ever. **Amen.**

2 Increase the faith of those who place their hope in you, O God, and graciously hear the prayers of those who call on you, that we, who today hold high these branches to hail Christ in his triumph, may bear fruit for you by good works accomplished in him. Who lives and reigns for ever and ever. **Amen.**

GOSPEL (Mark 11.1-10)

The Lord be with you. **And with your spirit.**
A reading from the holy Gospel according to Mark. **Glory to you, O Lord.**

When they were approaching Jerusalem, at Bethphage and Bethany, near the Mount of Olives, Jesus sent two of his disciples and said to them, "Go into the village ahead of you, and immediately as you enter it, you will find tied there a colt that has never been ridden; untie it and bring it. If anyone says to you, 'Why are you doing this?' just say this, 'The Lord needs it and will send it back here immediately.'"

They went away and found a colt tied near a door, outside in the street. As they were untying it, some of the bystanders said to them, "What are you doing, untying the colt?" The disciples told them what Jesus had said; and they allowed them to take it.

Then they brought the colt to Jesus and threw their cloaks on it; and he sat on it. Many people spread their cloaks on the road, and others spread leafy branches that they had cut in the fields.

Then those who went ahead and those who followed were shouting, "Hosanna! Blessed is the one who comes in the name of the Lord! Blessed is the coming kingdom of our father David! Hosanna in the highest heaven!"

The Gospel of the Lord. **Praise to you, Lord Jesus Christ.**

or

GOSPEL *(John 12.12-16)*

The Lord be with you. **And with your spirit.**
A reading from the holy Gospel according to John. **Glory to you, O Lord.**

The great crowd that had come to the festival heard that Jesus was coming to Jerusalem. So they took branches of palm trees and went out to meet him, shouting, "Hosanna! Blessed is the one who comes in the name of the Lord — the King of Israel!"

Jesus found a young donkey and sat on it; as it is written: "Do not be afraid, daughter of Zion. Look, your king is coming, sitting on a donkey's colt!"

His disciples did not understand these things at first; but when Jesus was glorified, then they remembered that these things had been written of him and had been done to him.

The Gospel of the Lord. **Praise to you, Lord Jesus Christ.**

PROCESSION

1 Dear brothers and sisters, like the crowds who acclaimed Jesus in Jerusalem, let us go forth in peace.

2 Let us go forth in peace. **In the name of Christ. Amen.**

All process to the church singing a hymn in honour of Christ the King. Mass continues with the Collect *(p. 245).*

SECOND FORM: The Solemn Entrance

The blessing of branches and proclamation of the Gospel take place, as above, but in the church. After the Gospel, the priest moves solemnly through the church to the sanctuary, while all sing. Mass continues with the Collect *(p. 245).*

THIRD FORM: The Simple Entrance

The people gather in the church as usual. While the priest goes to the altar, the following Entrance Antiphon *or a suitable hymn is sung.*

ENTRANCE ANTIPHON

(Cf. John 12.1, 12-13; Psalm 23.9-10)

Six days before the Passover, when the Lord came into the city of Jerusalem, the children ran to meet him; in their hands they carried palm branches and with a loud voice cried out:

Hosanna in the highest!
Blessed are you, who have come
in your abundant mercy!

O gates, lift high your heads;
grow higher, ancient doors.

Let him enter, the king of glory!
Who is this king of glory?
He, the Lord of hosts, he is the king of glory.

Hosanna in the highest!
Blessed are you, who have come
  in your abundant mercy!

INTRODUCTORY RITES *(p. 5)*

COLLECT

Almighty ever-living God, who as an example of humility for the human race to follow caused our Saviour to take flesh and submit to the Cross, graciously grant that we may heed his lesson of patient suffering and so merit a share in his Resurrection. Who lives and reigns with you in the unity of the Holy Spirit, one God, for ever and ever. **Amen.**

FIRST READING *(Isaiah 50.4-7)*

The servant of the Lord said: "The Lord God has given me the tongue of a teacher, that I may know how to sustain the weary with a word. Morning by morning he wakens — wakens my ear to listen as those who are taught. The Lord God has opened my ear, and I was not rebellious, I did not turn backward.

"I gave my back to those who struck me, and my cheeks to those who pulled out the beard; I did not hide my face from insult and spitting.

"The Lord God helps me; therefore I have not been disgraced; therefore I have set my face like flint, and I know that I shall not be put to shame."

The word of the Lord. **Thanks be to God.**

RESPONSORIAL PSALM *(Psalm 22)*

℟. **My God, my God, why have you forsaken me?**

All who see me · **mock_at_me;**
they make mouths at me, they shake ·
their heads;
"Commit your cause to the Lord;
let him de-·**liver;**
let him rescue the one in whom he · **de-**lights!" ℟.

For dogs are all a-·**round_me;**
a company of evildoers · **en-**circles_me.
My hands and feet have · **shrivelled;**
I can count all · **my** bones. ℟.

They divide my clothes a-·**mong_themselves,**
and for my clothing they · **cast** lots.
But you, O Lord, do not be far a-·**way!**
O my help, come quickly · **to_my** aid! ℟.

I will tell of your name to my brothers and
sisters; in the midst of the congregation
I will · **praise_you:**
You who fear the · **Lord,** praise_him!
All you offspring of Jacob, · **glorify_him;**
stand in awe of him, all you offspring
· **of** Israel! ℟.

©2009 Gordon Johnston/Novalis

SECOND READING *(Philippians 2.6-11)*

Christ Jesus, though he was in the form of God, did not regard equality with God as something to be exploited, but emptied himself, taking the form of a slave, being born in human likeness. And being found in human form, he humbled himself and became obedient to the point of death — even death on a cross.

Therefore God highly exalted him and gave him the name that is above every name, so that at the name of Jesus every knee should bend, in heaven and on earth and under the earth, and every tongue should confess that Jesus Christ is Lord, to the glory of God the Father.

The word of the Lord. **Thanks be to God.**

GOSPEL ACCLAMATION *(Philippians 2.8-9)*

Praise and honour to you, Lord Jesus Christ! Christ became obedient for us to death, even death on a Cross. Therefore God exalted him and gave him the name above every name. **Praise and honour to you, Lord Jesus Christ!**

GOSPEL *(Mark 14.1 – 15.47)*

Several readers may proclaim the passion narrative today. N indicates the narrator, J the words of Jesus, and S the words of other speakers.

N The Passion of our Lord Jesus Christ according to Mark.

It was two days before the Passover and the festival of Unleavened Bread. The chief priests and the scribes were looking for a way to arrest Jesus by stealth and kill him; for they said,

S *Not during the festival, or there may be a riot among the people.*

N While Jesus was at Bethany in the house of Simon the leper, as he sat at the table, a woman came with an alabaster jar of very costly ointment of nard, and she broke open the jar and poured the ointment on his head. But some were there who said to one another in anger,

S *Why was the ointment wasted in this way? For this ointment could have been sold for more than three hundred denarii, and the money given to the poor.*

N And they scolded her. But Jesus said,

J **Let her alone; why do you trouble her? She has performed a good service for me. For you always have the poor with you, and you can show kindness to them whenever you wish; but you will not always have me. She has done what she could; she has anointed my body beforehand for its burial. Truly I tell you, wherever the good news is proclaimed in the whole world, what she has done will be told in remembrance of her.**

N Then Judas Iscariot, who was one of the twelve, went to the chief priests in order to betray him to them. When they heard it, they were greatly pleased, and promised to give him money. So he began to look for an opportunity to betray him.

On the first day of Unleavened Bread, when the Passover lamb is sacrificed, the disciples said to Jesus,

S *Where do you want us to go and make the preparations for you to eat the Passover?*

N So he sent two of his disciples, saying to them,

J **Go into the city, and a man carrying a jar of water will meet you; follow him, and wherever he enters, say to the owner of the house, "The Teacher asks, 'Where is my guest room where I may eat the Passover with my disciples?'" He will show you a large room upstairs, furnished and ready. Make preparations for us there.**

N So the disciples set out and went to the city, and found everything as he had told them; and they prepared the Passover meal.

When it was evening, Jesus came with the twelve. And when they had taken their places and were eating, Jesus said,

J **Truly I tell you, one of you will betray me, one who is eating with me.**

N They began to be distressed and to say to him one after another,

S *Surely, not I?*

J **It is one of the twelve, one who is dipping bread into the bowl with me. For the Son of Man goes as it is written of him, but woe to that one by whom the Son of Man is betrayed! It would have been better for that one not to have been born.**

N While they were eating, he took a loaf of bread, and after blessing it he broke it, gave it to them, and said,

J **Take; this is my Body.**

N Then he took a cup, and after giving thanks he gave it to them, and all of them drank from it. He said to them,

J **This is my Blood of the covenant, which is poured out for many. Truly I tell you, I will never again drink of the fruit of the vine until that day when I drink it new in the kingdom of God.**

N When they had sung the hymn, they went out to the Mount of Olives. And Jesus said to them,

J **You will all become deserters; for it is written, "I will strike the shepherd, and the sheep will be scattered." But after I am raised up, I will go before you to Galilee.**

N Peter said to him,

S *Even though all become deserters, I will not.*

J **Truly I tell you, this day, this very night, before the cock crows twice, you will deny me three times.**

N But he said vehemently,

S *Even though I must die with you, I will not deny you.*

N And all of them said the same.

*At this point all may join in singing
an appropriate acclamation.*

Ky - ri - e,   Chris - te,   Ky - ri - e   e - le - i - son!

Text: Didier Rimaud, © *CNPL.* **Music:** Jacques Berthier
Source: © *Éditions Musicales Studio SM,* 060794-2

N They went to a place called Gethsemane; and Jesus said to his disciples,

J **Sit here while I pray.**

N He took with him Peter and James and John, and began to be distressed and agitated. And he said to them,

J **I am deeply grieved, even to death; remain here, and keep awake.**

N And going a little farther, he threw himself on the ground and prayed that, if it were possible, the hour might pass from him.

J **Abba, Father, for you all things are possible; remove this cup from me; yet, not what I want, but what you want.**

N Jesus came and found them sleeping; and he said to Peter,

J **Simon, are you asleep? Could you not keep awake one hour? Keep awake and pray that you may not come into temptation; the spirit indeed is willing, but the flesh is weak.**

N And again he went away and prayed, saying the same words. And once more he came and found them sleeping, for their eyes were very heavy; and they did not know what to say to him.

He came a third time and said to them,

J **Are you still sleeping and taking your rest? Enough! The hour has come; the Son of Man is betrayed into the hands of sinners. Get up, let us be going. See, my betrayer is at hand.**

N Immediately, while he was still speaking, Judas, one of the twelve, arrived; and with him there was a crowd with swords and clubs, from the chief priests, the scribes, and the elders. Now the betrayer had given them a sign, saying,

S *The one I will kiss is the man; arrest him and lead him away under guard.*

N So when he came, he went up to Jesus at once and said,

S *"Rabbi!"*

N and kissed him. Then they laid hands on him and arrested him. But one of those who stood near drew his sword and struck the slave of the high priest, cutting off his ear. Then Jesus said to them,

J **Have you come out with swords and clubs to arrest me as though I were a bandit? Day after day I was with you in the temple teaching, and you did not arrest me. But let the Scriptures be fulfilled.**

N All of them deserted him and fled.

A certain young man was following Jesus, wearing nothing but a linen cloth. They caught hold of him, but he left the linen cloth and ran off naked.

They took Jesus to the high priest; and all the chief priests, the elders, and the scribes were assembled.

Peter had followed him at a distance, right into the courtyard of the high priest; and he was sitting with the guards, warming himself at the fire.

Now the chief priests and the whole council were looking for testimony against Jesus to put him to death; but they found none. For many gave false testimony against him, and their testimony did not agree. Some stood up and gave false testimony against him, saying,

S *We heard him say, "I will destroy this temple that is made with hands, and in three days I will build another, not made with hands."*

N But even on this point their testimony did not agree. Then the high priest stood up before them and asked Jesus,

S *Have you no answer? What is it that they testify against you?*

N But he was silent and did not answer. Again the high priest asked him,

S *Are you the Christ, the Son of the Blessed One?*

J **I am; and "you will see the Son of Man seated at the right hand of the Power," and "coming with the clouds of heaven."**

N Then the high priest tore his clothes and said,

S *Why do we still need witnesses? You have heard his blasphemy! What is your decision?*

N All of them condemned him as deserving death. Some began to spit on him, to blindfold him, and to strike him, saying to him,

S *Prophesy!*

N The guards also took him over and beat him.

While Peter was below in the courtyard, one of the servant girls of the high priest came by. When she saw Peter warming himself, she stared at him and said,

S *You also were with Jesus, the man from Nazareth.*

N But he denied it, saying,

S *I do not know or understand what you are talking about.*

N And he went out into the forecourt. Then the cock crowed. And the servant girl, on seeing him, began again to say to the bystanders,

S *This man is one of them.*

N But again he denied it. Then after a little while the bystanders again said to Peter,

S *Certainly you are one of them; for you are a Galilean.*

N But he began to curse, and he swore an oath,

S *I do not know this man you are talking about.*

N At that moment the cock crowed for the second time. Then Peter remembered that Jesus had said to him, "Before the cock crows twice, you will deny me three times." And he broke down and wept.

*At this point all may join in singing
an appropriate acclamation.*

Ky - ri - e,   Chris - te,   Ky - ri - e   e - le - i - son!

Text: Didier Rimaud, © *CNPL*. **Music:** Jacques Berthier
Source: © *Éditions Musicales Studio SM*, 060794-2

N As soon as it was morning, the chief priests held a consultation with the elders and scribes and the whole council. They bound Jesus, led him away, and handed him over to Pilate. Pilate asked him,

S *Are you the King of the Jews?*

J *You say so.*

N Then the chief priests accused him of many things. Pilate asked him again,

S *Have you no answer? See how many charges they bring against you.*

N But Jesus made no further reply, so that Pilate was amazed.

Now at the festival Pilate used to release a prisoner for them, anyone for whom they asked. Now a man called Barabbas was in prison with the rebels who had committed murder during the insurrection. So the crowd came and began to ask Pilate to do for them according to his custom. Then he answered them,

S *Do you want me to release for you the King of the Jews?*

N For he realized that it was out of jealousy that the chief priests had handed him over. But the chief priests stirred up the crowd to have him release Barabbas for them instead. Pilate spoke to them again,

S *Then what do you wish me to do with the man you call the King of the Jews?*

N They shouted back,

S *Crucify him!*

N Pilate asked them,

S *Why, what evil has he done?*

N But they shouted all the more,

S *Crucify him!*

N So Pilate, wishing to satisfy the crowd, released Barabbas for them; and after flogging Jesus, he handed him over to be crucified. Then the soldiers led him into the courtyard of the palace, (that is, the governor's headquarters); and they called together the whole cohort. And they clothed him in a purple cloak; and after twisting

some thorns into a crown, they put it on him. And
they began saluting him,

S *Hail, King of the Jews!*

N They struck his head with a reed, spat upon him,
and knelt down in homage to him. After mocking
him, they stripped him of the purple cloak and
put his own clothes on him. Then they led him
out to crucify him.

They compelled a passer-by, who was coming
in from the country, to carry his Cross; it was
Simon of Cyrene, the father of Alexander and
Rufus. Then they brought Jesus to the place called
Golgotha, (which means the Place of a Skull).
And they offered him wine mixed with myrrh;
but he did not take it. And they crucified him,
and divided his clothes among them, casting lots
to decide what each should take.

It was nine o'clock in the morning when they
crucified him. The inscription of the charge
against him read, "The King of the Jews." And
with him they crucified two bandits, one on his
right and one on his left. Those who passed by
derided him, shaking their heads and saying,

S *Aha! You would destroy the temple and build
it in three days; save yourself, and come down
from the Cross!*

N In the same way the chief priests, along with the
scribes, were also mocking him among themselves and saying,

S *He saved others; he cannot save himself. Let the
Christ, the King of Israel, come down from the
Cross now, so that we may see and believe.*

N Those who were crucified with him also taunted him.

When it was noon, darkness came over the whole land until three in the afternoon. At three o'clock Jesus cried out with a loud voice,

J **Eloi, Eloi, lema sabachthani?**

N which means, "My God, my God, why have you forsaken me?" When some of the bystanders heard it, they said,

S *Listen, he is calling for Elijah.*

N And someone ran, filled a sponge with sour wine, put it on a stick, and gave it to him to drink, saying,

S *Wait, let us see whether Elijah will come to take him down.*

N Then Jesus gave a loud cry and breathed his last.

Here all kneel and pause for a short time.

N And the curtain of the temple was torn in two, from top to bottom. Now when the centurion, who stood facing him, saw that in this way he breathed his last, he said,

S *Truly this man was God's Son!*

N There were also women looking on from a distance; among them were Mary Magdalene, and Mary the mother of James the younger and of Joses, and Salome. These used to follow him and provided for him when he was in Galilee; and there were many other women who had come up with him to Jerusalem.

When evening had come, and since it was the day of Preparation, that is, the day before the Sabbath, Joseph of Arimathea, a respected member of the council, who was also himself waiting expectantly for the kingdom of God, went boldly to Pilate and asked for the body of Jesus. Then Pilate wondered if he were already dead; and summoning the centurion, he asked him whether he had been dead for some time. When he learned from the centurion that Jesus was dead, he granted the body to Joseph.

Then Joseph bought a linen cloth, and taking down the body, wrapped it in the linen cloth, and laid it in a tomb that had been hewn out of the rock. He then rolled a stone against the door of the tomb. Mary Magdalene and Mary the mother of Joses saw where the body was laid.

The readers return to their places in silence.

PROFESSION OF FAITH *(p. 11)*

PRAYER OF THE FAITHFUL

The following intentions are suggestions only. There are more suggestions at www.livingwithchrist.ca

R. **Lord, hear our prayer.**

For the Church, living presence of God's compassion, we pray to the Lord: R.

For civic and world leaders, builders of a just society, we pray to the Lord: R.

For the special needs of all who suffer in any way this day, we pray to the Lord: R.

For the community of faith gathered today, we pray to the Lord: R.

PREPARATION OF THE GIFTS *(p. 14)*

PRAYER OVER THE OFFERINGS
Through the Passion of your Only Begotten Son, O Lord, may our reconciliation with you be near at hand, so that, though we do not merit it by our own deeds, yet by this sacrifice made once for all, we may feel already the effects of your mercy. Through Christ our Lord. **Amen.**

PREFACE *(Passion Sunday, p. 22)*

COMMUNION ANTIPHON *(Matthew 26.42)*
Father, if this chalice cannot pass without my drinking it, your will be done.

PRAYER AFTER COMMUNION
Nourished with these sacred gifts, we humbly beseech you, O Lord, that, just as through the death of your Son you have brought us to hope for what we believe, so by his Resurrection you may lead us to where you call. Through Christ our Lord. **Amen.**

PRAYER OVER THE PEOPLE
Look, we pray, O Lord, on this your family, for whom our Lord Jesus Christ did not hesitate to be delivered into the hands of the wicked and submit to the agony of the Cross. Who lives and reigns for ever and ever. **Amen.**

SOLEMN BLESSING — PASSION OF THE LORD
(Optional)

Bow down for the blessing.

May God, the Father of mercies, who has given you an example of love in the Passion of his Only Begotten Son, grant that, by serving God and your neighbour, you may lay hold of the wondrous gift of his blessing. **Amen.**

So that you may receive the reward of everlasting life from him, through whose earthly Death you believe that you escape eternal death. **Amen.**

And by following the example of his self-abasement, may you possess a share in his Resurrection. **Amen.**

And may the blessing of almighty God, the Father, and the Son, and the Holy Spirit, come down on you and remain with you for ever. **Amen.**

DISMISSAL *(p. 71)*

March 29
Holy Thursday
Mass of the Lord's Supper

"You will never wash my feet!"

I wonder how many of us say something like this to God, usually at critical moments in our lives. "This is not what I expected! This is not what I wanted!"

Peter, like us, has listened to Jesus, seen his power and acknowledged him as Messiah. But he reacts strongly to his Lord and Messiah humbling himself!

Most of us, I suspect, are not overly thrilled with God's humility, with the simple truth that God humbles himself to speak to us and offer himself as food for our journey. We want a 'bigger' God, an 'action' God. Indeed, many people today reject God because God does not meet their expectations or demands.

Nonetheless, the Eucharist is the pinnacle of God's gentle humility, of letting go of divinity to become human, to become food for a starving people. In this peaceful oasis we encounter our humble, incarnate, healing God, reaching out to us in love and offering us his Spirit – and asking us to trust him, united to his Son.

"Do this in remembrance of me" is not just a memory; it should be the beginning of a daily prayer: "Lord, I accept that you wash my feet; help me wash the feet of my brothers and sisters, to become more like you."

Fr. Mark Miller, CSsR
Toronto, ON

ENTRANCE ANTIPHON *(Cf. Galatians 6.14)*
We should glory in the Cross of our Lord Jesus Christ,
in whom is our salvation, life and resurrection,
through whom we are saved and delivered.

INTRODUCTORY RITES *(p. 5)*

COLLECT
O God, who have called us to participate in this
most sacred Supper, in which your Only Begotten
Son, when about to hand himself over to death, entrusted to the Church a sacrifice new for all eternity,
the banquet of his love, grant, we pray, that we may
draw from so great a mystery, the fullness of charity and of life. Through our Lord Jesus Christ, your
Son, who lives and reigns with you in the unity of
the Holy Spirit, one God, for ever and ever. **Amen.**

FIRST READING *(Exodus 12.1-8, 11-14)*
The Lord said to Moses and Aaron in the land of
Egypt: This month shall mark for you the beginning
of months; it shall be the first month of the year for
you. Tell the whole congregation of Israel that on
the tenth of this month they are to take a lamb for
each family, a lamb for each household. If a household is too small for a whole lamb, it shall join its
closest neighbour in obtaining one; the lamb shall
be divided in proportion to the number of people
who eat of it.

Your lamb shall be without blemish, a year-old
male; you may take it from the sheep or from the
goats. You shall keep it until the fourteenth day of
this month; then the whole assembled congregation

of Israel shall slaughter it at twilight. They shall take some of the blood and put it on the two doorposts and the lintel of the houses in which they eat it. They shall eat the lamb that same night; they shall eat it roasted over the fire with unleavened bread and bitter herbs.

This is how you shall eat it: your loins girded, your sandals on your feet, and your staff in your hand; and you shall eat it hurriedly. It is the Passover of the Lord. For I will pass through the land of Egypt that night, and I will strike down every firstborn in the land of Egypt, both human beings and animals; on all the gods of Egypt I will execute judgments: I am the Lord.

The blood shall be a sign for you on the houses where you live: when I see the blood, I will pass over you, and no plague shall destroy you when I strike the land of Egypt.

This day shall be a day of remembrance for you. You shall celebrate it as a festival to the Lord; throughout your generations you shall observe it as a perpetual ordinance.

The word of the Lord. **Thanks be to God.**

RESPONSORIAL PSALM *(Psalm 116)*

The cup of bless-ing that we bless
is a shar-ing in the Blood of Christ.

R̰. **The cup of blessing that we bless
is a sharing in the Blood of Christ.**

What shall I return to the · **Lord**
for all his bounty to · **me?**
I will lift up the cup of sal-**vation**
and call on the name · **of_the** Lord. R̰.

Precious in the sight of the · **Lord**
is the death of his · **faithful_ones.**
I am your servant, the son
    of your · **serving_girl.**
You have loosed · **my** bonds. R̰.

I will offer to you a thanksgiving · **sacrifice**
and call on the name of the · **Lord.**
I will pay my vows to the · **Lord**
in the presence of all · **his** people. R̰.

©2009 Gordon Johnston/Novalis

To hear the Sunday Psalms, visit www.livingwithchrist.ca.

SECOND READING *(1 Corinthians 11.23-26)*
Brothers and sisters: I received from the Lord what I also handed on to you, that the Lord Jesus on the night when he was betrayed took a loaf of bread, and when he had given thanks, he broke it and said, "This is my Body that is for you. Do this in remembrance of me."

In the same way he took the cup also, after supper, saying, "This cup is the new covenant in my Blood. Do this, as often as you drink it, in remembrance of me." For as often as you eat this bread and drink the cup, you proclaim the Lord's death until he comes.

The word of the Lord. **Thanks be to God.**

GOSPEL ACCLAMATION *(John 13.34)*
Praise and honour to you, Lord Jesus Christ! I give you a new commandment: love one another as I have loved you. **Praise and honour to you, Lord Jesus Christ!**

GOSPEL *(John 13.1-15)*
The Lord be with you. **And with your spirit.**
A reading from the holy Gospel according to John. **Glory to you, O Lord.**

Before the festival of the Passover, Jesus knew that his hour had come to depart from this world and go to the Father. Having loved his own who were in the world, he loved them to the end.

The devil had already put it into the heart of Judas, son of Simon Iscariot, to betray him. And during supper Jesus, knowing that the Father had given all things into his hands, and that he had come from

God and was going to God, got up from the table, took off his outer robe, and tied a towel around himself. Then he poured water into a basin and began to wash the disciples' feet and to wipe them with the towel that was tied around him.

He came to Simon Peter, who said to him, "Lord, are you going to wash my feet?" Jesus answered, "You do not know now what I am doing, but later you will understand." Peter said to him, "You will never wash my feet." Jesus answered, "Unless I wash you, you have no share with me." Simon Peter said to him, "Lord, not my feet only but also my hands and my head!" Jesus said to him, "One who has bathed does not need to wash, except for the feet, but is entirely clean. And you are clean, though not all of you." For he knew who was to betray him; for this reason he said, "Not all of you are clean."

After he had washed their feet, put on his robe, and returned to the table, Jesus said to them, "Do you know what I have done to you? You call me Teacher and Lord — and you are right, for that is what I am. So if I, your Lord and Teacher, have washed your feet, you also ought to wash one another's feet. For I have set you an example, that you also should do as I have done to you."

The Gospel of the Lord. **Praise to you, Lord Jesus Christ.**

The Profession of Faith *is omitted.*

THE WASHING OF FEET *(Optional)*

During the washing of feet, an appropriate song may be sung.

PRAYER OF THE FAITHFUL

The following intentions are suggestions only. There are more suggestions at www.livingwithchrist.ca

R. **Lord, hear our prayer.**

For the healing of divisions in the Christian Church, we pray to the Lord: R.

For world leaders who listen to those who cry out for peace and justice, we pray to the Lord: R.

For all who have died and for those who mourn their loss, we pray to the Lord: R.

For those in our community who are suffering, and for those who reach out to ease their suffering, we pray to the Lord: R.

PREPARATION OF THE GIFTS *(p. 14)*

PRAYER OVER THE OFFERINGS

Grant us, O Lord, we pray, that we may participate worthily in these mysteries, for whenever the memorial of this sacrifice is celebrated, the work of our redemption is accomplished. Through Christ our Lord. **Amen.**

PREFACE *(Holy Eucharist I, p. 27)*

COMMUNION ANTIPHON *(1 Corinthians 11.24-25)*

This is the Body that will be given up for you; this is the Chalice of the new covenant in my Blood, says the Lord; do this, whenever you receive it, in memory of me.

PRAYER AFTER COMMUNION

Grant, almighty God, that, just as we are renewed
by the Supper of your Son in this present age, so we
may enjoy his banquet for all eternity. Who lives and
reigns for ever and ever. **Amen.**

The Blessing *and* Dismissal *are omitted tonight.*

TRANSFER OF THE HOLY EUCHARIST

*The Blessed Sacrament is carried through the church to the
place of repose. During the procession, the hymn* Pange
Lingua *(p. 269, stanzas 1-4) or another eucharistic song is
sung. At the place of repose, the presider incenses the Blessed
Sacrament, while* Tantum ergo Sacramentum *(Pange Lingua,
stanzas 5-6) or another eucharistic song is sung. The tabernacle of repose is then closed.*

*After a period of silent adoration, the priests and ministers of
the altar retire. The faithful are encouraged to continue adoration before the Blessed Sacrament for a suitable period of time.
There should be no solemn adoration after midnight.*

HAIL OUR SAVIOUR'S GLORIOUS BODY
(Pange Lingua)

Hail our Sa-viour's glo-rious Bo-dy,

Which his Vir-gin Mo-ther bore;

Hail the Blood which, shed for sin-ners,

Did a bro-ken world re-store;

Hail the sac-ra-ment most ho-ly,

Flesh and Blood of Christ a-dore.

A - men.

2. To the Virgin, for our healing,
   His own Son the Father sends;
   From the Father's love proceeding
   Sower, seed and word descends;
   Wondrous life of Word incarnate
   With his greatest wonder ends.

3. On that paschal evening see him
   With the chosen twelve recline,
   To the old law still obedient
   In its feast of love divine;
   Love divine, the new law giving,
   Gives himself as Bread and Wine.

4. By his word the Word almighty
   Makes of bread his flesh indeed;
   Wine becomes his very life-blood;
   Faith God's living Word must heed!
   Faith alone may safely guide us
   Where the senses cannot lead!

At the incensing of the Blessed Sacrament:

5. Come, adore this wondrous presence;
   Bow to Christ, the source of grace!
   Here is kept the ancient promise
   Of God's earthly dwelling place!
   Sight is blind before God's glory,
   Faith alone may see God's face.

6. Glory be to God the Father,
   Praise to his co-equal Son,
   Adoration to the Spirit,
   Bond of love in God-head one!
   Blest be God by all creation
   Joyously while ages run! Amen.

Text: *Pange Lingua,* Thomas Aquinas, 1227-74; tr. James Quinn, SJ (1919-2010). Used by permission of Oregon Catholic Press. **Tune:** PANGE LINGUA, 87.87.87. **Music:** CBW II 583; CBW III 381

March 30
Good Friday
Celebration of the Passion of the Lord

Alone. Abandoned. Forsaken.

How must it have felt for Jesus on that fateful Friday? The day that we have come to call 'Good'; the first day in the celebration of the Lord's Passion. Taken prisoner the night before, handed over to the Romans and betrayed by someone close to him, he now faced horrible torture and death.

His crime? He healed the sick; he embraced the poor; he made the lame walk and blind see; he spoke of love, justice and mercy. The Way of the Cross is a journey that each of us will make in our own way. For some, it has been one that called them to sacrifice their lives to be tortured and imprisoned for the sake of justice, so that others might live free from oppression.

For most, our Way is often that of keeping vigil over loved ones in palliative care, or struggling to ensure that there is food on the table and a decent place for our children to live, or helping others who struggle to live day-by-day.

Good Friday reminds us that Jesus is our rock, our refuge, our safe harbour (Psalm 31). He knows what suffering and feeling helpless means. We need only call on him to find the strength and the grace to help us on our way.

Jack Panozzo
Toronto, ON

National Collection for the Church in the Holy Land

PRAYER

1 Remember your mercies, O Lord, and with your
   eternal protection sanctify your servants, for
   whom Christ your Son, by the shedding of his
   Blood, established the Paschal Mystery. Who
   lives and reigns for ever and ever. **Amen.**

2 O God, who by the Passion of Christ your Son, our
   Lord, abolished the death inherited from ancient
   sin by every succeeding generation, grant that
   just as, being conformed to him, we have borne
   by the law of nature the image of the man of earth,
   so by the sanctification of grace we may bear the
   image of the Man of heaven. Through Christ our
   Lord. **Amen.**

LITURGY OF THE WORD

FIRST READING *(Isaiah 52.13 – 53.12)*

See, my servant shall prosper; he shall be exalted
and lifted up, and shall be very high.

Just as there were many who were astonished at
him — so marred was his appearance, beyond human
semblance, and his form beyond that of the sons of
man — so he shall startle many nations; kings shall
shut their mouths because of him; for that which had
not been told them they shall see, and that which
they had not heard they shall contemplate. Who has
believed what we have heard? And to whom has the
arm of the Lord been revealed?

For he grew up before the Lord like a young plant,
and like a root out of dry ground; he had no form or
majesty that we should look at him, nothing in his

appearance that we should desire him. He was despised and rejected by men; a man of suffering and acquainted with infirmity; and as one from whom others hide their faces he was despised, and we held him of no account.

Surely he has borne our infirmities and carried our diseases; yet we accounted him stricken, struck down by God, and afflicted. But he was wounded for our transgressions, crushed for our iniquities; upon him was the punishment that made us whole, and by his bruises we are healed.

All we like sheep have gone astray; each has turned to their own way and the Lord has laid on him the iniquity of us all.

He was oppressed, and he was afflicted, yet he did not open his mouth; like a lamb that is led to the slaughter, and like a sheep that before its shearers is silent, so he did not open his mouth.

By a perversion of justice he was taken away. Who could have imagined his future? For he was cut off from the land of the living, stricken for the transgression of my people. They made his grave with the wicked and his tomb with the rich, although he had done no violence, and there was no deceit in his mouth.

Yet it was the will of the Lord to crush him with pain. When you make his life an offering for sin, he shall see his offspring, and shall prolong his days; through him the will of the Lord shall prosper. Out of his anguish he shall see light; he shall find satisfaction through his knowledge. The righteous one, my servant, shall make many righteous, and he shall bear their iniquities.

Therefore I will allot him a portion with the great, and he shall divide the spoil with the strong; because he poured out himself to death, and was numbered with the transgressors; yet he bore the sin of many, and made intercession for the transgressors.

The word of the Lord. **Thanks be to God.**

RESPONSORIAL PSALM *(Psalm 31)*

Fa-ther, in-to your hands   I com-mend my spir-it.

R̰. **Father, into your hands I commend my spirit.**

In you, O Lord, I seek refuge;
    do not let me ever be put · **to** shame;
in your righteousness · **de**-liver_me.
Into your hand I commit · **my** spirit;
    you have redeemed me,
      O Lord, · **faith**-ful God. R̰.

I am the scorn of all my adversaries,
    a horror to my neighbours,
      an object of dread to my · **ac**-quaintances.
Those who see me in the · **street** flee_from_me.
I have passed out of mind like one
    who · **is** dead;
I have become like a · **bro**-ken vessel. R̰.

But I trust in you, · **O** Lord;
I say, "You are · **my** God."
My times are in · **your** hand;
deliver me from the hand
   of my · **enemies** and persecutors. ℟.

Let your face shine upon · **your** servant;
save me in your stead·-**fast** love.
Be strong, and let your heart · **take** courage,
all you who wait · **for** the Lord. ℟.

©2009 Gordon Johnston/Novalis

To hear the Sunday Psalms, visit www.livingwithchrist.ca.

SECOND READING *(Hebrews 4.14-16; 5.7-9)*
Brothers and sisters: Since we have a great high priest who has passed through the heavens, Jesus, the Son of God, let us hold fast to our confession. For we do not have a high priest who is unable to sympathize with our weaknesses, but we have one who in every respect has been tested as we are, yet without sin. Let us therefore approach the throne of grace with boldness, so that we may receive mercy and find grace to help in time of need.

In the days of his flesh, Jesus offered up prayers and supplications, with loud cries and tears, to the one who was able to save him from death, and he was heard because of his reverent submission. Although he was a Son, he learned obedience through what he suffered; and having been made perfect, he became the source of eternal salvation for all who obey him.

The word of the Lord. **Thanks be to God.**

GOSPEL ACCLAMATION *(Philippians 2.8-9)*
Praise and honour to you, Lord Jesus Christ! Christ became obedient for us to death, even death on a Cross. Therefore God exalted him and gave him the name above every name. **Praise and honour to you, Lord Jesus Christ!**

GOSPEL *(John 18.1 – 19.42)*
Several readers may proclaim the passion narrative today. N indicates the narrator, J the words of Jesus, and S the words of other speakers.

N The Passion of our Lord Jesus Christ according to John.

  After they had eaten the supper, Jesus went out with his disciples across the Kidron valley to a place where there was a garden, which he and his disciples entered. Now Judas, who betrayed him, also knew the place, because Jesus often met there with his disciples. So Judas brought a detachment of soldiers together with police from the chief priests and the Pharisees, and they came there with lanterns and torches and weapons.

  Then Jesus, knowing all that was to happen to him, came forward and asked them,

J **Whom are you looking for?**
N They answered,
S *Jesus of Nazareth.*
J **I am he.**
N Judas, who betrayed him, was standing with them. When Jesus said to them, "I am he," they stepped back and fell to the ground. Again he asked them,

J **Whom are you looking for?**

S *Jesus of Nazareth.*

J **I told you that I am he. So if you are looking for me, let these men go.**

N This was to fulfill the word that he had spoken, "I did not lose a single one of those whom you gave me."

Then Simon Peter, who had a sword, drew it, struck the high priest's slave, and cut off his right ear. The slave's name was Malchus. Jesus said to Peter,

J **Put your sword back into its sheath. Am I not to drink the cup that the Father has given me?**

N So the soldiers, their officer, and the Jewish police arrested Jesus and bound him. First they took him to Annas, who was the father-in-law of Caiaphas, the high priest that year. Caiaphas was the one who had advised the Jews that it was better to have one person die for the people.

Simon Peter and another disciple followed Jesus. Since that disciple was known to the high priest, he went with Jesus into the courtyard of the high priest, but Peter was standing outside at the gate. So the other disciple, who was known to the high priest, went out, spoke to the woman who guarded the gate, and brought Peter in. The woman said to Peter,

S *You are not also one of this man's disciples, are you?*

N Peter said,

S *I am not.*

N Now the slaves and the police had made a charcoal fire because it was cold, and they were standing around it and warming themselves. Peter also was standing with them and warming himself.

Then the high priest questioned Jesus about his disciples and about his teaching. Jesus answered,

J **I have spoken openly to the world; I have always taught in synagogues and in the temple, where all the Jews come together. I have said nothing in secret. Why do you ask me? Ask those who heard what I said to them; they know what I said.**

N When he had said this, one of the police standing nearby struck Jesus on the face, saying,

S *Is that how you answer the high priest?*

J **If I have spoken wrongly, testify to the wrong. But if I have spoken rightly, why do you strike me?**

N Then Annas sent him bound to Caiaphas the high priest.

Now Simon Peter was standing and warming himself. They asked him,

S *You are not also one of his disciples, are you?*

N He denied it and said,

S *I am not.*

N One of the slaves of the high priest, a relative of the man whose ear Peter had cut off, asked,

S *Did I not see you in the garden with him?*

N Again Peter denied it, and at that moment the cock crowed.

*At this point all may join in singing
an appropriate acclamation.*

Ky - ri - e, Chris - te, Ky - ri - e e - le - i - son!

Text: Didier Rimaud, © *CNPL*. **Music:** Jacques Berthier
Source: © *Éditions Musicales Studio SM*, 060794-2

N Then they took Jesus from Caiaphas to Pilate's headquarters. It was early in the morning. They themselves did not enter the headquarters, so as to avoid ritual defilement and to be able to eat the Passover. So Pilate went out to them and said,

S *What accusation do you bring against this man?*

N They answered,

S *If this man were not a criminal, we would not have handed him over to you.*

N Pilate said to them,

S *Take him yourselves and judge him according to your law.*

N They replied,

S *We are not permitted to put anyone to death.*

N This was to fulfill what Jesus had said when he indicated the kind of death he was to die.
Then Pilate entered the headquarters again, summoned Jesus, and asked him,

S *Are you the King of the Jews?*

J **Do you ask this on your own, or did others tell you about me?**

S *I am not a Jew, am I? Your own nation and the chief priests have handed you over to me. What have you done?*

J **My kingdom is not from this world. If my kingdom were from this world, my followers** would be fighting to keep me from being handed over to the Jews. But as it is, my kingdom is not from here.

S *So you are a king?*

J You say that I am a king. For this I was born, and for this I came into the world, to testify to the truth. Everyone who belongs to the truth listens to my voice.

S *What is truth?*

N After he had said this, Pilate went out to the Jews again and told them,

S *I find no case against him. But you have a custom that I release someone for you at the Passover. Do you want me to release for you the King of the Jews?*

N They shouted in reply,

S *Not this man, but Barabbas!*

N Now Barabbas was a bandit. Then Pilate took Jesus and had him flogged. And the soldiers wove a crown of thorns and put it on his head, and they dressed him in a purple robe. They kept coming up to him, saying,

S *"Hail, King of the Jews!"*

N and they struck him on the face. Pilate went out again and said to them,

S *Look, I am bringing him out to you to let you know that I find no case against him.*

N So Jesus came out, wearing the crown of thorns and the purple robe. Pilate said to them,

S *Here is the man!*

N When the chief priests and the police saw him, they shouted,

S *Crucify him! Crucify him!*

N Pilate said to them,

S *Take him yourselves and crucify him; I find no case against him.*

N They answered him,

S *We have a law, and according to that law he ought to die because he has claimed to be the Son of God.*

N Now when Pilate heard this, he was more afraid than ever. He entered his headquarters again and asked Jesus,

S *Where are you from?*

N But Jesus gave him no answer. Pilate therefore said to him,

S *Do you refuse to speak to me? Do you not know that I have power to release you, and power to crucify you?*

J **You would have no power over me unless it had been given you from above; therefore the one who handed me over to you is guilty of a greater sin.**

N From then on Pilate tried to release him, but the Jews cried out,

S *If you release this man, you are no friend of the emperor. Everyone who claims to be a king sets himself against the emperor.*

N When Pilate heard these words, he brought Jesus outside and sat on the judge's bench at a place called "The Stone Pavement," or in Hebrew "Gabbatha."

Now it was the day of Preparation for the Passover; and it was about noon. Pilate said to the Jews,

S *Here is your King!*
N They cried out,
S *Away with him! Away with him! Crucify him!*
N Pilate asked them,
S *Shall I crucify your King?*
N The chief priests answered,
S *We have no king but the emperor.*

*At this point all may join in singing
an appropriate acclamation.*

Ky - ri - e,   Chris - te,   Ky - ri - e   e - le - i - son!

Text: Didier Rimaud, © *CNPL.* **Music:** Jacques Berthier
Source: © *Éditions Musicales Studio SM,* 060794-2

N Then Pilate handed Jesus over to them to be
crucified. So they took Jesus; and carrying the
Cross by himself, he went out to what is called
The Place of the Skull, which in Hebrew is called
Golgotha. There they crucified him, and with him
two others, one on either side, with Jesus between
them.

Pilate also had an inscription written and put
on the Cross. It read, "Jesus of Nazareth, the King
of the Jews." Many of the people read this inscription, because the place where Jesus was crucified
was near the city; and it was written in Hebrew,
in Latin, and in Greek. Then the chief priests of
the Jews said to Pilate,
S *Do not write, "The King of the Jews," but, "This
man said, I am King of the Jews."*
N Pilate answered,

S *What I have written I have written.*

N When the soldiers had crucified Jesus, they took his clothes and divided them into four parts, one for each soldier. They also took his tunic; now the tunic was seamless, woven in one piece from the top. So they said to one another,

S *Let us not tear it, but cast lots for it to see who will get it.*

N This was to fulfill what the Scripture says, "They divided my clothes among themselves, and for my clothing they cast lots." And that is what the soldiers did.

Meanwhile, standing near the Cross of Jesus were his mother, and his mother's sister, Mary the wife of Clopas, and Mary Magdalene. When Jesus saw his mother and the disciple whom he loved standing beside her, he said to his mother,

J **Woman, here is your son.**

N Then he said to the disciple,

J **Here is your mother.**

N And from that hour the disciple took her into his own home.

After this, when Jesus knew that all was now finished, in order to fulfill the Scripture, he said,

J **I am thirsty.**

N A jar full of sour wine was standing there. So they put a sponge full of the wine on a branch of hyssop and held it to his mouth.

When Jesus had received the wine, he said,

J **It is finished.**

N Then he bowed his head and gave up his spirit.

Here all kneel and pause for a short time.

N Since it was the day of Preparation, the Jews did
not want the bodies left on the cross during the
Sabbath, especially because that Sabbath was a day
of great Solemnity. So they asked Pilate to have the
legs of the crucified men broken and the bodies removed. Then the soldiers came and broke the legs
of the first and of the other who had been crucified
with him. But when they came to Jesus and saw
that he was already dead, they did not break his
legs. Instead, one of the soldiers pierced his side
with a spear, and at once blood and water came out.

(He who saw this has testified so that you also
may believe. His testimony is true, and he knows
that he tells the truth.) These things occurred so
that the Scripture might be fulfilled, "None of his
bones shall be broken." And again another passage of Scripture says, "They will look on the one
whom they have pierced."

After these things, Joseph of Arimathea, who
was a disciple of Jesus, though a secret one because
of his fear of the Jews, asked Pilate to let him take
away the body of Jesus. Pilate gave him permission;
so he came and removed his body.

Nicodemus, who had at first come to Jesus by
night, also came, bringing a mixture of myrrh and
aloes, weighing about a hundredweight. They
took the body of Jesus and wrapped it with the
spices in linen cloths, according to the burial
custom of the Jews. Now there was a garden in the
place where he was crucified, and in the garden
there was a new tomb in which no one had ever

been laid. And so, because it was the Jewish day of Preparation, and the tomb was nearby, they laid Jesus there.

The readers return to their places in silence.

THE SOLEMN INTERCESSIONS

For Holy Church

Let us pray, dearly beloved, for the holy Church of God, that our God and Lord be pleased to give her peace, to guard her and to unite her throughout the whole world and grant that, leading our life in tranquillity and quiet, we may glorify God the Father almighty. *(Pause)*

Almighty ever-living God, who in Christ revealed your glory to all the nations, watch over the works of your mercy, that your Church, spread throughout all the world, may persevere with steadfast faith in confessing your name. Through Christ our Lord. **Amen.**

For the Pope

Let us pray also for our most Holy Father Pope N., that our God and Lord, who chose him for the Order of Bishops, may keep him safe and unharmed for the Lord's holy Church, to govern the holy People of God. *(Pause)*

Almighty ever-living God, by whose decree all things are founded, look with favour on our prayers and in your kindness protect the Pope chosen for us, that, under him, the Christian people, governed by you their maker, may grow in merit by reason of their faith. Through Christ our Lord. **Amen.**

For all orders and degrees of the faithful
Let us pray also for our Bishop N., for all Bishops, Priests, and Deacons of the Church and for the whole of the faithful people. *(Pause)*

Almighty ever-living God, by whose Spirit the whole body of the Church is sanctified and governed, hear our humble prayer for your ministers, that, by the gift of your grace, all may serve you faithfully. Through Christ our Lord. **Amen.**

For catechumens
Let us pray also for (our) catechumens, that our God and Lord may open wide the ears of their inmost hearts and unlock the gates of his mercy, that, having received forgiveness of all their sins through the waters of rebirth, they, too, may be one with Christ Jesus our Lord. *(Pause)*

Almighty ever-living God, who make your Church ever fruitful with new offspring, increase the faith and understanding of (our) catechumens, that, reborn in the font of Baptism, they may be added to the number of your adopted children. Through Christ our Lord. **Amen.**

For the unity of Christians
Let us pray also for all our brothers and sisters who believe in Christ, that our God and Lord may be pleased, as they live the truth, to gather them together and keep them in his one Church. *(Pause)*

Almighty ever-living God, who gather what is scattered and keep together what you have gathered, look kindly on the flock of your Son, that those whom one Baptism has consecrated may be joined together by integrity of faith and united in the bond of charity. Through Christ our Lord. **Amen.**

For the Jewish people
Let us pray also for the Jewish people, to whom the Lord our God spoke first, that he may grant them to advance in love of his name and in faithfulness to his covenant. *(Pause)*

Almighty ever-living God, who bestowed your promises on Abraham and his descendants, graciously hear the prayers of your Church, that the people you first made your own may attain the fullness of redemption. Through Christ our Lord. **Amen.**

For those who do not believe in Christ
Let us pray also for those who do not believe in Christ, that, enlightened by the Holy Spirit, they, too, may enter on the way of salvation. *(Pause)*

Almighty ever-living God, grant to those who do not confess Christ that, by walking before you with a sincere heart, they may find the truth and that we ourselves, being constant in mutual love and striving to understand more fully the mystery of your life, may be made more perfect witnesses to your love in the world. Through Christ our Lord. **Amen.**

For those who do not believe in God
Let us pray also for those who do not acknowledge God, that, following what is right in sincerity of heart, they may find the way to God himself. *(Pause)*

Almighty ever-living God, who created all people to seek you always by desiring you and, by finding you, come to rest, grant, we pray, that, despite every harmful obstacle, all may recognize the signs of your fatherly love and the witness of the good works done by those who believe in you, and so in gladness confess you, the one true God and Father of our human race. Through Christ our Lord. **Amen.**

For those in public office
Let us pray also for those in public office, that our God and Lord may direct their minds and hearts according to his will for the true peace and freedom of all. *(Pause)*

Almighty ever-living God, in whose hand lies every human heart and the rights of peoples, look with favour, we pray, on those who govern with authority over us, that throughout the whole world, the prosperity of peoples, the assurance of peace, and freedom of religion may through your gift be made secure. Through Christ our Lord. **Amen.**

For those in tribulation
Let us pray, dearly beloved, to God the Father almighty, that he may cleanse the world of all errors, banish disease, drive out hunger, unlock prisons, loosen fetters, granting to travellers safety, to pilgrims return, health to the sick, and salvation to the dying. *(Pause)*

Almighty ever-living God, comfort of mourners, strength of all who toil, may the prayers of those who cry out in any tribulation come before you, that all may rejoice, because in their hour of need your mercy was at hand. Through Christ our Lord. **Amen.**

ADORATION OF THE HOLY CROSS

Three times the priest or deacon invites the assembly to proclaim its faith:

Cantor

Be - hold__ the wood of the Cross,

on which hung the salvation of the world.

Assembly

Come,__ let us__ a - dore.__

Behold the wood of the Cross, on which hung the salvation of the world. **Come, let us adore.**

After each response all adore the Cross briefly in silence. After the third response, the Cross and the candles are placed at the entrance to the sanctuary and the people approach, moving as in procession, to adore the Cross. They may make a simple genuflection or perform some other appropriate sign of reverence according to local custom.

During the adoration, suitable songs may be sung. All who have already adored the Cross remain seated. Where large numbers of people make individual adoration difficult, the priest may raise the Cross briefly for all to adore in silence.

HOLY COMMUNION

LORD'S PRAYER *(p. 69)*

PRAYER AFTER COMMUNION
Almighty ever-living God, who have restored us to
life by the blessed Death and Resurrection of your
Christ, preserve in us the work of your mercy, that,
by partaking of this mystery, we may have a life unceasingly devoted to you. Through Christ our Lord.
Amen.

PRAYER OVER THE PEOPLE AND DISMISSAL
Bow down for the blessing.

May abundant blessing, O Lord, we pray, descend
upon your people, who have honoured the Death of
your Son in the hope of their resurrection: may pardon come, comfort be given, holy faith increase, and
everlasting redemption be made secure. Through
Christ our Lord. **Amen.**

All genuflect to the Cross, then depart in silence.

March 31
Easter Vigil
Resurrection of the Lord

The history of God's people recounted in tonight's Liturgy of the Word is bookended by two particularly powerful readings. The Genesis 1 story shows God creating and delighting in all that is. From dark emptiness the Master Artist calls forth light, land and sea, vegetation, animals and humanity, "and indeed, it was very good."

In Mark's resurrection account, the focus narrows to a dark and empty tomb. The dominant feeling here is fear, as the women confront the inexplicable. And yet this scene is as cosmically significant as the Creation story. For in rising from the dead Jesus has overcome our greatest enemy, death itself.

But the story does not end here. In a world still crying out for wholeness and healing, we are continually called to cooperate with God in the ongoing work of creation and redemption. In his encyclical *Laudato si*, Pope Francis reminds us of our duty to care for both our planet and our brothers and sisters, especially those who are in most need. This is what it means to be an Easter people. As we rejoice in the Resurrection we cannot give in to complacency. May the risen Jesus renew in us the courage and faith needed to be co-creators and co-redeemers with our God in the light of the Holy Spirit.

Krystyna Higgins
Guelph, ON

SOLEMN BEGINNING OF THE VIGIL
(Lucernarium)

GREETING

The priest and the ministers, one of whom carries the unlit paschal candle, approach the fire.

In the name of the Father, and of the Son, and of the Holy Spirit. **Amen.**

1 The grace of our Lord Jesus Christ, and the love of God, and the communion of the Holy Spirit be with you all.
2 Grace to you and peace from God our Father and the Lord Jesus Christ.
3 The Lord be with you.
And with your spirit.

BLESSING OF THE FIRE

Dear brothers and sisters, on this most sacred night, in which our Lord Jesus Christ passed over from death to life, the Church calls upon her sons and daughters, scattered throughout the world, to come together to watch and pray. If we keep the memorial of the Lord's paschal solemnity in this way, listening to his word and celebrating his mysteries, then we shall have the sure hope of sharing his triumph over death and living with him in God.

Let us pray. O God, who through your Son bestowed upon the faithful the fire of your glory, sanctify this new fire, we pray, and grant that, by these paschal celebrations, we may be so inflamed with heavenly desires, that with minds made pure we may attain festivities of unending splendour. Through Christ our Lord. **Amen.**

PREPARATION AND LIGHTING OF THE CANDLE

The priest cuts a cross in the paschal candle and traces the Greek letters alpha (A) and omega (Ω) and the numerals 2018, saying:

Christ yesterday and today, the Beginning and the End, the Alpha and the Omega. All time belongs to him, and all the ages. To him be glory and power, through every age and for ever. Amen.

When the marks have been made, the priest may insert five grains of incense into the candle in the form of a cross, saying:

By his holy and glorious wounds, may Christ our Lord guard us and protect us. Amen.

The priest lights the paschal candle from the new fire, saying:

May the light of Christ rising in glory dispel the darkness of our hearts and minds.

PROCESSION WITH THE PASCHAL CANDLE

The deacon or another suitable minister holds the paschal candle and, three times during the procession to the altar, lifts it high and sings.

Deacon/Cantor   Assembly

The Light of Christ.   Thanks be to God.

The Light of Christ. **Thanks be to God.**

After the first response, the priest lights his candle from the paschal candle.

After the second response, all the people light their candles from the flame of the paschal candle.

After the third response, all the lights in the church are lit, except for the altar candles.

EASTER PROCLAMATION *(EXSULTET)*

For the shorter version, omit the indented parts.
Exult, let them exult, the hosts of heaven,
exult, let Angel ministers of God exult,
let the trumpet of salvation
sound aloud our mighty King's triumph!
Be glad, let earth be glad, as glory floods her,
ablaze with light from her eternal King,
let all corners of the earth be glad,
knowing an end to gloom and darkness.
Rejoice, let Mother Church also rejoice,
arrayed with the lightning of his glory,
let this holy building shake with joy,
filled with the mighty voices of the peoples.

> (Therefore, dearest friends,
> standing in the awesome glory of this holy light,
> invoke with me, I ask you,
> the mercy of God almighty,
> that he, who has been pleased to number me,
> though unworthy, among the Levites,
> may pour into me his light unshadowed,
> that I may sing this candle's perfect praises.)

(The Lord be with you. **And with your spirit.**)
Lift up your hearts. **We lift them up to the Lord.**
Let us give thanks to the Lord our God. **It is right and just.**

It is truly right and just,
with ardent love of mind and heart
and with devoted service of our voice,
to acclaim our God invisible, the almighty Father,
and Jesus Christ, our Lord, his Son, his Only Begotten.

Who for our sake paid Adam's debt to the eternal Father,
and, pouring out his own dear Blood,
wiped clean the record of our ancient sinfulness.
These, then, are the feasts of Passover,
in which is slain the Lamb, the one true Lamb,
whose Blood anoints the doorposts of believers.

This is the night
when once you led our forebears, Israel's children,
from slavery in Egypt
and made them pass dry-shod through the Red Sea.
This is the night
that with a pillar of fire
banished the darkness of sin.
This is the night
that even now, throughout the world,
sets Christian believers apart from worldly vices
and from the gloom of sin,
leading them to grace
and joining them to his holy ones.
This is the night
when Christ broke the prison-bars of death
and rose victorious from the underworld.

> Our birth would have been no gain,
> had we not been redeemed.

O wonder of your humble care for us!
O love, O charity beyond all telling,
to ransom a slave you gave away your Son!
O truly necessary sin of Adam,
destroyed completely by the Death of Christ!
O happy fault
that earned so great, so glorious a Redeemer!

longer version:

O truly blessed night,
worthy alone to know
the time and hour when
Christ rose from the
underworld!

This is the night of
which it is written: The
night shall be as bright
as day, dazzling is the
night for me, and full
of gladness.

The sanctifying power
of this night dispels
wickedness, washes
faults away, restores
innocence to the fallen,
and joy to mourners,
drives out hatred, fos-
ters concord, and brings
down the mighty.

On this, your night of
grace, O holy Father, ac-
cept this candle, a sol-
emn offering, the work
of bees and of your serv-
ants' hands, an evening
sacrifice of praise, this
gift from your most holy
Church.

shorter version:

The sanctifying power
of this night dispels
wickedness, washes
faults away, restores
innocence to the fallen,
and joy to mourners.

O truly blessed night,
when things of heaven
are wed to those of
earth and divine to
the human.

On this, your night of
grace, O holy Father, ac-
cept this candle, a sol-
emn offering, the work
of bees and of your serv-
ants' hands, an evening
sacrifice of praise, this
gift from your most holy
Church.

But now we know the
praises of this pillar,
which glowing fire
ignites for God's
honour, a fire into
many flames divided,
yet never dimmed by
sharing of its light,
for it is fed by melting
wax, drawn out by
mother bees to build
a torch so precious.

O truly blessed night,
when things of heaven
are wed to those of
earth, and divine to
the human.

Therefore, O Lord,
we pray you that this candle,
hallowed to the honour of your name,
may persevere undimmed,
to overcome the darkness of this night.
Receive it as a pleasing fragrance,
and let it mingle with the lights of heaven.
May this flame be found still burning
by the Morning Star:
the one Morning Star who never sets,
Christ your Son,
who, coming back from death's domain,
has shed his peaceful light on humanity,
and lives and reigns for ever and ever. **Amen.**

LITURGY OF THE WORD

Dear brothers and sisters, now that we have begun our solemn Vigil, let us listen with quiet hearts to the Word of God. Let us meditate on how God in times past saved his people and in these, the last days, has sent us his Son as our Redeemer. Let us pray that our God may complete this paschal work of salvation by the fullness of redemption.

FIRST READING *(Genesis 1.1 – 2.2)*

For the shorter version, omit the indented parts.

In the beginning when God created the heavens and the earth,

the earth was a formless void and darkness covered the face of the deep, while the spirit of God swept over the face of the waters. Then God said, "Let there be light"; and there was light. And God saw that the light was good; and God separated the light from the darkness. God called the light "Day," and the darkness he called "Night." And there was evening and there was morning, the first day.

And God said, "Let there be a dome in the midst of the waters, and let it separate the waters from the waters." So God made the dome and separated the waters that were under the dome from the waters that were above the dome. And it was so. God called the dome "Sky." And there was evening and there was morning, the second day.

And God said, "Let the waters under the sky be gathered together into one place, and let the dry land appear." And it was so. God called the dry land "Earth," and the waters that were gathered together he called "Seas." And God saw that it was good.

Then God said, "Let the earth put forth vegetation: plants yielding seed, and fruit trees of every kind on earth that bear fruit with the seed in it." And it was so. The earth brought forth vegetation: plants yielding seed of every kind, and trees of every kind bearing fruit with the seed in it. And God saw that it was good. And there was evening and there was morning, the third day.

And God said, "Let there be lights in the dome of the sky to separate the day from the night; and let them be for signs and for seasons and for days and years, and let them be lights in the dome of the sky to give light upon the earth." And it was so.

God made the two great lights — the greater light to rule the day and the lesser light to rule the night — and the stars. God set them in the dome of the sky to give light upon the earth, to rule over the day and over the night, and to separate the light from the darkness. And God saw that it was good. And there was evening and there was morning, the fourth day.

And God said, "Let the waters bring forth swarms of living creatures, and let birds fly above the earth across the dome of the sky." So God created the great sea monsters and every living creature that moves, of every kind, with which the waters swarm, and every winged bird of every kind. And God saw that it was good. God blessed them, saying, "Be fruitful and multiply and fill the waters in the seas, and let birds multiply on the earth." And there was evening and there was morning, the fifth day.

And God said, "Let the earth bring forth living creatures of every kind: cattle and creeping things and wild animals of the earth of every kind." And it was so. God made the wild animals of the earth of every kind, and the cattle of every kind, and everything that creeps upon the ground of every kind. And God saw that it was good. Then God said, "Let us make man in our image, according to our likeness; and let them have dominion over the fish of the sea, and over the birds of the air, and over the cattle, and over all the wild animals of the earth, and over every creeping thing that creeps upon the earth." So God created man in his image, in the image of God he created him; male and female he created them.

God blessed them, and God said to them, "Be fruitful and multiply, and fill the earth and subdue it; and have dominion over the fish of the sea and over the birds of the air and over every living thing that moves upon the earth."

God said, "See, I have given you every plant yielding seed that is upon the face of all the earth, and every tree with seed in its fruit; you shall have them for food. And to every beast of the earth, and to every bird of the air, and to everything that creeps on the earth, everything that has the breath of life, I have given every green plant for food." And it was so.

God saw everything that he had made, and indeed, it was very good. And there was evening and there was morning, the sixth day.

Thus the heavens and the earth were finished, and all their multitude. And on the seventh day God finished the work that he had done, and he rested on the seventh day from all the work that he had done. The word of the Lord. **Thanks be to God.**

An alternate psalm follows.

RESPONSORIAL PSALM *(Psalm 104)*

R. **Lord, send forth your Spirit,
and renew the face of the earth.**

Bless the Lord, O · **my** soul.
O Lord my God, you are very · **great.**
You are clothed with · **honour** and majesty,
wrapped in light as with · **a** garment. R.

You set the earth on its · **foun-**dations,
so that it shall never be · **shaken.**
You cover it with the deep as · **with** a garment;
the waters stood above · **the** mountains. R.

You make springs gush forth in · **the** valleys;
they flow between the · **hills.**
By the streams the birds of the air
    have their · **ha-**bi-tation;
they sing among · **the** branches. ℟

From your lofty abode you water · **the** mountains;
the earth is satisfied with the fruit of your · **work.**
You cause the grass to · **grow_for** the cattle,
and plants for people to use,
    to bring forth food from · **the** earth. ℟

O Lord, how manifold are · **your** works!
In wisdom you have made them · **all;**
the earth is · **full_of** your creatures.
Bless the Lord, O · **my** soul. ℟

©2009 Gordon Johnston/Novalis

or

RESPONSORIAL PSALM *(Psalm 33)*

The earth is full of the stead-fast love of the Lord.

℟ **The earth is full of the steadfast love of the Lord.**

The word of the Lord · **is** upright,
and all his work is done · **in** faithfulness.
He loves righteousness · **and** justice;
the earth is full of the steadfast love of · **the** Lord. ℟

By the word of the Lord
the heavens · **were** made,
and all their host by the breath of · **his** mouth.
He gathered the waters of the sea
as in · **a** bottle;
he put the deeps · **in** storehouses. R.

Blessed is the nation whose God is · **the** Lord,
the people whom he has chosen
as · **his** heritage.
The Lord looks down · **from** heaven;
he sees all · **human** beings. R.

Our soul waits for · **the** Lord;
he is our help · **and** shield.
Let your steadfast love, O Lord, be · **up**-on_us,
even as we hope · **in** you. R.

©2009 Gordon Johnston/Novalis

PRAYER

Let us pray. *(Pause)*

1 Almighty ever-living God, who are wonderful in the ordering of all your works, may those you have redeemed understand that there exists nothing more marvellous than the world's creation in the beginning except that, at the end of the ages, Christ our Passover has been sacrificed. Who lives and reigns for ever and ever. **Amen.**

2 O God, who wonderfully created human nature and still more wonderfully redeemed it, grant us, we pray, to set our minds against the enticements of sin, that we may merit to attain eternal joys. Through Christ our Lord. **Amen.**

SECOND READING *(Genesis 22.1-18)*

For the shorter version, omit the indented parts.

God tested Abraham. He said to him, "Abraham!" And Abraham said, "Here I am." God said, "Take your son, your only son Isaac, whom you love, and go to the land of Moriah, and offer him there as a burnt offering on one of the mountains that I shall show you."

So Abraham rose early in the morning, saddled his donkey, and took two of his young men with him, and his son Isaac; he cut the wood for the burnt offering, and set out and went to the place in the distance that God had shown him.

On the third day Abraham looked up and saw the place far away. Then Abraham said to his young men, "Stay here with the donkey; the boy and I will go over there; we will worship, and then we will come back to you." Abraham took the wood of the burnt offering and laid it on his son Isaac, and he himself carried the fire and the knife. So the two of them walked on together.

Isaac said to his father Abraham, "Father!" And Abraham said, "Here I am, my son." Isaac said, "The fire and the wood are here, but where is the lamb for a burnt offering?" Abraham said, "God himself will provide the lamb for a burnt offering, my son." So the two of them walked on together.

When Abraham and Isaac came to the place that God had shown him, Abraham built an altar there and laid the wood in order. He bound his son Isaac, and laid him on the altar, on top of the wood. Then

Abraham reached out his hand and took the knife to kill his son.

But the Angel of the Lord called to him from heaven, and said, "Abraham, Abraham!" And he said, "Here I am." The Angel said, "Do not lay your hand on the boy or do anything to him; for now I know that you fear God, since you have not withheld your son, your only son, from me." And Abraham looked up and saw a ram, caught in a thicket by its horns. Abraham went and took the ram and offered it up as a burnt offering instead of his son.

So Abraham called that place "The Lord will provide"; as it is said to this day, "On the mount of the Lord it shall be provided."

The Angel of the Lord called to Abraham a second time from heaven, and said, "By myself I have sworn, says the Lord: Because you have done this, and have not withheld your son, your only son, I will indeed bless you, and I will make your offspring as numerous as the stars of heaven and as the sand that is on the seashore. And your offspring shall possess the gate of their enemies, and by your offspring shall all the nations of the earth gain blessing for themselves, because you have obeyed my voice."

The word of the Lord. **Thanks be to God.**

RESPONSORIAL PSALM *(Psalm 16)*

Pro-tect me, O God,—— for in you I take re-fuge.——

R̰. **Protect me, O God, for in you I take refuge.**

The Lord is my chosen portion · **and_my** cup;
you hold · **my** lot.
I keep the Lord always · **be**-fore_me;
because he is at my right hand,
    I shall · **not** be moved. R̰.

Therefore my heart is glad,
    and my soul · **re**-joices;
my body also rests · **se**-cure.
For you do not give me up · **to** Sheol,
or let your faithful one · **see** the Pit. R̰.

You show me the path · **of** life.
In your presence there is fullness · **of** joy;
in your right hand · **are** pleasures
for--**ev**-er-more. R̰.

©2009 Gordon Johnston/Novalis

PRAYER

Let us pray. *(Pause)* O God, supreme Father of the
faithful, who increase the children of your promise
by pouring out the grace of adoption throughout the
whole world and who through the Paschal Mystery

make your servant Abraham father of nations, as once you swore, grant, we pray, that your peoples may enter worthily into the grace to which you call them. Through Christ our Lord. **Amen.**

THIRD READING (*Exodus 14.15-31; 15.20, 1*)
The Lord said to Moses, "Why do you cry out to me? Tell the children of Israel to go forward. But you, lift up your staff, and stretch out your hand over the sea and divide it, that the children of Israel may go into the sea on dry ground. Then I will harden the hearts of the Egyptians so that they will go in after them; and so I will gain glory for myself over Pharaoh and all his army, his chariots, and his chariot drivers. And the Egyptians shall know that I am the Lord, when I have gained glory for myself over Pharaoh, his chariots, and his chariot drivers."

The Angel of God who was going before the Israelite army moved and went behind them; and the pillar of cloud moved from in front of them and took its place behind them. It came between the army of Egypt and the army of Israel. And so the cloud was there with the darkness, and it lit up the night; one did not come near the other all night. Then Moses stretched out his hand over the sea. The Lord drove the sea back by a strong east wind all night, and turned the sea into dry land; and the waters were divided. The children of Israel went into the sea on dry ground, the waters forming a wall for them on their right and on their left.

The Egyptians pursued, and went into the sea after them, all of Pharaoh's horses, chariots, and chariot drivers. At the morning watch, the Lord in the pillar of fire and cloud looked down upon the Egyptian army, and threw the Egyptian army into panic. He clogged their chariot wheels so that they turned with difficulty. The Egyptians said, "Let us flee from the children of Israel, for the Lord is fighting for them against Egypt."

Then the Lord said to Moses, "Stretch out your hand over the sea, so that the water may come back upon the Egyptians, upon their chariots and chariot drivers." So Moses stretched out his hand over the sea, and at dawn the sea returned to its normal depth. As the Egyptians fled before it, the Lord tossed the Egyptians into the sea. The waters returned and covered the chariots and the chariot drivers, the entire army of Pharaoh that had followed them into the sea; not one of them remained.

But the children of Israel walked on dry ground through the sea, the waters forming a wall for them on their right and on their left. Thus the Lord saved Israel that day from the Egyptians; and Israel saw the Egyptians dead on the seashore. Israel saw the great work that the Lord did against the Egyptians. So the people feared the Lord and believed in the Lord and in his servant Moses.

The Prophet Miriam, Aaron's sister, took a tambourine in her hand; and all the women went out after her with tambourines and with dancing. Moses and the children of Israel sang this song to the Lord:

RESPONSORIAL PSALM *(Exodus 15)*

Let us sing to the Lord; he has cov-ered him-self in glo-ry.

℟. **Let us sing to the Lord;
he has covered himself in glory.**

I will sing to the Lord,
    for he has triumphed · **gloriously;**
horse and rider he has thrown into · **the** sea.
The Lord is my strength and my · **might,**
and he has become my · **sal**-vation;
this is my God, and I will · **praise_him,**
my father's God, and I will · **ex**-alt_him. ℟.

The Lord is a · **warrior;**
the Lord is · **his** name.
Pharaoh's chariots and his army
    he cast into the · **sea;**
his picked officers were sunk in the · **Red** Sea.
The floods · **covered_them;**
they went down into the depths
    · **like_a** stone. ℟.

Your right hand, O Lord, glorious in · **power;**
your right hand, O Lord, shattered · **the** enemy.
In the greatness of your · **majesty**
you overthrew · **your** adversaries;
you sent out your · **fury,**
it consumed them · **like** stubble. R.

You brought your people · **in**
and plant·-**ed** them
on the mountain of your own pos·-**session,**
the place, O Lord, that you made your · **a**-bode,
the sanctuary, O Lord, that your hands
    have es·-**tablished.**
The Lord will reign forever · **and** ever. R.

©2009 Gordon Johnston/Novalis

PRAYER
Let us pray. *(Pause)*
1 O God, whose ancient wonders remain undimmed in splendour even in our day, for what
  you once bestowed on a single people, freeing
  them from Pharaoh's persecution by the power
  of your right hand, now you bring about as the
  salvation of the nations through the waters of
  rebirth, grant, we pray, that the whole world may
  become children of Abraham and inherit the
  dignity of Israel's birthright. Through Christ our
  Lord. **Amen.**
2 O God, who by the light of the New Testament
  have unlocked the meaning of wonders worked
  in former times, so that the Red Sea prefigures the
  sacred font and the nation delivered from slavery

foreshadows the Christian people, grant, we pray, that all nations, obtaining the privilege of Israel by merit of faith, may be reborn by partaking of your Spirit. Through Christ our Lord. **Amen.**

FOURTH READING (Isaiah 54.5-14)

Thus says the Lord, the God of hosts. Your Maker is your husband, the Lord of hosts is his name; the Holy One of Israel is your Redeemer, the God of the whole earth he is called. For the Lord has called you like a wife forsaken and grieved in spirit, like the wife of a man's youth when she is cast off, says your God.

For a brief moment I abandoned you, but with great compassion I will gather you. In overflowing wrath for a moment I hid my face from you, but with everlasting love I will have compassion on you, says the Lord, your Redeemer.

This is like the days of Noah to me: Just as I swore that the waters of Noah would never again go over the earth, so I have sworn that I will not be angry with you and will not rebuke you. For the mountains may depart and the hills be removed, but my steadfast love shall not depart from you, and my covenant of peace shall not be removed, says the Lord, who has compassion on you.

O afflicted one, storm-tossed, and not comforted, I am about to set your stones in antimony, and lay your foundations with sapphires. I will make your pinnacles of rubies, your gates of jewels, and all your walls of precious stones.

All your children shall be taught by the Lord, and great shall be the prosperity of your children. In righteousness you shall be established; you shall be far from oppression, for you shall not fear; and from terror, for it shall not come near you.

The word of the Lord. **Thanks be to God.**

RESPONSORIAL PSALM *(Psalm 30)*

I will ex-tol you, Lord, for you have raised me up.

R̲. **I will extol you, Lord,**
for you have raised me up.

I will extol you, O Lord, for you have
      drawn me · **up,**
and did not let my foes rejoice · **over_me.**
O Lord, you brought up my soul from · **Sheol,**
restored me to life from among those gone
      down · **to_the** Pit. R̲.

Sing praises to the Lord,
      O you his · **faithful_ones,**
and give thanks to his holy · **name.**
For his anger is but for a moment;
      his favour is for a · **lifetime.**
Weeping may linger for the night,
      but joy comes · **with_the** morning. R̲.

Hear, O Lord, and be gracious to · **me!**
O Lord, be my · **helper!**
You have turned my mourning into · **dancing.**
O Lord my God, I will give thanks
   to you · **for**-ever. R.

©2009 Gordon Johnston/Novalis

PRAYER

Let us pray. *(Pause)* Almighty ever-living God, surpass, for the honour of your name, what you pledged to the Patriarchs by reason of their faith, and through sacred adoption increase the children of your promise, so that what the Saints of old never doubted would come to pass your Church may now see in great part fulfilled. Through Christ our Lord. **Amen.**

FIFTH READING *(Isaiah 55.1-11)*

Thus says the Lord: "Everyone who thirsts, come to the waters; and you that have no money, come, buy and eat! Come, buy wine and milk without money and without price. Why do you spend your money for that which is not bread, and your labour for that which does not satisfy? Listen carefully to me, and eat what is good, and delight yourselves in rich food. Incline your ear, and come to me; listen, so that you may live. I will make with you an everlasting covenant, my steadfast, sure love for David.

"See, I made him a witness to the peoples, a leader and commander for the peoples. See, you shall call nations that you do not know, and nations that do not know you shall run to you, because of the Lord your God, the Holy One of Israel, for he has glorified you.

"Seek the Lord while he may be found, call upon him while he is near; let the wicked person forsake their way, and the unrighteous person their thoughts; let that person return to the Lord that he may have mercy on them, and to our God, for he will abundantly pardon.

"For my thoughts are not your thoughts, nor are your ways my ways, says the Lord. For as the heavens are higher than the earth, so are my ways higher than your ways and my thoughts than your thoughts. For as the rain and the snow come down from heaven, and do not return there until they have watered the earth, making it bring forth and sprout, giving seed to the sower and bread to the one who eats, so shall my word be that goes out from my mouth; it shall not return to me empty, but it shall accomplish that which I purpose, and succeed in the thing for which I sent it."

The word of the Lord. **Thanks be to God.**

RESPONSORIAL PSALM *(Isaiah 12)*

With joy you will draw wa-ter___ from the wells of sal-va-tion.___

R̥. **With joy you will draw water
from the wells of salvation.**

Surely God is my salvation;
  I will trust, and will not · **be** a-fraid,
for the Lord God is my strength and my might;
  he has be--**come_my** sal-vation.
With joy · **you_will** draw water
from the wells · **of** sal-vation. R̥.

Give thanks · **to** the Lord,
call · **on** his name;
make known his deeds a--**mong** the nations;
proclaim that his · **name_is** ex-alted. R̥.

Sing praises to the Lord,
  for he · **has** done gloriously;
let this be known in · **all** the earth.
Shout aloud and sing for joy, O · **roy-**al Zion,
for great in your midst
  is the Holy · **One** of Israel. R̥.

©2009 Gordon Johnston/Novalis

To hear the Sunday Psalms, visit www.livingwithchrist.ca.

PRAYER

Let us pray. *(Pause)* Almighty ever-living God, sole hope of the world, who by the preaching of your Prophets unveiled the mysteries of this present age, graciously increase the longing of your people, for only at the prompting of your grace do the faithful progress in any kind of virtue. Through Christ our Lord. **Amen.**

SIXTH READING *(Baruch 3.9-15, 32 – 4.4)*

Hear the commandments of life, O Israel; give ear, and learn wisdom! Why is it, O Israel, why is it that you are in the land of your enemies, that you are growing old in a foreign country, that you are defiled with the dead, that you are counted among those in Hades? You have forsaken the fountain of wisdom. If you had walked in the way of God, you would be living in peace forever.

Learn where there is wisdom, where there is strength, where there is understanding, so that you may at the same time discern where there is length of days, and life, where there is light for the eyes, and peace. Who has found her place? And who has entered her storehouses?

But the one who knows all things knows her, he found her by his understanding. The one who prepared the earth for all time filled it with four-footed creatures; the one who sends forth the light, and it goes; he called it, and it obeyed him, trembling; the stars shone in their watches, and were glad; he called them, and they said, "Here we are!" They shone with gladness for him who made them.

This is our God; no other can be compared to him. He found the whole way to knowledge, and gave her to his servant Jacob and to Israel, whom he loved. Afterward she appeared on earth and lived with humanity. She is the book of the commandments of God, the law that endures forever. All who hold her fast will live, and those who forsake her will die. Turn, O Jacob, and take her; walk toward the shining of her light. Do not give your glory to another, or your advantages to an alien people.

Happy are we, O Israel, for we know what is pleasing to God.

The word of the Lord. **Thanks be to God.**

RESPONSORIAL PSALM *(Psalm 19)*

Lord, you have the words of e - ter - nal life.

℟. **Lord, you have the words of eternal life.**

The law of the Lord is · **perfect,**
reviving the · **soul;**
the decrees of the Lord are · **sure,**
making · **wise** the simple. ℟.

The precepts of the Lord are · **right,**
rejoicing the · **heart;**
the commandment of the Lord is · **clear,**
en-·**lightening** the eyes. ℟.

The fear of the Lord is · **pure,**
enduring for--**ever;**
the ordinances of the Lord are · **true**
and righteous · **al-**to-gether. R.

More to be desired are they than · **gold,**
even much fine · **gold;**
sweeter also than · **honey,**
and drippings · **of** the honeycomb. R.

©2009 Gordon Johnston/Novalis

To hear the Sunday Psalms, visit www.livingwithchrist.ca.

PRAYER

Let us pray. *(Pause)* O God, who constantly increase your Church by your call to the nations, graciously grant to those you wash clean in the waters of Baptism the assurance of your unfailing protection. Through Christ our Lord. **Amen.**

SEVENTH READING *(Ezekiel 36.16-17a, 18-28)*

The word of the Lord came to me: Son of man, when the house of Israel lived on their own soil, they defiled it with their ways and their deeds; their conduct in my sight was unclean. So I poured out my wrath upon them for the blood that they had shed upon the land, and for the idols with which they had defiled it. I scattered them among the nations, and they were dispersed through the countries; in accordance with their conduct and their deeds I judged them.

But when they came to the nations, wherever they came, they profaned my holy name, in that it was said of them, "These are the people of the Lord, and yet they had to go out of his land."

But I had concern for my holy name, which the house of Israel had profaned among the nations to which they came. Therefore say to the house of Israel, Thus says the Lord God: It is not for your sake, O house of Israel, that I am about to act, but for the sake of my holy name, which you have profaned among the nations to which you came.

I will sanctify my great name, which has been profaned among the nations, and which you have profaned among them; and the nations shall know that I am the Lord, says the Lord God, when through you I display my holiness before their eyes.

I will take you from the nations, and gather you from all the countries, and bring you into your own land.

I will sprinkle clean water upon you, and you shall be clean from all your uncleanness, and from all your idols I will cleanse you.

A new heart I will give you, and a new spirit I will put within you; and I will remove from your body the heart of stone and give you a heart of flesh. I will put my spirit within you, and make you follow my statutes and be careful to observe my ordinances. Then you shall live in the land that I gave to your ancestors; and you shall be my people, and I will be your God.

The word of the Lord. **Thanks be to God.**

An alternate psalm follows. When baptism is celebrated, sing Isaiah 12 (p. 315).

RESPONSORIAL PSALM *(Psalm 42; 43)*

R. **As a deer longs for flowing streams,**
my soul longs for you, O God.

My soul thirsts for · **God,**
for the living · **God.**
When shall I · **come**
and behold the face · **of** God? R.

I went with the · **throng,**
and led them in procession
    to the house of · **God,**
with glad shouts and songs of · **thanksgiving,**
a multitude · **keeping** festival. R.

O send out your light and your · **truth;**
let them · **lead_me;**
let them bring me to your holy · **mountain**
and to · **your** dwelling. R.

Then I will go to the altar of · **God,**
to God my exceeding · **joy;**
and I will praise you with the · **harp,**
O God, · **my** God. R.

©2009 Gordon Johnston/Novalis

or

RESPONSORIAL PSALM *(Psalm 51)*

Cre-ate in me a clean heart,— O God.

R︲. **Create in me a clean heart, O God.**

Create in me a clean heart, · **O** God,
and put a new and right spirit · **with**-in_me.
Do not cast me away from · **your** presence,
and do not take your holy · **spirit** from me. R︲.

Restore to me the joy of your · **sal**-vation,
and sustain in me a will·-**ing** spirit.
Then I will teach transgressors · **your** ways,
and sinners will re·-**turn** to you. R︲.

For you have no delight · **in** sacrifice;
if I were to give a burnt offering,
    you would not · **be** pleased.
The sacrifice acceptable to God
    is a bro·-**ken** spirit;
a broken and contrite heart, O God,
    you will · **not** de-spise. R︲.

©2009 Gordon Johnston/Novalis

PRAYER

Let us pray. *(Pause)*

1 O God of unchanging power and eternal light, look with favour on the wondrous mystery of the whole Church and serenely accomplish the work of human salvation, which you planned from all eternity; may the whole world know and see that what was cast down is raised up, what had become old is made new, and all things are restored to integrity through Christ, just as by him they came into being. Who lives and reigns for ever and ever. **Amen**.

2 O God, who by the pages of both Testaments instruct and prepare us to celebrate the Paschal Mystery, grant that we may comprehend your mercy, so that the gifts we receive from you this night may confirm our hope of the gifts to come. Through Christ our Lord. **Amen.**

GLORY TO GOD *(p. 10)*

COLLECT

Let us pray. O God, who make this most sacred night radiant with the glory of the Lord's Resurrection, stir up in your Church a spirit of adoption, so that, renewed in body and mind, we may render you undivided service. Through our Lord Jesus Christ, your Son, who lives and reigns with you in the unity of the Holy Spirit, one God, for ever and ever. **Amen.**

EPISTLE *(Romans 6.3-11)*

Brothers and sisters: Do you not know that all of us who have been baptized into Christ Jesus were baptized into his death? Therefore we have been buried with him by baptism into death, so that, just as Christ was raised from the dead by the glory of the Father, so we too might walk in newness of life. For if we have been united with him in a death like his, we will certainly be united with him in a resurrection like his.

We know that our old self was crucified with him so that the body of sin might be destroyed, and we might no longer be enslaved to sin. For whoever has died is freed from sin. But if we have died with Christ, we believe that we will also live with him.

We know that Christ, being raised from the dead, will never die again; death no longer has dominion over him. The death he died, he died to sin, once for all; but the life he lives, he lives to God. So you also must consider yourselves dead to sin and alive to God in Christ Jesus.

The word of the Lord. **Thanks be to God.**

SOLEMN ALLELUIA *(Psalm 118)*

Al - le-lu - ia! Al - le - lu - ia! Al - le-lu - ia!

℟. **Alleluia! Alleluia! Alleluia!**

O give thanks to the Lord, for · **he** is good;
his steadfast love en-·**dures** for-ever.
Let Is-·**rael** say,
"His steadfast love en-·**dures** for-ever." ℟.

"The right hand of the Lord · **is** ex-alted;
the right hand of the · **Lord** does valiantly."
I shall not die, but · **I_shall** live,
and recount the · **deeds_of** the Lord. ℞

The stone that the · **builders** re-jected
has become · **the** chief cornerstone.
This is the · **Lord's** doing;
it is marvellous · **in** our eyes. ℞

©2009 Gordon Johnston/Novalis

GOSPEL *(Mark 16.1-8)*

The Lord be with you. **And with your spirit.**
A reading from the holy Gospel according to Mark.
Glory to you, O Lord.

When the Sabbath was over, Mary Magdalene, and Mary the Mother of James, and Salome bought spices, so that they might go and anoint Jesus. And very early on the first day of the week, when the sun had risen, they went to the tomb. They had been saying to one another, "Who will roll away the stone for us from the entrance to the tomb?" When they looked up, they saw that the stone, which was very large, had already been rolled back.

As they entered the tomb, they saw a young man, dressed in a white robe, sitting on the right side; and they were alarmed. But he said to them, "Do not be alarmed; you are looking for Jesus of Nazareth, who was crucified. He has been raised; he is not here. Look, there is the place they laid him.

"But go, tell his disciples and Peter that he is going ahead of you to Galilee; there you will see him, just as he told you." So they went out and fled from the tomb, for terror and amazement had seized them; and they said nothing to anyone, for they were afraid.

The Gospel of the Lord. **Praise to you, Lord Jesus Christ.**

BAPTISMAL LITURGY

This celebration combines text from The Roman Missal *(2011) and the* Rite of Christian Initiation of Adults *(1987), where appropriate.*

INTRODUCTION

1 *If there are candidates for baptism:*
Dearly beloved, with one heart and one soul, let us by our prayers come to the aid of these our brothers and sisters in their blessed hope, so that, as they approach the font of rebirth, the almighty Father may bestow on them all his merciful help.

2 *If there are no candidates for baptism:*
Dearly beloved, let us humbly invoke upon this font the grace of God the almighty Father, that those who from it are born anew may be numbered among the children of adoption in Christ.

3 *If there are no candidates for baptism and the font is not to be blessed, proceed to the* Blessing of Water, *p. 333.*

LITANY OF THE SAINTS

Lord, have mer - cy.   Lord, have mer - cy.

Lord, have mercy. **Lord, have mercy.**
Christ, have mercy. **Christ, have mercy.**
Lord, have mercy. **Lord, have mercy.**

Holy Mary, Mother of God,   pray__   for   us.

Holy Mary, Mother of God, **pray for us.**
Saint Michael,
Holy Angels of God,
Saint John the Baptist,
Saint Joseph,
Saint Peter and Saint Paul,
Saint Andrew,
Saint John,
Saint Mary Magdalene,
Saint Stephen,
Saint Ignatius of Antioch,
Saint Lawrence,
Saint Perpetua and Saint Felicity,
Saint Agnes,
Saint Gregory,
Saint Augustine,
Saint Athanasius,
Saint Basil,
Saint Martin,
Saint Benedict,

Saint Francis and Saint Dominic,
Saint Francis Xavier,
Saint John Vianney,
Saint Catherine of Siena,
Saint Teresa of Jesus,
(other saints)
All holy men and women, Saints of God,

Lord, be mer - ci - ful, Lord, de - liv - er us, we pray.

Lord, be merciful, **Lord, deliver us, we pray.**
From all evil,
From every sin,
From everlasting death,
By your Incarnation,
By your Death and Resurrection,
By the outpouring of the Holy Spirit,

Be merciful to us sin-ners, Lord, we ask you, hear our prayer.

Be merciful to us sinners,
Lord, we ask you, hear our prayer.
1 *If there are candidates for baptism:*
  Bring these chosen ones to new birth through
  the grace of Baptism,
  Lord, we ask you, hear our prayer.
2 *If there are no candidates for baptism:*
  Make this font holy by your grace for the new
  birth of your children,
  Lord, we ask you, hear our prayer.

Jesus, Son of the living God,
Lord, we ask you, hear our prayer.

Christ, hear us.
Christ, hear us.
Christ, graciously hear us.
Christ, graciously hear us.

If there are candidates for baptism, the priest prays:
Almighty ever-living God, be present by the mysteries of your great love and send forth the spirit of adoption to create the new peoples brought to birth for you in the font of Baptism, so that what is to be carried out by our humble service may be brought to fulfillment by your mighty power. Through Christ our Lord. **Amen.**

BLESSING OF BAPTISMAL WATER
O God, who by invisible power accomplish a wondrous effect through sacramental signs and who in many ways have prepared water, your creation, to show forth the grace of Baptism;

O God, whose Spirit in the first moments of the world's creation hovered over the waters, so that the very substance of water would even then take to itself the power to sanctify;

O God, who by the outpouring of the flood fore-shadowed regeneration, so that from the mystery of one and the same element of water would come an end to vice and a beginning of virtue;

O God, who caused the children of Abraham to pass dry-shod through the Red Sea, so that the chosen people, set free from slavery to Pharaoh, would prefigure the people of the baptized;

O God, whose Son, baptized by John in the waters of the Jordan, was anointed with the Holy Spirit, and, as he hung upon the Cross, gave forth water from his side along with blood, and after his Resurrection, commanded his disciples: "Go forth, teach all nations, baptizing them in the name of the Father and of the Son and of the Holy Spirit," look now, we pray, upon the face of your Church and graciously unseal for her the fountain of Baptism. May this water receive by the Holy Spirit the grace of your Only Begotten Son, so that human nature, created in your image and washed clean through the Sacrament of Baptism from all the squalor of the life of old, may be found worthy to rise to the life of newborn children through water and the Holy Spirit.

May the power of the Holy Spirit, O Lord, we pray, come down through your Son into the fullness of this font, so that all who have been buried with Christ by Baptism into death may rise again to life with him. Who lives and reigns with you in the unity of the Holy Spirit, one God, for ever and ever. **Amen.**

**Springs of water, bless the Lord;
praise and exalt him above all for ever.**

RENUNCIATION OF SIN

Using one of the following formularies, the priest questions all the candidates together or individually.

1 Do you reject sin so as to live in the freedom of God's children? **I do.**
  Do you reject the glamour of evil, and refuse to be mastered by sin? **I do.**
  Do you reject Satan, father of sin and prince of darkness? **I do.**

2 Do you reject Satan, and all his works, and all his empty promises? **I do.**

3 Do you reject Satan? **I do.**
  And all his works? **I do.**
  And all his empty promises? **I do.**

Adult candidates may now be anointed with the Oil of Catechumens.

We anoint you with the oil of salvation in the name of Christ our Saviour. May he strengthen you with his power. **Amen.**

PROFESSION OF FAITH

N., do you believe in God, the Father almighty, creator of heaven and earth? **I do.**

Do you believe in Jesus Christ, his only Son, our Lord, who was born of the Virgin Mary, was crucified, died, and was buried, rose from the dead, and is now seated at the right hand of the Father? **I do.**

Do you believe in the Holy Spirit, the holy catholic Church, the communion of saints, the forgiveness of sins, the resurrection of the body, and the life everlasting? **I do.**

BAPTISM

The priest baptizes each candidate either by immersion or by the pouring of water.

N., I baptize you in the name of the Father, and of the Son, and of the Holy Spirit.

ANOINTING AFTER BAPTISM

Any newly baptized infants are anointed now with chrism.

The God of power and Father of our Lord Jesus Christ has freed you from sin and brought you to new life through water and the Holy Spirit.

He now anoints you with the chrism of salvation, so that, united with his people, you may remain for ever a member of Christ who is Priest, Prophet, and King. **Amen.**

CLOTHING WITH A BAPTISMAL GARMENT

All the newly baptized receive a white garment.

N. and N., you have become a new creation and have clothed yourselves in Christ. Receive this baptismal garment and bring it unstained to the judgment seat of our Lord Jesus Christ, so that you may have ever-lasting life. **Amen.**

PRESENTATION OF A LIGHTED CANDLE

Godparents, please come forward to give to the newly baptized the light of Christ.

A godparent of each of the newly baptized lights a candle from the paschal candle and presents it to the newly baptized.

You have been enlightened by Christ. Walk always as children of the light and keep the flame of faith alive in your hearts. When the Lord comes, may you go out to meet him with all the saints in the heavenly kingdom. **Amen.**

CONFIRMATION OF ADULTS

The newly baptized adults with their godparents stand before the priest.

My dear candidates for confirmation, by your baptism you have been born again in Christ and you have become members of Christ and of his priestly people. Now you are to share in the outpouring of the Holy Spirit among us, the Spirit sent by the Lord upon his apostles at Pentecost and given by them and their successors to the baptized.

The promised strength of the Holy Spirit, which you are to receive, will make you more like Christ and help you to be witnesses to his suffering, death, and resurrection. It will strengthen you to be active members of the Church and to build up the Body of Christ in faith and love.

My dear friends, let us pray to God our Father, that he will pour out the Holy Spirit on these candidates for confirmation to strengthen them with his gifts and anoint them to be more like Christ, the Son of God.

LAYING ON OF HANDS

All-powerful God, Father of our Lord Jesus Christ, by water and the Holy Spirit you freed your sons and daughters from sin and gave them new life.

Send your Holy Spirit upon them to be their helper and guide.

Give them the spirit of wisdom and understanding, the spirit of right judgment and courage, the spirit of knowledge and reverence. Fill them with the spirit of wonder and awe in your presence. We ask this through Christ our Lord. **Amen.**

ANOINTING WITH CHRISM

During the conferral of the sacrament an appropriate song may be sung.

N., be sealed with the Gift of the Holy Spirit. **Amen.**
Peace be with you. **And with your spirit.**

BLESSING OF WATER

(when no one is to be baptized)

Dear brothers and sisters, let us humbly beseech the Lord our God to bless this water he has created, which will be sprinkled upon us as a memorial of our Baptism. May he graciously renew us, that we may remain faithful to the Spirit whom we have received. *(Pause)*

Lord our God, in your mercy be present to your people who keep vigil on this most sacred night, and, for us who recall the wondrous work of our creation and the still greater work of our redemption, graciously bless this water. For you created water to make the fields fruitful and to refresh and cleanse our bodies. You also made water the instrument of your mercy: for through water you freed your people from slavery and quenched their thirst in the desert; through water the Prophets proclaimed the new covenant you were to enter upon with the human race; and last of all, through water, which Christ made holy in the Jordan, you have renewed our corrupted nature in the bath of regeneration.

Therefore, may this water be for us a memorial of the Baptism we have received, and grant that we may share in the gladness of our brothers and sisters, who at Easter have received their Baptism. Through Christ our Lord. **Amen.**

RENEWAL OF BAPTISMAL PROMISES

While holding lit candles, the entire community renews its baptismal promises, if it has not already done so.

Dear brothers and sisters, through the Paschal Mystery we have been buried with Christ in Baptism, so that we may walk with him in newness of life. And so, now that our Lenten observance is concluded, let us renew the promises of Holy Baptism, by which we once renounced Satan and his works and promised to serve God in the holy Catholic Church.

And so I ask you:

1   Do you renounce Satan? **I do.**
    And all his works? **I do.**
    And all his empty show? **I do.**

2 Do you renounce sin, so as to live in the freedom of the children of God? **I do.**

Do you renounce the lure of evil, so that sin may have no mastery over you? **I do.**

Do you renounce Satan, the author and prince of sin? **I do.**

3 Do you reject sin so as to live in the freedom of God's children? **I do.**

Do you reject the glamour of evil, and refuse to be mastered by sin? **I do.**

Do you reject Satan, father of sin and prince of darkness? **I do.**

The community professes its faith:

Do you believe in God, the Father almighty, Creator of heaven and earth? **I do.**

Do you believe in Jesus Christ, his only Son, our Lord, who was born of the Virgin Mary, suffered death and was buried, rose again from the dead and is seated at the right hand of the Father? **I do.**

Do you believe in the Holy Spirit, the holy catholic Church, the communion of saints, the forgiveness of sins, the resurrection of the body, and life everlasting? **I do.**

And may almighty God, the Father of our Lord Jesus Christ, who has given us new birth by water and the Holy Spirit and bestowed on us forgiveness of our sins, keep us by his grace, in Christ Jesus our Lord, for eternal life. **Amen.**

The priest sprinkles the people with blessed water, while an appropriate song is sung.

PRAYER OF THE FAITHFUL

The following intentions are suggestions only. There are more suggestions at www.livingwithchrist.ca

R. **Lord, hear our prayer.**

For the Church, proclaiming the Good News of the Resurrection in word and in deed, we pray to the Lord: R.

For world leaders making wise choices to safeguard all of God's creation, we pray to the Lord: R.

For those baptized this night into Christ's death and resurrection, called as Christ's body to witness to the Good News, we pray to the Lord: R.

For all of us gathered here, living witnesses to the truth of the Resurrection, we pray to the Lord: R.

LITURGY OF THE EUCHARIST

PREPARATION OF THE GIFTS *(p. 14)*

PRAYER OVER THE OFFERINGS

Accept, we ask, O Lord, the prayers of your people with the sacrificial offerings, that what has begun in the paschal mysteries may, by the working of your power, bring us to the healing of eternity. Through Christ our Lord. **Amen.**

PREFACE *(Easter I, p. 23)*

COMMUNION ANTIPHON *(1 Corinthians 5.7-8)*
Christ our Passover has been sacrificed; therefore let us keep the feast with the unleavened bread of purity and truth, alleluia.

PRAYER AFTER COMMUNION

Pour out on us, O Lord, the Spirit of your love, and in your kindness make those you have nourished by this paschal Sacrament one in mind and heart. Through Christ our Lord. **Amen.**

SOLEMN BLESSING — EASTER

Bow down for the blessing.

May almighty God bless you through today's Easter Solemnity and, in his compassion, defend you from every assault of sin. **Amen.**

And may he, who restores you to eternal life in the Resurrection of his Only Begotten, endow you with the prize of immortality. **Amen.**

Now that the days of the Lord's Passion have drawn to a close, may you who celebrate the gladness of the Paschal Feast come with Christ's help, and exulting in spirit, to those feasts that are celebrated in eternal joy. **Amen.**

And may the blessing of almighty God, the Father, and the Son, and the Holy Spirit, come down on you and remain with you for ever. **Amen.**

DISMISSAL

1 Go forth, the Mass is ended, alleluia, alleluia!
2 Go in peace, alleluia, alleluia!

Thanks be to God, al-le-lu-ia, al-le - lu - ia!_

R̶. **Thanks be to God, alleluia, alleluia!**

April Saints' Days

The following saints are traditionally remembered in April in Canada.

2 Saint Francis of Paola

4 Saint Isidore

5 Saint Vincent Ferrer

7 Saint John Baptist de la Salle

11 Saint Stanislaus

13 Saint Martin I

17 Saint Kateri Tekakwitha

18 Blessed Marie-Anne Blondin

21 Saint Anselm

23 Saint George
Saint Adalbert

24 Saint Fidelis of Sigmaringen

25 Saint Mark

26 Our Lady of Good Counsel

28 Saint Peter Chanel
Saint Louis Grignion de Montfort

29 Saint Catherine of Siena

30 Saint Marie of the Incarnation

April 1
Easter Sunday
Resurrection of the Lord

Reading today's Gospel, on this most holy day, I marvel at Mary Magdalene's tenacity in seeking Jesus and her transformation when she sees his promise fulfilled.

As you hear the Gospel proclaimed today, imagine her blinding grief. She watched her beloved Rabbi being tortured, witnessed his crucifixion, and finds his tomb empty. Notice how Mary comes so early in the morning that it is still dark and she is the only one there. How greatly must she love him to go to the tomb alone, unafraid when all the others were?

Her faith is a wondrous thing. Even in grief and bewilderment, Mary stays by the empty tomb in the hope of finding out what happened to Jesus. Jesus appears to her first, to announce his resurrection before he has even fully ascended.

Don't we all encounter these moments in our life, when we need God but do not feel his presence? Mary Magdalene's unwavering faith teaches us discipleship, that if we seek him with love and faith, we will find him. Mary's faith transforms her grief to joy when she is the first to meet Jesus, eventually becoming an apostle to the apostles.

This Easter, let us remember that we are here to rejoice in a promise fulfilled and the transformative power of God who draws us close to him in love.

Saskia Sivananthan
Vancouver, BC

ENTRANCE ANTIPHON *(Cf. Psalm 138.18, 5-6)*
I have risen, and I am with you still, alleluia. You have laid your hand upon me, alleluia. Too wonderful for me, this knowledge, alleluia, alleluia.

or (Luke 24.34; cf. Revelation 1.6)
The Lord is truly risen, alleluia. To him be glory and power for all the ages of eternity, alleluia, alleluia.

INTRODUCTORY RITES *(p. 5)*

COLLECT
O God, who on this day, through your Only Begotten Son, have conquered death and unlocked for us the path to eternity, grant, we pray, that we who keep the solemnity of the Lord's Resurrection may, through the renewal brought by your Spirit, rise up in the light of life. Through our Lord Jesus Christ, your Son, who lives and reigns with you in the unity of the Holy Spirit, one God, for ever and ever. **Amen.**

FIRST READING *(Acts 10.34a, 37-43)*
Peter began to speak: "You know the message that spread throughout Judea, beginning in Galilee after the baptism that John announced: how God anointed Jesus of Nazareth with the Holy Spirit and with power; how he went about doing good and healing all who were oppressed by the devil, for God was with him.

"We are witnesses to all that he did both in Judea and in Jerusalem. They put him to death by hanging him on a tree; but God raised him on the third day and allowed him to appear, not to all the people but to us who were chosen by God as witnesses, and who ate and drank with him after he rose from the dead.

"He commanded us to preach to the people and to testify that he is the one ordained by God as judge of the living and the dead. All the Prophets testify about him that everyone who believes in him receives forgiveness of sins through his name."

The word of the Lord. **Thanks be to God.**

RESPONSORIAL PSALM *(Psalm 118)*

This is the day the Lord has made;
let us re - joice and be glad.

R. **This is the day the Lord has made;
let us rejoice and be glad.**
or **Alleluia! Alleluia! Alleluia!**

O give thanks to the Lord, for · **he** is good;
his steadfast love en·**-dures** for-ever.
Let Is·**-rael** say,
"His steadfast love en·**-dures** for-ever." R.

"The right hand of the Lord · **is** ex-alted;
the right hand of the · **Lord** does valiantly."
I shall not die, but · **I_shall** live,
and recount the · **deeds_of** the Lord. R.

The stone that the · **builders** re-jected
has become · **the** chief cornerstone.
This is the · **Lord's** doing;
it is marvellous · **in** our eyes. R.

©2009 Gordon Johnston/Novalis

To hear the Sunday Psalms, visit www.livingwithchrist.ca.

An alternate reading follows.

SECOND READING *(Colossians 3.1-4)*
Brothers and sisters: If you have been raised with
Christ, seek the things that are above, where Christ
is, seated at the right hand of God. Set your minds on
things that are above, not on things that are on earth,
for you have died, and your life is hidden with Christ
in God. When Christ who is your life is revealed,
then you also will be revealed with him in glory.

The word of the Lord. **Thanks be to God.**
or

SECOND READING *(1 Corinthians 5.6b-8)*
Do you not know that a little yeast leavens the whole
batch of dough? Clean out the old yeast so that you
may be a new batch, as you really are unleavened.
For our paschal lamb, Christ, has been sacrificed.
Therefore, let us celebrate the festival, not with the
old yeast, the yeast of malice and evil, but with the
unleavened bread of sincerity and truth.

The word of the Lord. **Thanks be to God.**

EASTER SEQUENCE

On this day the following sequence is sung. An earlier version can be found at CBW II 202.

1. Christians, praise the paschal victim!
   Offer thankful sacrifice!

2. Christ the Lamb has saved the sheep,
   Christ the just one paid the price,
   Reconciling sinners to the Father.

3. Death and life fought bitterly
   For this wondrous victory;
   The Lord of life who died reigns glorified!

4. "O Mary, come and say
   what you saw at break of day."

5. "The empty tomb of my living Lord!
   I saw Christ Jesus risen and adored!

6. "Bright Angels testified,
   Shroud and grave clothes side by side!

7. "Yes, Christ my hope rose gloriously.
   He goes before you into Galilee."

8. Share the Good News, sing joyfully:
   His death is victory!
   Lord Jesus, Victor King, show us mercy.

Text: *Victimae Paschali Laudes;* tr. © 1983 *Peter J. Scagnelli.*
Tune: VICTIMAE PASCHALI LAUDES. **Music:** *CBW III* 690

GOSPEL ACCLAMATION *(1 Corinthians 5.7-8)*
Alleluia. Alleluia. Christ, our Paschal Lamb, has been sacrificed; let us feast with joy in the Lord. **Alleluia.**

The Gospel from the Easter Vigil (p. 324) may be read instead. For an afternoon or evening Mass, see p. 345.

GOSPEL *(John 20.1-18)*
The shorter version ends at the asterisks.

The Lord be with you. **And with your spirit.** A reading from the holy Gospel according to John. **Glory to you, O Lord.**

Early on the first day of the week, while it was still dark, Mary Magdalene came to the tomb and saw that the stone had been removed from the tomb. So she ran and went to Simon Peter and the other disciple, the one whom Jesus loved, and said to them, "They have taken the Lord out of the tomb, and we do not know where they have laid him."

Then Peter and the other disciple set out and went toward the tomb. The two were running together, but the other disciple outran Peter and reached the tomb first. He bent down to look in and saw the linen wrappings lying there, but he did not go in.

Then Simon Peter came, following him, and went into the tomb. He saw the linen wrappings lying there, and the cloth that had been on Jesus' head, not lying with the linen wrappings but rolled up in a place by itself. Then the other disciple, who reached the tomb first, also went in, and he saw and believed; for as yet they did not understand the Scripture, that he must rise from the dead.

* * *

Then the disciples returned to their homes. But Mary Magdalene stood weeping outside the tomb. As she wept, she bent over to look into the tomb; and she saw two Angels in white, sitting where the body of Jesus had been lying, one at the head and the other at the feet. They said to her, "Woman, why are you weeping?" She said to them, "They have taken away my Lord, and I do not know where they have laid him."

When she had said this, she turned around and saw Jesus standing there, but she did not know that it was Jesus. Jesus said to her, "Woman, why are you weeping? Whom are you looking for?" Supposing him to be the gardener, she said to him, "Sir, if you have carried him away, tell me where you have laid him, and I will take him away."

Jesus said to her, "Mary!" She turned and said to him in Hebrew, "Rabbouni!" which means Teacher. Jesus said to her, "Do not hold on to me, because I have not yet ascended to the Father. But go to my brothers and say to them, 'I am ascending to my Father and your Father, to my God and your God.'"

Mary Magdalene went and announced to the disciples, "I have seen the Lord," and she told them that he had said these things to her.

The Gospel of the Lord. **Praise to you, Lord Jesus Christ.**

Alternate Gospel for an afternoon or evening Mass:

GOSPEL *(Luke 24.13-35)*
The Lord be with you. **And with your spirit.**
A reading from the holy Gospel according to Luke.
Glory to you, O Lord.

On the first day of the week, two of the disciples were going to a village called Emmaus, about eleven kilometres from Jerusalem, and talking with each other about all these things that had happened. While they were talking and discussing, Jesus himself came near and went with them, but their eyes were kept from recognizing him.

And he said to them, "What are you discussing with each other while you walk along?" They stood still, looking sad. Then one of them, whose name was Cleopas, answered him, "Are you the only stranger in Jerusalem who does not know the things that have taken place there in these days?"

He asked them, "What things?" They replied, "The things about Jesus of Nazareth, who was a Prophet mighty in deed and word before God and all the people, and how our chief priests and leaders handed him over to be condemned to death and crucified him. But we had hoped that he was the one to redeem Israel. Yes, and besides all this, it is now the third day since these things took place. Moreover, some women of our group astounded us. They were at the tomb early this morning, and when they did not find his body there, they came back and told us that they had indeed seen a vision of Angels who said that he was alive. Some of those who were with us went to the tomb and found it just as the women had said; but they did not see him."

Then he said to them, "Oh, how foolish you are, and how slow of heart to believe all that the Prophets have declared! Was it not necessary that the Christ should suffer these things and then enter into his glory?"

Then beginning with Moses and all the Prophets, he interpreted to them the things about himself in all the Scriptures. As they came near the village to which they were going, he walked ahead as if he were going on. But they urged him strongly, saying, "Stay with us, because it is almost evening and the day is now nearly over." So he went in to stay with them.

When he was at the table with them, he took bread, blessed and broke it, and gave it to them. Then their eyes were opened, and they recognized him; and he vanished from their sight.

They said to each other, "Were not our hearts burning within us while he was talking to us on the road, while he was opening the Scriptures to us?"

That same hour they got up and returned to Jerusalem; and they found the eleven and their companions gathered together. These were saying, "The Lord has risen indeed, and he has appeared to Simon!"

Then they told what had happened on the road, and how he had been made known to them in the breaking of the bread.

The Gospel of the Lord. **Praise to you, Lord Jesus Christ.**

RENEWAL OF BAPTISMAL PROMISES (p. 334)

PRAYER OF THE FAITHFUL

The following intentions are suggestions only. There are more suggestions at www.livingwithchrist.ca

R. **Lord, hear our prayer.**

For the Church, sign of Christ's continuing presence among us, we pray to the Lord: R.

For peace and reconciliation in the world, we pray to the Lord: R.

For those who have no hope, we pray to the Lord: R.

For all of us here today, called to proclaim Jesus' Resurrection, we pray to the Lord: R.

PREPARATION OF THE GIFTS *(p. 14)*

PRAYER OVER THE OFFERINGS
Exultant with paschal gladness, O Lord, we offer the sacrifice by which your Church is wondrously reborn and nourished. Through Christ our Lord. **Amen.**

PREFACE *(Easter I, p. 23)*

COMMUNION ANTIPHON *(1 Corinthians 5.7-8)*
Christ our Passover has been sacrificed, alleluia; therefore let us keep the feast with the unleavened bread of purity and truth, alleluia, alleluia.

PRAYER AFTER COMMUNION
Look upon your Church, O God, with unfailing love and favour, so that, renewed by the paschal mysteries, she may come to the glory of the resurrection. Through Christ our Lord. **Amen.**

SOLEMN BLESSING *(Optional)*
AND DISMISSAL *(p. 337)*

April 8
2nd Sunday of Easter
Divine Mercy

One cold, grey Argentine morning, amidst rubbish piles, a small, scruffy child bent over a small fire trying to mend the strap on one of his plastic sandals. This is only one of a thousand mental images I have, will always have, of the poverty and brokenness in our world today. Aren't we called to something better?

Thomas felt the mercy and forgiveness of Jesus whom he had followed so eagerly but doubted so quickly. We all need the comfort of knowing we can be forgiven over and over again when we fail to take to heart "his commandments" which we know deep in our hearts "are not burdensome."

Yet still we doubt. We vainly try to tightly hold on to what earthly riches we have knowing full well that material possessions will not bring us closer to our ultimate goal. Simple lessons like the more we give, the more we will receive just do not seem to stick and need to be re-learned over and over again.

The early Christian community recognized the path. "There was not a needy person among them," because they shared their wealth. "It was distributed to each as any had need."

The risen Jesus entered the locked room and said, "Peace be with you." Can we hear his voice today? "This is the victory that conquers the world, our faith."

Michael Dougherty
Whitehorse, YT

ENTRANCE ANTIPHON *(1 Peter 2.2)*
Like newborn infants, you must long for the pure, spiritual milk, that in him you may grow to salvation, alleluia.

    or (4 Esdras 2.36-37)
Receive the joy of your glory, giving thanks to God, who has called you into the heavenly kingdom, alleluia.

INTRODUCTORY RITES *(p. 5)*

COLLECT
God of everlasting mercy, who in the very recurrence of the paschal feast kindle the faith of the people you have made your own, increase, we pray, the grace you have bestowed, that all may grasp and rightly understand in what font they have been washed, by whose Spirit they have been reborn, by whose Blood they have been redeemed. Through our Lord Jesus Christ, your Son, who lives and reigns with you in the unity of the Holy Spirit, one God, for ever and ever. **Amen.**

FIRST READING *(Acts 4.32-35)*
The whole group of those who believed were of one heart and soul, and no one claimed private ownership of any possessions, but everything they owned was held in common.

    With great power the Apostles gave their testimony to the resurrection of the Lord Jesus, and great grace was upon them all.

    There was not a needy person among them, for as many as owned lands or houses sold them and brought the proceeds of what was sold. They laid it at the Apostles' feet, and it was distributed to each as any had need.

The word of the Lord. **Thanks be to God.**

RESPONSORIAL PSALM *(Psalm 118)*

Give thanks to the Lord for he is good;

his stead-fast love en-dures for-ev-er.

R̥. **Give thanks to the Lord, for he is good;**
his steadfast love endures forever.
or **Alleluia!**

Let Israel · **say,**
"His steadfast love endures for--**ever.**"
Let the house of Aaron · **say,**
"His steadfast love endures for--**ever.**"
Let those who fear the Lord · **say,**
"His steadfast love endures for--**ever.**" R̥.

"The right hand of the Lord is ex--**alted;**
the right hand of the Lord does · **valiantly.**"
I shall not die, but I shall · **live,**
and recount the deeds of the · **Lord.**
The Lord has punished me se--**verely,**
but he did not give me over to · **death.** R̥.

The stone that the builders re-**jected**
has become the chief · **cornerstone.**
This is the Lord's · **doing;**
it is marvellous in our · **eyes.**
This is the day that the Lord has · **made;**
let us rejoice and be glad in · **it.** R̲.

©2009 Gordon Johnston/Novalis

SECOND READING *(1 John 5.1-6)*
Beloved: Everyone who believes that Jesus is the
Christ has been born of God, and everyone who loves
the parent loves the child.

By this we know that we love the children of
God, when we love God and obey his commandments. For the love of God is this, that we obey his
commandments. And his commandments are not
burdensome, for whatever is born of God conquers
the world. And this is the victory that conquers the
world, our faith.

Who is it that conquers the world but the one
who believes that Jesus is the Son of God? This is
the one who came by water and blood, Jesus Christ,
not with the water only but with the water and the
blood. And the Spirit is the one that testifies, for the
Spirit is the truth.

The word of the Lord. **Thanks be to God.**

GOSPEL ACCLAMATION *(See John 20.29)*
Alleluia. Alleluia. You believed, Thomas, because
you have seen me; blessed are those who have not
seen and yet believe. **Alleluia.**

GOSPEL *(John 20.19-31)*

The Lord be with you. **And with your spirit.**
A reading from the holy Gospel according to John.
Glory to you, O Lord.

It was evening on the day Jesus rose from the dead, the first day of the week, and the doors of the house where the disciples had met were locked for fear of the Jews. Jesus came and stood among them and said, "Peace be with you." After he said this, he showed them his hands and his side. Then the disciples rejoiced when they saw the Lord.

Jesus said to them again, "Peace be with you. As the Father has sent me, so I send you." When he had said this, he breathed on them and said to them, "Receive the Holy Spirit. If you forgive the sins of any, they are forgiven them; if you retain the sins of any, they are retained."

But Thomas, who was called the Twin, one of the twelve, was not with them when Jesus came. So the other disciples told him, "We have seen the Lord." But he said to them, "Unless I see the mark of the nails in his hands, and put my finger in the mark of the nails and my hand in his side, I will not believe."

After eight days his disciples were again in the house, and Thomas was with them. Although the doors were shut, Jesus came and stood among them and said, "Peace be with you." Then he said to Thomas, "Put your finger here and see my hands. Reach out your hand and put it in my side. Do not doubt but believe." Thomas answered him, "My Lord and my God!"

Jesus said to him, "Have you believed because you have seen me? Blessed are those who have not seen and yet have come to believe."

Now Jesus did many other signs in the presence of his disciples, which are not written in this book. But these are written so that you may come to believe that Jesus is the Christ, the Son of God, and that through believing you may have life in his name.

The Gospel of the Lord. **Praise to you, Lord Jesus Christ.**

PROFESSION OF FAITH (p. 11)

PRAYER OF THE FAITHFUL

The following intentions are suggestions only. There are more suggestions at www.livingwithchrist.ca

R. **Lord, hear our prayer.**

For the Church, called to be a sign of God's forgiveness and love, we pray to the Lord: R.

For leaders of governments, dedicated to exercising wisdom for the well-being of all, we pray to the Lord: R.

For those among us who struggle with fears, regrets and doubts, we pray to the Lord: R.

For ourselves during this Easter Time, invited to enter into the grace of the Resurrection, we pray to the Lord: R.

PREPARATION OF THE GIFTS (p. 14)

PRAYER OVER THE OFFERINGS

Accept, O Lord, we pray, the oblations of your people (and of those you have brought to new birth), that, renewed by confession of your name and by Baptism, they may attain unending happiness. Through Christ our Lord. **Amen.**

PREFACE (Easter I, p. 23)

COMMUNION ANTIPHON (Cf. John 20.27)

Bring your hand and feel the place of the nails, and do not be unbelieving but believing, alleluia.

PRAYER AFTER COMMUNION

Grant, we pray, almighty God, that our reception of this paschal Sacrament may have a continuing effect in our minds and hearts. Through Christ our Lord. **Amen.**

SOLEMN BLESSING — EASTER TIME (Optional)

Bow down for the blessing.

May God, who by the Resurrection of his Only Begotten Son was pleased to confer on you the gift of redemption and of adoption, give you gladness by his blessing. **Amen.**

May he, by whose redeeming work you have received the gift of everlasting freedom, make you heirs to an eternal inheritance. **Amen.**

And may you, who have already risen with Christ in Baptism through faith, by living in a right manner on this earth, be united with him in the homeland of heaven. **Amen.**

And may the blessing of almighty God, the Father, and the Son, and the Holy Spirit, come down on you and remain with you for ever. **Amen.**

DISMISSAL

1 Go forth, the Mass is ended, alleluia, alleluia!
2 Go in peace, alleluia, alleluia!

Thanks be to God, al-le-lu-ia,   al-le - lu - ia!

℟. **Thanks be to God, alleluia, alleluia!**

April 15
3rd Sunday of Easter

Imagine being one of the disciples in today's Gospel. You have just heard of Jesus's appearance on the road to Emmaus, which, along with the amazing story of the tomb, has given you a surge of hope. However, the grief and fear you felt during the crucifixion still remain in your heart. You want to believe that he has risen as he said, but a pall of paralyzing uncertainty hangs over everything.

Suddenly, he's in the room, standing right in front of you. Of course, he knows what you are feeling. "Why are you frightened, and why do doubts arise in your hearts?" he asks. "Touch me and see." You do see.

Appearing before the disciples, Jesus gave them precisely what they needed for the next phase of their mission. He reassured and strengthened them by replacing their fear and uncertainty with peace and joy. He made the scriptures intelligible to them so that they'd be able to pass on his wisdom.

Why do fear and doubt arise in our hearts when Jesus calls us to something new? His death was the ultimate proof that his love for us knows no bounds. Just as he prepared the disciples for their mission, so he will prepare us for ours.

Kate Larson
Ottawa, ON

ENTRANCE ANTIPHON *(Cf. Psalm 65.1-2)*
Cry out with joy to God, all the earth; O sing to the glory of his name. O render him glorious praise, alleluia.

INTRODUCTORY RITES *(p. 5)*

COLLECT
May your people exult for ever, O God, in renewed youthfulness of spirit, so that, rejoicing now in the restored glory of our adoption, we may look forward in confident hope to the rejoicing of the day of resurrection. Through our Lord Jesus Christ, your Son, who lives and reigns with you in the unity of the Holy Spirit, one God, for ever and ever. **Amen.**

FIRST READING *(Acts 3.13-15, 17-19)*
At the temple gate, Peter addressed the people: "The God of Abraham, the God of Isaac, and the God of Jacob, the God of our fathers has glorified his servant Jesus, whom you handed over and rejected in the presence of Pilate, though he had decided to release him.

"But you rejected the Holy and Righteous One and asked to have a murderer given to you, and you killed the Author of life, whom God raised from the dead. To this we are witnesses.

"And now, brothers and sisters, I know that you acted in ignorance, as did also your rulers. In this way God fulfilled what he had foretold through all the Prophets, that his Christ would suffer.

"Repent therefore, and turn to God so that your sins may be wiped out."

The word of the Lord. **Thanks be to God.**

RESPONSORIAL PSALM *(Psalm 4)*

Let the light of your face shine on us, O Lord.

R. **Let the light of your face shine on us, O Lord.**
or **Alleluia!**

Answer me when I call, O God of · **my** right!
You gave me room when I was in · **dis**-tress.
Be gracious to me, and · **hear** my prayer. R.

But know that the Lord has set · **a**-part
the faithful for · **him**-self;
the Lord hears when I · **call** to him. R.

There are many · **who** say,
"O that we might see · **some** good!
Let the light of your face shine on · **us**, O Lord!" R.

I will both lie down and sleep · **in** peace;
for you alone, · **O** Lord,
make me lie · **down** in safety. R.

©2009 Gordon Johnston/Novalis

SECOND READING *(1 John 2.1-5)*
My little children, I am writing these things to you
so that you may not sin. But if anyone does sin, we
have an advocate with the Father, Jesus Christ the
righteous; and he is the atoning sacrifice for our
sins, and not for ours only but also for the sins of
the whole world.

Now by this we may be sure that we know him, if we obey his commandments. Whoever says, "I have come to know him," but does not obey his commandments, is a liar, and in such a person the truth does not exist; but whoever obeys his word, truly in this person the love of God has reached perfection. By this we may be sure that we are in him.

The word of the Lord. **Thanks be to God.**

GOSPEL ACCLAMATION *(See Luke 24.32)*
Alleluia. Alleluia. Lord Jesus, open the Scriptures to us: make our hearts burn with love when you speak. **Alleluia.**

GOSPEL *(Luke 24.35-48)*
The Lord be with you. **And with your spirit.** A reading from the holy Gospel according to Luke. **Glory to you, O Lord.**

The two disciples told the eleven and their companions what had happened on the road to Emmaus, and how Jesus had been made known to them in the breaking of the bread.

While they were talking about this, Jesus himself stood among them and said to them, "Peace be with you." They were startled and terrified, and thought that they were seeing a ghost. He said to them, "Why are you frightened, and why do doubts arise in your hearts? Look at my hands and my feet; see that it is I myself. Touch me and see; for a ghost does not have flesh and bones as you see that I have."

And when he had said this, he showed them his hands and his feet. While in their joy they were disbelieving and still wondering, he said to them, "Have you anything here to eat?" They gave him a piece of broiled fish, and he took it and ate in their presence.

Then he said to them, "These are my words that I spoke to you while I was still with you — that everything written about me in the Law of Moses, the Prophets, and the Psalms must be fulfilled." Then he opened their minds to understand the Scriptures, and he said to them, "Thus it is written, that the Christ is to suffer and to rise from the dead on the third day, and that repentance and forgiveness of sins is to be proclaimed in his name to all nations, beginning from Jerusalem. You are witnesses of these things."

The Gospel of the Lord. **Praise to you, Lord Jesus Christ.**

PROFESSION OF FAITH *(p. 11)*

PRAYER OF THE FAITHFUL

The following intentions are suggestions only. There are more suggestions at www.livingwithchrist.ca

R. **Lord, hear our prayer.**

For the Church during this Easter Time, calling us to see Jesus in our brothers and sisters everywhere, we pray to the Lord: R.

For world leaders working together to find solutions to our common global problems, we pray to the Lord: R.

For all who call out in their need and for those who respond, we pray to the Lord: R.

For all the members of this community, working to be faithful followers of Jesus, we pray to the Lord: ℟.

PREPARATION OF THE GIFTS (p. 14)

PRAYER OVER THE OFFERINGS
Receive, O Lord, we pray, these offerings of your exultant Church, and, as you have given her cause for such great gladness, grant also that the gifts we bring may bear fruit in perpetual happiness. Through Christ our Lord. **Amen.**

PREFACE (Easter, p. 23)

COMMUNION ANTIPHON (Luke 24.35)
The disciples recognized the Lord Jesus in the breaking of the bread, alleluia.
   or (Luke 24.46-47)
The Christ had to suffer and on the third day rise from the dead; in his name repentance and remission of sins must be preached to all the nations, alleluia.

PRAYER AFTER COMMUNION
Look with kindness upon your people, O Lord, and grant, we pray, that those you were pleased to renew by eternal mysteries may attain in their flesh the incorruptible glory of the resurrection. Through Christ our Lord. **Amen.**

SOLEMN BLESSING (Optional, p. 355)

DISMISSAL (p. 71)

April 22
4th Sunday of Easter
World Day of Prayer for Vocations

Today's readings are especially poignant to the western world. North American culture is over-saturated with marketing. Advertisers promote the message that if we buy their products, we will be complete. Most of us have experienced the disappointment of a newly purchased item falling short of our expectations.

Today's readings, especially the Gospel, contrast God's true love with worldly promises of love that fade. Jesus uses the analogy of the Good Shepherd and compares his authentic concern for the flock with that of the hired help who only care about their pay cheque. They flee the scene at the first sign of danger, leaving the sheep to fend for themselves. This message is also present in the other readings. In the first reading, from Acts, Peter states that "there is salvation in no one else." To put our faith in others, whether they be advertisers or celebrities, will lead to disappointment. In Psalm 118, the psalmist praises God who has protected him when all else failed.

God promises us a greater love than we can imagine. As the ultimate sign of this, he sent Christ into the world to call us. During this Easter season, and today on World Day of Prayer for Vocations, we pray that Jesus' message will be embraced by all people searching for immortal and timeless love.

Andrew Hume
Toronto, ON

ENTRANCE ANTIPHON *(Cf. Psalm 32.5-6)*
The merciful love of the Lord fills the earth; by the word of the Lord the heavens were made, alleluia.

INTRODUCTORY RITES *(p. 5)*

COLLECT
Almighty ever-living God, lead us to a share in the joys of heaven, so that the humble flock may reach where the brave Shepherd has gone before. Who lives and reigns with you in the unity of the Holy Spirit, one God, for ever and ever. **Amen.**

FIRST READING *(Acts 4.7-12)*
While Peter and John were speaking to the people about the resurrection of Jesus, the captain of the temple arrested them and placed them in custody.

The next day the rulers, elders and scribes assembled. When they had made the prisoners stand in their midst, they inquired, "By what power or by what name did you do this?" Then Peter, filled with the Holy Spirit, said to them, "Rulers of the people and elders, if we are questioned today because of a good deed done to someone who was sick and are asked how this man has been healed, let it be known to all of you, and to all the people of Israel, that this man is standing before you in good health by the name of Jesus Christ of Nazareth, whom you crucified, whom God raised from the dead.

"This Jesus is 'the stone that was rejected by you, the builders; it has become the cornerstone.' There is salvation in no one else, for there is no other name under heaven given among human beings by which we must be saved."

The word of the Lord. **Thanks be to God.**

RESPONSORIAL PSALM *(Psalm 118)*

R. **The stone that the builders rejected**
has become the cornerstone.
or **Alleluia!**

O give thanks to the Lord, for he is · **good;**
his steadfast love endures · **for**-ever!
It is better to take refuge in the · **Lord**
than to put confidence · **in** humans.
It is better to take refuge in the · **Lord**
than to put confidence · **in** princes. R.

I thank you that you have · **answered_me**
and have become my · **sal**-vation.
The stone that the builders re-·**jected**
has become the · **chief** cornerstone.
This is the Lord's · **doing;**
it is marvellous in · **our** eyes. R.

Blessed is the one who comes in the name of
    the · **Lord.**
We bless you from the house of · **the** Lord.
You are my God, and I will give · **thanks_to_you;**
you are my God, I will · **ex**-tol_you.
O give thanks to the Lord, for he is · **good,**
for his steadfast love endures · **for**-ever. ℟

©2009 Gordon Johnston/Novalis

SECOND READING *(1 John 3.1-2)*
Beloved: See what love the Father has given us, that
we should be called children of God; and that is what
we are. The reason the world does not know us is
that it did not know him.

Beloved, we are God's children now; what we will
be has not yet been revealed. What we do know is
this: when he is revealed, we will be like him, for
we will see him as he is.

The word of the Lord. **Thanks be to God.**

GOSPEL ACCLAMATION *(John 10.14)*
Alleluia. Alleluia. I am the good shepherd, says
the Lord; I know my own, and my own know me.
Alleluia.

GOSPEL *(John 10.11-18)*
The Lord be with you. **And with your spirit.**
A reading from the holy Gospel according to John.
Glory to you, O Lord.

Jesus said: "I am the good shepherd. The good
shepherd lays down his life for the sheep. The hired
hand, who is not the shepherd and does not own the

sheep, sees the wolf coming and leaves the sheep and runs away — and the wolf snatches them and scatters them. The hired hand runs away because a hired hand does not care for the sheep.

"I am the good shepherd. I know my own and my own know me, just as the Father knows me and I know the Father. And I lay down my life for the sheep. I have other sheep that do not belong to this fold. I must bring them also, and they will listen to my voice. So there will be one flock, one shepherd.

"For this reason the Father loves me, because I lay down my life in order to take it up again. No one takes it from me, but I lay it down of my own accord. I have power to lay it down, and I have power to take it up again. I have received this command from my Father."

The Gospel of the Lord. **Praise to you, Lord Jesus Christ.**

PROFESSION OF FAITH (p. 11)

PRAYER OF THE FAITHFUL

The following intentions are suggestions only. There are more suggestions at www.livingwithchrist.ca

R. **Lord, hear our prayer.**

For all who bring the Spirit of God to us each day, we pray to the Lord: R.

For the world as it continues to struggle to find peace, we pray to the Lord: R.

In gratitude for all the special people in our lives who have acted as mentors and guides, we pray to the Lord: R.

For this flock, called together by the Good Shepherd, we pray to the Lord: R̷.

PREPARATION OF THE GIFTS *(p. 14)*

PRAYER OVER THE OFFERINGS

Grant, we pray, O Lord, that we may always find delight in these paschal mysteries, so that the renewal constantly at work within us may be the cause of our unending joy. Through Christ our Lord. **Amen.**

PREFACE *(Easter, p. 23)*

COMMUNION ANTIPHON

The Good Shepherd has risen, who laid down his life for his sheep and willingly died for his flock, alleluia.

PRAYER AFTER COMMUNION

Look upon your flock, kind Shepherd, and be pleased to settle in eternal pastures the sheep you have redeemed by the Precious Blood of your Son. Who lives and reigns for ever and ever. **Amen.**

SOLEMN BLESSING *(Optional, p. 355)*

DISMISSAL *(p. 71)*

April 29
5th Sunday of Easter

God calls us daily into an intimate union with him. Today's readings remind us of this and that our souls thirst for God and his love. He is the only source of eternal life and apart from him we will never be satisfied.

In this Easter season we rejoice in the Lord's resurrection and we continue to reflect on his unfailing and everlasting love for us. Today, we are called to go deeper in our relationship with Jesus and surrender our lives to him so we can be who we were created to be. As the branch needs to be attached to the vine, we need to be attached to Jesus to produce fruit. As we grow in faith and love for others, God will prune us so we can produce more fruit.

The more time we spend with Jesus, the more we will learn to love others and ourselves as he does. We will be faithful to his commandments and abide in him.

Today, let's open our hearts to Jesus and receive his love, especially during Communion. Let's take today's readings home and meditate on them – especially the Gospel. It's a great passage to use for a *Lectio Divina* with family or friends.

Sarah Escobar
Ottawa, ON

ENTRANCE ANTIPHON *(Cf. Psalm 97.1-2)*
O sing a new song to the Lord, for he has worked
wonders; in the sight of the nations he has shown
his deliverance, alleluia.

INTRODUCTORY RITES *(p. 5)*

COLLECT
Almighty ever-living God, constantly accomplish
the Paschal Mystery within us, that those you were
pleased to make new in Holy Baptism may, under
your protective care, bear much fruit and come to the
joys of life eternal. Through our Lord Jesus Christ,
your Son, who lives and reigns with you in the unity
of the Holy Spirit, one God, for ever and ever. **Amen.**

FIRST READING *(Acts 9.26-31)*
When Saul had come to Jerusalem, he attempted to
join the disciples; and they were all afraid of him,
for they did not believe that he was a disciple. But
Barnabas took him, brought him to the Apostles, and
described for them how on the road he had seen the
Lord, who had spoken to him, and how in Damascus
Saul had spoken boldly in the name of Jesus.

So Saul went in and out among them in Jerusalem,
speaking boldly in the name of the Lord. He spoke and
argued with the Hellenists; but they were attempting to
kill him. When the believers learned of it, they brought
Saul down to Caesarea and sent him off to Tarsus.

Meanwhile the Church throughout Judea, Galilee,
and Samaria had peace and was built up. Living in
the fear of the Lord and in the comfort of the Holy
Spirit, it increased in numbers.

The word of the Lord. **Thanks be to God.**

RESPONSORIAL PSALM *(Psalm 22)*

R̲. **Lord, from you comes my praise**
in the great congregation.
or **Alleluia!**

My vows I will pay before those who · **fear_him.**
The poor shall eat · **and** be satisfied;
those who seek him shall · **praise** the Lord.
May your hearts live · **for**-ever. R̲.

All the ends of the earth shall remember and
    turn to the · **Lord;**
and all the families of the nations shall wor-
    ship be-fore_him.
To him, indeed, shall all who sleep in the · **earth**
    bow down;
before him shall bow all who go down to · **the**
    dust. R̲.

I shall live for him. Posterity will · **serve_him;**
future generations will be told a-·**bout** the Lord,
and proclaim his deliverance to a people · **yet**
    un-born,
saying that he · **has** done_it. R̲.

©2009 Gordon Johnston/Novalis

SECOND READING *(1 John 3.18-24)*

Little children, let us love, not in word or speech, but in truth and action. And by this we will know that we are from the truth and will reassure our hearts before him whenever our hearts condemn us; for God is greater than our hearts, and God knows everything.

Beloved, if our hearts do not condemn us, we have boldness before God; and we receive from him whatever we ask, because we obey his commandments and do what pleases him.

And this is his commandment, that we should believe in the name of his Son Jesus Christ and love one another, just as he has commanded us. Whoever obeys his commandments abides in him, and he abides in them. And by this we know that he abides in us, by the Spirit that he has given us.

The word of the Lord. **Thanks be to God.**

GOSPEL ACCLAMATION *(John 15.4, 5)*

Alleluia. Alleluia. Abide in me as I abide in you, says the Lord; my branches bear much fruit. **Alleluia.**

GOSPEL *(John 15.1-8)*

The Lord be with you. **And with your spirit.**
A reading from the holy Gospel according to John.
Glory to you, O Lord.

Jesus said to his disciples: "I am the true vine, and my Father is the vinegrower. He removes every branch in me that bears no fruit. Every branch that bears fruit he prunes to make it bear more fruit. You have already been cleansed by the word that I have spoken to you.

"Abide in me as I abide in you. Just as the branch cannot bear fruit by itself unless it abides in the vine, neither can you unless you abide in me. I am the vine, you are the branches. Whoever abides in me and I in them bears much fruit, because apart from me you can do nothing.

"Whoever does not abide in me is thrown away like a branch and withers; such branches are gathered, thrown into the fire, and burned.

"If you abide in me, and my words abide in you, ask for whatever you wish, and it will be done for you. My Father is glorified by this, that you bear much fruit and become my disciples."

The Gospel of the Lord. **Praise to you, Lord Jesus Christ.**

PROFESSION OF FAITH (p. 11)

PRAYER OF THE FAITHFUL

The following intentions are suggestions only. There are more suggestions at www.livingwithchrist.ca

R. **Lord, hear our prayer.**

For the Church, striving to share the Good News of the Resurrection, we pray to the Lord: R.

For all who make decisions that affect the lives of others, we pray to the Lord: R.

For all who remain entombed in darkness and for all who seek to liberate them, we pray to the Lord: R.

For Easter hope in our eucharistic community, we pray to the Lord: R.

PREPARATION OF THE GIFTS *(p. 14)*

PRAYER OVER THE OFFERINGS

O God, who by the wonderful exchange effected in this sacrifice have made us partakers of the one supreme Godhead, grant, we pray, that, as we have come to know your truth, we may make it ours by a worthy way of life. Through Christ our Lord. **Amen.**

PREFACE *(Easter, p. 23)*

COMMUNION ANTIPHON *(Cf. John 15.1, 5)*

I am the true vine and you are the branches, says the Lord. Whoever remains in me, and I in him, bears fruit in plenty, alleluia.

PRAYER AFTER COMMUNION

Graciously be present to your people, we pray, O Lord, and lead those you have imbued with heavenly mysteries to pass from former ways to newness of life. Through Christ our Lord. **Amen.**

SOLEMN BLESSING *(Optional, p. 355)*

DISMISSAL *(p. 71)*

May Saints' Days

The following saints are traditionally remembered in May in Canada.

1 Saint Joseph the Worker
Saint Pius V

2 Saint Athanasius

3 Saints Philip and James

4 Blessed Marie-Léonie Paradis

6 Saint François de Laval

8 Blessed Catherine of Saint Augustine

12 Saints Nereus and Achilleus
Saint Pancras

13 Our Lady of Fatima

14 Saint Matthias

18 Saint John I

20 Saint Bernardine of Siena

21 Saint Christopher Magallanes & Companions
Saint Eugène de Mazenod

22 Saint Rita of Cascia

24 Blessed Louis-Zéphirin Moreau

25 Saint Bede the Venerable
Saint Gregory VII
Saint Mary Magdalene de' Pazzi

26 Saint Philip Neri

27 Saint Augustine of Canterbury

May 6
6th Sunday of Easter

In today's Gospel, Jesus calls his disciples and us his friends. Friendship is a valuable gift. It requires generosity, honesty and mutual love. A true friend understands us even when we remain silent and accepts us as we are. Jesus' self-giving love for us, his friends, forms the model for the love we are to have for one another.

Jesus has no secrets with his disciples. He opens his heart to them, revealing to them the knowledge the Father has given him and his love for each of them. He demonstrates his profound love and that of his Father by laying down his life for us, suffering and dying on the cross for our salvation. His love has no limits, embracing everyone and giving everything. Jesus invites us to enter into his love and to express this love in our daily lives. This challenging love consists in making sacrifices and reaching out to others freely. It involves loving to the end, with Jesus' same compassion and selflessness. Only if we love one another as he has loved us can we be his true friends.

Jesus offers us his love and friendship, a relationship that will transform our lives and give us true joy. Let us accept his offer today by having faith in him and sharing his merciful love with others.

Nada Mazzei
Toronto, ON

ENTRANCE ANTIPHON (Cf. Isaiah 48.20)
Proclaim a joyful sound and let it be heard; proclaim to the ends of the earth: The Lord has freed his people, alleluia.

INTRODUCTORY RITES (p. 5)

COLLECT
Grant, almighty God, that we may celebrate with heartfelt devotion these days of joy, which we keep in honour of the risen Lord, and that what we relive in remembrance we may always hold to in what we do. Through our Lord Jesus Christ, your Son, who lives and reigns with you in the unity of the Holy Spirit, one God, for ever and ever. **Amen.**

FIRST READING (Acts 10.25-26, 34-35, 44-48)
On Peter's arrival, Cornelius, a centurion of the Italian cohort, met him, and falling at his feet, worshipped him. But Peter made him get up, saying, "Stand up; I am only a man."

Then Peter began to speak, "I truly understand that God shows no partiality, but in every nation anyone who fears him and does what is right is acceptable to him."

While Peter was still speaking, the Holy Spirit fell upon all who heard the word. The circumcised believers who had come with Peter were astounded that the gift of the Holy Spirit had been poured out even on the Gentiles, for they heard them speaking in tongues and extolling God.

Then Peter said, "Can anyone withhold the water for baptizing these people who have received the Holy Spirit just as we have?" So he ordered them to be baptized in the name of Jesus Christ. Then they invited him to stay for several days.

The word of the Lord. **Thanks be to God.**

RESPONSORIAL PSALM *(Psalm 98)*

R. **The Lord has revealed his victory**
   in the sight of the nations.
or **Alleluia!**

O sing to the Lord · **a new song,**
for he has done · **marvel**-lous things.
His right hand and his · **ho**-ly arm
have · **brought** him victory. R.

The Lord has made · **known** his victory;
he has revealed his vindication in the · **sight_of**
   the nations.
He has remembered his · **stead**-fast love
and faithfulness to the · **house** of Israel. R.

All the ends of the · **earth** have seen
the victory · **of** our God.
Make a joyful noise to the Lord, · **all** the earth;
break forth into joyous · **song_and** sing praises. R.

©2009 Gordon Johnston/Novalis

SECOND READING *(1 John 4.7-10)*
Beloved, let us love one another, because love is from God; everyone who loves is born of God and knows God. Whoever does not love does not know God, for God is love.

God's love was revealed among us in this way: God sent his only-begotten Son into the world so that we might live through him. In this is love, not that we loved God but that he loved us and sent his Son to be the atoning sacrifice for our sins.

The word of the Lord. **Thanks be to God.**

GOSPEL ACCLAMATION *(John 14.23)*
Alleluia. Alleluia. Those who love me will keep my word, and my Father will love them, and we will come to them. **Alleluia.**

GOSPEL *(John 15.9-17)*
The Lord be with you. **And with your spirit.** A reading from the holy Gospel according to John. **Glory to you, O Lord.**

Jesus said to his disciples: "As the Father has loved me, so I have loved you; abide in my love. If you keep my commandments, you will abide in my love, just as I have kept my Father's commandments and abide in his love.

"I have said these things to you so that my joy may be in you, and that your joy may be complete. This is my commandment, that you love one another as I have loved you. No one has greater love than this, to lay down one's life for one's friends.

"You are my friends if you do what I command you. I do not call you servants any longer, because the servant does not know what the master is doing; but I have called you friends, because I have made known to you everything that I have heard from my Father.

"You did not choose me but I chose you. And I appointed you to go and bear fruit, fruit that will last, so that the Father will give you whatever you ask him in my name. I am giving you these commands so that you may love one another."

The Gospel of the Lord. **Praise to you, Lord Jesus Christ.**

PROFESSION OF FAITH *(p. 11)*

PRAYER OF THE FAITHFUL

The following intentions are suggestions only. There are more suggestions at www.livingwithchrist.ca

R. **Lord, hear our prayer.**

For the Church, witness to the saving life, death and Resurrection of Jesus, we pray to the Lord: R.

For just and sound stewardship of God's creation, we pray to the Lord: R.

For those among us who suffer silently, we pray to the Lord: R.

For the special needs of this community gathered here today, we pray to the Lord: R.

PREPARATION OF THE GIFTS *(p. 14)*

PRAYER OVER THE OFFERINGS

May our prayers rise up to you, O Lord, together with the sacrificial offerings, so that, purified by your graciousness, we may be conformed to the mysteries of your mighty love. Through Christ our Lord. **Amen.**

PREFACE *(Easter, p. 23)*

COMMUNION ANTIPHON *(John 14.15-16)*

If you love me, keep my commandments, says the Lord, and I will ask the Father and he will send you another Paraclete, to abide with you for ever, alleluia.

PRAYER AFTER COMMUNION

Almighty ever-living God, who restore us to eternal life in the Resurrection of Christ, increase in us, we pray, the fruits of this paschal Sacrament and pour into our hearts the strength of this saving food. Through Christ our Lord. **Amen.**

SOLEMN BLESSING *(Optional, p. 355)*

DISMISSAL *(p. 71)*

May 13
Ascension of the Lord
World Communications Day

On this feast of the Ascension of the Lord, the Church pays special attention to communication in our world, and encourages us to spread the good news of God's saving grace, revealed in Jesus and made present through the power of the Holy Spirit.

The accounts of the ascension in both Acts and Mark entrust us, as Jesus himself entrusted the eleven, to share the good news. The sacraments equip us wonderfully for the task of witnessing to the "whole of creation." In Baptism, we became light to the world. In Confirmation, we received the gifts of the Holy Spirit that empower us to be the Christ-bearers of unity. And through the celebration of the Eucharist, we are nourished and strengthened for our mission.

Communicating the good news is a work in progress. There has never been a time in history when people did not need the news of salvation. When much of the communication around us tears down rather than builds up, we have the opportunity to build bridges through our encounters with others.

Jesus is the benchmark for all of our communications. Following his example, may our lives communicate God's love and mercy and be a sign of hope to the world.

Louise McEwan
Trail, BC

ENTRANCE ANTIPHON (Acts 1.11)
Men of Galilee, why gaze in wonder at the heavens? This Jesus whom you saw ascending into heaven will return as you saw him go, alleluia.

INTRODUCTORY RITES (p. 5)

COLLECT
Gladden us with holy joys, almighty God, and make us rejoice with devout thanksgiving, for the Ascension of Christ your Son is our exaltation, and, where the Head has gone before in glory, the Body is called to follow in hope. Through our Lord Jesus Christ, your Son, who lives and reigns with you in the unity of the Holy Spirit, one God, for ever and ever. **Amen.**
  or
Grant, we pray, almighty God, that we, who believe that your Only Begotten Son, our Redeemer, ascended this day to the heavens, may in spirit dwell already in heavenly realms. Who lives and reigns with you in the unity of the Holy Spirit, one God, for ever and ever. **Amen.**

FIRST READING (Acts 1.1-11)
In the first book, Theophilus, I wrote about all that Jesus did and taught from the beginning until the day when he was taken up to heaven, after giving instructions through the Holy Spirit to the Apostles whom he had chosen. After his suffering he presented himself alive to them by many convincing proofs, appearing to them during forty days and speaking about the kingdom of God.

While staying with them, he ordered them not to leave Jerusalem, but to wait there for the promise of the Father. "This," he said, "is what you have heard from me; for John baptized with water, but you will be baptized with the Holy Spirit not many days from now."

So when they had come together, they asked him, "Lord, is this the time when you will restore the kingdom to Israel?" He replied, "It is not for you to know the times or periods that the Father has set by his own authority. But you will receive power when the Holy Spirit has come upon you; and you will be my witnesses in Jerusalem, in all Judea and Samaria, and to the ends of the earth."

When he had said this, as they were watching, he was lifted up, and a cloud took him out of their sight. While he was going and they were gazing up toward heaven, suddenly two men in white robes stood by them. They said, "Men of Galilee, why do you stand looking up toward heaven? This Jesus, who has been taken up from you into heaven, will come in the same way as you saw him go into heaven."

The word of the Lord. **Thanks be to God.**

RESPONSORIAL PSALM *(Psalm 47)*

God has gone up with a shout, ____ the
Lord with the sound of a trum - pet. ____

R̰. **God has gone up with a shout,**
   the Lord with the sound of a trumpet.
or **Alleluia!**

Clap your hands, all · **you** peoples;
shout to God with loud songs · **of** joy.
For the Lord, the Most High, · **is** awesome,
a great king over · **all** the earth. R̰.

God has gone up · **with_a** shout,
the Lord with the sound of · **a** trumpet.
Sing praises to God, · **sing** praises;
sing praises to our · **King,** sing praises. R̰.

For God is the king of all · **the** earth;
sing praises · **with_a** Psalm.
God is king over · **the** nations;
God sits on his · **ho**-ly throne. R̰.

©*2009 Gordon Johnston/Novalis*

To hear the Sunday Psalms, visit www.livingwithchrist.ca.

An alternate reading follows.

SECOND READING *(Ephesians 1.17-23)*

Brothers and sisters: I pray that the God of our Lord Jesus Christ, the Father of glory, may give you a spirit of wisdom and revelation as you come to know him, so that, with the eyes of your heart enlightened, you may know what is the hope to which he has called you, what are the riches of his glorious inheritance among the saints, and what is the immeasurable greatness of his power for us who believe, according to the working of his great power.

God put this power to work in Christ when he raised him from the dead and seated him at his right hand in the heavenly places, far above all rule and authority and power and dominion, and above every name that is named, not only in this age but also in the age to come.

And he has put all things under his feet and has made him the head over all things for the Church, which is his body, the fullness of him who fills all in all.

The word of the Lord. **Thanks be to God.**

or

SECOND READING *(Ephesians 4.1-13)*

For the shorter version, omit the indented parts.

Brothers and sisters: I, the prisoner in the Lord, beg you to lead a life worthy of the calling to which you have been called, with all humility and gentleness, with patience, bearing with one another in love, making every effort to maintain the unity of the Spirit in the bond of peace.

There is one body and one Spirit, just as you were called to the one hope of your calling, one Lord, one faith, one baptism, one God and Father of all, who is above all and through all and in all. But each of us was given grace according to the measure of Christ's gift.

Therefore it is said, "When he ascended on high he made captivity itself a captive; he gave gifts to his people."

When it says, "He ascended," what does it mean but that he had also descended into the lower parts of the earth?

He who descended is the same one who ascended far above all the heavens, so that he might fill all things.

The gifts he gave were that some would be Apostles, some Prophets, some evangelists, some pastors and teachers, to equip the saints for the work of ministry, for building up the body of Christ, until all of us come to the unity of the faith and of the knowledge of the Son of God, to maturity, to the measure of the full stature of Christ.

The word of the Lord. **Thanks be to God.**

GOSPEL ACCLAMATION *(Matthew 28.19, 20)*
Alleluia. Alleluia. Go make disciples of all nations. I am with you always, to the end of the age. **Alleluia.**

GOSPEL *(Mark 16.15-20)*
The Lord be with you. **And with your spirit.**
A reading from the holy Gospel according to Mark. **Glory to you, O Lord.**

Jesus appeared to the eleven, and he said to them, "Go into all the world and proclaim the good news to the whole creation. The one who believes and is baptized will be saved; but the one who does not believe will be condemned. And these signs will accompany those who believe: by using my name they will cast out demons; they will speak in new tongues; they will pick up snakes in their hands, and if they drink any deadly thing, it will not hurt them; they will lay their hands on the sick, and they will recover."

So then the Lord Jesus, after he had spoken to them, was taken up into heaven and sat down at the right hand of God. And they went out and proclaimed the good news everywhere, while the Lord worked with them and confirmed the message by the signs that accompanied it.

The Gospel of the Lord. **Praise to you, Lord Jesus Christ.**

PROFESSION OF FAITH *(p. 11)*

PRAYER OF THE FAITHFUL

The following intentions are suggestions only. There are more suggestions at www.livingwithchrist.ca

R. **Lord, hear our prayer.**

For the Church, sent to proclaim the Good News to all, we pray to the Lord: R.

On this World Communications Day, for people in the different forms of media working to build a just society, we pray to the Lord: R.

For the sick, the dying and all who suffer, we pray to the Lord: ℟.

For mothers everywhere, nurturing the next generation, and for those who share in childrearing, we pray to the Lord: ℟.

For the members of this community, formed by our encounters with the risen Lord and sent forth to serve, we pray to the Lord: ℟.

PREPARATION OF THE GIFTS *(p. 14)*

PRAYER OVER THE OFFERINGS
We offer sacrifice now in supplication, O Lord, to honour the wondrous Ascension of your Son: grant, we pray, that through this most holy exchange we, too, may rise up to the heavenly realms. Through Christ our Lord. **Amen.**

PREFACE *(Ascension, p. 25)*

COMMUNION ANTIPHON *(Matthew 28.20)*
Behold, I am with you always, even to the end of the age, alleluia.

PRAYER AFTER COMMUNION
Almighty ever-living God, who allow those on earth to celebrate divine mysteries, grant, we pray, that Christian hope may draw us onward to where our nature is united with you. Through Christ our Lord. **Amen.**

SOLEMN BLESSING — ASCENSION *(Optional)*

Bow down for the blessing.

May almighty God bless you, for on this very day his Only Begotten Son pierced the heights of heaven and unlocked for you the way to ascend to where he is. **Amen.**

May he grant that, as Christ after his Resurrection was seen plainly by his disciples, so when he comes as Judge he may show himself merciful to you for all eternity. **Amen.**

And may you, who believe he is seated with the Father in his majesty, know with joy the fulfillment of his promise to stay with you until the end of time. **Amen.**

And may the blessing of almighty God, the Father, and the Son, and the Holy Spirit, come down on you and remain with you for ever. **Amen.**

DISMISSAL *(p. 71)*

May 20
Pentecost Sunday

In the 1950s, we said "Holy Ghost." And in school, as exam time approached, we prayed to the Holy Ghost that we might study the right stuff; then, on the day of the exam, we prayed for help to remember what we had studied. This always struck me as a trivialization of the mighty and treasured gifts of knowledge, wisdom and understanding promised on the day of my confirmation. But, being an obedient – and sometimes desperate – student, I prayed anyway; and, lo and behold, I passed!

Today, as we ponder the larger-than-usual selection of readings offered for today, we see a much richer picture of the One we now call "Holy Spirit." This Spirit has the power of wind and fire, but is conveyed on a breath. This Spirit comes bearing truth. This Spirit comes to turn societal values upside-down: self-centredness and divisions give way to love and peace.

This Spirit first came to transform and energize Jesus' followers to bear Christ's presence in and to the world – to be his body. The Spirit's work continues in the Church to this day. We feel it most at work in and among us during our Sunday celebration, praying "Grant that we, who are nourished by the Body and Blood of your Son and filled with his Holy Spirit, may become one body, one spirit in Christ."

Margaret Bick
Toronto, ON

ENTRANCE ANTIPHON *(Wisdom 1.7)*
The Spirit of the Lord has filled the whole world and that which contains all things understands what is said, alleluia.

or (Romans 5.5; cf. 8.11)
The love of God has been poured into our hearts through the Spirit of God dwelling within us, alleluia.

INTRODUCTORY RITES *(p. 5)*

COLLECT
O God, who by the mystery of today's great feast sanctify your whole Church in every people and nation, pour out, we pray, the gifts of the Holy Spirit across the face of the earth and, with the divine grace that was at work when the Gospel was first proclaimed, fill now once more the hearts of believers. Through our Lord Jesus Christ, your Son, who lives and reigns with you in the unity of the Holy Spirit, one God, for ever and ever. **Amen.**

FIRST READING *(Acts 2.1-11)*
When the day of Pentecost had come, they were all together in one place. And suddenly from heaven there came a sound like the rush of a violent wind, and it filled the entire house where they were sitting. Divided tongues, as of fire, appeared among them, and a tongue rested on each of them. All of them were filled with the Holy Spirit and began to speak in other languages, as the Spirit gave them ability.

Now there were devout Jews from every nation under heaven living in Jerusalem. And at this sound the crowd gathered and was bewildered, because each one heard them speaking in their own language. Amazed and astonished, they asked, "Are not all these who are speaking Galileans? And how is it that we hear, each of us, in our own language? Parthians, Medes, Elamites, and residents of Mesopotamia, Judea and Cappadocia, Pontus and Asia, Phrygia and Pamphylia, Egypt and the parts of Libya belonging to Cyrene, and visitors from Rome, both Jews and converts, Cretans and Arabs — in our own languages we hear them speaking about God's deeds of power."

The word of the Lord. **Thanks be to God.**

RESPONSORIAL PSALM *(Psalm 104)*

Lord, send forth your Spir - it,

and re - new the face of the earth.

℟. **Lord, send forth your Spirit,**
   and renew the face of the earth.
or **Alleluia!**

Bless the Lord, O · **my** soul.
O Lord my God, you are very · **great.**
O Lord, how manifold · **are** your works!
The earth is full of · **your** creatures. ℟.

When you take away · **their** breath,
they die and return to their · **dust.**
When you send forth your spirit, they · **are** cre-ated;
and you renew the face of · **the** earth. R.

May the glory of the Lord endure · **for**-ever;
may the Lord rejoice in his · **works.**
May my meditation be · **pleasing** to him,
for I rejoice in · **the** Lord. R.

©*2009 Gordon Johnston/Novalis*

To hear the Sunday Psalms, visit www.livingwithchrist.ca.

An alternate reading follows.

SECOND READING *(1 Corinthians 12.3b-7, 12-13)*
Brothers and sisters: No one can say "Jesus is Lord"
except by the Holy Spirit.

Now there are varieties of gifts, but the same Spirit; and there are varieties of services, but the same
Lord; and there are varieties of activities, but it is the
same God who activates all of them in everyone. To
each is given the manifestation of the Spirit for the
common good.

For just as the body is one and has many members,
and all the members of the body, though many, are
one body, so it is with Christ. For in the one Spirit
we were all baptized into one body — Jews or Greeks,
slaves or free — and we were all made to drink of
one Spirit.

The word of the Lord. **Thanks be to God.**

or

SECOND READING *(Galatians 5.16-25)*

Brothers and sisters: Live by the Spirit, I say, and do not gratify the desires of the flesh. For what the flesh desires is opposed to the Spirit, and what the Spirit desires is opposed to the flesh; for these are opposed to each other, to prevent you from doing what you want.

But if you are led by the Spirit, you are not subject to the law. Now the works of the flesh are obvious: fornication, impurity, licentiousness, idolatry, sorcery, enmities, strife, jealousy, anger, quarrels, dissensions, factions, envy, drunkenness, carousing, and things like these. I am warning you, as I warned you before: those who do such things will not inherit the kingdom of God.

By contrast, the fruit of the Spirit is love, joy, peace, patience, kindness, generosity, faithfulness, gentleness, and self-control. There is no law against such things. And those who belong to Christ Jesus have crucified the flesh with its passions and desires. If we live by the Spirit, let us also be guided by the Spirit.

The word of the Lord. Thanks be to God.

SEQUENCE

1. Ho - ly Spir - it, Lord di - vine,
2. Come, O Fa - ther of the poor,

Come from heights of heav'n and shine,
Come, whose treas - ured gifts en - sure,

Come with bless - ed ra - diance bright!
Come, our heart's un - fail - ing light!

3. Of consolers, wisest, best,
   And our soul's most welcome guest,
   Sweet refreshment, sweet repose.

4. In our labour, rest most sweet,
   Pleasant coolness in the heat,
   Consolation in our woes.

5. Light most blessed, shine with grace
   In our heart's most secret place,
   Fill your faithful through and through.

6. Left without your presence here,
   Life itself would disappear,
   Nothing thrives apart from you!

7. Cleanse our soiled hearts of sin,
   Arid souls refresh within,
   Wounded lives to health restore.

8. On the faithful who are true
   and profess their faith in you,
   In your sev'nfold gift descend!

9. Bend the stubborn heart and will,
   Melt the frozen, warm the chill,
   Guide the wayward home once more!

10. Give us virtue's sure reward,
    Give us your salvation, Lord,
    Give us joys that never end!

Text: *Veni Sancte Spiritus; tr. E. Caswell; adapt.* © *Peter J. Scagnelli.* **Tune:** © *1995 Albert Dunn*

GOSPEL ACCLAMATION

Alleluia. Alleluia. Come, Holy Spirit, fill the hearts of your faithful and kindle in them the fire of your love. **Alleluia.**

An alternate Gospel follows.

GOSPEL *(John 20.19-23)*

The Lord be with you. **And with your spirit.** A reading from the holy Gospel according to John. **Glory to you, O Lord.**

It was evening on the day Jesus rose from the dead, the first day of the week, and the doors of the house where the disciples had met were locked for fear of the Jews. Jesus came and stood among them and said, "Peace be with you." After he said this, he showed them his hands and his side. Then the disciples rejoiced when they saw the Lord.

Jesus said to them again, "Peace be with you. As the Father has sent me, so I send you."

When he had said this, he breathed on them and said to them, "Receive the Holy Spirit. If you forgive the sins of any, they are forgiven them; if you retain the sins of any, they are retained."

The Gospel of the Lord. **Praise to you, Lord Jesus Christ.**

or

GOSPEL *(John 15.26-27; 16.12-15)*
The Lord be with you. **And with your spirit.**
A reading from the holy Gospel according to John. **Glory to you, O Lord.**

Jesus said to the disciples: "When the Advocate comes, whom I will send to you from the Father, the Spirit of truth who comes from the Father, he will testify on my behalf. You also are to testify because you have been with me from the beginning.

"I still have many things to say to you, but you cannot bear them now. When the Spirit of truth comes, he will guide you into all the truth; for he will not speak on his own, but will speak whatever he hears, and he will declare to you the things that are to come. He will glorify me, because he will take what is mine and declare it to you.

"All that the Father has is mine. For this reason I said that he will take what is mine and declare it to you."

The Gospel of the Lord. **Praise to you, Lord Jesus Christ.**

PROFESSION OF FAITH *(p. 11)*

PRAYER OF THE FAITHFUL

The following intentions are suggestions only. There are more suggestions at www.livingwithchrist.ca

R. **Send forth your Spirit, O Lord.**

For wisdom and courage among leaders in the Church, addressing the needs of the suffering and forgotten, we pray to the Lord: R.

For youth, eager to be of service to their neighbour in need, we pray to the Lord: R.

For the newest members of the Church, inspiring joy and faithful witness to the mission of Jesus in the world, we pray to the Lord: R.

For ourselves, guided by the Holy Spirit to renew the face of the earth, we pray to the Lord: R.

PREPARATION OF THE GIFTS *(p. 14)*

PRAYER OVER THE OFFERINGS

Grant, we pray, O Lord, that, as promised by your Son, the Holy Spirit may reveal to us more abundantly the hidden mystery of this sacrifice and graciously lead us into all truth. Through Christ our Lord. **Amen.**

PREFACE *(Pentecost, p. 26)*

COMMUNION ANTIPHON *(Acts 2.4, 11)*
They were all filled with the Holy Spirit and spoke of the marvels of God, alleluia.

PRAYER AFTER COMMUNION

O God, who bestow heavenly gifts upon your Church, safeguard, we pray, the grace you have given, that the gift of the Holy Spirit poured out upon her may retain all its force and that this spiritual food may gain her abundance of eternal redemption. Through Christ our Lord. **Amen.**

SOLEMN BLESSING — THE HOLY SPIRIT
(Optional)

Bow down for the blessing.

May God, the Father of lights, who was pleased to enlighten the disciples' minds by the outpouring of the Spirit, the Paraclete, grant you gladness by his blessing and make you always abound with the gifts of the same Spirit. **Amen.**

May the wondrous flame that appeared above the disciples powerfully cleanse your hearts from every evil and pervade them with its purifying light. **Amen.**

And may God, who has been pleased to unite many tongues in the profession of one faith, give you perseverance in that same faith and, by believing, may you journey from hope to clear vision. **Amen.**

And may the blessing of almighty God, the Father, and the Son, and the Holy Spirit, come down on you and remain with you for ever. **Amen.**

DISMISSAL
1   Go forth, the Mass is ended, alleluia, alleluia!
2   Go in peace, alleluia, alleluia!

Thanks be to God, al-le-lu - ia, al - le - lu - ia!

R. **Thanks be to God, alleluia, alleluia!**

May 27
Trinity Sunday

Trinity Sunday is a day to reflect upon and celebrate just who our God is. God is revealed to us first and foremost as a saving God. That is what today's first reading celebrates. The Jewish people knew their God's identity because of his saving acts.

Christian belief in the Trinity was not the result of philosophical reflection on the nature of God. Rather, it developed as Christians reflected on their experience of salvation in Jesus Christ and the presence of his spirit – the spirit crying out to God, revealed by Christ as "Abba, Father" – within their very souls.

Jesus and the Holy Spirit were experienced as doing what only God can do – saving us – and so they must be divine. But good Jews knew that God is one. This is the origin of the doctrine of the Trinity.

Only later did philosophical precision give us language like "three persons," "one nature," "hypostatic union," etc. These are important to keep Christian faith from being misunderstood, but they are not the core of our faith in the Trinity. The core is that the same God who saved the Jewish people from slavery in Egypt has also saved us from slavery to sin through his Son Jesus Christ, and that we can experience that salvation even today, even at this Mass, through the ministry of their Holy Spirit.

Brett Salkeld
Regina, SK

ENTRANCE ANTIPHON
Blest be God the Father, and the Only Begotten Son of God, and also the Holy Spirit, for he has shown us his merciful love.

INTRODUCTORY RITES *(p. 5)*

COLLECT
God our Father, who by sending into the world the Word of truth and the Spirit of sanctification made known to the human race your wondrous mystery, grant us, we pray, that in professing the true faith, we may acknowledge the Trinity of eternal glory and adore your Unity, powerful in majesty. Through our Lord Jesus Christ, your Son, who lives and reigns with you in the unity of the Holy Spirit, one God, for ever and ever. **Amen.**

FIRST READING *(Deuteronomy 4.32-34, 39-40)*
Moses spoke to the people saying, "Ask now about former ages, long before your own, ever since the day that God created man on the earth; ask from one end of heaven to the other: 'Has anything so great as this ever happened or has its like ever been heard of?'

"Has any people ever heard the voice of a god speaking out of a fire, as you have heard, and lived? Or has any god ever attempted to go and take a nation for himself from the midst of another nation, by trials, by signs and wonders, by war, by a mighty hand and an outstretched arm, and by terrifying displays of power, as the Lord your God did for you in Egypt before your very eyes?

"So acknowledge today and take to heart that the Lord is God in heaven above and on the earth beneath; there is no other. Keep his statutes and his commandments, which I am commanding you today for your own well-being and that of your descendants after you, so that you may long remain in the land that the Lord your God is giving you for all time."

The word of the Lord. **Thanks be to God.**

RESPONSORIAL PSALM *(Psalm 33)*

Bless-ed the peo-ple the Lord has chos-en as his her-it-age.

R. **Blessed the people the Lord has chosen as his heritage.**

The word of the · **Lord** is upright,
and all his work is · **done** in faithfulness.
He loves · **righteousness** and justice;
the earth is full of the steadfast · **love_of** the
    Lord. R.

By the word of the Lord the · **heavens** were made,
and all their host by the breath · **of** his mouth.
For he spoke, and it · **came** to be;
he commanded, and · **it** stood firm. R.

Truly the eye of the Lord is on · **those** who fear_
   him,
on those who hope in his · **stead**-fast love,
to deliver their · **souls** from death,
and to keep them a·-**live** in famine. R̶.

Our soul waits · **for** the Lord;
he is our · **help** and shield.
Let your steadfast love, O Lord, · **be** up-on_us,
even as we · **hope** in you. R̶.

©2009 Gordon Johnston/Novalis

SECOND READING *(Romans 8.14-17)*

Brothers and sisters: All who are led by the Spirit of
God are sons and daughters of God. For you did not
receive a spirit of slavery to fall back into fear, but
you have received a spirit of adoption to sonship.
When we cry, "Abba! Father!" it is that very Spirit
bearing witness with our spirit that we are children
of God, and if children, then heirs, heirs of God and
joint heirs with Christ — if in fact, we suffer with him
so that we may also be glorified with him.
   The word of the Lord. **Thanks be to God.**

GOSPEL ACCLAMATION *(See Revelation 1.8)*

Alleluia. Alleluia. Glory to the Father, the Son, and
the Holy Spirit: to God who is, who was, and who is
to come. **Alleluia.**

GOSPEL *(Matthew 28.16-20)*

The Lord be with you. **And with your spirit.**
A reading from the holy Gospel according to Matthew. **Glory to you, O Lord.**

The eleven disciples went to Galilee, to the mountain to which Jesus had directed them. When they saw him, they worshipped him; but some doubted.

And Jesus came and said to them, "All authority in heaven and on earth has been given to me. Go therefore and make disciples of all nations, baptizing them in the name of the Father and of the Son and of the Holy Spirit, and teaching them to obey everything that I have commanded you.

"And remember, I am with you always, to the end of the age."

The Gospel of the Lord. **Praise to you, Lord Jesus Christ.**

PROFESSION OF FAITH (*p. 11*)

PRAYER OF THE FAITHFUL

The following intentions are suggestions only. There are more suggestions at www.livingwithchrist.ca

R. **Lord, hear our prayer.**

For the People of God, striving to embody the love of the Trinity, we pray to the Lord: R.

For leaders of nations, working for peace in war-torn regions of the world, we pray to the Lord: R.

For families responding to the call to be a community of God's love, we pray to the Lord: R.

For our parish community, especially in our efforts to reflect God's love, we pray to the Lord: R.

PREPARATION OF THE GIFTS (*p. 14*)

PRAYER OVER THE OFFERINGS

Sanctify by the invocation of your name, we pray, O Lord our God, this oblation of our service, and by it make of us an eternal offering to you. Through Christ our Lord. **Amen.**

PREFACE *(Trinity, p. 27)*

COMMUNION ANTIPHON *(Galatians 4.6)*

Since you are children of God, God has sent into your hearts the Spirit of his Son, the Spirit who cries out: Abba, Father.

PRAYER AFTER COMMUNION

May receiving this Sacrament, O Lord our God, bring us health of body and soul, as we confess your eternal holy Trinity and undivided Unity. Through Christ our Lord. **Amen.**

BLESSING AND DISMISSAL *(p. 71)*

June Saints' Days

The following saints are traditionally remembered in June in Canada.

1. Saint Justin
2. Saints Marcellinus and Peter
3. Saint Charles Lwanga and Companions
5. Saint Boniface
6. Saint Norbert
9. Saint Ephrem
11. Saint Barnabas
13. Saint Anthony of Padua
19. Saint Romuald
21. Saint Aloysius Gonzaga
22. Saint Paulinus of Nola
    Saints John Fisher and Thomas More
24. The Nativity of Saint John the Baptist
27. Blesseds Nykyta Budka and
    Vasyl Velychkowsky
    Saint Cyril of Alexandria
28. Saint Irenaeus
29. Saints Peter and Paul
30. The First Martyrs of the Holy Roman Church

June 3
Body and Blood of Christ

Today we celebrate the great gift that Jesus left us before ascending to his Father, the gift of his real abiding presence, and of his body and blood that we are invited to consume during the celebration of the Eucharist. What more could our God give to us? What more could we ask of our God?

Whenever we eat and drink, we are transformed. Most food is good for our body; it feeds our mind and enlivens our spirits. In fact, we feel better after we have eaten a good meal; we are full, satisfied and energized.

Unexplainable food for life, the holy bread and wine fills us though we do not know how. Relying on our faith to believe that the true presence of our God makes his home in our body, heart and soul, we come back again and again for more of this holy food. We have been invited to come, from here and from there, to eat and to drink, as one in Christ.

On this great Feast of the Body and Blood of Christ, we gather not to explain how this mystery happens, but to fall on our knees in profound adoration, to celebrate with deep joy that God is truly present to each one of us.

Fr. Matthew Durham, CSB
Windsor, ON

ENTRANCE ANTIPHON *(Cf. Psalm 80.17)*
He fed them with the finest wheat and satisfied them with honey from the rock.

INTRODUCTORY RITES *(p. 5)*

COLLECT
O God, who in this wonderful Sacrament have left us a memorial of your Passion, grant us, we pray, so to revere the sacred mysteries of your Body and Blood that we may always experience in ourselves the fruits of your redemption. Who live and reign with God the Father in the unity of the Holy Spirit, one God, for ever and ever. **Amen.**

FIRST READING *(Exodus 24.3-8)*
Moses came and told the people all the words of the Lord and all the ordinances; and all the people answered with one voice, and said, "All the words that the Lord has spoken we will do."

And Moses wrote down all the words of the Lord. He rose early in the morning, and built an altar at the foot of the mountain, and set up twelve pillars, corresponding to the twelve tribes of Israel. He sent young men of the children of Israel, who offered burnt offerings and sacrificed oxen as offerings of well-being to the Lord. Moses took half of the blood and put it in basins, and half of the blood he dashed against the altar.

Then he took the book of the covenant, and read it in the hearing of the people; and they said, "All that the Lord has spoken we will do, and we will be obedient."

Moses took the blood and dashed it on the people, and said, "See the blood of the covenant that the Lord has made with you in accordance with all these words."

The word of the Lord. **Thanks be to God.**

RESPONSORIAL PSALM *(Psalm 116)*

I will lift up the cup of sal-va-tion,

and call on the name of the Lord.

R҃. **I will lift up the cup of salvation,**
   and call on the name of the Lord.
or **Alleluia!**

What shall I return to the · **Lord**
for all his bounty to · **me?**
I will lift up the cup of sal-**vation**
and call on the name · **of_the** Lord. R҃.

Precious in the sight of the · **Lord**
is the death of his · **faithful_ones.**
O Lord, I am your servant, the son of your ·
   serving_girl.
You have loosed · **my** bonds. R҃.

I will offer to you a thanksgiving · **sacrifice**
and call on the name of the · **Lord.**
I will pay my vows to the · **Lord**
in the presence of all · **his** people. R.

©2009 Gordon Johnston/Novalis

SECOND READING (Hebrews 9.11-15)

Brothers and sisters: When Christ came as a high priest of the good things that have come, then through the greater and perfect tent — not made with hands, that is, not of this creation — he entered once for all into the Holy Place, not with the blood of goats and calves, but with his own blood, thus obtaining eternal redemption.

For if the blood of goats and bulls, with the sprinkling of the ashes of a heifer, sanctifies those who have been defiled so that their flesh is purified, how much more will the blood of Christ, who through the eternal Spirit offered himself without blemish to God, purify our conscience from dead works to worship the living God!

For this reason Christ is the mediator of a new covenant, so that those who are called may receive the promised eternal inheritance, because a death has occurred that redeems them from the transgressions under the first covenant.

The word of the Lord. **Thanks be to God.**

SEQUENCE *(Optional)*

This sequence is to be sung. The shorter version begins at the asterisks (p. 414). An earlier version of this Sequence is set to music in CBW III, 693.

1. Laud, O Sion, your salvation,
   laud with hymns of exultation
   Christ, your King and Shepherd true:
   Bring him all the praise you know,
   He is more than you bestow;
   never can you reach his due.

2. Wondrous theme for glad thanksgiving
   is the living and life-giving
   Bread today before you set,
   from his hands of old partaken,
   As we know, by faith unshaken,
   where the Twelve at supper met.

3. Full and clear ring out your chanting,
   let not joy nor grace be wanting.
   From your heart let praises burst.
   For this day the Feast is holden,
   When the institution olden
   of that Supper was rehearsed.

4. Here the new law's new oblation,
   by the new King's revelation,
   Ends the forms of ancient rite.
   Now the new the old effaces,
   Substance now the shadow chases,
   light of day dispels the night.

5. What he did at supper seated,
   Christ ordained to be repeated,
   His remembrance not to cease.
   And his rule for guidance taking,
   Bread and wine we hallow, making,
   thus, our sacrifice of peace.

6. This the truth each Christian learns:
   bread into his own flesh Christ turns,
   To his precious Blood the wine.
   Sight must fail, no thought conceives,
   But a steadfast faith believes,
   resting on a power divine.

7. Here beneath these signs are hidden
   priceless things to sense forbidden.
   Signs alone, not things, we see:
   Blood and flesh as wine, bread broken;
   Yet beneath each wondrous token,
   Christ entire we know to be.

8. All who of this great food partake,
   they sever not the Lord, nor break:
   Christ is whole to all that taste.
   Be one or be a thousand fed
   They eat alike that living Bread,
   eat of him who cannot waste.

9. Good and guilty likewise sharing,
   though their different ends preparing:
   timeless death, or blessed life.
   Life to these, to those damnation,
   Even like participation
   is with unlike outcomes rife.

10. When the sacrament is broken,
    doubt not, but believe as spoken,
    That each severed outward token
    does the very whole contain.
    None that precious gift divides,
    breaking but the sign betides.
    Jesus still the same abides,
    still unbroken he remains.

* * *

11. Hail, the food of Angels given
    to the pilgrim who has striven,
    to the child as bread from heaven,
    food alone for spirit meant:
    Now the former types fulfilling —
    Isaac bound, a victim willing,
    Paschal Lamb, its life-blood spilling,
    manna to the ancients sent.

12. Bread yourself, good Shepherd, tend us;
    Jesus, with your love befriend us.
    You refresh us and defend us;
    to your lasting goodness send us
    That the land of life we see.
    Lord, who all things both rule and know,
    who on this earth such food bestow,
    Grant that with your saints we follow
    to that banquet ever hallow,
    With them heirs and guests to be.

Text: *translation ©2009 Concacan Inc.*

GOSPEL ACCLAMATION *(John 6.51-52)*

Alleluia. Alleluia. I am the living bread that came down from heaven, says the Lord; whoever eats of this bread will live forever. **Alleluia.**

GOSPEL *(Mark 14.12-16, 22-26)*

The Lord be with you. **And with your spirit.** A reading from the holy Gospel according to Mark. **Glory to you, O Lord.**

On the first day of Unleavened Bread, when the Passover lamb is sacrificed, the disciples said to Jesus, "Where do you want us to go and make the preparations for you to eat the Passover?"

So he sent two of his disciples, saying to them, "Go into the city, and a man carrying a jar of water will meet you; follow him, and wherever he enters, say to the owner of the house, 'The Teacher asks, "Where is my guest room where I may eat the Passover with my disciples?"' He will show you a large room upstairs, furnished and ready. Make preparations for us there."

So the disciples set out and went to the city, and found everything as he had told them; and they prepared the Passover meal.

While they were eating, he took a loaf of bread, and after blessing it he broke it, gave it to them, and said, "Take; this is my Body." Then he took a cup, and after giving thanks he gave it to them, and all of them drank from it. He said to them, "This is my Blood of the covenant, which is poured out for many. Truly I tell you, I will never again drink of the fruit of the vine until that day when I drink it new in the kingdom of God."

When they had sung the hymn, they went out to the Mount of Olives.

The Gospel of the Lord. **Praise to you, Lord Jesus Christ.**

PROFESSION OF FAITH *(p. 11)*

PRAYER OF THE FAITHFUL

The following intentions are suggestions only. There are more suggestions at www.livingwithchrist.ca —

R. **Lord, hear our prayer.**

For the Church, striving to be bread for the world, we pray to the Lord: R.

For people who hunger and thirst for justice, we pray to the Lord: R.

For the sick and the dying, and for those who are lonely, we pray to the Lord: R.

For our parish community, meditating on the Word of Life and walking the path of action, we pray to the Lord: R.

PREPARATION OF THE GIFTS *(p. 14)*

PRAYER OVER THE OFFERINGS

Grant your Church, O Lord, we pray, the gifts of unity and peace, whose signs are to be seen in mystery in the offerings we here present. Through Christ our Lord. **Amen.**

PREFACE *(Holy Eucharist II-I, p. 27)*

COMMUNION ANTIPHON *(John 6.57)*

Whoever eats my flesh and drinks my blood remains in me and I in him, says the Lord.

PRAYER AFTER COMMUNION

Grant, O Lord, we pray, that we may delight for all eternity in that share in your divine life, which is foreshadowed in the present age by our reception of your precious Body and Blood. Who live and reign for ever and ever. **Amen.**

BLESSING AND DISMISSAL *(p. 71)*

June 10
10th Sunday in Ordinary Time

Today's readings are about faith and hope, virtues that are much needed in a world where people suffer the 'demons' of poverty, racial inequality, fear of strangers, or fear of anyone who is different from what is accepted as 'normal.' When our safety and security are threatened, we try to hold on desperately to what we have and what we know.

Jesus gave freedom to those oppressed by demons because he was rooted in the love of God. The Pharisees, being rooted in the letter of the law, were not able to bring freedom to those who were suffering. They sought safety in the law: it was familiar and tried. Jesus stepped outside those boundaries and turned to the indulgent love of God to free the suffering.

We, like the Pharisees, are sometimes trapped by our fears and, not being rooted in the love of God, cannot think and act as Jesus did. In order to ask critical questions about why injustice exists, or to step outside of our comfort zone to try something different to alleviate suffering, we must be rooted in God.

In today's Eucharist, let us pray for grace to be rooted in God so that we, like Jesus, can confront evil and bring freedom to those who suffer.

Anthony Chezzi
Sudbury, ON

ENTRANCE ANTIPHON *(Cf. Psalm 26.1-2)*
The Lord is my light and my salvation; whom shall
I fear? The Lord is the stronghold of my life; whom
should I dread? When those who do evil draw near,
they stumble and fall.

INTRODUCTORY RITES *(p. 5)*

COLLECT
O God, from whom all good things come, grant
that we, who call on you in our need, may at your
prompting discern what is right, and by your guidance do it. Through our Lord Jesus Christ, your Son,
who lives and reigns with you in the unity of the
Holy Spirit, one God, for ever and ever. **Amen.**

FIRST READING *(Genesis 3.8-15)*
After the woman and the man had eaten from the
tree, they heard the sound of the Lord God walking
in the garden at the time of the evening breeze, and
the man and his wife hid themselves from the presence of the Lord God among the trees of the garden.
But the Lord God called to the man, and said to him,
"Where are you?" He said, "I heard the sound of you
in the garden, and I was afraid, because I was naked;
and I hid myself." God said, "Who told you that you
were naked? Have you eaten from the tree of which
I commanded you not to eat?"

The man said, "The woman whom you gave to be
with me, she gave me fruit from the tree, and I ate."

Then the Lord God said to the woman, "What is
this that you have done?" The woman said, "The
serpent tricked me, and I ate."

The Lord God said to the serpent, "Because you have done this, cursed are you among all animals and among all wild creatures; upon your belly you shall go, and dust you shall eat all the days of your life. I will put enmity between you and the woman, and between your offspring and hers; he will strike your head, and you will strike his heel."

The word of the Lord. **Thanks be to God.**

RESPONSORIAL PSALM *(Psalm 130)*

With the Lord there is stead-fast love, and great pow'r to re-deem.

R̺. **With the Lord there is steadfast love,
and great power to redeem.**

Out of the depths I cry to you, O · **Lord.**
Lord, hear · **my** voice!
Let your ears be at-·**tentive**
to the voice of my sup-·**pli-**cations! R̺.

If you, O Lord, should mark in-·**iquities,**
Lord, who · **could** stand?
But there is forgiveness with · **you,**
so that you may be · **re-**vered. R̺.

I wait for the · **Lord,**
my soul waits, and in his word · **I** hope;
my soul waits for the · **Lord**
more than watchmen for · **the** morning. ℟.

For with the Lord there is steadfast · **love,**
and with him is great power to · **re-**deem.
It is he who will redeem · **Israel**
from all its · **in-**iquities. ℟.

©2009 Gordon Johnston/Novalis

SECOND READING *(2 Corinthians 4.13 – 5.1)*
Brothers and sisters: Just as we have the same spirit
of faith that is in accordance with Scripture — "I
believe, and so I spoke" — we also believe, and so
we speak, because we know that the one who raised
the Lord Jesus will raise us also with Jesus, and will
bring us with you into his presence. Yes, everything
is for your sake, so that grace, as it extends to more
and more people, may increase thanksgiving, to the
glory of God.

So we do not lose heart. Even though our outer
self is wasting away, our inner self is being renewed
day by day. For this slight momentary affliction is
preparing us for an eternal weight of glory beyond
all measure, because we look not at what can be seen
but at what cannot be seen; for what can be seen is
temporary, but what cannot be seen is eternal.

For we know that if the earthly tent we live in is
destroyed, we have a building from God, a house not
made with hands, eternal in the heavens.

The word of the Lord. **Thanks be to God.**

GOSPEL ACCLAMATION *(John 12.31-32)*
Alleluia. Alleluia. Now the ruler of this world will be driven out, and when I am lifted up from the earth, I will draw all people to myself. **Alleluia.**

GOSPEL *(Mark 3.20-35)*
The Lord be with you. **And with your spirit.**
A reading from the holy Gospel according to Mark.
Glory to you, O Lord.

Jesus went home and the crowd came together again, so that they could not even eat. When his family heard it, they went out to restrain him, for people were saying, "He has gone out of his mind."

And the scribes who came down from Jerusalem said, "He has Beelzebul, and by the ruler of the demons he casts out demons."

And Jesus called them to him, and spoke to them in parables, "How can Satan cast out Satan? If a kingdom is divided against itself, that kingdom cannot stand. And if a house is divided against itself, that house will not be able to stand. And if Satan has risen up against himself and is divided, he cannot stand, but his end has come. But no one can enter a strong man's house and plunder his property without first tying up the strong man; then indeed the house can be plundered.

"Truly I tell you, people will be forgiven for their sins and whatever blasphemies they utter; but whoever blasphemes against the Holy Spirit can never have forgiveness, but is guilty of an eternal sin" — for they had said, "He has an unclean spirit."

Then his mother and his brothers came; and standing outside, they sent to him and called him. A crowd was sitting around him; and they said to him, "Your mother and your brothers and sisters are outside, asking for you."

And Jesus replied, "Who are my mother and my brothers?" And looking at those who sat around him, he said, "Here are my mother and my brothers! Whoever does the will of God is my brother and sister and mother."

The Gospel of the Lord. **Praise to you, Lord Jesus Christ.**

PROFESSION OF FAITH (p. 11)

PRAYER OF THE FAITHFUL

The following intentions are suggestions only. There are more suggestions at www.livingwithchrist.ca

R. **Lord, hear our prayer.**

For the Church, a sign of God's compassion for the world, we pray to the Lord: R.

For nations and peoples seeking justice and peace, we pray to the Lord: R.

For love and forgiveness in our families, we pray to the Lord: R.

For our faith community as we strive to live with one heart, one mind and one spirit, we pray to the Lord: R.

PREPARATION OF THE GIFTS (p. 14)

PRAYER OVER THE OFFERINGS

Look kindly upon our service, O Lord, we pray, that
what we offer may be an acceptable oblation to you
and lead us to grow in charity. Through Christ our
Lord. **Amen.**

PREFACE *(Sundays in Ordinary Time, p. 29)*

COMMUNION ANTIPHON *(Psalm 17.3)*

**The Lord is my rock, my fortress, and my deliverer;
my God is my saving strength.**

or (1 John 4.16)

**God is love, and whoever abides in love abides in
God, and God in him.**

PRAYER AFTER COMMUNION

May your healing work, O Lord, free us, we pray,
from doing evil and lead us to what is right. Through
Christ our Lord. **Amen.**

BLESSING AND DISMISSAL *(p. 71)*

June 17
11th Sunday in Ordinary Time

"He explained everything in private to his disciples."

The closing words of today's Gospel capture the essence of our need for a personal and private prayer life. Everything starts to make sense when we are alone with our Lord.

Sitting quietly with Jesus, we consider the profound wisdom of his message: simply sow small seeds. Each word or action is a small seed: we have no idea when or where it will sprout and grow. We don't have to. The grain will eventually mature, ready for harvest. The tree will one day branch out, ready to support a nest.

With faith, we listen attentively as Jesus speaks to us. We ponder how and where to scatter the seeds given to us. We delight in all that is green and growing. We learn what is complete, what is now ready for harvest.

Jesus offers simple words and everyday images: trees, plants and birds. In the Eucharist, we offer bread and wine, gifts of the harvest, each offering once hidden in a very tiny seed.

As we gather in a community and receive the gift of the word, our common faith is strengthened and supported. Privately, one at a time, we receive the Lord into our very being; the harvest of grain and vine nourishing both body and soul. We come forward, with open hands, and we are blessed. We give thanks.

Brenda Merk Hildebrand
Campbell River, BC

ENTRANCE ANTIPHON *(Cf. Psalm 26.7, 9)*

O Lord, hear my voice, for I have called to you; be my help. Do not abandon or forsake me, O God, my Saviour!

INTRODUCTORY RITES *(p. 5)*

COLLECT

O God, strength of those who hope in you, graciously hear our pleas, and, since without you mortal frailty can do nothing, grant us always the help of your grace, that in following your commands we may please you by our resolve and our deeds. Through our Lord Jesus Christ, your Son, who lives and reigns with you in the unity of the Holy Spirit, one God, for ever and ever. **Amen.**

FIRST READING *(Ezekiel 17.22-24)*

Thus says the Lord God:

"I myself will take a sprig from the lofty top of a cedar; I will set it out. I will break off a tender one from the topmost of its young twigs; I myself will plant it on a high and lofty mountain.

"On the mountain height of Israel I will plant it, in order that it may produce boughs and bear fruit, and become a noble cedar. Under it every kind of bird will live; in the shade of its branches will nest winged creatures of every kind.

"All the trees of the field shall know that I am the Lord. I bring low the high tree, I make high the low tree; I dry up the green tree and make the dry tree flourish. I the Lord have spoken; I will accomplish it."

The word of the Lord. **Thanks be to God.**

RESPONSORIAL PSALM *(Psalm 92)*

Lord, it is good to give thanks to   you.

R. **Lord, it is good to give thanks to you.**

It is good to give thanks · **to** the Lord,
to sing praises to your name, · **O** Most High;
to declare your steadfast love · **in** the morning,
and your · **faithfulness** by night. R.

The righteous flourish · **like** the palm_tree,
and grow like a · **cedar** in Lebanon.
They are planted in the house · **of** the Lord;
they flourish in the · **courts_of** our God. R.

In old age they · **still_pro**-duce fruit;
they are always green and · **full** of sap,
showing that the · **Lord** is upright;
he is my rock, and there is no un-·**righteousness**
  in him. R.

©2009 Gordon Johnston/Novalis

SECOND READING *(2 Corinthians 5.6-10)*
Brothers and sisters, we are always confident, even
though we know that while we are at home in the
body we are away from the Lord — for we walk by
faith, not by sight. Yes, we do have confidence, and
we would rather be away from the body and at home
with the Lord.

So whether we are at home or away, we make it our aim to please him. For all of us must appear before the judgment seat of Christ, so that each may receive recompense for what he or she has done in the body, whether good or evil.

The word of the Lord. **Thanks be to God.**

GOSPEL ACCLAMATION

Alleluia. Alleluia. The seed is the word of God, Christ is the sower; all who come to him will live for ever. **Alleluia.**

GOSPEL (Mark 4.26-34)

The Lord be with you. **And with your spirit.** A reading from the holy Gospel according to Mark. **Glory to you, O Lord.**

Such a large crowd gathered around Jesus that he got into a boat and began to teach them using many parables.

Jesus said: "The kingdom of God is as if a man would scatter seed on the ground, and would sleep and rise night and day, and the seed would sprout and grow, without his knowing how. The earth produces of itself, first the stalk, then the head, then the full grain in the head. But when the grain is ripe, at once he goes in with the sickle, because the harvest has come."

Jesus also said, "With what can we compare the kingdom of God, or what parable will we use for it? It is like a mustard seed, which, when sown upon the ground, is the smallest of all the seeds on earth; yet when it is sown it grows up and becomes the greatest of all shrubs, and puts forth large branches, so that the birds of the air can make nests in its shade."

With many such parables Jesus spoke the word to them, as they were able to hear it; he did not speak to them except in parables, but he explained everything in private to his disciples.

The Gospel of the Lord. **Praise to you, Lord Jesus Christ.**

PROFESSION OF FAITH (p. 11)

PRAYER OF THE FAITHFUL

The following intentions are suggestions only. There are more suggestions at www.livingwithchrist.ca

R. **Lord, hear our prayer.**

For the Church, on the road to unity, we pray to the Lord: R.

For all world leaders in their commitment to peace and justice, we pray to the Lord: R.

For all who are disabled by fear, we pray to the Lord: R.

For fathers everywhere, called to model love and care, we pray to the Lord: R.

For this community, celebrating the love, joy and peace of Christ, we pray to the Lord: R.

PREPARATION OF THE GIFTS (p. 14)

PRAYER OVER THE OFFERINGS

O God, who in the offerings presented here provide for the twofold needs of human nature, nourishing us with food and renewing us with your Sacrament, grant, we pray, that the sustenance they provide may not fail us in body or in spirit. Through Christ our Lord. **Amen.**

PREFACE *(Sundays in Ordinary Time, p. 29)*

COMMUNION ANTIPHON *(Psalm 26.4)*
There is one thing I ask of the Lord, only this do I seek: to live in the house of the Lord all the days of my life.
or (John 17.11)
Holy Father, keep in your name those you have given me, that they may be one as we are one, says the Lord.

PRAYER AFTER COMMUNION

As this reception of your Holy Communion, O Lord, foreshadows the union of the faithful in you, so may it bring about unity in your Church. Through Christ our Lord. **Amen.**

BLESSING AND DISMISSAL *(p. 71)*

June 24
Nativity of Saint John the Baptist

The Church celebrates John the Baptist's natural birth by a festival of his 'nativity,' assigned exactly six months before the nativity of Christ. The fact that Christ praised John the Baptist so highly encouraged a special veneration.

Today's first reading is the second of the four "Servant of the Lord" songs of the prophet Isaiah. John was the Servant made ready and fit for the preaching of God's word. John was the sharp-edged sword who pointed out the true light to the nations, the one whose salvation would reach to the ends of the earth. Saint Paul spoke of John who heralded the Messiah's coming by proclaiming a baptism of repentance to all the people of Israel.

Because John represents the old, he is born of an elderly couple; because he represents the new, he is revealed as a prophet in his mother's womb. John's preceding Jesus was clearly fixed in the Christian tradition, so much that in two of the three Gospels that begin their story before the public ministry with Jesus' first appearance on earth, John the Baptist is brought forth to precede the appearance as well.

John always defined his humanity in terms of its limitations. He came to teach us that there is a way out of the darkness and sadness of the world and of the human condition, and that way is Jesus himself.

Fr. Thomas Rosica, CSB
Toronto, ON

ENTRANCE ANTIPHON *(John 1.6-7; Luke 1.17)*

A man was sent from God, whose name was John. He came to testify to the light, to prepare a people fit for the Lord.

INTRODUCTORY RITES *(p. 5)*

COLLECT

O God, who raised up Saint John the Baptist to make ready a nation fit for Christ the Lord, give your people, we pray, the grace of spiritual joys and direct the hearts of all the faithful into the way of salvation and peace. Through our Lord Jesus Christ, your Son, who lives and reigns with you in the unity of the Holy Spirit, one God, for ever and ever. **Amen.**

FIRST READING *(Isaiah 49.1-6)*

Listen to me, O coastlands,
pay attention, you peoples from far away!
The Lord called me before I was born,
while I was in my mother's womb he named me.

He made my mouth like a sharp sword,
in the shadow of his hand he hid me;
he made me a polished arrow,
in his quiver he hid me away.

And the Lord said to me,
"You are my servant, Israel, in whom I will be
    glorified."
But I said, "I have laboured in vain,
I have spent my strength for nothing and vanity;
yet surely my cause is with the Lord,
and my reward with my God."

And now the Lord says,
who formed me in the womb to be his servant,
to bring Jacob back to him,
and that Israel might be gathered to him,
for I am honoured in the sight of the Lord,
and my God has become my strength.

He says,
"It is too small a thing that you should be my servant
to raise up the tribes of Jacob
and to restore the survivors of Israel;
I will give you as a light to the nations,
that my salvation may reach to the end of the earth."

The word of the Lord. **Thanks be to God.**

RESPONSORIAL PSALM (Psalm 139)

I praise you, ___ for I am won-der-ful-ly made.

R. **I praise you, for I am wonderfully made.**

O Lord, you have searched me and · **known_me.**
You know when I sit down and when I · **rise** up;
you discern my thoughts from far a·-**way.**
You search out my path and my lying down,
and are acquainted with all · **my** ways. R.

For it was you who formed my inward · **parts;**
you knit me together in my · **mother's** womb.
I · **praise_you,**
for I am fearfully and · **wonderfully** made. R̟

Wonderful are your works; that I know very · **well.**
My frame was not hidden · **from** you,
when I was being made in · **secret,**
intricately woven in the depths of · **the** earth. R̟

©2009 Gordon Johnston/Novalis

SECOND READING *(Acts 13.22-26)*
In those days, Paul said: "God made David king of
our ancestors. In his testimony about him God said,
'I have found David, son of Jesse, to be a man after
my heart, who will carry out all my wishes.'

"Of this man's posterity God has brought to Israel
a Saviour, Jesus, as he promised; before his coming
John had already proclaimed a baptism of repentance to all the people of Israel. And as John was
finishing his work, he said, 'What do you suppose
that I am? I am not he. No, but one is coming after
me; I am not worthy to untie the thong of the sandals
on his feet.'

"You descendants of Abraham's family, and others who fear God, to us the message of this salvation
has been sent."

The word of the Lord. **Thanks be to God.**

GOSPEL ACCLAMATION *(Luke 1.76)*
Alleluia. Alleluia. You, child, will be called the
Prophet of the Most High; for you will go before the
Lord to prepare his ways. **Alleluia.**

GOSPEL *(Luke 1.57-66, 80)*

The Lord be with you. **And with your spirit.**
A reading from the holy Gospel according to Luke.
Glory to you, O Lord.

The time came for Elizabeth to give birth, and she bore a son. Her neighbours and relatives heard that the Lord had shown his great mercy to her, and they rejoiced with her.

On the eighth day they came to circumcise the child, and they were going to name him Zechariah after his father. But his mother said, "No; he is to be called John." They said to her, "None of your relatives has this name." Then they began motioning to his father to find out what name he wanted to give him.

He asked for a writing tablet and wrote, "His name is John." And all of them were amazed. Immediately his mouth was opened and his tongue freed, and he began to speak, praising God.

Fear came over all their neighbours, and all these things were talked about throughout the entire hill country of Judea. All who heard them pondered them and said, "What then will this child become?" For, indeed, the hand of the Lord was with him.

The child grew and became strong in spirit, and he was in the wilderness until the day he appeared publicly to Israel.

The Gospel of the Lord. **Praise to you, Lord Jesus Christ.**

PROFESSION OF FAITH *(p. 11)*

PRAYER OF THE FAITHFUL

The following intentions are suggestions only. There are more suggestions at www.livingwithchrist.ca

℟. **Lord, hear our prayer.**

For the Church, calling for lasting peace among nations, we pray to the Lord: ℟.

For world leaders in their commitment to peace and justice, we pray to the Lord: ℟.

For leaders of youth who accept the responsibility to model in faith the life of Christ, we pray to the Lord: ℟.

For parents seeking to provide love, guidance and a secure home, we pray to the Lord: ℟.

PREPARATION OF THE GIFTS *(p. 14)*

PRAYER OVER THE OFFERINGS

We place these offerings on your altar, O Lord, to celebrate with fitting honour the nativity of him who both foretold the coming of the world's Saviour and pointed him out when he came. Who lives and reigns for ever and ever. **Amen.**

PREFACE *(John the Baptist, p. 29)*

COMMUNION ANTIPHON *(Cf. Luke 1.78)*
Through the tender mercy of our God, the Dawn from on high will visit us.

PRAYER AFTER COMMUNION

Having feasted at the banquet of the heavenly Lamb, we pray, O Lord, that, finding joy in the nativity of Saint John the Baptist, your Church may know as the author of her rebirth the Christ whose coming John foretold. Who lives and reigns for ever and ever. **Amen.**

BLESSING AND DISMISSAL *(p. 71)*

July Saints' Days

The following saints are traditionally remembered in July in Canada.

3 Saint Thomas

4 Saint Elizabeth of Portugal

5 Saint Anthony Zaccaria

6 Saint Maria Goretti

9 Saint Augustine Zhao Rong
and Companions

11 Saint Benedict

13 Saint Henry

14 Saint Camillus de Lellis

15 Saint Bonaventure

16 Our Lady of Mount Carmel

20 Saint Apollinaris

21 Saint Lawrence of Brindisi

22 Saint Mary Magdalene

23 Saint Bridget

24 Saint Sharbel Makhlüf

25 Saint James

26 Saint Anne and Saint Joachim

29 Saint Martha

30 Saint Peter Chrysologus

31 Saint Ignatius of Loyola

July 1
13th Sunday in Ordinary Time
Canada Day

As I began to understand scripture, I was often struck by the many paradoxes I read. Jesus says one thing but means the opposite. He said one would find his life when he loses it. This made my head spin. What did those words mean? What was Jesus trying to teach me?

In today's Gospel, Jesus says, "Do not fear, only believe" – another paradox. He is challenging me to walk by faith, not by sight, even when I do not understand. Jesus is calling me to believe him when I am searching for and trying to find answers to my questions. I am a 'doubting Thomas' many times. I am beginning to realize that believing Jesus is not just hearing his words but absorbing them. My faith develops and grows as I gain insight from the words and example of Jesus. I begin to understand what's behind and beyond the words he proclaims. I realize there is much more than meets the eye in what Jesus is saying.

Today's Gospel clearly shows us who Jesus truly is. He is the Son of God. He could sense the "power had gone forth from him" when the hemorrhaging woman touched his garment. Yet, he was fully human – again, a paradox. Jesus is inviting and challenging us to walk in faith. May we begin to live not according to our limited view but by God's limitless possibilities.

Gerry Sobie
Nelson, BC

ENTRANCE ANTIPHON *(Psalm 46.2)*
All peoples, clap your hands. Cry to God with shouts of joy!

INTRODUCTORY RITES *(p. 5)*

COLLECT
O God, who through the grace of adoption chose us to be children of light, grant, we pray, that we may not be wrapped in the darkness of error but always be seen to stand in the bright light of truth. Through our Lord Jesus Christ, your Son, who lives and reigns with you in the unity of the Holy Spirit, one God, for ever and ever. **Amen.**

FIRST READING *(Wisdom 1.13-15; 2.23-24)*
God did not make death, and he does not delight in the death of the living. For he created all things so that they might exist; the generative forces of the world are wholesome, and there is no destructive poison in them, and the dominion of Hades is not on earth. For righteousness is immortal.

For God created man for incorruption, and made him in the image of his own eternity, but through the devil's envy death entered the world, and those who belong to his company experience it.

The word of the Lord. **Thanks be to God.**

RESPONSORIAL PSALM *(Psalm 30)*

I will ex-tol you, Lord, for you have raised me up.

R. **I will extol you, Lord, for you have raised me up.**

I will extol you, O Lord, for you have drawn
     me · **up,**
and did not let my foes rejoice · **over_me.**
O Lord, you brought up my soul from · **Sheol,**
restored me to life from among those gone down
     · **to_the** Pit. R.

Sing praises to the Lord, O you his · **faithful_ones,**
and give thanks to his holy · **name.**
For his anger is but for a moment; his favour is
     for a · **lifetime.**
Weeping may linger for the night, but joy comes
     · **with_the** morning. R.

Hear, O Lord, and be gracious to · **me!**
O Lord, be my · **helper!**
You have turned my mourning into · **dancing.**
O Lord my God, I will give thanks to you ·
     for-ever. R.

©2009 Gordon Johnston/Novalis

SECOND READING *(2 Corinthians 8.7, 9, 13-15)*
Brothers and sisters: Now as you excel in everything — in faith, in speech, in knowledge, in utmost eagerness, and in our love for you — so we want you to excel also in this generous undertaking.

For you know the generous act of our Lord Jesus Christ, that though he was rich, yet for your sakes he became poor so that by his poverty you might become rich.

I do not mean that there should be relief for others and pressure on you, but it is a question of a fair balance between your present abundance and their need, so that their abundance may be for your need, in order that there may be a fair balance.

As it is written, "The one who had much did not have too much, and the one who had little did not have too little."

The word of the Lord. **Thanks be to God.**

GOSPEL ACCLAMATION *(2 Timothy 1.10)*
Alleluia. Alleluia. Our Saviour Jesus Christ has abolished death and has brought us life through the Gospel. **Alleluia.**

GOSPEL *(Mark 5.21-43)*
For the shorter version, omit the indented parts.
The Lord be with you. **And with your spirit.**
A reading from the holy Gospel according to Mark. **Glory to you, O Lord.**

When Jesus had crossed in the boat to the other side, a great crowd gathered around him; and he was by the sea. Then one of the synagogue leaders named

Jairus came and, when he saw Jesus, fell at his feet and begged him repeatedly, "My little daughter is at the point of death. Come and lay your hands on her, so that she may be made well, and live." So Jesus went with him. And a large crowd followed him.

and pressed in on him. Now there was a woman who had been suffering from hemorrhages for twelve years. She had endured much under many physicians, and had spent all that she had; and she was no better, but rather grew worse. She had heard about Jesus, and came up behind him in the crowd and touched his cloak, for she said, "If I but touch his clothes, I will be made well." Immediately her hemorrhage stopped; and she felt in her body that she was healed of her disease.

Immediately aware that power had gone forth from him, Jesus turned about in the crowd and said, "Who touched my clothes?" And his disciples said to him, "You see the crowd pressing in on you; how can you say, 'Who touched me'?" He looked all around to see who had done it. But the woman, knowing what had happened to her, came in fear and trembling, fell down before him, and told him the whole truth. Jesus said to her, "Daughter, your faith has made you well; go in peace, and be healed of your disease." While Jesus was still speaking,

Some people came from the leader's house to say, "Your daughter is dead. Why trouble the teacher any further?" But overhearing what they said, Jesus said to the leader of the synagogue, "Do not fear, only believe."

Jesus allowed no one to follow him. When they came to the house of the leader of the synagogue, he saw a commotion, people weeping and wailing loudly. When he had entered, he said to them, "Why do you make a commotion and weep? The child is not dead but sleeping." And they laughed at him.

Then Jesus put them all outside, and took the child's father and mother and those who were with him, and went in where the child was. He took her by the hand and said to her, "Talitha cum," which means, "Little girl, get up!" And immediately the girl got up and began to walk about for she was twelve years of age.

At this they were overcome with amazement. He strictly ordered them that no one should know this, and told them to give her something to eat.

The Gospel of the Lord. **Praise to you, Lord Jesus Christ.**

PROFESSION OF FAITH (*p. 11*)

PRAYER OF THE FAITHFUL

The following intentions are suggestions only. There are more suggestions at www.livingwithchrist.ca

R. **Lord, hear our prayer.**

For the Church, embraced by Jesus' unconditional love and acceptance, we pray to the Lord: R.

For public authorities bound to protect and meet the needs of all, we pray to the Lord: R.

For all who seek equality and justice, we pray to the Lord: R.

For our community, reaching out to others with the healing touch of God, we pray to the Lord: R⁀.

PREPARATION OF THE GIFTS *(p. 14)*

PRAYER OVER THE OFFERINGS

O God, who graciously accomplish the effects of your mysteries, grant, we pray, that the deeds by which we serve you may be worthy of these sacred gifts. Through Christ our Lord. **Amen.**

PREFACE *(Sundays in Ordinary Time, p. 29)*

COMMUNION ANTIPHON *(Cf. Psalm 102.1)*

Bless the Lord, O my soul, and all within me, his holy name.

or (John 17.20-21)

O Father, I pray for them, that they may be one in us, that the world may believe that you have sent me, says the Lord.

PRAYER AFTER COMMUNION

May this divine sacrifice we have offered and received fill us with life, O Lord, we pray, so that, bound to you in lasting charity, we may bear fruit that lasts for ever. Through Christ our Lord. **Amen.**

BLESSING AND DISMISSAL *(p. 71)*

July 8
14th Sunday in Ordinary Time

In serving the Lord, we may find that we are rejected by those closest to us. We may suffer hardships for simply trying to do what is right. Jesus encourages us in these moments. He reminds us that our suffering is not meaningless. In experiencing hurt and isolation we also come to realize our own limitations, our weaknesses and our need for God's help. This is the beginning of true maturity in faith.

Like an attentive gardener, God prunes us of the need to seek the approval of others – he rids us of our pride. When we no longer are dependent on the approval of others we become freer to seek God's approval. When God's approval is what our heart seeks, we begin to see the world more for what it is, and to have an accurate understanding of our role in it.

Dependency on the approval of others is a form of pride, which distorts reality, making us less resilient. To suffer for Christ also means to be healed from our pride. We must remember that in our sufferings we remain in good company. Many of the saints suffered slander and persecution by those closest to them. Intimacy with the Lord means we will share in his suffering; but we will also share in greater freedom and ultimately – joy.

Cheridan Sanders
Toronto, ON

ENTRANCE ANTIPHON *(Cf. Psalm 47.10-11)*
Your merciful love, O God, we have received in the midst of your temple. Your praise, O God, like your name, reaches the ends of the earth; your right hand is filled with saving justice.

INTRODUCTORY RITES *(p. 5)*

COLLECT
O God, who in the abasement of your Son have raised up a fallen world, fill your faithful with holy joy, for on those you have rescued from slavery to sin you bestow eternal gladness. Through our Lord Jesus Christ, your Son, who lives and reigns with you in the unity of the Holy Spirit, one God, for ever and ever. **Amen.**

FIRST READING *(Ezekiel 2.3-5)*
A spirit entered into me and set me on my feet; and I heard one speaking to me: "Son of man, I am sending you to the children of Israel, to a nation of rebels who have rebelled against me; they and their ancestors have transgressed against me to this very day. The descendants are impudent and stubborn. I am sending you to them, and you shall say to them, 'Thus says the Lord God.' Whether they hear or refuse to hear (for they are a rebellious house), they shall know that there has been a Prophet among them."

The word of the Lord. **Thanks be to God.**

RESPONSORIAL PSALM *(Psalm 123)*

Our eyes look to the Lord, un-til he has mer-cy up-

on us.

R. **Our eyes look to the Lord,**
until he has mercy upon us.

To you I lift up my · **eyes** —
O you who are enthroned in · **the** heavens —
as the eyes of · **servants**
look to the hand of · **their** master. R.

As the eyes of a · **maid**
to the hand of · **her** mistress,
so our eyes look to the Lord our · **God**,
until he has mercy · **up**-on_us. R.

Have mercy upon us, O Lord, have · **mercy**,
for we have had more than enough of · **con**-tempt.
Our soul has had more than its fill of the · **scorn**
of those who are at ease, of the contempt of · **the**
proud. R.

©2009 Gordon Johnston/Novalis

SECOND READING *(2 Corinthians 12.7-10)*
Brothers and sisters: Considering the exceptional character of the revelations, to keep me from being too elated, a thorn was given me in the flesh, a messenger of Satan to torment me, to keep me from being too elated.

Three times I appealed to the Lord about this, that it would leave me, but he said to me, "My grace is sufficient for you, for power is made perfect in weakness."

So, I will boast all the more gladly of my weaknesses, so that the power of Christ may dwell in me. Therefore I am content with weaknesses, insults, hardships, persecutions, and calamities for the sake of Christ; for whenever I am weak, then I am strong.

The word of the Lord. **Thanks be to God.**

GOSPEL ACCLAMATION *(Luke 4.18)*
Alleluia. Alleluia. The Spirit of the Lord is upon me; he has sent me to bring good news to the poor. **Alleluia.**

GOSPEL *(Mark 6.1-6)*
The Lord be with you. **And with your spirit.** A reading from the holy Gospel according to Mark. **Glory to you, O Lord.**

Jesus came to his hometown, and his disciples followed him. On the Sabbath he began to teach in the synagogue, and many who heard him were astounded. They said, "Where did this man get all this? What is this wisdom that has been given to him? What deeds of power are being done by his hands! Is not this the carpenter, the son of Mary and brother of James and Joses and Judas and Simon, and are not his sisters here with us?" And they took offence at him.

Then Jesus said to them, "A Prophet is not without honour, except in his hometown, and among his own kin, and in his own house."

And Jesus could do no deed of power there, except that he laid his hands on a few sick people and cured them. And Jesus was amazed at their unbelief.

Then he went about among the villages teaching.

The Gospel of the Lord. **Praise to you, Lord Jesus Christ.**

PROFESSION OF FAITH (p. 11)

PRAYER OF THE FAITHFUL

The following intentions are suggestions only. There are more suggestions at www.livingwithchrist.ca

R̰. **Lord, hear our prayer.**

For the Body of Christ, called to proclaim the dignity and worth of every human being, we pray to the Lord: R̰.

For all the world's citizens, entitled to benefit from a just distribution of the planet's resources, we pray to the Lord: R̰.

For all who face challenges in their work, we pray to the Lord: R̰.

For ourselves, trusting in the Lord to help us in our efforts to live the Gospel, we pray to the Lord: R̰.

PREPARATION OF THE GIFTS (p. 14)

PRAYER OVER THE OFFERINGS

May this oblation dedicated to your name purify us, O Lord, and day by day bring our conduct closer to the life of heaven. Through Christ our Lord. **Amen.**

PREFACE *(Sundays in Ordinary Time, p. 29)*

COMMUNION ANTIPHON *(Psalm 33.9)*
Taste and see that the Lord is good; blessed the man
who seeks refuge in him.
   or (Matthew 11.28)
Come to me, all who labour and are burdened, and
I will refresh you, says the Lord.

PRAYER AFTER COMMUNION
Grant, we pray, O Lord, that, having been replenished by such great gifts, we may gain the prize of
salvation and never cease to praise you. Through
Christ our Lord. **Amen.**

BLESSING AND DISMISSAL *(p. 71)*

July 15
15th Sunday in Ordinary Time

It is frustrating to believe that you are right while no one seems to listen.

A parent can patiently point out the right direction to a teenage child who is yearning to break the yoke of blind obedience. The teen is still likely to take the wrong turn. Watching a friend make life-changing decisions that can lead to misery and ruin, you will find it impossible not to get involved and to offer advice. The warned friend will often stubbornly push ahead in the ruinous direction, showing only resentment for you and your cautionary message.

"Don't listen to me, then, you deserve whatever you get," you mutter angrily under your breath.

That is not the message that Jesus imparts to the apostles or to us as he sends us on our mission to spread the good word. We are unlikely to tell all that they should repent, cast out their demons, anoint and cure them, but the task that Jesus assigns us is not that different than his direction to the apostles.

Live simply and share the message of salvation as best you can. When that message falls on deaf ears, do not become irate and make a scene that will harden the hearts of those who refuse to listen. Shake the dust off your feet and leave the path open to try again.

Frank Campbell
Enfield, NS

ENTRANCE ANTIPHON *(Cf. Psalm 16.15)*
As for me, in justice I shall behold your face; I shall be filled with the vision of your glory.

INTRODUCTORY RITES *(p. 5)*

COLLECT
O God, who show the light of your truth to those who go astray, so that they may return to the right path, give all who for the faith they profess are accounted Christians the grace to reject whatever is contrary to the name of Christ and to strive after all that does it honour. Through our Lord Jesus Christ, your Son, who lives and reigns with you in the unity of the Holy Spirit, one God, for ever and ever. **Amen.**

FIRST READING *(Amos 7.12-15)*
Amaziah, the priest of Bethel, said to Amos, "O seer, go, flee away to the land of Judah, earn your bread there, and prophesy there; but never again prophesy at Bethel, for it is the king's sanctuary, and it is a temple of the kingdom."

Then Amos answered Amaziah, "I am no Prophet, nor a Prophet's son; but I am a herdsman, and a dresser of sycamore trees, and the Lord took me from following the flock, and the Lord said to me, 'Go, prophesy to my people Israel.'"

The word of the Lord. **Thanks be to God.**

RESPONSORIAL PSALM *(Psalm 85)*

Show us your stead - fast love, O Lord,

and grant us your sal - va - tion.

R. **Show us your steadfast love, O Lord,
and grant us your salvation.**

Let me hear what God the Lord will · **speak,**
for he will speak peace to his · **people.**
Surely his salvation is at hand for those who ·
    fear_him,
that his glory may dwell · **in_our** land. R.

Steadfast love and faithfulness will · **meet;**
righteousness and peace will · **kiss_each_other.**
Faithfulness will spring up from the · **ground,**
and righteousness will look down · **from_the**
    sky. R.

The Lord will give what is · **good,**
and our land will yield its · **increase.**
Righteousness will go be·-**fore_him,**
and will make a path · **for_his** steps. R.

©2009 Gordon Johnston/Novalis

SECOND READING *(Ephesians 1.3-14)*

The shorter version ends at the asterisks.

Blessed be the God and Father of our Lord Jesus Christ, who has blessed us in Christ with every spiritual blessing in the heavenly places, just as he chose us in Christ before the foundation of the world to be holy and blameless before him in love.

He destined us for adoption to sonship as his own through Jesus Christ, according to the good pleasure of his will, to the praise of his glorious grace that he freely bestowed on us in the Beloved.

In Christ we have redemption through his blood, the forgiveness of our trespasses, according to the riches of his grace that he lavished on us.

With all wisdom and insight God has made known to us the mystery of his will, according to his good pleasure that he set forth in Christ, as a plan for the fullness of time, to gather up all things in Christ, things in heaven and things on earth.

* * *

In Christ we have also obtained an inheritance, having been destined according to the purpose of him who accomplishes all things according to his counsel and will, so that we, who were the first to set our hope on Christ, might live for the praise of his glory.

In him you also, when you had heard the word of truth, the Gospel of your salvation, and had believed in him, were marked with the seal of the promised Holy Spirit.

This is the pledge of our inheritance toward redemption as God's own people, to the praise of his glory.

The word of the Lord. **Thanks be to God.**

GOSPEL ACCLAMATION *(See Ephesians 1.17-18)*
Alleluia. Alleluia. May the Father of our Lord Jesus
Christ enlighten the eyes of our heart that we may
know the hope to which we are called. **Alleluia.**

GOSPEL *(Mark 6.7-13)*
The Lord be with you. **And with your spirit.**
A reading from the holy Gospel according to Mark.
Glory to you, O Lord.

Jesus called the twelve and began to send them out
two by two, and gave them authority over the unclean
spirits. He ordered them to take nothing for their journey except a staff; no bread, no bag, no money in their
belts; but to wear sandals and not to put on two tunics.

Jesus said to them, "Wherever you enter a house,
stay there until you leave the place. If any place will
not welcome you and they refuse to hear you, as
you leave, shake off the dust that is on your feet as a
testimony against them."

So the twelve went out and proclaimed that all
should repent. They cast out many demons, and
anointed with oil many who were sick and cured them.

The Gospel of the Lord. **Praise to you, Lord Jesus
Christ.**

PROFESSION OF FAITH *(p. 11)*

PRAYER OF THE FAITHFUL
*The following intentions are suggestions only. There are more
suggestions at www.livingwithchrist.ca*

℟. **Lord, hear our prayer.**

For the Church, attentive to the needs of the marginalized persons in our midst, we pray to the Lord: ℟.

For leaders, heeding the cry of those who feel excluded from society, we pray to the Lord: ℟.

For the isolated of the world, especially those in institutions, hospitals or prisons, we pray to the Lord: ℟.

For this community, reaching out to those in need, we pray to the Lord: ℟.

PREPARATION OF THE GIFTS *(p. 14)*

PRAYER OVER THE OFFERINGS
Look upon the offerings of the Church, O Lord, as she makes her prayer to you, and grant that, when consumed by those who believe, they may bring ever greater holiness. Through Christ our Lord. **Amen.**

PREFACE *(Sundays in Ordinary Time, p. 29)*

COMMUNION ANTIPHON *(Cf. Psalm 83.4-5)*
The sparrow finds a home, and the swallow a nest for her young: by your altars, O Lord of hosts, my King and my God. Blessed are they who dwell in your house, for ever singing your praise.
or (John 6.57)
Whoever eats my flesh and drinks my blood remains in me and I in him, says the Lord.

PRAYER AFTER COMMUNION
Having consumed these gifts, we pray, O Lord, that, by our participation in this mystery, its saving effects upon us may grow. Through Christ our Lord. **Amen.**

BLESSING AND DISMISSAL *(p. 71)*

July 22
16th Sunday in Ordinary Time

Today we hear the beloved twenty-third psalm, "The Lord is my Shepherd." On my desk, I have a memorial card with this psalm and some pictures from the life of Melvin, a member of L'Arche Toronto for 33 years. In L'Arche, we normally conclude dinner by reciting the Lord's Prayer, but Melvin was Jewish and his housemates chose to stand with him in solidarity by reciting this psalm that Melvin loved.

Melvin had an intellectual disability. He also had the heart of a shepherd. He discovered his longing to help people who are poor when serving meals at the Good Shepherd refuge. He worked daily for many years at the food bank, travelling by bus and subway each way. People there loved him for his kindness and humour.

What does it mean to declare that the Lord is our Shepherd and we shall lack nothing? Is it true, or are these just beautiful words? Of course we will lack at times, perhaps desperately. In today's Gospel, Jesus and his followers badly needed a rest, but Jesus finds the compassion to teach the crowd. The answer is that even at such times, when God feeds us and leads us by still waters in our innermost being, it may take us some time to discover and trust this. Let us give thanks for God's faithfulness.

Beth Porter
Richmond Hill, ON

ENTRANCE ANTIPHON *(Psalm 53.6, 8)*
See, I have God for my help. The Lord sustains my soul. I will sacrifice to you with willing heart, and praise your name, O Lord, for it is good.

INTRODUCTORY RITES *(p. 5)*

COLLECT
Show favour, O Lord, to your servants and mercifully increase the gifts of your grace, that, made fervent in hope, faith and charity, they may be ever watchful in keeping your commands. Through our Lord Jesus Christ, your Son, who lives and reigns with you in the unity of the Holy Spirit, one God, for ever and ever. **Amen**.

FIRST READING *(Jeremiah 23.1-6)*
"Woe to the shepherds who destroy and scatter the sheep of my pasture!" says the Lord. Therefore, thus says the Lord, the God of Israel, concerning the shepherds who shepherd my people: It is you who have scattered my flock, and have driven them away, and you have not attended to them.

"So I will attend to you for your evil doings," says the Lord. "Then I myself will gather the remnant of my flock out of all the lands where I have driven them, and I will bring them back to their fold, and they shall be fruitful and multiply. I will raise up shepherds over them who will shepherd them, and they shall not fear any longer, or be dismayed, nor shall any be missing," says the Lord.

"The days are surely coming," says the Lord, "when I will raise up for David a righteous Branch, and he shall reign as king and deal wisely, and shall execute justice and righteousness in the land. In his days Judah will be saved and Israel will live in safety. And this is the name by which he will be called: "The Lord is our righteousness.'"

The word of the Lord. **Thanks be to God.**

RESPONSORIAL PSALM *(Psalm 23)*

The Lord is my shep-herd; I shall not want.

R. **The Lord is my shepherd; I shall not want.**

The Lord is my shepherd, I shall · **not** want.
He makes me lie down in · **green** pastures;
he leads me be-·side still waters;
he re-·**stores** my soul. R.

He leads me in right paths for his · **name's** sake.
Even though I walk through the darkest valley,
    I fear · **no** evil;
for · **you** are with_me;
your rod and your · **staff** — they comfort_me. R.

You prepare a table · **be**-fore_me
in the presence · **of_my** enemies;
you anoint my · **head** with oil;
my · **cup** over-flows. R.

Surely goodness and mercy · **shall** follow_me
all the days of · **my** life,
and I shall dwell in the · **house_of** the Lord
my · **whole** life long. ℟.

©2009 Gordon Johnston/Novalis

SECOND READING (Ephesians 2.13-18)

Brothers and sisters: Now in Christ Jesus you who once were far off have been brought near by the blood of Christ. For he is our peace; in his flesh he has made both Jews and Gentiles into one and has broken down the dividing wall, that is, the hostility between us.

He has abolished the law with its commandments and ordinances, that he might create in himself one New Man in place of the two, thus making peace, and might reconcile both groups to God in one body through the Cross, thus putting to death that hostility through it.

So Christ Jesus came and proclaimed peace to you who were far off and peace to those who were near; for through him both of us have access in one Spirit to the Father.

The word of the Lord. **Thanks be to God.**

GOSPEL ACCLAMATION (John 10.27)

Alleluia. Alleluia. My sheep hear my voice, says the Lord; I know them, and they follow me. **Alleluia.**

GOSPEL (Mark 6.30-34)

The Lord be with you. **And with your spirit.**
A reading from the holy Gospel according to Mark.
Glory to you, O Lord.

The Apostles returned from their mission. They gathered around Jesus, and told him all that they had done and taught.

He said to them, "Come away to a deserted place all by yourselves and rest a while." For many were coming and going, and they had no leisure even to eat. And they went away in the boat to a deserted place by themselves.

Now many saw them going and recognized them, and they hurried there on foot from all the towns and arrived ahead of them. As Jesus went ashore, he saw a great crowd; and he had compassion for them, because they were like sheep without a shepherd; and he began to teach them many things.

The Gospel of the Lord. **Praise to you, Lord Jesus Christ.**

PROFESSION OF FAITH (p. 11)

PRAYER OF THE FAITHFUL

The following intentions are suggestions only. There are more suggestions at www.livingwithchrist.ca

R. **Lord, hear our prayer.**

For the Church, a sign of Christ's compassion for the world, we pray to the Lord: R.

For public leaders working for justice and peace, we pray to the Lord: R.

For those who are sick, suffering or lonely, we pray to the Lord: R.

For the compassionate witness of this faith community, we pray to the Lord: R.

PREPARATION OF THE GIFTS *(p. 14)*

PRAYER OVER THE OFFERINGS

O God, who in the one perfect sacrifice brought to completion varied offerings of the law, accept, we pray, this sacrifice from your faithful servants and make it holy, as you blessed the gifts of Abel, so that what each has offered to the honour of your majesty may benefit the salvation of all. Through Christ our Lord. **Amen.**

PREFACE *(Sundays in Ordinary Time, p. 29)*

COMMUNION ANTIPHON *(Psalm 110.4-5)*

The Lord, the gracious, the merciful, has made a memorial of his wonders; he gives food to those who fear him.

or (Revelation 3.20)

Behold, I stand at the door and knock, says the Lord. If anyone hears my voice and opens the door to me, I will enter his house and dine with him, and he with me.

PRAYER AFTER COMMUNION

Graciously be present to your people, we pray, O Lord, and lead those you have imbued with heavenly mysteries to pass from former ways to newness of life. Through Christ our Lord. **Amen.**

BLESSING AND DISMISSAL *(p. 71)*

July 29
17th Sunday in Ordinary Time

In today's Gospel, Our Lord demonstrates his great compassion for us. Having created us to be both material and spiritual in nature, he knows intimately the needs of both our bodies and souls.

We hear that a great crowd was following him. He fed their souls by giving them hope. As the most perfect parent, however, he also cared for their bodies, feeding them with miraculous, overflowing generosity. "You open your hand to feed us, Lord; you satisfy all our needs."

He proves that his love for us is not just a theory, but also something tangible. What did the people in the crowd do to receive Jesus' generosity? They followed him closely and gave him all they had: five loaves and two fishes. No doubt this humble offering seemed woefully inadequate, but they brought it nonetheless. Jesus transformed it beyond all expectations.

Let us therefore always remember to stay close to him, to completely trust him, and to give him everything we have, even if it is very humble. He is the One who cares for us more than we can imagine. He takes five loaves and two fishes and turns them into a banquet. With the psalmist we acclaim: "All your works shall give thanks to you, O Lord, and all your faithful shall bless you."

Natalia Ljahovic
Mississauga, ON

ENTRANCE ANTIPHON *(Cf. Psalm 67.6-7, 36)*
God is in his holy place, God who unites those
who dwell in his house; he himself gives might and
strength to his people.

INTRODUCTORY RITES *(p. 5)*

COLLECT
O God, protector of those who hope in you, without
whom nothing has firm foundation, nothing is holy,
bestow in abundance your mercy upon us and grant
that, with you as our ruler and guide, we may use
the good things that pass in such a way as to hold
fast even now to those that ever endure. Through our
Lord Jesus Christ, your Son, who lives and reigns
with you in the unity of the Holy Spirit, one God,
for ever and ever. **Amen.**

FIRST READING *(2 Kings 4.42-44)*
A man came bringing food from the first fruits to
Elisha, the man of God: twenty loaves of barley and
fresh ears of grain in his sack. Elisha said, "Give it
to the people and let them eat."

But his servant said, "How can I set this before a
hundred people?" So Elisha repeated, "Give it to the
people and let them eat, for thus says the Lord, 'They
shall eat and have some left.'"

The servant set it before them, they ate, and had
some left, according to the word of the Lord.

The word of the Lord. **Thanks be to God.**

RESPONSORIAL PSALM *(Psalm 145)*

You o-pen your hand to feed us, Lord;
you sat-is-fy all our needs.

R. **You open your hand to feed us, Lord;
you satisfy all our needs.**

All your works shall give thanks to you, O · **Lord,**
and all your faithful shall · **bless_you.**
They shall speak of the glory of your · **kingdom,**
and tell of · **your** power. R.

The eyes of all look to · **you,**
and you give them their food in due · **season.**
You open your · **hand,**
satisfying the desire of every · **living** thing. R.

The Lord is just in all his · **ways,**
and kind in all his · **doings.**
The Lord is near to all who · **call_on_him,**
to all who call on him · **in** truth. R.

©2009 Gordon Johnston/Novalis

SECOND READING *(Ephesians 4.1-6)*

Brothers and sisters: I, the prisoner in the Lord, beg
you to lead a life worthy of the calling to which you
have been called, with all humility and gentleness,

with patience, bearing with one another in love, making every effort to maintain the unity of the Spirit in the bond of peace.

There is one body and one Spirit, just as you were called to the one hope of your calling, one Lord, one faith, one baptism, one God and Father of all, who is above all and through all and in all.

The word of the Lord. **Thanks be to God.**

GOSPEL ACCLAMATION (Luke 7.16)

Alleluia. Alleluia. A great Prophet has risen among us; God has looked favourably on his people. **Alleluia.**

GOSPEL (John 6.1-15)

The Lord be with you. **And with your spirit.** A reading from the holy Gospel according to John. **Glory to you, O Lord.**

Jesus went to the other side of the Sea of Galilee, also called the Sea of Tiberias. A large crowd kept following him, because they saw the signs that he was doing for the sick. Jesus went up the mountain and sat down there with his disciples. Now the Passover, the festival of the Jews, was near.

When he looked up and saw a large crowd coming toward him, Jesus said to Philip, "Where are we to buy bread for these people to eat?" He said this to test him, for he himself knew what he was going to do. Philip answered him, "Six months' wages would not buy enough bread for each of them to get a little."

One of his disciples, Andrew, Simon Peter's brother, said to Jesus, "There is a boy here who has five barley loaves and two fish. But what are they among so many people?" Jesus said, "Make the people sit down." Now there was a great deal of grass in the place; so they sat down, about five thousand in all.

Then Jesus took the loaves, and when he had given thanks, he distributed them to those who were seated; so also the fish, as much as they wanted. When they were satisfied, he told his disciples, "Gather up the fragments left over, so that nothing may be lost." So they gathered them up, and from the fragments of the five barley loaves, left by those who had eaten, they filled twelve baskets.

When the people saw the sign that he had done, they began to say, "This is indeed the Prophet who is to come into the world." When Jesus realized that they were about to come and take him by force to make him king, he withdrew again to the mountain by himself.

The Gospel of the Lord. **Praise to you, Lord Jesus Christ.**

PROFESSION OF FAITH *(p. 11)*

PRAYER OF THE FAITHFUL

The following intentions are suggestions only. There are more suggestions at www.livingwithchrist.ca

R̰. **Lord, hear our prayer.**

For the Church, embodying Christ's ministry of sharing and service, we pray to the Lord: R̰.

For young people discerning their vocation, we pray to the Lord: R̰.

For all those who hunger for food — food for the body, for the mind and for the soul, we pray to the Lord: R.

For this community, called to share our bread with others, we pray to the Lord: R.

PREPARATION OF THE GIFTS *(p. 14)*

PRAYER OVER THE OFFERINGS

Accept, O Lord, we pray, the offerings which we bring from the abundance of your gifts, that through the powerful working of your grace these most sacred mysteries may sanctify our present way of life and lead us to eternal gladness. Through Christ our Lord. **Amen.**

PREFACE *(Sundays in Ordinary Time, p. 29)*

COMMUNION ANTIPHON *(Psalm 102.2)*
Bless the Lord, O my soul, and never forget all his benefits.
or (Matthew 5.7-8)
Blessed are the merciful, for they shall receive mercy. Blessed are the clean of heart, for they shall see God.

PRAYER AFTER COMMUNION

We have consumed, O Lord, this divine Sacrament, the perpetual memorial of the Passion of your Son; grant, we pray, that this gift, which he himself gave us with love beyond all telling, may profit us for salvation. Through Christ our Lord. **Amen.**

BLESSING AND DISMISSAL *(p. 71)*

August Saints' Days

The following saints are traditionally remembered in August in Canada.

1 Saint Alphonsus Liguori
2 Saint Eusebius of Vercelli
   Saint Peter Julian Eymard
4 Saint John Mary Vianney
5 Blessed Frédéric Janssoone
7 Saint Sixtus II and Companions
   Saint Cajetan
8 Saint Dominic
9 Saint Teresa Benedicta of the Cross
10 Saint Lawrence
11 Saint Clare
12 Saint Jane Frances de Chantal
13 Saints Pontian and Hippolytus
14 Saint Maximilian Kolbe
16 Saint Stephen of Hungary
19 Saint John Eudes
20 Saint Bernard
21 Saint Pius X
23 Saint Rose of Lima
24 Saint Bartholomew
25 Saint Louis
   Saint Joseph Calasanz
27 Saint Monica
28 Saint Augustine

August 5
18th Sunday in Ordinary Time

I remember my difficult, three-day ski mountaineering trek with a friend where we encountered many challenges. First we used up our food supply sooner than expected. Then, on the third day, carrying a heavy pack and skiing our way back to our starting point, we stopped at lunchtime and the only thing we had left to eat was a sweet pudding powder. I experience a sugar rush but, half an hour later, I was just as famished as before.

What do we really feed on? Success? Being accepted by others? Perfectionism? Financial security? Status? These things may give us a "sugar rush" but they leave us just as famished as before. Today's Gospel invites us to seek what nourishes us, to strive after "the bread of God... [which] gives life to the world."

This life-giving food is a free gift. But how do we access this gift? Jesus tells each one of us today, "Whoever comes to me will never be hungry." Every day, as we grow in our personal relationship with the Lord, the words of the psalm can ring true for each one of us. The Lord wants to give us "food in abundance" so that we can proclaim the "glorious deeds of the Lord" in our daily lives.

Emmanuel Martel
Ottawa, ON

ENTRANCE ANTIPHON *(Psalm 69.2, 6)*
O God, come to my assistance; O Lord, make haste
to help me! You are my rescuer, my help; O Lord,
do not delay.

INTRODUCTORY RITES *(p. 5)*

COLLECT
Draw near to your servants, O Lord, and answer their
prayers with unceasing kindness, that, for those who
glory in you as their Creator and guide, you may restore what you have created and keep safe what you
have restored. Through our Lord Jesus Christ, your
Son, who lives and reigns with you in the unity of
the Holy Spirit, one God, for ever and ever. **Amen.**

FIRST READING *(Exodus 16.2-4, 12-15, 31a)*
The whole congregation of the children of Israel
complained against Moses and Aaron in the wilderness. The children of Israel said to them, "If only we
had died by the hand of the Lord in the land of Egypt,
when we sat by the fleshpots and ate our fill of bread;
for you have brought us out into this wilderness to
kill this whole assembly with hunger."

Then the Lord said to Moses, "I am going to rain
bread from heaven for you, and each day the people
shall go out and gather enough for that day. In that
way I will test them, whether they will follow my
instruction or not.

"I have heard the complaining of the children of
Israel; say to them, 'At twilight you shall eat meat,
and in the morning you shall have your fill of bread;
then you shall know that I am the Lord your God.'"

In the evening quails came up and covered the camp; and in the morning there was a layer of dew around the camp. When the layer of dew lifted, there on the surface of the wilderness was a fine flaky substance, as fine as frost on the ground.

When the children of Israel saw it, they said to one another, "What is it?" For they did not know what it was. Moses said to them, "It is the bread that the Lord has given you to eat."

The house of Israel called it manna.

The word of the Lord. **Thanks be to God.**

RESPONSORIAL PSALM *(Psalm 78)*

The Lord gave them the bread of heav-en.

R. **The Lord gave them the bread of heaven.**

Things that we have heard and known, that our
    ancestors have · **told_us,**
we will not · **hide;**
we will tell to the coming generation the glorious
    deeds of the Lord, and · **his** might,
and the wonders that he has · **done.** R.

He commanded the skies a·-**bove,**
and opened the doors of · **heaven;**
he rained down on them manna · **to** eat,
and gave them the bread of · **heaven.** R.

Man ate of the bread of · **Angels;**
he sent them food in a-·**bundance.**
And he brought them to his · **holy** hill,
to the mountain that his right hand had · **won.** R.

©2009 Gordon Johnston/Novalis

SECOND READING *(Ephesians 4.17, 20-24)*

Brothers and sisters: Now this I affirm and insist on in the Lord: you must no longer live as the Gentiles live, in the futility of their minds.

That is not the way you learned Christ! For surely you have heard about him and were taught in him, as truth is in Jesus.

You were taught to put away your former way of life, your old self, corrupt and deluded by its lusts, and to be renewed in the spirit of your minds, and to clothe yourselves with the New Man, created according to the likeness of God in true righteousness and holiness.

The word of the Lord. **Thanks be to God.**

GOSPEL ACCLAMATION *(Matthew 4.4)*

Alleluia. Alleluia. Man does not live by bread alone, but by every word that comes from the mouth of God. **Alleluia.**

GOSPEL *(John 6.24-35)*

The Lord be with you. **And with your spirit.**
A reading from the holy Gospel according to John.
Glory to you, O Lord.

When the crowd saw that neither Jesus nor his disciples were at the place where Jesus had given the bread, they themselves got into the boats and went to Capernaum looking for Jesus.

When they found him on the other side of the sea, they said to him, "Rabbi, when did you come here?" Jesus answered them, "Very truly, I tell you, you are looking for me, not because you saw signs, but because you ate your fill of the loaves. Do not work for the food that perishes, but for the food that endures for eternal life, which the Son of Man will give you. For it is on him that God the Father has set his seal."

Then they said to Jesus, "What must we do to perform the works of God?" Jesus answered them, "This is the work of God, that you believe in him whom he has sent." So they said to him, "What sign are you going to give us then, so that we may see it and believe you? What work are you performing? Our ancestors ate the manna in the wilderness; as it is written, 'He gave them bread from heaven to eat.'"

Then Jesus said to them, "Very truly, I tell you, it was not Moses who gave you the bread from heaven, but it is my Father who gives you the true bread from heaven. For the bread of God is that which comes down from heaven and gives life to the world."

They said to him, "Sir, give us this bread always." Jesus said to them, "I am the bread of life. Whoever comes to me will never be hungry, and whoever believes in me will never be thirsty."

The Gospel of the Lord. **Praise to you, Lord Jesus Christ.**

PROFESSION OF FAITH *(p. 11)*

PRAYER OF THE FAITHFUL

The following intentions are suggestions only. There are more suggestions at www.livingwithchrist.ca

R. **Lord, hear our prayer.**

For the Church, joyful witness to the Resurrection of Christ, we pray to the Lord: R.

For civic leaders, working for the true good of all their people, we pray to the Lord: R.

For all who hunger and thirst for acceptance, we pray to the Lord: R.

For Christian communities everywhere, embodying the triumph of life over death, we pray to the Lord: R.

PREPARATION OF THE GIFTS *(p. 14)*

PRAYER OVER THE OFFERINGS

Graciously sanctify these gifts, O Lord, we pray, and, accepting the oblation of this spiritual sacrifice, make of us an eternal offering to you. Through Christ our Lord. **Amen.**

PREFACE *(Sundays in Ordinary Time, p. 29)*

COMMUNION ANTIPHON *(Wisdom 16.20)*

You have given us, O Lord, bread from heaven, endowed with all delights and sweetness in every taste.
    or (John 6.35)
I am the bread of life, says the Lord; whoever comes to me will not hunger and whoever believes in me will not thirst.

PRAYER AFTER COMMUNION

Accompany with constant protection, O Lord, those you renew with these heavenly gifts and, in your never-failing care for them, make them worthy of eternal redemption. Through Christ our Lord. **Amen.**

BLESSING AND DISMISSAL *(p. 71)*

August 12
19th Sunday in Ordinary Time

We live in a world where suffering manifests itself in many ways, including the hunger for necessities like food, shelter, and work. Our suffering and hunger are not only material but also spiritual. Today's Gospel recounts the doubts the Jews had upon hearing Jesus' testimony: being the bread of life for those who believe in him. While the physical and superficial define many aspects of our lives, this Gospel and the readings inspire us to reflect on whether temporary fixes will truly satisfy our hunger and suffering. We need our faith in God, our refuge and redemption, to ultimately feed and sustain us on our journey to be with him in heaven.

Jesus highlights the power of faith that nourishes beyond the material sense of manna, provided by God as bread from heaven that sustained the Israelites in the wilderness. Jesus offers himself as the true manna, the Eucharist being the foundation of our spiritual life. He reveals that those who believe in him and take the Eucharist as the living bread will transcend the suffering in this world and live on with him in eternal life.

Even with our struggles and broken hearts, may we find the nourishment, faith and hope in true manna – Jesus and his promise of salvation.

Christl Dabu
Hamilton, ON

ENTRANCE ANTIPHON *(Cf. Psalm 73.20, 19, 22, 23)*
Look to your covenant, O Lord, and forget not the life of your poor ones for ever. Arise, O God, and defend your cause, and forget not the cries of those who seek you.

INTRODUCTORY RITES *(p. 5)*

COLLECT
Almighty ever-living God, whom, taught by the Holy Spirit, we dare to call our Father, bring, we pray, to perfection in our hearts the spirit of adoption as your sons and daughters, that we may merit to enter into the inheritance which you have promised. Through our Lord Jesus Christ, your Son, who lives and reigns with you in the unity of the Holy Spirit, one God, for ever and ever. **Amen.**

FIRST READING *(1 Kings 19.4-8)*
Elijah went a day's journey into the wilderness, and came and sat down under a solitary broom tree. He asked that he might die: "It is enough; now, O Lord, take away my life, for I am no better than my ancestors."

Then Elijah lay down under the broom tree and fell asleep. Suddenly an Angel touched him and said to him, "Get up and eat." He looked, and there at his head was a cake baked on hot stones, and a jar of water. He ate and drank, and lay down again.

The Angel of the Lord came a second time, touched him, and said, "Get up and eat, otherwise the journey will be too much for you." Elijah got up, and ate and drank; then he went in the strength of that food forty days and forty nights to Horeb the mountain of God.

The word of the Lord. **Thanks be to God.**

RESPONSORIAL PSALM *(Psalm 34)*

Taste and see that the Lord is good.

℟. **Taste and see that the Lord is good.**

I will bless the Lord at all · **times;**
his praise shall continually be in · **my** mouth.
My soul makes its boast in the · **Lord;**
let the humble hear and · **be** glad. ℟.

O magnify the Lord with · **me,**
and let us exalt his name · **to**-gether.
I sought the Lord, and he · **answered_me,**
and delivered me from all · **my** fears. ℟.

Look to him, and be · **radiant;**
so your faces shall never · **be_a**-shamed.
The poor one called, and the Lord · **heard,**
and saved that person from ev-**ery** trouble. ℟.

The Angel of the Lord en-**camps**
around those who fear him, and · **de**-livers_them.
O taste and see that the Lord is · **good;**
blessed is the one who takes refuge · **in** him. ℟.

©2009 Gordon Johnston/Novalis

SECOND READING *(Ephesians 4.30 – 5.2)*
Brothers and sisters: Do not grieve the Holy Spirit of God, with which you were marked with a seal for the day of redemption. Put away from you all bitterness and wrath and anger and wrangling and slander, together with all malice, and be kind to one another, tender-hearted, forgiving one another, as God in Christ has forgiven you.

Therefore be imitators of God, as beloved children, and live in love, as Christ loved us and gave himself up for us, a fragrant offering and sacrifice to God.

The word of the Lord. **Thanks be to God.**

GOSPEL ACCLAMATION *(John 6.51)*
Alleluia. Alleluia. I am the living bread that came down from heaven, says the Lord; whoever eats of this bread will live for ever. **Alleluia.**

GOSPEL *(John 6.41-51)*
The Lord be with you. **And with your spirit.**
A reading from the holy Gospel according to John. **Glory to you, O Lord.**

The people began to complain about Jesus because he said, "I am the bread that came down from heaven." They were saying, "Is not this Jesus, the son of Joseph, whose father and mother we know? How can he now say, 'I have come down from heaven'?"

Jesus answered them, "Do not complain among yourselves. No one can come to me unless the Father who sent me draw them; and I will raise that person up on the last day. It is written in the Prophets, 'And they shall all be taught by God.' Everyone who has heard and learned from the Father comes to me. Not that anyone has seen the Father except the one who is from God; he has seen the Father. Very truly, I tell you, whoever believes has eternal life.

"I am the bread of life. Your ancestors ate the manna in the wilderness, and they died. This is the bread that comes down from heaven, so that one may eat of it and not die. I am the living bread that came down from heaven. Whoever eats of this bread will live forever; and the bread that I will give for the life of the world is my flesh."

The Gospel of the Lord. **Praise to you, Lord Jesus Christ.**

PROFESSION OF FAITH (p. 11)

PRAYER OF THE FAITHFUL

The following intentions are suggestions only. There are more suggestions at www.livingwithchrist.ca

R. **Lord, hear our prayer.**

For the Church, called to celebrate healing and sustenance through the Eucharist, we pray to the Lord: R.

For leaders working to establish unity and peace among nations and peoples, we pray to the Lord: R.

For people suffering from mental and emotional distress, we pray to the Lord: R.

For our worshipping community gathered here today, we pray to the Lord: R.

PREPARATION OF THE GIFTS (p. 14)

PRAYER OVER THE OFFERINGS
Be pleased, O Lord, to accept the offerings of your Church, for in your mercy you have given them to be offered and by your power you transform them into the mystery of our salvation. Through Christ our Lord. **Amen.**

PREFACE (Sundays in Ordinary Time, p. 29)

COMMUNION ANTIPHON (Psalm 147.12, 14)
O Jerusalem, glorify the Lord, who gives you your fill of finest wheat.
   or (Cf. John 6.51)
The bread that I will give, says the Lord, is my flesh for the life of the world.

PRAYER AFTER COMMUNION
May the communion in your Sacrament that we have consumed, save us, O Lord, and confirm us in the light of your truth. Through Christ our Lord. **Amen.**

BLESSING AND DISMISSAL (p. 71)

August 19
20th Sunday in Ordinary Time

Today's readings invite us to consider the parallel paradoxes and promises of our faith: wisdom and foolishness, eating and being satisfied, boasting and humility, fear and courage, dying and living forever, eating Jesus' flesh and blood for salvation.

We die in order to live. We surrender to suffering in order to lessen the hold our pain has on us. We give in to the common good to be free as individuals. We lay aside our childish desires so as to become adults who can revel in the joy and gift of mature insight into our own condition.

I remember when my first child was about eight months old and was 'helping' me with the laundry. As soon as I folded a shirt or towel, Grace pulled it out and 'folded' it again. I was beginning to get frustrated and wondered if I should leave it until she was asleep. I looked at her face shining with joy and purpose and at once I realized that the joy, the loving, and the wisdom was in the fun and the mess. This was surely the bread and wine, the flesh and blood of mothering. And so, gradually, I learned to drink and eat of it and live. Today, I pray that we all have the eyes to see these moments of invitation and accept them.

Maureen Wicken
Vancouver, BC

ENTRANCE ANTIPHON *(Psalm 83.10-11)*
Turn your eyes, O God, our shield; and look on the face of your anointed one; one day within your courts is better than a thousand elsewhere.

INTRODUCTORY RITES *(p. 5)*

COLLECT
O God, who have prepared for those who love you good things which no eye can see, fill our hearts, we pray, with the warmth of your love, so that, loving you in all things and above all things, we may attain your promises, which surpass every human desire. Through our Lord Jesus Christ, your Son, who lives and reigns with you in the unity of the Holy Spirit, one God, for ever and ever. **Amen.**

FIRST READING *(Proverbs 9.1-6)*
Wisdom has built her house,
she has hewn her seven pillars.
She has slaughtered her animals,
she has mixed her wine,
she has also set her table.
She has sent out her servant girls,
she calls from the highest places in the town,
"You that are simple, turn in here!"

To those without sense she says,
"Come, eat of my bread
and drink of the wine I have mixed.
Lay aside immaturity, and live,
and walk in the way of insight."

The word of the Lord. **Thanks be to God.**

RESPONSORIAL PSALM *(Psalm 34)*

Taste and see that the Lord is good.

R̶. **Taste and see that the Lord is good.**

I will bless the Lord at all · **times;**
his praise shall continually be in · **my** mouth.
My soul makes its boast in the · **Lord;**
let the humble hear and · **be** glad. R̶.

O fear the Lord, you his · **holy_ones,**
for those who fear him have · **no** want.
The young lions suffer want and · **hunger,**
but those who seek the Lord lack no · **good**
    thing. R̶.

Come, O children, · **listen_to_me;**
I will teach you the fear of · **the** Lord.
Which of you desires · **life,**
and covets many days to en·-**joy** good? R̶.

Keep your tongue from · **evil,**
and your lips from speaking · **de**-ceit.
Depart from evil, and do · **good;**
seek peace, and · **pur**-sue_it. R̶.

©2009 Gordon Johnston/Novalis

SECOND READING *(Ephesians 5.15-20)*

Brothers and sisters, be careful how you live, not as unwise people but as wise, making the most of the time, because the days are evil. So do not be foolish, but understand what the will of the Lord is.

Do not get drunk with wine, for that is debauchery; but be filled with the Spirit, as you sing Psalms and hymns and spiritual songs among yourselves, singing and making music to the Lord in your hearts, giving thanks to God the Father at all times and for everything in the name of our Lord Jesus Christ.

The word of the Lord. **Thanks be to God.**

GOSPEL ACCLAMATION *(John 6.56)*

Alleluia. Alleluia. Whoever eats my flesh and drinks my blood abides in me, and I in them, says the Lord. **Alleluia.**

GOSPEL *(John 6.51-58)*

The Lord be with you. **And with your spirit.** A reading from the holy Gospel according to John. **Glory to you, O Lord.**

Jesus said to the people: "I am the living bread that came down from heaven. Whoever eats of this bread will live forever; and the bread that I will give for the life of the world is my flesh."

The people then disputed among themselves, saying, "How can this man give us his flesh to eat?"

So Jesus said to them, "Very truly, I tell you, unless you eat the flesh of the Son of Man and drink his blood, you have no life in you. Whoever eats my flesh and drinks my blood has eternal life, and I will raise them up on the last day; for my flesh is true food and my blood is true drink. Whoever eats my flesh and drinks my blood abides in me, and I in them.

"Just as the living Father sent me, and I live because of the Father, so whoever eats me will live because of me. This is the bread that came down from heaven, not like that which your ancestors ate, and they died. But the one who eats this bread will live forever."

The Gospel of the Lord. **Praise to you, Lord Jesus Christ.**

PROFESSION OF FAITH (p. 11)

PRAYER OF THE FAITHFUL

The following intentions are suggestions only. There are more suggestions at www.livingwithchrist.ca

R. **Lord, hear our prayer.**

For the Church, whose very life proclaims the joy of the kingdom, we pray to the Lord: R.

For leaders of nations, seeking justice for their people, we pray to the Lord: R.

For the poor who lack the basic necessities of life, we pray to the Lord: R.

For our community, striving to be a model of fullness of life in Christ, we pray to the Lord: R.

PREPARATION OF THE GIFTS (p. 14)

PRAYER OVER THE OFFERINGS
Receive our oblation, O Lord, by which is brought
about a glorious exchange, that, by offering what you
have given, we may merit to receive your very self.
Through Christ our Lord. **Amen.**

PREFACE *(Sundays in Ordinary Time, p. 29)*

COMMUNION ANTIPHON *(Psalm 129.7)*
**With the Lord there is mercy; in him is plentiful
redemption.**

or (John 6.51-52)

**I am the living bread that came down from heaven,
says the Lord. Whoever eats of this bread will live
for ever.**

PRAYER AFTER COMMUNION
Made partakers of Christ through these Sacraments,
we humbly implore your mercy, Lord, that, conformed to his image on earth, we may merit also to
be his co-heirs in heaven. Who lives and reigns for
ever and ever. **Amen.**

BLESSING AND DISMISSAL *(p. 71)*

August 26
21st Sunday in Ordinary Time

To do or not to do? That is the question. Everyday we are faced with countless choices and decisions to make. As Christians headed toward eternal life, we are called to align our lives and choices to the example and teachings that Jesus provided.

It's not easy. Jesus' disciples experienced the difficulty of keeping faith, and some doubted and left. Sometimes following Jesus is hard. We also have left him many times. However after wondering aimlessly, we realize once again that Jesus was right.

There is something truly heart-warming about someone saying "I'm sorry" in all sincerity. Small children are likely to express remorse most authentically. When my four year old looks at me and says, "Mama, I'm sorry," my heart melts and my only possible response is to scoop him up in a big hug.

I imagine it is similar with our heavenly Father. His only response to our failure and regret is pure compassion and unconditional love. If we allow ourselves to receive his love, we in turn become more compassionate and more loving ourselves. God wastes no opportunities for our good.

The beauty of the Eucharist is that as we continue on our earthly pilgrimage, he gives us the nourishment we need to continue, to grow stronger and to eventually reach our eternal destination.

Natalia Kononenko
Toronto, ON

ENTRANCE ANTIPHON *(Cf. Psalm 85.1-3)*
Turn your ear, O Lord, and answer me; save the
servant who trusts in you, my God. Have mercy on
me, O Lord, for I cry to you all the day long.

INTRODUCTORY RITES *(p. 5)*

COLLECT
O God, who cause the minds of the faithful to unite
in a single purpose, grant your people to love what
you command and to desire what you promise, that,
amid the uncertainties of this world, our hearts may
be fixed on that place where true gladness is found.
Through our Lord Jesus Christ, your Son, who lives
and reigns with you in the unity of the Holy Spirit,
one God, for ever and ever. **Amen.**

FIRST READING *(Joshua 24.1-2a, 15-17, 18b)*
Joshua gathered all the tribes of Israel to Shechem,
and summoned the elders, the heads, the judges, and
the officers of Israel; and they presented themselves
before God.

And Joshua said to all the people, "If you are un-
willing to serve the Lord, choose this day whom you
will serve, whether the gods your ancestors served in
the region beyond the River or the gods of the Amor-
ites in whose land you are living. As for me and my
household, we will serve the Lord."

Then the people answered, "Far be it from us that
we should forsake the Lord to serve other gods; for it
is the Lord our God who brought us and our ancestors
up from the land of Egypt, out of the house of slavery,
and who did those great signs in our sight. He pro-

tected us along all the way that we went, and among all the peoples through whom we passed. Therefore we also will serve the Lord, for he is our God."

The word of the Lord. **Thanks be to God.**

RESPONSORIAL PSALM *(Psalm 34)*

Taste and see that the Lord is good.

R̷. **Taste and see that the Lord is good.**

I will bless the Lord at all · **times;**
his praise shall continually be in · **my** mouth.
My soul makes its boast in the · **Lord;**
let the humble hear and · **be** glad. R̷.

The eyes of the Lord are on the · **righteous,**
and his ears are open · **to_their** cry.
The face of the Lord is against · **evildoers,**
to cut off the remembrance of them · **from_the**
    earth. R̷.

When the righteous cry for help, the Lord · **hears,**
and rescues them from all · **their** troubles.
The Lord is near to the broken--**hearted,**
and saves the crushed · **in** spirit. R̷.

Many are the afflictions of the · **righteous_one,**
but the Lord rescues him from · **them** all.
He keeps all his · **bones;**
not one of them will · **be** broken. R̷.

Evil brings death to the · **wicked,**
and those who hate the righteous will be ·
   con-demned.
The Lord redeems the life of his · **servants;**
none of those who take refuge in him will be ·
   con-demned. R.

©2009 Gordon Johnston/Novalis

SECOND READING *(Ephesians 4.32 – 5.1-2, 21-32)*
Brothers and sisters: Be kind to one another, tender-hearted, forgiving one another, as God in Christ has forgiven you. Therefore be imitators of God, as beloved children, and live in love, as Christ loved us and gave himself up for us, a fragrant offering and sacrifice to God. Be subject to one another out of reverence for Christ.

Wives, be subject to your husbands as you are to the Lord. For the husband is the head of the wife just as Christ is the head of the Church, the body of which he is the Saviour. Just as the Church is subject to Christ, so also wives ought to be, in everything, to their husbands.

Husbands, love your wives, just as Christ loved the Church and gave himself up for her, in order to make her holy by cleansing her with the washing of water by the word, so as to present the Church to himself in splendour, without a spot or wrinkle or anything of the kind — yes, so that she may be holy and without blemish. In the same way, husbands should love their wives as they do their own bodies. He who loves his wife loves himself. For no one ever hates his own body, but he nourishes and tenderly cares for it, just as Christ does for the Church, because we are members of his body.

For this reason a man will leave his father and mother and be joined to his wife, and the two will become one flesh. This is a great mystery, and I am applying it to Christ and the Church.

The word of the Lord. **Thanks be to God.**

GOSPEL ACCLAMATION *(John 6.63, 68)*

Alleluia. Alleluia. Your words, Lord, are spirit and life; you have the words of eternal life. **Alleluia.**

GOSPEL *(John 6.53, 60-69)*

The Lord be with you. **And with your spirit.** A reading from the holy Gospel according to John. **Glory to you, O Lord.**

Jesus said to the people: "Very truly, I tell you, unless you eat the flesh of the Son of Man and drink his blood, you have no life in you."

When many of his disciples heard this, they said: "This teaching is difficult; who can accept it?"

But Jesus, being aware that his disciples were complaining about it, said to them, "Does this offend you? Then what if you were to see the Son of Man ascending to where he was before? It is the spirit that gives life; the flesh is useless. The words that I have spoken to you are spirit and life. But among you there are some who do not believe." For Jesus knew from the first who were the ones that did not believe, and who was the one that would betray him.

And he said, "For this reason I have told you that no one can come to me unless it is granted them by my Father."

Because of this many of his disciples turned back, and no longer went about with him. So Jesus asked the twelve, "Do you also wish to go away?"

Simon Peter answered him, "Lord, to whom can we go? You have the words of eternal life. We have come to believe and know that you are the Holy One of God."

The Gospel of the Lord. **Praise to you, Lord Jesus Christ.**

PROFESSION OF FAITH (p. 11)

PRAYER OF THE FAITHFUL

The following intentions are suggestions only. There are more suggestions at www.livingwithchrist.ca

R. **Lord, hear our prayer.**

For the Church, witness to God's mercy and love, we pray to the Lord: R.

For leaders of nations working for the peace and well-being of all citizens, we pray to the Lord: R.

For the sick and suffering, and for those who care for them, we pray to the Lord: R.

For all of us gathered here in faith, hope and love, we pray to the Lord: R.

PREPARATION OF THE GIFTS (p. 14)

PRAYER OVER THE OFFERINGS

O Lord, who gained for yourself a people by adoption through the one sacrifice offered once for all, bestow graciously on us, we pray, the gifts of unity and peace in your Church. Through Christ our Lord. **Amen.**

PREFACE *(Sundays in Ordinary Time, p. 29)*

COMMUNION ANTIPHON *(Cf. Psalm 103.13-15)*

The earth is replete with the fruits of your work, O Lord; you bring forth bread from the earth and wine to cheer the heart.

or (Cf. John 6.54)

Whoever eats my flesh and drinks my blood has eternal life, says the Lord, and I will raise him up on the last day.

PRAYER AFTER COMMUNION

Complete within us, O Lord, we pray, the healing work of your mercy and graciously perfect and sustain us, so that in all things we may please you. Through Christ our Lord. **Amen.**

BLESSING AND DISMISSAL *(p. 71)*

September Saints' Days

The following saints are traditionally remembered in September in Canada.

2   Blessed André Grasset

3   Saint Gregory the Great

4   Blessed Dina Bélanger

9   Saint Peter Claver

13   Saint John Chrysostom

15   Our Lady of Sorrows

16   Saints Cornelius and Cyprian

17   Saint Robert Bellarmine

19   Saint Januarius

20   Saints Andrew Kim Tae-gon, Paul Chong Ha-sang and Companions

21   Saint Matthew

23   Saint Pius of Pietrelcina

24   Blessed Émilie Tavernier-Gamelin

25   Saints Cosmas and Damian

26   Saints John de Brébeuf, Isaac Jogues and Companions, Secondary Patrons of Canada

27   Saint Vincent de Paul

28   Saint Wenceslaus
     Saint Lawrence Ruiz and Companions

29   Saints Michael, Gabriel and Raphael

30   Saint Jerome

September 2
22nd Sunday in Ordinary Time

Jesus said, "Listen to me, all of you, and understand." What I hear Jesus saying here, is: listen with all your mind and with all your heart.

Being in the pew on Sunday does not mean we have listened or understood the scripture readings of the day. To help us focus and to help us to internalize the Word of God that we hear on Sunday, we may need to invest a bit more time and preparation throughout the preceding week.

For example, on Wednesday we can pray for openness of heart, to be able to receive the Good News more generously: "Come Holy Spirit, help me to listen and understand." Then, over the next few days, we can read and re-read the coming Sunday's readings so that they become more and more familiar in our mind and have an opportunity to touch our heart. For additional help, we can invest in a scripture commentary or read one online.

Our exercise of internalizing the Word of God will require some patience, persistence and being reflective. But if we are willing to invest more of ourselves by spending more time on the Word of God, we may find that it starts to change how we think, how we see the world around us, how we act and, generally, how we live – becoming the very person God wishes us to be.

Harry McAvoy
Newmarket, ON

ENTRANCE ANTIPHON *(Cf. Psalm 85.3, 5)*
Have mercy on me, O Lord, for I cry to you all the day long. O Lord, you are good and forgiving, full of mercy to all who call to you.

INTRODUCTORY RITES *(p. 5)*

COLLECT
God of might, giver of every good gift, put into our hearts the love of your name, so that, by deepening our sense of reverence, you may nurture in us what is good and, by your watchful care, keep safe what you have nurtured. Through our Lord Jesus Christ, your Son, who lives and reigns with you in the unity of the Holy Spirit, one God, for ever and ever. **Amen.**

FIRST READING *(Deuteronomy 4.1-2, 6-8)*
"Now, Israel, give heed to the statutes and ordinances that I am teaching you to observe, so that you may live to enter and occupy the land that the Lord, the God of your fathers, is giving you. You must neither add anything to what I command you nor take away anything from it, but keep the commandments of the Lord your God with which I am charging you.

"You must observe them diligently, for this will show your wisdom and discernment to the peoples, who, when they hear all these statutes, will say, 'Surely this great nation is a wise and discerning people!' For what other great nation has a god so near to it as the Lord our God is whenever we call to him? And what other great nation has statutes and ordinances as just as this entire law that I am setting before you today?"

The word of the Lord. **Thanks be to God.**

RESPONSORIAL PSALM *(Psalm 15)*

O Lord, who may a-bide in your tent?

℟. **O Lord, who may abide in your tent?**

Whoever walks · **blamelessly,**
and does what is · **right,**
and speaks the truth from their · **heart;**
whoever does not slander · **with_their** tongue. ℟.

Whoever does no evil to a · **friend,**
nor takes up a reproach against a · **neighbour;**
in whose eyes the wicked one is de·-**spised,**
but who honours those who fear · **the** Lord. ℟.

Whoever stands by their oath even to their · **hurt;**
who does not lend money at · **interest,**
and does not take a bribe against the · **innocent.**
One who does these things shall never · **be**
    moved. ℟.

©2009 Gordon Johnston/Novalis

SECOND READING *(James 1.17-18, 21-22, 27)*
Every generous act of giving, with every perfect
gift, is from above, coming down from the Father of
lights, with whom there is no variation or shadow
due to change. In fulfillment of his own purpose he
gave us birth by the word of truth, so that we would
become a kind of first fruits of his creatures.

Welcome with meekness the implanted word that has the power to save your souls. But be doers of the word, and not merely hearers who deceive themselves.

Religion that is pure and undefiled before God, the Father, is this: to care for orphans and widows in their distress, and to keep oneself unstained by the world.

The word of the Lord. **Thanks be to God.**

GOSPEL ACCLAMATION (James 1.18)
Alleluia. Alleluia. The Father gave us birth by the word of truth, that we would become first fruits of his creation. **Alleluia.**

GOSPEL (Mark 7.1-8, 14-15, 21-23)
The Lord be with you. **And with your spirit.**
A reading from the holy Gospel according to Mark. **Glory to you, O Lord.**

When the Pharisees and some of the scribes who had come from Jerusalem gathered around Jesus, they noticed that some of his disciples were eating with defiled hands, that is, without washing them. For the Pharisees, and all the Jews, do not eat unless they thoroughly wash their hands, thus observing the tradition of the elders; and they do not eat anything from the market unless they wash it; and there are also many other traditions that they observe, the washing of cups, pots, and bronze kettles. So the Pharisees and the scribes asked him, "Why do your disciples not live according to the tradition of the elders, but eat with defiled hands?"

Jesus said to them, "Isaiah prophesied rightly about you hypocrites, as it is written, 'This people honours me with their lips, but their hearts are far from me; in vain do they worship me, teaching human precepts as doctrines.' You abandon the commandment of God and hold to human tradition."

Then Jesus called the crowd again and said to them, "Listen to me, all of you, and understand: there is nothing outside a person that by going in can defile them, but the things that come out of a person are what defile them.

"For it is from within, from the human heart, that evil intentions come: fornication, theft, murder, adultery, avarice, wickedness, deceit, licentiousness, envy, slander, pride, folly. All these evil things come from within, and they defile a person."

The Gospel of the Lord. **Praise to you, Lord Jesus Christ.**

PROFESSION OF FAITH (p. 11)

PRAYER OF THE FAITHFUL

The following intentions are suggestions only. There are more suggestions at www.livingwithchrist.ca

R. **Lord, hear our prayer.**

For the Church, witness to the kingdom of God throughout the world, we pray to the Lord: R.

For civic leaders, working for the good of all people, we pray to the Lord: R.

For people living in poverty, pain and injustice, we pray to the Lord: R.

For our community, diligently striving to live the commandment of love, we pray to the Lord: ℟.

PREPARATION OF THE GIFTS *(p. 14)*

PRAYER OVER THE OFFERINGS
May this sacred offering, O Lord, confer on us always the blessing of salvation, that what it celebrates in mystery it may accomplish in power. Through Christ our Lord. **Amen.**

PREFACE *(Sundays in Ordinary Time, p. 29)*

COMMUNION ANTIPHON *(Psalm 30.20)*
How great is the goodness, Lord, that you keep for those who fear you.
or (Matthew 5.9-10)
Blessed are the peacemakers, for they shall be called children of God. Blessed are they who are persecuted for the sake of righteousness, for theirs is the Kingdom of Heaven.

PRAYER AFTER COMMUNION
Renewed by this bread from the heavenly table, we beseech you, Lord, that, being the food of charity, it may confirm our hearts and stir us to serve you in our neighbour. Through Christ our Lord. **Amen.**

BLESSING AND DISMISSAL *(p. 71)*

September 9
23rd Sunday in Ordinary Time

Isaiah calls forth courage in each of us. "Be strong, do not fear," for God will save, giving sight to the blind and hearing to the deaf. During the exile in Babylon, the Israelites must have felt abandoned and alone. Isaiah's news of God's everlasting love was a glimmer of light in the darkness

In today's Gospel, God shows, through Jesus, his love to his people by overcoming social barriers and healing through touch. In a time of stringent laws of purity, this was a bold act of mercy. Illness and disability were seen as a sign of the presence of sin. Jesus reaches across this social boundary and wipes it away, healing the broken and demonstrating his love for the marginalized.

Saint James calls each of us to follow in Jesus' footsteps – may we participate in the kingdom by reaching beyond barriers in order to show kindness and love to others. The sign of God's miraculous love is present to us every day through words and deeds that, inspired by grace, bring healing and comfort. These small miracles bring God's light to the places of darkness in our world. If we open our hearts to this visceral love, won't we too want to zealously share the Good News?

Vanessa and Michael Nicholas-Schmidt
Toronto, ON

ENTRANCE ANTIPHON *(Psalm 118.137, 124)*
You are just, O Lord, and your judgment is right; treat
your servant in accord with your merciful love.

INTRODUCTORY RITES *(p. 5)*

COLLECT
O God, by whom we are redeemed and receive
adoption, look graciously upon your beloved sons
and daughters, that those who believe in Christ may
receive true freedom and an everlasting inheritance.
Through our Lord Jesus Christ, your Son, who lives
and reigns with you in the unity of the Holy Spirit,
one God, for ever and ever. **Amen.**

FIRST READING *(Isaiah 35.4-7)*
Say to those who are of a fearful heart,
"Be strong, do not fear!
Here is your God.
He will come with vengeance,
with terrible recompense.
He will come and save you."

Then the eyes of the blind shall be opened,
and the ears of the deaf unstopped;
then the lame shall leap like a deer,
and the tongue of the mute sing for joy.

For waters shall break forth in the wilderness,
and streams in the desert;
the burning sand shall become a pool,
and the thirsty ground springs of water.

The word of the Lord. **Thanks be to God.**

RESPONSORIAL PSALM *(Psalm 146)*

Praise the Lord, O my soul!

R. **Praise the Lord, O my soul!**
or **Alleluia!**

It is the Lord who keeps faith for-**ever,**
who executes justice for the op-**pressed;**
who gives food to the · **hungry.**
The Lord sets the · **prisoners** free. R.

The Lord opens the eyes of the · **blind**
and lifts up those who are bowed · **down;**
the Lord loves the · **righteous**
and watches over · **the** strangers. R.

The Lord upholds the orphan and the · **widow,**
but the way of the wicked he brings to · **ruin.**
The Lord will reign for-**ever,**
your God, O Zion, for all · **gener**-ations. R.

©2009 Gordon Johnston/Novalis

SECOND READING *(James 2.1-5)*

My brothers and sisters, do you with your acts of
favouritism really believe in our glorious Lord Jesus Christ? For if a man with gold rings and in fine
clothes comes into your assembly, and if a poor person in dirty clothes also comes in, and if you take
notice of the one wearing the fine clothes and say,
"Have a seat here, please," while to the one who is

poor you say, "Stand there," or, "Sit at my feet," have you not made distinctions among yourselves, and become judges with evil thoughts?

Listen, my beloved brothers and sisters. Has not God chosen the poor in the world to be rich in faith and to be heirs of the kingdom that he has promised to those who love him?

The word of the Lord. **Thanks be to God.**

GOSPEL ACCLAMATION *(Matthew 4.23)*
Alleluia. Alleluia. Jesus proclaimed the good news of the kingdom and cured every sickness among the people. **Alleluia.**

GOSPEL *(Mark 7.31-37)*
The Lord be with you. **And with your spirit.**
A reading from the holy Gospel according to Mark. **Glory to you, O Lord.**

Returning from the region of Tyre, Jesus went by way of Sidon towards the Sea of Galilee, in the region of the Decapolis.

They brought to him a man who was deaf and who had an impediment in his speech; and they begged him to lay his hand on him. Jesus took him aside in private, away from the crowd, and put his fingers into his ears, and he spat and touched his tongue. Then looking up to heaven, he sighed and said to him, "Ephphatha," that is, "Be opened." And immediately the man's ears were opened, his tongue was released, and he spoke plainly.

Then Jesus ordered them to tell no one; but the more he ordered them, the more zealously they proclaimed it. They were astounded beyond measure, saying, "He has done everything well; he even makes the deaf to hear and the mute to speak."

The Gospel of the Lord. **Praise to you, Lord Jesus Christ.**

PROFESSION OF FAITH *(p. 11)*

PRAYER OF THE FAITHFUL

The following intentions are suggestions only. There are more suggestions at www.livingwithchrist.ca

R. **Lord, hear our prayer.**

For the Church, welcoming all God's children, we pray to the Lord: R.

For world leaders, bringing strength and wisdom to their care for the poor, we pray to the Lord: R.

For all who hunger and thirst for acceptance, we pray to the Lord: R.

For God's people gathered here, we pray to the Lord: R.

PREPARATION OF THE GIFTS *(p. 14)*

PRAYER OVER THE OFFERINGS

O God, who give us the gift of true prayer and of peace, graciously grant that, through this offering, we may do fitting homage to your divine majesty and, by partaking of the sacred mystery, we may be faithfully united in mind and heart. Through Christ our Lord. **Amen.**

PREFACE *(Sundays in Ordinary Time, p. 29)*

COMMUNION ANTIPHON *(Cf. Psalm 41.2-3)*
Like the deer that yearns for running streams, so my soul is yearning for you, my God; my soul is thirsting for God, the living God.

or (John 8.12)
I am the light of the world, says the Lord; whoever follows me will not walk in darkness, but will have the light of life.

PRAYER AFTER COMMUNION
Grant that your faithful, O Lord, whom you nourish and endow with life through the food of your Word and heavenly Sacrament, may so benefit from your beloved Son's great gifts that we may merit an eternal share in his life. Who lives and reigns for ever and ever. **Amen.**

BLESSING AND DISMISSAL *(p. 71)*

September 16
24th Sunday in Ordinary Time

Jesus and his disciples set out for the villages of Caesarea in Philippi. These journeys would not have been easy by our modern standards. Dusty, uneven terrain, hot and all on foot. Yet that is when he asked his disciples: "Who do people say that I am?"

Walking with Christ is a spiritual journey fed by prayer, scripture reading and the Eucharist. However, it is revealed by works. Jesus does not ask us to arrive at our destination before we begin doing acts of mercy. The Christian journey is always about imperfect people bringing Christ to an imperfect world, now, through him.

When your acts of mercy defend the unborn, the sick, the dying, marriage, the cost of this discipleship can be high. It can be lonely and overwhelming. God's plan is not that we do this in our own strength. He is able to do within us, whatever he has called us to do, whether to serve, to speak the truth, or to stand and defend.

Let the Mass today be your prayerful next step; then give God glory and praise as you boldly proclaim the Messiah in our broken world.

Johanne Brownrigg
Orleans, ON

ENTRANCE ANTIPHON *(Cf. Sirach 36.18)*
Give peace, O Lord, to those who wait for you, that your prophets be found true. Hear the prayers of your servant, and of your people Israel.

INTRODUCTORY RITES *(p. 5)*

COLLECT
Look upon us, O God, Creator and ruler of all things, and, that we may feel the working of your mercy, grant that we may serve you with all our heart. Through our Lord Jesus Christ, your Son, who lives and reigns with you in the unity of the Holy Spirit, one God, for ever and ever. **Amen.**

FIRST READING *(Isaiah 50.5-9)*
The Lord God has opened my ear,
and I was not rebellious, I did not turn backward.
I gave my back to those who struck me,
and my cheeks to those who pulled out the beard;
I did not hide my face from insult and spitting.

The Lord God helps me;
therefore I have not been disgraced;
therefore I have set my face like flint,
and I know that I shall not be put to shame;
he who vindicates me is near.

Who will contend with me? Let us stand up together.
Who are my adversaries? Let them confront me.
It is the Lord God who helps me;
who will declare me guilty?

The word of the Lord. **Thanks be to God.**

RESPONSORIAL PSALM *(Psalm 116)*

I will walk be-fore the Lord, in the land of the liv-ing.

℟. **I will walk before the Lord,**
   in the land of the living.
or **Alleluia!**

I love the Lord, because he has · **heard**
my voice and my · **suppli**-cations.
Because he inclined his ear to · **me**,
therefore I will call on him as long as · **I** live. ℟.

The snares of death encompassed me; the pangs
of Sheol laid · **hold_on_me**;
I suffered distress · **and** anguish.
Then I called on the name of the · **Lord:**
"O Lord, I pray, save · **my** life!" ℟.

Gracious is the Lord, and · **righteous;**
our God · **is** merciful.
The Lord protects the · **simple;**
when I was brought low, · **he** saved_me. ℟.

For you have delivered my soul from · **death,**
my eyes from tears, my feet · **from** stumbling.
I will walk before the · **Lord**
in the land of · **the** living. ℟.

©2009 Gordon Johnston/Novalis

SECOND READING *(James 2.14-18)*
What good is it, my brothers and sisters, if you say you have faith but do not have works? Can faith save you?

If a brother or a sister is without clothing and lacks daily food, and one of you says to them, "Go in peace; keep warm and eat your fill," and yet you do not supply their bodily needs, what is the good of that? So faith by itself, if it has no works, is dead.

But someone will say, "You have faith and I have works." Show me your faith apart from your works, and I by my works will show you my faith.

The word of the Lord. **Thanks be to God.**

GOSPEL ACCLAMATION *(Galatians 6.14)*
Alleluia. Alleluia. May I never boast of anything except the Cross of the Lord, by which the world has been crucified to me, and I to the world. **Alleluia.**

GOSPEL *(Mark 8.27-35)*
The Lord be with you. **And with your spirit.**
A reading from the holy Gospel according to Mark.
Glory to you, O Lord.

Jesus went on with his disciples to the villages of Caesarea Philippi; and on the way he asked his disciples, "Who do people say that I am?" And they answered him, "John the Baptist; and others, Elijah; and still others, one of the Prophets."

Jesus asked them, "But who do you say that I am?" Peter answered him, "You are the Christ." And he sternly ordered them not to tell anyone about him.

Then he began to teach them that the Son of Man must undergo great suffering, and be rejected by the elders, the chief priests, and the scribes, and be killed, and after three days rise again. He said all this quite openly.

And Peter took Jesus aside and began to rebuke him. But turning and looking at his disciples, he rebuked Peter and said, "Get behind me, Satan! For you are thinking not as God does, but as humans do."

Jesus called the crowd with his disciples, and said to them, "Whoever wants to become my follower, let him deny himself and take up his cross and follow me. For whoever wants to save their life will lose it, and whoever loses their life for my sake, and for the sake of the Gospel, will save it."

The Gospel of the Lord. **Praise to you, Lord Jesus Christ.**

PROFESSION OF FAITH (p. 11)

PRAYER OF THE FAITHFUL

The following intentions are suggestions only. There are more suggestions at www.livingwithchrist.ca

R. **Lord, hear our prayer.**

For the Church, walking in the presence of the Lord, we pray to the Lord: R.

For world leaders who work for justice, peace and the integrity of creation, we pray to the Lord: R.

For those suffering from illness, violence, poverty or hunger, we pray to the Lord: R.

For the members of this community, called to listen for the stirrings of God's spirit, we pray to the Lord: R.

PREPARATION OF THE GIFTS (p. 14)

PRAYER OVER THE OFFERINGS
Look with favour on our supplications, O Lord, and in your kindness accept these, your servants' offerings, that what each has offered to the honour of your name may serve the salvation of all. Through Christ our Lord. **Amen.**

PREFACE (Sundays in Ordinary Time, p. 29)

COMMUNION ANTIPHON (Cf. Psalm 35.8)
How precious is your mercy, O God! The children of men seek shelter in the shadow of your wings.
or (Cf. 1 Corinthians 10.16)
The chalice of blessing that we bless is a communion in the Blood of Christ; and the bread that we break is a sharing in the Body of the Lord.

PRAYER AFTER COMMUNION
May the working of this heavenly gift, O Lord, we pray, take possession of our minds and bodies, so that its effects, and not our own desires, may always prevail in us. Through Christ our Lord. **Amen.**

BLESSING AND DISMISSAL (p. 71)

September 23
25th Sunday in Ordinary Time

Christianity is often castigated for teaching that God is an angry God whose wrath at human sin required a perfect human sacrifice to appease his bad temper. And we can even admit that some Christians do misrepresent the gospel in this way. But today's readings tell a very different story.

It is not God who demands the death of the innocent, but us. The reading from Wisdom lays bare the human response to innocence. It makes us uncomfortable. And so, when God comes to us as an innocent man, we cannot bear his presence and we crucify him.

In the letter of James, and in today's Gospel, we see the human dynamics that underlie our propensity to sacrifice the innocent. But we also see Christ's answer to those dynamics. If we are not to be people who sacrifice the innocent, we must be, as James says "peaceable, gentle, willing to yield, full of mercy and good fruits, without a trace of partiality or hypocrisy," or, as Jesus says, "Whoever wants to be first must be last of all and servant of all."

The sacrifice we offer at Mass today, then, is not an innocent victim presented to an angry God, but a loving victim who offered himself to God precisely by offering himself to us, even as we "condemned him to a shameful death."

Brett Salkeld
Regina, SK

ENTRANCE ANTIPHON
I am the salvation of the people, says the Lord. Should they cry to me in any distress, I will hear them, and I will be their Lord for ever.

INTRODUCTORY RITES *(p. 5)*

COLLECT
O God, who founded all the commands of your sacred Law upon love of you and of our neighbour, grant that, by keeping your precepts, we may merit to attain eternal life. Through our Lord Jesus Christ, your Son, who lives and reigns with you in the unity of the Holy Spirit, one God, for ever and ever. **Amen.**

FIRST READING *(Wisdom 2.12, 17-20)*
The godless say, "Let us lie in wait for the righteous one, who makes life inconvenient to us and opposes our actions; who reproaches us for sins against the law, and accuses us of sins against our training.

"Let us see if his words are true, and let us test what will happen at the end of his life; for if the righteous one is God's son, God will help him, and will deliver him from the hand of his adversaries.

"Let us test him with insult and torture, so that we may find out how gentle he is, and make trial of his forbearance. Let us condemn him to a shameful death, for, according to what he says, he will be protected."

The word of the Lord. **Thanks be to God.**

RESPONSORIAL PSALM *(Psalm 54)*

The Lord up-holds my life.

R. **The Lord upholds my life.**

Save me, O God, by your · **name,**
and vindicate me by · **your** might.
Hear my prayer, O · **God;**
give ear to the words of · **my** mouth. R.

1 - For the insolent have risen a-·**gainst_me,**
2 - the ruthless seek · **my** life;
4 - they do not set God · **be**-fore_them. R.

But surely, God is my · **helper;**
the Lord is the upholder of · **my** life.
With a freewill offering I will · **sacrifice_to_you;**
I will give thanks to your name, for · **it_is** good. R.

©2009 Gordon Johnston/Novalis

SECOND READING *(James 3.16 – 4.3)*

Beloved: Where there is envy and selfish ambition, there will also be disorder and wickedness of every kind. But the wisdom from above is first pure, then peaceable, gentle, willing to yield, full of mercy and good fruits, without a trace of partiality or hypocrisy. And a harvest of righteousness is sown in peace for those who make peace.

Those conflicts and disputes among you, where do they come from? Do they not come from your cravings that are at war within you? You want something and do not have it; so you commit murder. And you covet something and cannot obtain it; so you engage in disputes and conflicts.

You do not have, because you do not ask. You ask and do not receive, because you ask wrongly, in order to spend what you get on your pleasures.

The word of the Lord. **Thanks be to God.**

GOSPEL ACCLAMATION *(2 Thessalonians 2.14)*
Alleluia. Alleluia. God has called us through the good news, to obtain the glory of our Lord Jesus Christ. **Alleluia.**

GOSPEL *(Mark 9.30-37)*
The Lord be with you. **And with your spirit.**
A reading from the holy Gospel according to Mark. **Glory to you, O Lord.**

After leaving the mountain Jesus and his disciples went on from there and passed through Galilee. He did not want anyone to know it; for he was teaching his disciples, saying to them, "The Son of Man is to be betrayed into the hands of men, and they will kill him, and three days after being killed, he will rise again." But they did not understand what he was saying and were afraid to ask him.

Then they came to Capernaum; and when he was in the house Jesus asked them, "What were you arguing about on the way?" But they were silent, for on the way they had argued with one another who was the greatest.

Jesus sat down, called the twelve, and said to them, "Whoever wants to be first must be last of all and servant of all."

Then he took a little child and put it among them; and taking it in his arms, he said to them, "Whoever welcomes one such child in my name welcomes me, and whoever welcomes me welcomes not me but the one who sent me."

The Gospel of the Lord. **Praise to you, Lord Jesus Christ.**

PROFESSION OF FAITH (p. 11)

PRAYER OF THE FAITHFUL

The following intentions are suggestions only. There are more suggestions at www.livingwithchrist.ca

R. **Lord, hear our prayer.**

For the Church, called to be a humble servant of all, we pray to the Lord: R.

For discerning service by all those who hold public office, we pray to the Lord: R.

For children everywhere, blessed and loved by God, we pray to the Lord: R.

For this community, called to welcome children in the name of Jesus, we pray to the Lord: R.

PREPARATION OF THE GIFTS (p. 14)

PRAYER OVER THE OFFERINGS
Receive with favour, O Lord, we pray, the offerings of your people, that what they profess with devotion and faith may be theirs through these heavenly mysteries. Through Christ our Lord. **Amen.**

PREFACE *(Sundays in Ordinary Time, p. 29)*

COMMUNION ANTIPHON *(Psalm 118.4-5)*
You have laid down your precepts to be carefully kept; may my ways be firm in keeping your statutes.
or (John 10.14)
I am the Good Shepherd, says the Lord; I know my sheep, and mine know me.

PRAYER AFTER COMMUNION
Graciously raise up, O Lord, those you renew with this Sacrament, that we may come to possess your redemption both in mystery and in the manner of our life. Through Christ our Lord. **Amen.**

BLESSING AND DISMISSAL *(p. 71)*

September 30
26th Sunday in Ordinary Time

Today's readings make a clear distinction between our desires for worldly riches versus the riches that we receive as a result of just living by following God's law. The riches of the world easily seem more appealing at first glance – status, power, wealth, material things. They seem to bring with them freedom, opportunities and comfort. Wealth in and of itself is not a bad thing. What matters is how one acquires it and what one does with it.

Pope John Paul I once said "It is not wrong to want to live better; what is wrong is a style of life which is presumed to be better when it is directed towards 'having' rather than 'being,' and which wants to have more, not in order to *be* more but in order to spend life in enjoyment as an end in itself." The reading from James sends a warning specifically to the rich who oppress others for their own benefit.

If we can re-direct our worldly riches and possessions (we all have some!) to serve us in the way that helps us to gather eternal treasures, we can be rewarded with eternal life in the kingdom of God. This has already begun here on earth through the good fruits that result from spiritually-healthy choices and just actions: peace, joy, kindness, goodness, charity and well-being. May God bless all of our good efforts!

Natalia Kononenko
Toronto, ON

ENTRANCE ANTIPHON *(Daniel 3.31, 29, 30, 43, 42)*
All that you have done to us, O Lord, you have done
with true judgment, for we have sinned against you
and not obeyed your commandments. But give glory
to your name and deal with us according to the
bounty of your mercy.

INTRODUCTORY RITES *(p. 5)*

COLLECT
O God, who manifest your almighty power above all
by pardoning and showing mercy, bestow, we pray,
your grace abundantly upon us and make those hastening to attain your promises heirs to the treasures
of heaven. Through our Lord Jesus Christ, your Son,
who lives and reigns with you in the unity of the
Holy Spirit, one God, for ever and ever. **Amen.**

FIRST READING *(Numbers 11.25-29)*
The Lord came down in the cloud, took some of
the spirit that was on Moses and put it on the seventy elders. When the spirit rested upon them, they
prophesied. But they did not do so again.

Two men remained in the camp, one named Eldad,
and the other named Medad, and the spirit rested on
them; they were among those registered, but they had
not gone out to the tent, and so they prophesied in
the camp. A young man ran and told Moses, "Eldad
and Medad are prophesying in the camp."

Joshua son of Nun, the assistant of Moses, one of
his chosen men, said, "My lord Moses, stop them!"
But Moses said to him, "Are you jealous for my sake?

Would that all the Lord's people were Prophets, and that the Lord would put his spirit on them!"

The word of the Lord. **Thanks be to God.**

RESPONSORIAL PSALM *(Psalm 19)*

R̶ **The precepts of the Lord are right,**
and give joy to the heart.

The law of the Lord is · **perfect,**
reviving the · **soul;**
the decrees of the Lord are · **sure,**
making wise · **the** simple. R̶

The fear of the Lord is · **pure,**
enduring for-**ever;**
the ordinances of the Lord are · **true**
and righteous · **alto**-gether. R̶

By them is your servant · **warned;**
in keeping them there is great re-**ward.**
But who can detect unmindful · **errors?**
Clear me from · **hidden** faults. R̶

Keep back your servant also from the · **insolent;**
do not let them have dominion · **over_me.**
Then I shall be · **blameless,**
and innocent of · **great_trans**-gression. R̶

©*2009 Gordon Johnston/Novalis*

SECOND READING *(James 5.1-6)*
Come now, you rich people, weep and wail for the miseries that are coming to you. Your riches have rotted, and your clothes are moth-eaten. Your gold and silver have rusted, and their rust will be evidence against you, and it will eat your flesh like fire.

You have laid up treasure for the last days. Listen! The wages of the labourers who mowed your fields, which you kept back by fraud, cry out, and the cries of the harvesters have reached the ears of the Lord of hosts.

You have lived on the earth in luxury and in pleasure; you have fattened your hearts in a day of slaughter. You have condemned and murdered the righteous one, who does not resist you.

The word of the Lord. **Thanks be to God.**

GOSPEL ACCLAMATION *(John 17.17)*
Alleluia. Alleluia. Your word, O Lord, is truth; sanctify us in the truth. **Alleluia.**

GOSPEL *(Mark 9.38-43, 45, 47-48)*
The Lord be with you. **And with your spirit.** A reading from the holy Gospel according to Mark. **Glory to you, O Lord.**

After Jesus had finished teaching the disciples, John said to him, "Teacher, we saw someone casting out demons in your name, and we tried to stop him, because he was not following us." But Jesus said, "Do not stop him; for no one who does a deed of power in my name will be able soon afterward to speak evil of me. Whoever is not against us is for us.

"For truly I tell you, whoever gives you a cup of water to drink because you bear the name of Christ will by no means lose the reward.

"If any of you put a stumbling block before one of these little ones who believe in me, it would be better for you if a great millstone were hung around your neck and you were thrown into the sea.

"If your hand causes you to stumble, cut it off; it is better for you to enter life maimed than to have two hands and to go to hell, to the unquenchable fire. And if your foot causes you to stumble, cut it off; it is better for you to enter life lame than to have two feet and to be thrown into hell. And if your eye causes you to stumble, tear it out; it is better for you to enter the kingdom of God with one eye than to have two eyes and to be thrown into hell, where their worm never dies, and the fire is never quenched."

The Gospel of the Lord. **Praise to you, Lord Jesus Christ.**

PROFESSION OF FAITH *(p. 11)*

PRAYER OF THE FAITHFUL

The following intentions are suggestions only. There are more suggestions at www.livingwithchrist.ca

R. **Lord, hear our prayer.**

For all religious leaders who seek to foster love and forgiveness in the world, we pray to the Lord: R.

For leaders of nations, working to bring peace and security to troubled areas of the world, we pray to the Lord: R.

For those who keep the flame of hope burning in the midst of injustice and need, we pray to the Lord: ℟.

For this assembly, always striving to live the Good News, we pray to the Lord: ℟.

PREPARATION OF THE GIFTS *(p. 14)*

PRAYER OVER THE OFFERINGS

Grant us, O merciful God, that this our offering may find acceptance with you and that through it the wellspring of all blessing may be laid open before us. Through Christ our Lord. **Amen.**

PREFACE *(Sundays in Ordinary Time, p. 29)*

COMMUNION ANTIPHON *(Cf. Psalm 118.49-50)*

Remember your word to your servant, O Lord, by which you have given me hope. This is my comfort when I am brought low.

or (1 John 3.16)

By this we came to know the love of God: that Christ laid down his life for us; so we ought to lay down our lives for one another.

PRAYER AFTER COMMUNION

May this heavenly mystery, O Lord, restore us in mind and body, that we may be co-heirs in glory with Christ, to whose suffering we are united whenever we proclaim his Death. Who lives and reigns for ever and ever. **Amen.**

BLESSING AND DISMISSAL *(p. 71)*

October Saints' Days

The following saints are traditionally remembered in October in Canada.

1   Saint Thérèse of the Child Jesus

2   The Holy Guardian Angels

4   Saint Francis of Assisi

6   Blessed Marie-Rose Durocher
    Saint Bruno

7   Our Lady of the Rosary

9   Saint Denis and Companions
    Saint John Leonardi

11   Saint John XXIII

14   Saint Callistus I

15   Saint Teresa of Jesus

16   Saint Marguerite d'Youville

17   Saint Ignatius of Antioch

18   Saint Luke

19   Saint Paul of the Cross

20   Saint Hedwig
     Saint Margaret Mary Alacoque

22   Saint John Paul II

23   Saint John of Capistrano

24   Saint Anthony Mary Claret

28   Saints Simon and Jude

October 7
27th Sunday in Ordinary Time

Given the increasingly secular times in which we live, one can imagine how fragile conversations centered on marriage and family can be. That said, as Catholics, we are called to humbly and lovingly share God's teachings and reinforce our faith's mission in a world not always open to or familiar with the Good News.

Since the dawning of creation, God designed man and woman to both complement and unite with one another, bearing children as fruits of their love. In essence, two reciprocal halves are to become whole and combine to create new blessings.

In today's Gospel Jesus states clearly that marriage is to be an eternal bond between man and woman, with a loving and committed heart shared by both spouses. Any experience outside of this context or any human dissolution of this union, we can deduce, contravenes the will of God.

While marriage is designed to be unitive, Jesus illustrates its pro-creative nature when he embraces the children. His blessing and assurance of their entry into heaven invite us to equally welcome them as gifts of God.

While being sensitive and supportive to those in difficult situations, let us wholeheartedly strive to follow God's will for marriage and family, united as Jesus unites with his bride, the Church.

Matt Charbonneau
Ottawa, ON

ENTRANCE ANTIPHON (Cf. Esther 4.17)

Within your will, O Lord, all things are established, and there is none that can resist your will. For you have made all things, the heaven and the earth, and all that is held within the circle of heaven; you are the Lord of all.

INTRODUCTORY RITES (p. 5)

COLLECT

Almighty ever-living God, who in the abundance of your kindness surpass the merits and the desires of those who entreat you, pour out your mercy upon us to pardon what conscience dreads and to give what prayer does not dare to ask. Through our Lord Jesus Christ, your Son, who lives and reigns with you in the unity of the Holy Spirit, one God, for ever and ever. **Amen.**

FIRST READING (Genesis 2.7ab, 15, 18-24)

The Lord God formed man from the dust of the ground, and breathed into his nostrils the breath of life, and put him in the garden of Eden to till it and keep it.

Then the Lord God said, "It is not good that the man should be alone; I will make him a helper as his partner." So out of the ground the Lord God formed every animal of the field and every bird of the air, and brought them to the man to see what he would call them; and whatever the man called every living creature, that was its name. The man gave names to all cattle, and to the birds of the air, and to every animal of the field; but for the man there was not found a helper as his partner.

So the Lord God caused a deep sleep to fall upon the man, and he slept; then he took one of his ribs and closed up its place with flesh. And the rib that the Lord God had taken from the man he made into a woman and brought her to the man.

Then the man said, "This at last is bone of my bones and flesh of my flesh; this one shall be called Woman, for out of Man this one was taken."

Therefore a man leaves his father and his mother and clings to his wife, and they become one flesh.

The word of the Lord. **Thanks be to God.**

RESPONSORIAL PSALM *(Psalm 128)*

May the Lord bless us all the days of   our lives.

R. **May the Lord bless us all the days of our lives.**

Blessed is everyone who fears · **the** Lord,
who walks in · **his** ways.
You shall eat the fruit of the labour of · **your**
   hands;
you shall be happy, and it shall go well ·
   with you. R.

Your wife will be like a fruit·-**ful** vine
within · **your** house;
your children will be · **like** olive_shoots
around · **your** table. R.

Thus shall the man be blessed who fears ·
the Lord.
The Lord bless you · **from** Zion.
May you see the prosperity of · **Je**-rusalem
all the days of · **your** life. R.

©2009 Gordon Johnston/Novalis

SECOND READING (Hebrews 2.9-11)

We do indeed see Jesus, who for a little while was
made lower than the Angels, now crowned with
glory and honour because of the suffering of death,
so that by the grace of God he might taste death for
everyone.

It was fitting that God, for whom and through
whom all things exist, in bringing many sons and
daughters to glory should make the pioneer of their
salvation perfect through sufferings. For the one who
sanctifies and those who are sanctified are all from
one. For this reason he is not ashamed to call them
brothers and sisters.

The word of the Lord. **Thanks be to God.**

GOSPEL ACCLAMATION (1 John 4.12)

Alleluia. Alleluia. If we love one another, God will
live in us in perfect love. **Alleluia.**

GOSPEL (Mark 10.2-16)

The shorter version ends at the asterisks.
The Lord be with you. **And with your spirit.**
A reading from the holy Gospel according to Mark.
Glory to you, O Lord.

Some Pharisees came, and to test Jesus they asked, "Is it lawful for a man to divorce his wife?" Jesus answered them, "What did Moses command you?" They said, "Moses allowed a man to write a certificate of dismissal and to divorce her."

But Jesus said to them, "Because of your hardness of heart he wrote this commandment for you. But from the beginning of creation, 'God made them male and female.' 'For this reason a man shall leave his father and mother and be joined to his wife, and the two shall become one flesh.' So they are no longer two, but one flesh. Therefore what God has joined together, let no one separate."

Then in the house the disciples asked him again about this matter. Jesus said to them, "Whoever divorces his wife and marries another commits adultery against her; and if she divorces her husband and marries another, she commits adultery."

* * *

People were bringing little children to him in order that Jesus might touch them; and the disciples spoke sternly to them. But when Jesus saw this, he was indignant and said to them, "Let the little children come to me; do not stop them: for it is to such as these that the kingdom of God belongs. Truly I tell you, whoever does not receive the kingdom of God as a little child will never enter it."

And Jesus took them up in his arms, laid his hands on them, and blessed them.

The Gospel of the Lord. **Praise to you, Lord Jesus Christ.**

PROFESSION OF FAITH *(p. 11)*

PRAYER OF THE FAITHFUL

The following intentions are suggestions only. There are more suggestions at www.livingwithchrist.ca

R. **Lord, hear our prayer.**

For the Church, instrument of God's healing, we pray to the Lord: R.

For corporate and political leaders who have the power to promote peace, we pray to the Lord: R.

For healing for all victims of abuse and violence, we pray to the Lord: R.

For the community of faith gathered here today, we pray to the Lord: R.

PREPARATION OF THE GIFTS *(p. 14)*

PRAYER OVER THE OFFERINGS

Accept, O Lord, we pray, the sacrifices instituted by your commands and, through the sacred mysteries, which we celebrate with dutiful service, graciously complete the sanctifying work by which you are pleased to redeem us. Through Christ our Lord. **Amen.**

PREFACE *(Sundays in Ordinary Time, p. 29)*

COMMUNION ANTIPHON *(Lamentations 3.25)*
The Lord is good to those who hope in him, to the soul that seeks him.

or (Cf. 1 Corinthians 10.17)
Though many, we are one bread, one body, for we all partake of the one Bread and one Chalice.

PRAYER AFTER COMMUNION
Grant us, almighty God, that we may be refreshed and nourished by the Sacrament which we have received, so as to be transformed into what we consume. Through Christ our Lord. **Amen.**

BLESSING AND DISMISSAL *(p. 71)*

October 14
28th Sunday in Ordinary Time

"What must I do?" asked the rich man. Jesus' answer is a challenge. It is not just one more thing the man must add to his 'to do' list, but the essential thing. Jesus asks him to give up everything and follow him. It is not a simple question or a simple answer. The rich man had accomplished much and was ready to do more. But Jesus' reply knocks the wind out of his sails. Jesus is calling the man, and us, to trust more deeply – to sacrifice and be transformed.

It is easy to get caught up in depending upon ourselves, but our relationship with Jesus calls us to a radical trust. Give up our plans, our back-up plans, our safety nets and our stockpiles. Put Jesus first and let everything else go. Until we lay down our lives, we are still serving only in part.

Jesus' answer, said with love, convicts the man of holding back. His words shock the man out of his illusion that he on his way to eternal life, for "the word of God is living and active, sharper than any two-edged sword" – he must accept the challenge to go deeper. It is no easy thing – he must sacrifice everything to follow Jesus. It seemed impossible to him. What happened to the man? Did he accept the challenge? Do we? For with God, "all things are possible."

Kelly Bourke
Victoria, BC

ENTRANCE ANTIPHON *(Psalm 129.3-4)*
If you, O Lord, should mark iniquities, Lord, who could stand? But with you is found forgiveness, O God of Israel.

INTRODUCTORY RITES *(p. 5)*

COLLECT
May your grace, O Lord, we pray, at all times go before us and follow after and make us always determined to carry out good works. Through our Lord Jesus Christ, your Son, who lives and reigns with you in the unity of the Holy Spirit, one God, for ever and ever. **Amen.**

FIRST READING *(Wisdom 7.7-11)*
I prayed, and understanding was given me;
I called on God, and the spirit of wisdom came to me.

I preferred her to sceptres and thrones,
and I accounted wealth as nothing in comparison
    with her.
Neither did I liken to her any priceless gem,
because all gold is but a little sand in her sight,
and silver will be accounted as clay before her.

I loved her more than health and beauty,
and I chose to have her rather than light,
because her radiance never ceases.
All good things came to me along with her,
and in her hands uncounted wealth.

The word of the Lord. **Thanks be to God.**

RESPONSORIAL PSALM *(Psalm 90)*

Fill us with your love, O Lord,
that we may rejoice and be glad.

R̠ **Fill us with your love, O Lord,**
that we may rejoice and be glad.

Teach us to count our · **days**
that we may gain a wise · **heart.**
Turn, O Lord! How · **long?**
Have compassion · **on_your** servants! R̠

Satisfy us in the morning with your steadfast ·
love,
so that we may rejoice and be glad all our · **days.**
Make us glad as many days as you have
af--**flicted_us,**
and as many years as we have · **seen** evil. R̠

Let your work be manifest to your · **servants,**
and your glorious power to their · **children.**
Let the favour of the Lord our God be up--**on_us,**
and prosper for us the work of · **our** hands. R̠

©2009 Gordon Johnston/Novalis

SECOND READING *(Hebrews 4.12-13)*

The word of God is living and active, sharper than any two-edged sword, piercing until it divides soul from spirit, joints from marrow; it is able to judge the thoughts and intentions of the heart.

And before God no creature is hidden, but all are naked and laid bare to the eyes of the one to whom we must render an account.

The word of the Lord. **Thanks be to God.**

GOSPEL ACCLAMATION *(Matthew 5.3)*

Alleluia. Alleluia. Blessed are the poor in spirit; for theirs is the kingdom of heaven! **Alleluia.**

GOSPEL *(Mark 10.17-30)*

The shorter version ends at the asterisks.

The Lord be with you. **And with your spirit.** A reading from the holy Gospel according to Mark. **Glory to you, O Lord.**

As Jesus was setting out on a journey, a man ran up and knelt before him, and asked him, "Good Teacher, what must I do to inherit eternal life?"

Jesus said to him, "Why do you call me good? No one is good but God alone. You know the commandments: 'You shall not murder; You shall not commit adultery; You shall not steal; You shall not bear false witness; You shall not defraud; Honour your father and mother.'"

He said to Jesus, "Teacher, I have kept all these since my youth." Jesus, looking at him, loved him and said, "You lack one thing; go, sell what you own, and give the money to the poor, and you will have treasure in heaven; then come, follow me."

When the man heard this, he was shocked and went away grieving, for he had many possessions.

Then Jesus looked around and said to his disciples, "How hard it will be for those who have wealth to enter the kingdom of God!" And the disciples were perplexed at these words. But Jesus said to them again, "Children, how hard it is to enter the kingdom of God! It is easier for a camel to go through the eye of a needle than for someone who is rich to enter the kingdom of God."

They were greatly astounded and said to one another, "Then who can be saved?" Jesus looked at them and said, "For humans it is impossible, but not for God; for God all things are possible."

* * *

Peter began to say to him, "Look, we have left everything and followed you." Jesus said, "Truly I tell you, there is no one who has left house or brothers or sisters or mother or father or children or fields, for my sake and for the sake of the good news, who will not receive a hundredfold now in this age — houses, brothers and sisters, mothers and children, and fields — but with persecutions — and in the age to come, eternal life."

The Gospel of the Lord. **Praise to you, Lord Jesus Christ.**

PROFESSION OF FAITH *(p. 11)*

PRAYER OF THE FAITHFUL

The following intentions are suggestions only. There are more suggestions at www.livingwithchrist.ca

R. **Lord, hear our prayer.**

For all God's people, open to responding to the call of Jesus, we pray to the Lord: R.

For all leaders, summoned by God to help bring about the reign of love, we pray to the Lord: R.

For persons who struggle with poverty, and for those who choose to live in voluntary simplicity, we pray to the Lord: R.

For God's People gathered here, called to recognize God among us, we pray to the Lord: R.

PREPARATION OF THE GIFTS *(p. 14)*

PRAYER OVER THE OFFERINGS

Accept, O Lord, the prayers of your faithful with the sacrificial offerings, that, through these acts of devotedness, we may pass over to the glory of heaven. Through Christ our Lord. **Amen.**

PREFACE *(Sundays in Ordinary Time, p. 29)*

COMMUNION ANTIPHON *(Cf. Psalm 33.11)*
The rich suffer want and go hungry, but those who seek the Lord lack no blessing.

or (1 John 3.2)

When the Lord appears, we shall be like him, for we shall see him as he is.

PRAYER AFTER COMMUNION

We entreat your majesty most humbly, O Lord, that, as you feed us with the nourishment which comes from the most holy Body and Blood of your Son, so you may make us sharers of his divine nature. Who lives and reigns for ever and ever. **Amen.**

BLESSING AND DISMISSAL *(p. 71)*

October 21
29th Sunday in Ordinary Time
World Mission Sunday

"Teacher, we want you to do for us whatever we ask of you." We can often identify with both James and John from this Gospel passage when we directly ask God for what we want. Or perhaps we do it indirectly. We attend Mass regularly, act more obediently, and secretly hope that God is noticing and will make our requests come to fruition.

I think of how often I have treated Jesus like that one friend who people call only when they need something. Imagine if your phone rang only when people needed something from you. It would become pretty tiresome. However, Jesus does not scold his disciples, or us, for these requests.

Jesus makes reference to his ultimate sacrifice. He tries to tell them that he has come to die on the cross, to pay for the sins of the world, so that we may have a loving relationship with God.

God hears all of our requests. He knows exactly what we need and when we need it. I, myself, have made some pretty steep requests, and while God might not seem to answer when I want him to, he answers when I need it. He gives me so much more than what I asked for. He gave the ultimate sacrifice of his only Son.

Jacki Lavigne
Kitchener, ON

ENTRANCE ANTIPHON *(Cf. Psalm 16.6, 8)*
To you I call; for you will surely heed me, O God; turn your ear to me; hear my words. Guard me as the apple of your eye; in the shadow of your wings protect me.

INTRODUCTORY RITES *(p. 5)*

COLLECT
Almighty ever-living God, grant that we may always conform our will to yours and serve your majesty in sincerity of heart. Through our Lord Jesus Christ, your Son, who lives and reigns with you in the unity of the Holy Spirit, one God, for ever and ever. **Amen.**

FIRST READING *(Isaiah 53.10-11)*
It was the will of the Lord to crush him with pain. When you make his life an offering for sin, he shall see his offspring, and shall prolong his days; through him the will of the Lord shall prosper. Out of his anguish he shall see light; he shall find satisfaction through his knowledge. The righteous one, my servant, shall make many righteous, and he shall bear their iniquities.
    The word of the Lord. **Thanks be to God.**

RESPONSORIAL PSALM *(Psalm 33)*

Let your love be up-on us, Lord, e-ven as we hope in you.

R̷. **Let your love be upon on us, Lord, even as we hope in you.**

The word of the Lord is · **upright,**
and all his work is done in · **faithfulness.**
He loves righteousness and · **justice;**
the earth is full of the steadfast love of the ·
Lord. R̷.

Truly the eye of the Lord is on those who ·
fear_him,
on those who hope in his steadfast · **love,**
to deliver their soul from · **death,**
and to keep them alive in · **famine.** R̷.

Our soul waits for the · **Lord;**
he is our help and · **shield.**
Let your steadfast love, O Lord, be up-·**on_us,**
even as we hope in · **you.** R̷.

©2009 Gordon Johnston/Novalis

SECOND READING *(Hebrews 4.14-16)*
Brothers and sisters: Since we have a great high
priest who has passed through the heavens, Jesus,
the Son of God, let us hold fast to our confession.
For we do not have a high priest who is unable to

sympathize with our weaknesses, but we have one who in every respect has been tested as we are, yet without sin.

Let us therefore approach the throne of grace with boldness, so that we may receive mercy and find grace to help in time of need.

The word of the Lord. **Thanks be to God.**

GOSPEL ACCLAMATION *(Mark 10.45)*
Alleluia. Alleluia. The Son of Man came to serve and to give his life as a ransom for many. **Alleluia.**

GOSPEL *(Mark 10.35-45)*
The shorter version begins at the asterisks.

The Lord be with you. **And with your spirit.**
A reading from the holy Gospel according to Mark.
Glory to you, O Lord.

James and John, the sons of Zebedee, came forward to Jesus and said to him, "Teacher, we want you to do for us whatever we ask of you." And Jesus said to them, "What is it you want me to do for you?" And they said to him, "Grant us to sit, one at your right hand and one at your left, in your glory."

But Jesus said to them, "You do not know what you are asking. Are you able to drink the cup that I drink, or be baptized with the baptism that I am baptized with?" They replied, "We are able."

Then Jesus said to them, "The cup that I drink you will drink; and with the baptism with which I am baptized, you will be baptized; but to sit at my right hand or at my left is not mine to grant, but it is for those for whom it has been prepared."

When the ten heard this, they began to be angry with James and John.

* * *

So Jesus called them and said to them, "You know that among the Gentiles those whom they recognize as their rulers lord it over them, and their great ones are tyrants over them. But it is not so among you; whoever wishes to become great among you must be your servant, and whoever wishes to be first among you must be slave of all. For the Son of Man came not to be served but to serve, and to give his life as a ransom for many."

The Gospel of the Lord. **Praise to you, Lord Jesus Christ.**

PROFESSION OF FAITH (p. 11)

PRAYER OF THE FAITHFUL

The following intentions are suggestions only. There are more suggestions at www.livingwithchrist.ca

R. **Lord, hear our prayer.**

For the mission of the Church in the world, we pray to the Lord: R.

For leaders who work for justice and peace in the world, we pray to the Lord: R.

For all who suffer from poverty or isolation, we pray to the Lord: R.

For each of us called to witness to God's love and compassion, we pray to the Lord: R.

PREPARATION OF THE GIFTS *(p. 14)*

PRAYER OVER THE OFFERINGS
Grant us, Lord, we pray, a sincere respect for your gifts, that, through the purifying action of your grace, we may be cleansed by the very mysteries we serve. Through Christ our Lord. **Amen.**

PREFACE *(Sundays in Ordinary Time, p. 29)*

COMMUNION ANTIPHON *(Cf. Psalm 32.18-19)*
Behold, the eyes of the Lord are on those who fear him, who hope in his merciful love, to rescue their souls from death, to keep them alive in famine.
or (Mark 10.45)
The Son of Man has come to give his life as a ransom for many.

PRAYER AFTER COMMUNION
Grant, O Lord, we pray, that, benefiting from participation in heavenly things, we may be helped by what you give in this present age and prepared for the gifts that are eternal. Through Christ our Lord. **Amen.**

BLESSING AND DISMISSAL *(p. 71)*

October 28
30th Sunday in Ordinary Time

Do you know what you want? Really want? Sometimes we act like we want things that we do not need, which might be harmful for us. Or are we blind because we have not thought it through, are being impulsive, or have not dug deep enough into our heart and soul to see what we want.

Try keeping it simple – an act that requires confidence and humility.

Bartimaeus follows this principle. He knows what he wants – his sight. Furthermore, he has faith that he will get his sight even before he asks for the miracle from Jesus. He casts aside his cloak – hardly an act of a blind person who could not find anything within reach. Jesus uses the same economy; he cures Bartimaeus and reveals the key to the cure.

How many of us cling to things that interfere with getting closer to God? Often, we wear them like a cloak – envy, gluttony, greed or avarice, lust, pride, sloth and wrath. These sins are often confused with what we need and want, and we sometimes try to justify hanging onto them. But in the end, we find that they distance us from God.

The miraculous key that Jesus identified is faith. Do we have the courage to fling off the cloak? It is that simple – faith can help us find the way when we are blinded by confusion over what is important. Faith will save us.

Patrick M. Doyle
Carleton Place, ON

ENTRANCE ANTIPHON *(Cf. Psalm 104.3-4)*
Let the hearts that seek the Lord rejoice; turn to the
Lord and his strength; constantly seek his face.

INTRODUCTORY RITES *(p. 5)*

COLLECT
Almighty ever-living God, increase our faith, hope
and charity, and make us love what you command,
so that we may merit what you promise. Through
our Lord Jesus Christ, your Son, who lives and reigns
with you in the unity of the Holy Spirit, one God, for
ever and ever. **Amen.**

FIRST READING *(Jeremiah 31.7-9)*
Thus says the Lord:
"Sing aloud with gladness for Jacob,
and raise shouts for the chief of the nations;
proclaim, give praise, and say,
'Save, O Lord, your people,
the remnant of Israel.'

"See, I am going to bring them from the land of the
    north,
and gather them from the farthest parts of the earth,
among them those who are blind and those who
    are lame,
those with child and those in labour, together;
a great company, they shall return here.

"With weeping they shall come,
and with consolations I will lead them back,
I will let them walk by brooks of water,
in a straight path in which they shall not stumble;

for I have become a father to Israel,
and Ephraim is my firstborn."

The word of the Lord. **Thanks be to God.**

RESPONSORIAL PSALM *(Psalm 126)*

The Lord has done great things for us; we are filled with

joy.

R. **The Lord has done great things for us;
we are filled with joy.**

When the Lord restored the fortunes of · **Zion,**
we were like those who · **dream.**
Then our mouth was filled with · **laughter,**
and our tongue with shouts · **of** joy. R.

Then it was said among the · **nations,**
"The Lord has done great things for · **them."**
The Lord has done great things for · **us,**
and we · **re**-joiced. R.

Restore our fortunes, O · **Lord,**
like the watercourses in the desert of the · **Negev.**
May those who sow in · **tears**
reap with shouts · **of** joy. R.

Those who go out · **weeping,**
bearing the seed for · **sowing,**
shall come home with shouts of · **joy,**
carrying · **their** sheaves. R.

©2009 Gordon Johnston/Novalis

SECOND READING *(Hebrews 5.1-6)*

Every high priest chosen from among men is put in charge of things pertaining to God on their behalf, to offer gifts and sacrifices for sins. He is able to deal gently with the ignorant and wayward, since he himself is subject to weakness; and because of this he must offer sacrifice for his own sins as well as for those of the people. And one does not presume to take this honour, but takes it only when called by God, just as Aaron was.

So also Christ did not glorify himself in becoming a high priest, but was appointed by the one who said to him, "You are my Son, today I have begotten you"; as he says also in another place, "You are a priest forever, according to the order of Melchizedek."

The word of the Lord. **Thanks be to God.**

GOSPEL ACCLAMATION *(2 Timothy 1.10)*
Alleluia. Alleluia. Our Saviour Jesus Christ has abolished death and brought us life through the Gospel. **Alleluia.**

GOSPEL *(Mark 10.46-52)*
The Lord be with you. **And with your spirit.**
A reading from the holy Gospel according to Mark. **Glory to you, O Lord.**

As Jesus and his disciples and a large crowd were leaving Jericho, Bartimaeus son of Timaeus, a blind beggar, was sitting by the roadside. When he heard that it was Jesus of Nazareth, he began to shout out and say, "Jesus, Son of David, have mercy on me!" Many sternly ordered him to be quiet, but he cried out even more loudly, "Son of David, have mercy on me!"

Jesus stood still and said, "Call him here." And they called the blind man, saying to him, "Take heart; get up, he is calling you." So throwing off his cloak, he sprang up and came to Jesus.

Then Jesus said to him, "What do you want me to do for you?" The blind man said to him, "My teacher, let me see again." Jesus said to him, "Go; your faith has made you well."

Immediately the man regained his sight and followed Jesus on the way.

The Gospel of the Lord. **Praise to you, Lord Jesus Christ.**

PROFESSION OF FAITH (p. 11)

PRAYER OF THE FAITHFUL

The following intentions are suggestions only. There are more suggestions at www.livingwithchrist.ca

℟. **Lord, hear our prayer.**

For the Church, striving to grow in holiness, we pray to the Lord: ℟.

For world leaders, called to govern with wisdom, mercy and compassion, we pray to the Lord: ℟.

For all who hunger for the justice denied to them, we pray to the Lord: ℟.

For young people and their families in their desire to live and grow in discipleship with Jesus, we pray to the Lord: ℟.

PREPARATION OF THE GIFTS (p. 14)

PRAYER OVER THE OFFERINGS
Look, we pray, O Lord, on the offerings we make to your majesty, that whatever is done by us in your service may be directed above all to your glory. Through Christ our Lord. **Amen.**

PREFACE (Sundays in Ordinary Time, p. 29)

COMMUNION ANTIPHON (Cf. Psalm 19.6)
We will ring out our joy at your saving help and exult in the name of our God.
or (Ephesians 5.2)
Christ loved us and gave himself up for us, as a fragrant offering to God.

PRAYER AFTER COMMUNION
May your Sacraments, O Lord, we pray, perfect in us what lies within them, that what we now celebrate in signs we may one day possess in truth. Through Christ our Lord. **Amen.**

BLESSING AND DISMISSAL (p. 71)

November Saints' Days

The following saints are traditionally remembered in November in Canada.

1 All Saints
2 All Souls' Day
3 Saint Martin de Porres
4 Saint Charles Borromeo
10 Saint Leo the Great
11 Saint Martin of Tours
12 Saint Josaphat
15 Saint Albert the Great
16 Saint Margaret of Scotland
Saint Gertrude
17 Saint Elizabeth of Hungary
22 Saint Cecilia
23 Saint Clement I
Saint Columban
24 Saint Andrew Düng-Lac and Companions
25 Saint Catherine of Alexandria
30 Saint Andrew

November 4
31st Sunday in Ordinary Time

I have been spending time with people who know the law enough to know that they have broken it. From the beginning of time, they have been told by those around them that they are damaged goods, not worthy of care and attention. Some of them have been shamed in the core of their being and their law-abiding communities have attempted to straighten them out even if it kills them.

The "damaged goods" people cope with the bad news of not being good enough by using drugs or other ways of numbing their pain; then they sell their bodies to use more drugs; some get pregnant and end their pregnancy; and to survive the shame and the guilt that is choking them they then use even more drugs.

If Christ came today, he would come again for such as these. He would spend time with them and love them in their "as is" state. When the law-abiding neighbours would approach him with their mistrust and disapproval, he would remind them of the good news that the Law is Love. If they loved God full-time and cared for their neighbour for the rest of the time, the reign of God would be theirs here and now.

Mária Karajovanova
Toronto, ON

ENTRANCE ANTIPHON *(Cf. Psalm 37.22-23)*
Forsake me not, O Lord, my God; be not far from me! Make haste and come to my help, O Lord, my strong salvation!

INTRODUCTORY RITES *(p. 5)*

COLLECT
Almighty and merciful God, by whose gift your faithful offer you right and praiseworthy service, grant, we pray, that we may hasten without stumbling to receive the things you have promised. Through our Lord Jesus Christ, your Son, who lives and reigns with you in the unity of the Holy Spirit, one God, for ever and ever. **Amen.**

FIRST READING *(Deuteronomy 6.2-6)*
Moses spoke to the people: "May you and your children and your children's children fear the Lord your God all the days of your life, and keep all his decrees and his commandments that I am commanding you, so that your days may be long.

"Hear therefore, O Israel, and observe them diligently, so that it may go well with you, and so that you may multiply greatly in a land flowing with milk and honey, as the Lord, the God of your Fathers, has promised you.

"Hear, O Israel: The Lord is our God, the Lord alone. You shall love the Lord your God with all your heart, and with all your soul, and with all your might. Keep these words that I am commanding you today in your heart."

The word of the Lord. **Thanks be to God.**

RESPONSORIAL PSALM *(Psalm 18)*

R. **I love you, O Lord, my strength.**

I love you, O Lord, my · **strength.**
The Lord is my rock, my fortress, and my de-·
   liverer.
My God, my rock in whom I take · **refuge,**
my shield, and the source of my salvation, · **my**
   stronghold. R.

I call upon the Lord, who is worthy to be ·
   praised,
so I shall be saved from my · **enemies.**
From his temple he heard my · **voice,**
and my cry to him reached · **his** ears. R.

The Lord lives! Blessed be my · **rock,**
and exalted be the God of my sal-·**vation.**
Great triumphs he gives to his · **king,**
and shows steadfast love to · **his_a-**nointed. R.

©2009 Gordon Johnston/Novalis

SECOND READING *(Hebrews 7.23-28)*
The priests of the first covenant were many in number, because they were prevented by death from
continuing in office; but Jesus holds his priesthood
permanently, because he continues forever. Con-

sequently he is able for all time to save those who approach God through him, since he always lives to make intercession for them.

For it was fitting that we should have such a high priest, holy, blameless, undefiled, separated from sinners, and exalted above the heavens. Unlike the other high priests, he has no need to offer sacrifices day after day, first for his own sins, and then for those of the people; this he did once for all when he offered himself.

For the law appoints as high priests those who are subject to weakness, but the word of the oath, which came later than the law, appoints a Son who has been made perfect forever.

The word of the Lord. **Thanks be to God.**

GOSPEL ACCLAMATION *(John 14.23)*
Alleluia. Alleluia. Whoever loves me will keep my word, and my Father will love him, and we will come to him. **Alleluia.**

GOSPEL *(Mark 12.28-34)*
The Lord be with you. **And with your spirit.**
A reading from the holy Gospel according to Mark.
Glory to you, O Lord.

One of the scribes came near and heard the religious authorities disputing with one another, and seeing that Jesus answered them well, he asked him, "Which commandment is the first of all?"

Jesus answered, "The first is, 'Hear, O Israel: the Lord our God, the Lord is one; you shall love the Lord your God with all your heart, and with all your soul, and with all your mind, and with all your strength.'

The second is this, 'You shall love your neighbour as yourself.' There is no other commandment greater than these."

Then the scribe said to him, "You are right, Teacher; you have truly said that 'he is one, and besides him there is no other'; and 'to love him with all the heart, and with all the understanding, and with all the strength,' and 'to love one's neighbour as oneself,' — this is much more important than all whole burnt offerings and sacrifices."

When Jesus saw that the scribe answered wisely, he said to him, "You are not far from the kingdom of God."

After that no one dared to ask Jesus any question.

The Gospel of the Lord. **Praise to you, Lord Jesus Christ.**

PROFESSION OF FAITH *(p. 11)*

PRAYER OF THE FAITHFUL

The following intentions are suggestions only. There are more suggestions at www.livingwithchrist.ca

R. **Lord, hear our prayer.**

For the Church and its mission of justice and peace, we pray to the Lord: R.

For a fair distribution of resources, talent, time and possessions in our society, we pray to the Lord: R.

For those excluded from sharing in the fullness of creation, we pray to the Lord: R.

For a strong witness to the greatest commandment in this faith community, we pray to the Lord: R.

PREPARATION OF THE GIFTS *(p. 14)*

PRAYER OVER THE OFFERINGS
May these sacrificial offerings, O Lord, become for you a pure oblation, and for us a holy outpouring of your mercy. Through Christ our Lord. **Amen.**

PREFACE *(Sundays in Ordinary Time, p. 29)*

COMMUNION ANTIPHON *(Cf. Psalm 15.11)*
You will show me the path of life, the fullness of joy in your presence, O Lord.
or (John 6.58)
Just as the living Father sent me and I have life because of the Father, so whoever feeds on me shall have life because of me, says the Lord.

PRAYER AFTER COMMUNION
May the working of your power, O Lord, increase in us, we pray, so that, renewed by these heavenly Sacraments, we may be prepared by your gift for receiving what they promise. Through Christ our Lord. **Amen.**

BLESSING AND DISMISSAL *(p. 71)*

November 11
32nd Sunday in Ordinary Time
Remembrance Day

The Gospel today cautions us: hypocrisy and inauthenticity are worse than useless. In fact, they are condemnable. Putting on a show of righteousness will fool no one, and it certainly does not do the deceiver any good. Instead, we should cultivate authentic giving, like the poor widow who gave her last coins. Our gifts and our lives should be offered with humility and abandonment. If we grip tightly onto our last coin, we block God, grace and the potential of being transformed for our greatest good. The tale of the poor widow is meant to spark a conversion of the heart. It calls us to great openness. It is a big risk to surrender everything of value; when we surrender to a merciful God, it is called trust.

Today is also Remembrance Day, a day when we honour men and women who gave their lives in the pursuit of peace. Their self-offering was an act of hope. This is also a day when we are reminded of the horrors of war and of some of the worst aspects of our shared human nature. Our Gospel today underlines the necessity of each person accepting, and relying on, God's grace and goodness. Peace comes in every moment of conversion (literally, "turning"), away from the darkness in our hearts and in the world. When we turn toward the Lord, and offer him everything, we make room for peace to break in.

Kate McGee
Toronto, ON

ENTRANCE ANTIPHON *(Cf. Psalm 87.3)*
Let my prayer come into your presence. Incline your ear to my cry for help, O Lord.

INTRODUCTORY RITES *(p. 5)*

COLLECT
Almighty and merciful God, graciously keep from us all adversity, so that, unhindered in mind and body alike, we may pursue in freedom of heart the things that are yours. Through our Lord Jesus Christ, your Son, who lives and reigns with you in the unity of the Holy Spirit, one God, for ever and ever. **Amen.**

FIRST READING *(1 Kings 17.10-16)*
Elijah, the Prophet, set out and went to Zarephath. When he came to the gate of the town, a widow was there gathering sticks; he called to her and said, "Bring me a little water in a vessel, so that I may drink." As she was going to bring it, he called to her and said, "Bring me a morsel of bread in your hand."

But she said, "As the Lord your God lives, I have nothing baked, only a handful of meal in a jar, and a little oil in a jug; I am now gathering a couple of sticks, so that I may go home and prepare it for myself and my son, that we may eat it, and die."

Elijah said to her, "Do not be afraid; go and do as you have said; but first make me a little cake of it and bring it to me, and afterwards make something for yourself and your son. For thus says the Lord the God of Israel: 'The jar of meal will not be emptied and the jug of oil will not fail until the day that the Lord sends rain on the earth.'"

She went and did as Elijah said, so that she as well as he and her household ate for many days. The jar of meal was not emptied, neither did the jug of oil fail, according to the word of the Lord that he spoke by Elijah.

The word of the Lord. Thanks be to God.

RESPONSORIAL PSALM *(Psalm 146)*

Praise the Lord, O my soul!

R̶. **Praise the Lord, O my soul!**
or **Alleluia!**

It is the Lord who keeps faith for·-**ever,**
who executes justice for the op·-**pressed;**
who gives food to the · **hungry.**
The Lord sets the · **prisoners** free. R̶.

The Lord opens the eyes of the · **blind**
and lifts up those who are bowed · **down;**
the Lord loves the · **righteous**
and watches over · **the** strangers. R̶.

The Lord upholds the orphan and the · **widow,**
but the way of the wicked he brings to · **ruin.**
The Lord will reign for·-**ever,**
your God, O Zion, for all · **gener**-ations. R̶.

©2009 Gordon Johnston/Novalis

SECOND READING *(Hebrews 9.24-28)*

Christ did not enter a sanctuary made by human hands, a mere copy of the true one, but he entered into heaven itself, now to appear in the presence of God on our behalf.

Nor was it to offer himself again and again, as the high priest enters the Holy Place year after year with blood that is not his own; for then he would have had to suffer again and again since the foundation of the world.

But as it is, he has appeared once for all at the end of the age to remove sin by the sacrifice of himself. And just as it is appointed for human beings to die once, and after that comes the judgment, so Christ, having been offered once to bear the sins of many, will appear a second time, not to deal with sin, but to save those who are eagerly waiting for him.

The word of the Lord. **Thanks be to God.**

GOSPEL ACCLAMATION *(Matthew 5.3)*

Alleluia. Alleluia. Blessed are the poor in spirit; for theirs is the kingdom of heaven! **Alleluia.**

GOSPEL *(Mark 12.38-44)*

The shorter version begins at the asterisks.

The Lord be with you. **And with your spirit.** A reading from the holy Gospel according to Mark. **Glory to you, O Lord.**

Jesus was teaching in the temple, and a large crowd was listening to him. He said, "Beware of the scribes, who like to walk around in long robes, and to be greeted with respect in the marketplaces, and to have the best seats in the synagogues and places of honour at banquets! They devour widows' houses and for the sake of appearance say long prayers. They will receive the greater condemnation."

* * *

Jesus sat down opposite the treasury, and watched the crowd putting money into the treasury. Many rich people put in large sums. A poor widow came and put in two small copper coins, which are worth a penny. Then he called his disciples and said to them, "Truly I tell you, this poor widow has put in more than all those who are contributing to the treasury. For all of them have contributed out of their abundance; but she out of her poverty has put in everything she had, all she had to live on."

The Gospel of the Lord. **Praise to you, Lord Jesus Christ.**

PROFESSION OF FAITH *(p. 11)*

PRAYER OF THE FAITHFUL

The following intentions are suggestions only. There are more suggestions at www.livingwithchrist.ca

R. **Lord, hear our prayer.**

For leaders in the Church, as they strive to serve their communities in fidelity and trust, we pray to the Lord: R.

For all who suffer from war, famine and other threats to their security, we pray to the Lord: R.

For those who live without adequate shelter, food or employment, we pray to the Lord: R.

For ourselves, called to fulfill our vocation as people of faith and hope, we pray to the Lord: R.

PREPARATION OF THE GIFTS (p. 14)

PRAYER OVER THE OFFERINGS
Look with favour, we pray, O Lord, upon the sacrificial gifts offered here, that, celebrating in mystery the Passion of your Son, we may honour it with loving devotion. Through Christ our Lord. **Amen.**

PREFACE (Sundays in Ordinary Time, p. 29)

COMMUNION ANTIPHON (Cf. Psalm 22.1-2)
The Lord is my shepherd; there is nothing I shall want. Fresh and green are the pastures where he gives me repose, near restful waters he leads me.
or (Cf. Luke 24.35)
The disciples recognized the Lord Jesus in the breaking of bread.

PRAYER AFTER COMMUNION
Nourished by this sacred gift, O Lord, we give you thanks and beseech your mercy, that, by the pouring forth of your Spirit, the grace of integrity may endure in those your heavenly power has entered. Through Christ our Lord. **Amen.**

BLESSING AND DISMISSAL (p. 71)

November 18
33rd Sunday in Ordinary Time

In this week's Gospel, Jesus reminds his disciples to learn the lesson of the fig tree, that summer will follow new leaves. He asks us to also be attentive to the end of things. At the close of the church year, we practise being attentive to the ends of things: suffering, darkness and things falling apart.

Jesus promised that when we see darkness and destruction, suffering and pain, "he is near, at the very gates." Ironically, in the most difficult times of our lives, many of us are more likely to feel alone and distanced from God. It is easy to see summer coming after the spring, and harder to recognize the winter as the birthplace of spring. Jesus is inviting his disciples, and us, to remember that he draws near now, in the messiness of our world.

The central mystery of our faith is that death is followed by rising. God brings new life from ashes, sends a baby to save the world, dies to death when he walks out of the tomb. No matter how messy life has become, God invites us to be the people who pay attention, who wait for and expect new life.

May our hearts turn with gratitude toward God in the midst of struggle, hoping to see what gifts he will bring out of the difficulty.

Leah Perrault
Saskatoon, SK

ENTRANCE ANTIPHON *(Jeremiah 29.11, 12, 14)*
The Lord said: I think thoughts of peace and not of affliction. You will call upon me, and I will answer you, and I will lead back your captives from every place.

INTRODUCTORY RITES *(p. 5)*

COLLECT
Grant us, we pray, O Lord our God, the constant gladness of being devoted to you, for it is full and lasting happiness to serve with constancy the author of all that is good. Through our Lord Jesus Christ, your Son, who lives and reigns with you in the unity of the Holy Spirit, one God, for ever and ever. **Amen.**

FIRST READING *(Daniel 12.1-3)*
At that time Michael, the great prince, the protector of your people, shall arise. There shall be a time of anguish, such as has never occurred since nations first came into existence. But at that time your people shall be delivered, everyone who is found written in the book. Many of those who sleep in the dust of the earth shall awake, some to everlasting life, and some to shame and everlasting contempt.

Those who are wise shall shine like the brightness of the sky, and those who lead many to righteousness, like the stars forever and ever.

The word of the Lord. **Thanks be to God.**

RESPONSORIAL PSALM *(Psalm 16)*

Pro-tect me, O God,— for in you I take re-fuge.—

R. **Protect me, O God, for in you I take refuge.**

The Lord is my chosen portion · **and_my** cup;
you hold · **my** lot.
I keep the Lord always · **be**-fore_me;
because he is at my right hand, I shall · **not** be
    moved. R.

Therefore my heart is glad, and my soul ·
    re-joices;
my body also rests · **se**-cure.
For you do not give me up · **to** Sheol,
or let your faithful one · **see** the Pit. R.

You show me the path · **of** life.
In your presence there is fullness · **of** joy;
in your right hand · **are** pleasures
for--**ev**-er-more. R.

©2009 Gordon Johnston/Novalis

SECOND READING *(Hebrews 10.11-14, 18)*
Every priest stands day after day at his service, offering again and again the same sacrifices that can
never take away sins.

But when Christ had offered for all time a single
sacrifice for sins, "he sat down at the right hand of

God," and since then has been waiting "until his enemies would be made a footstool for his feet." For by a single offering he has perfected for all time those who are sanctified.

Where there is forgiveness of sin and lawless deeds, there is no longer any offering for sin.

The word of the Lord. **Thanks be to God.**

GOSPEL ACCLAMATION *(Luke 21.36)*
Alleluia. Alleluia. Be alert at all times, praying that you may be able to stand before the Son of Man. **Alleluia.**

GOSPEL *(Mark 13.24-32)*
The Lord be with you. **And with your spirit.** A reading from the holy Gospel according to Mark. **Glory to you, O Lord.**

Jesus spoke to his disciples about the end which is to come:

"In those days, after the time of suffering, the sun will be darkened, and the moon will not give its light, and the stars will be falling from heaven, and the powers in the heavens will be shaken.

"Then they will see 'the Son of Man coming in clouds' with great power and glory. Then he will send out the Angels, and gather his elect from the four winds, from the ends of the earth to the ends of heaven.

"From the fig tree learn its lesson: as soon as its branch becomes tender and puts forth its leaves, you know that summer is near. So also, when you see these things taking place, you know that he is near, at the very gates.

"Truly I tell you, this generation will not pass away until all these things have taken place. Heaven and earth will pass away, but my words will not pass away.

"But about that day or hour no one knows, neither the Angels in heaven, nor the Son, but only the Father."

The Gospel of the Lord. **Praise to you, Lord Jesus Christ.**

PROFESSION OF FAITH *(p. 11)*

PRAYER OF THE FAITHFUL

The following intentions are suggestions only. There are more suggestions at www.livingwithchrist.ca

R̷. **Lord, hear our prayer.**

For the Church, working to overcome divisions between persons, races and nations, we pray to the Lord: R̷.

For the world, longing for its promised salvation, we pray to the Lord: R̷.

For all who desire freedom from oppression in their lives, we pray to the Lord: R̷.

For our parish community, striving each day to become a more authentic witness to the gospel, we pray to the Lord: R̷.

PREPARATION OF THE GIFTS *(p. 14)*

PRAYER OVER THE OFFERINGS
Grant, O Lord, we pray, that what we offer in the sight of your majesty may obtain for us the grace of being devoted to you and gain us the prize of everlasting happiness. Through Christ our Lord. **Amen.**

PREFACE *(Sundays in Ordinary Time, p. 29)*

COMMUNION ANTIPHON *(Psalm 72.28)*
To be near God is my happiness, to place my hope in God the Lord.
or (Mark 11.23-24)
Amen, I say to you: Whatever you ask in prayer, believe that you will receive, and it shall be given to you, says the Lord.

PRAYER AFTER COMMUNION
We have partaken of the gifts of this sacred mystery, humbly imploring, O Lord, that what your Son commanded us to do in memory of him may bring us growth in charity. Through Christ our Lord. **Amen.**

BLESSING AND DISMISSAL *(p. 71)*

November 25
Our Lord Jesus Christ, King of the Universe

In today's Gospel the kingdom of heaven and the kingdom of Earth clash. Although Pilate is not a king, he is the representative of the most powerful king in the world, Caesar. Therefore, this is the day that the "king" of Earth finally meets Christ the King face to face. We must all decide for ourselves to which of these kings we will pledge our allegiance, now and for eternity.

What does the king of Earth promise us? Just think of everything with which Satan tempted Jesus in the desert. Power, fame, worldly glory, material riches, pleasure and so on. He tempts us with these temporary gratifications all the time. Meanwhile Christ the King makes it clear that following him will be difficult. His subjects are certain to face trials and persecutions, and suffer for their loyalty to him.

Yet which king will make us happy? The short-term gratifications of the king of Earth are illusions. They do not lead to lasting joy or peace, but rather to loneliness, emptiness, misery and ultimately to hell. We are the children of God, made in his image and likeness. Only in him will the deepest longings of our soul be satisfied. Only in him will we find rest. The whole Bible boils down to a choice: to which king will you pledge allegiance? Give your life to Christ the King, who lives and reigns now and forever. Amen.

Connor Brownrigg
Ottawa, ON

ENTRANCE ANTIPHON *(Revelation 5.12; 1.6)*

How worthy is the Lamb who was slain, to receive power and divinity, and wisdom and strength and honour. To him belong glory and power for ever and ever.

INTRODUCTORY RITES *(p. 5)*

COLLECT

Almighty ever-living God, whose will is to restore all things in your beloved Son, the King of the universe, grant, we pray, that the whole creation, set free from slavery, may render your majesty service and ceaselessly proclaim your praise. Through our Lord Jesus Christ, your Son, who lives and reigns with you in the unity of the Holy Spirit, one God, for ever and ever. **Amen.**

FIRST READING *(Daniel 7.13-14)*

I had a dream and visions as I lay in bed. As I watched in the night visions, I saw one like a son of man coming with the clouds of heaven. And he came to the One who is Ancient of Days and was presented before him.

To him was given dominion and glory and kingship, that all peoples, nations and languages should serve him. His dominion is an everlasting dominion that shall not pass away, and his kingship is one that shall never be destroyed.

The word of the Lord. **Thanks be to God.**

RESPONSORIAL PSALM (Psalm 93)

The Lord is king; he is robed in maj-es-ty.

℟. **The Lord is king; he is robed in majesty.**

The Lord is king, he is robed · **in** majesty;
the Lord · **is** robed,
he is · **girded** with strength. ℟.

He has established the world; it shall never ·
be moved;
your throne is established · **from_of** old;
you are from · **ev**-er-lasting. ℟.

Your decrees are · **very** sure;
holiness befits · **your** house,
O Lord, for--**ev**-er-more. ℟.

©2009 Gordon Johnston/Novalis

SECOND READING (Revelation 1.5-8)

Jesus Christ is the faithful witness, the firstborn of the dead, and the ruler of the kings of the earth. To him who loves us and freed us from our sins by his blood, and made us to be a kingdom, priests serving his God and Father, to him be glory and dominion forever and ever. Amen.

Look! He is coming with the clouds; every eye will see him, even those who pierced him; and on his account all the tribes of the earth will lament. So it is to be. Amen.

"I am the Alpha and the Omega," says the Lord God, who is and who was and who is to come, the Almighty.

The word of the Lord. **Thanks be to God.**

GOSPEL ACCLAMATION *(Mark 11.9-10)*
Alleluia. Alleluia. Blessed is the coming kingdom of our father David; blessed is the one who comes in the name of the Lord! **Alleluia.**

GOSPEL *(John 18.33b-37)*
The Lord be with you. **And with your spirit.** A reading from the holy Gospel according to John. **Glory to you, O Lord.**

Pilate asked Jesus, "Are you the King of the Jews?"

Jesus answered, "Do you ask this on your own, or did others tell you about me?"

Pilate replied, "I am not a Jew, am I? Your own nation and the chief priests have handed you over to me. What have you done?"

Jesus answered, "My kingdom is not from this world. If my kingdom were from this world, my followers would be fighting to keep me from being handed over to the Jews. But as it is, my kingdom is not from here."

Pilate asked him, "So you are a king?"

Jesus answered, "You say that I am a king. For this I was born, and for this I came into the world, to testify to the truth. Everyone who belongs to the truth listens to my voice."

The Gospel of the Lord. **Praise to you, Lord Jesus Christ.**

PROFESSION OF FAITH *(p. 11)*

PRAYER OF THE FAITHFUL

The following intentions are suggestions only. There are more suggestions at www.livingwithchrist.ca

R. **Lord, hear our prayer.**

For the Church, called to work together to bring about God's kingdom of truth and love, we pray to the Lord: R.

For world leaders who follow Christ's example of humility and service, we pray to the Lord: R.

For those struggling with injustice, privation and a loss of hope, we pray to the Lord: R.

For this parish, working to build up the kingdom of God, we pray to the Lord: R.

PREPARATION OF THE GIFTS *(p. 14)*

PRAYER OVER THE OFFERINGS

As we offer you, O Lord, the sacrifice by which the human race is reconciled to you, we humbly pray that your Son himself may bestow on all nations the gifts of unity and peace. Through Christ our Lord. **Amen.**

PREFACE *(Christ the King, p. 33)*

COMMUNION ANTIPHON *(Psalm 28.10-11)*
The Lord sits as King for ever. The Lord will bless his people with peace.

PRAYER AFTER COMMUNION

Having received the food of immortality, we ask, O Lord, that, glorying in obedience to the commands of Christ, the King of the universe, we may live with him eternally in his heavenly Kingdom. Who lives and reigns for ever and ever. **Amen.**

BLESSING AND DISMISSAL *(p. 71)*

THE POPE'S PRAYER INTENTIONS FOR 2017-2018

DECEMBER 2017
Universal: The Elderly

That the elderly, sustained by families and Christian communities, may apply their wisdom and experience to spreading the faith and forming the new generations.

JANUARY 2018
Evangelization: Religious Minorities in Asia

That Christians, and other religious minorities in Asian countries, may be able to practise their faith in full freedom.

FEBRUARY 2018
Universal: Say "No" to Corruption

That those who have material, political or spiritual power may resist any lure of corruption.

MARCH 2018
Evangelization: Formation in Spiritual Discernment

That the Church may appreciate the urgency of formation in spiritual discernment, both on the personal and communitarian levels.

* For the Pope's Urgent Prayer Intention for each month, visit www.livingwithchrist.ca

APRIL 2018
Universal: For those who have Responsibility in Economic Matters

That economists may have the courage to reject any economy of exclusion and know how to open new paths.

MAY 2018
Evangelization: The Mission of the Laity

That the lay faithful may fulfill their specific mission, by responding with creativity to the challenges that face the world today.

JUNE 2018
Universal: Social Networks

That social networks may work towards that inclusiveness which respects others for their differences.

JULY 2018
Evangelization: Priests and their Pastoral Ministry

That priests, who experience fatigue and loneliness in their pastoral work, may find help and comfort in their intimacy with the Lord and in their friendship with their brother priests.

AUGUST 2018
Universal: The Treasure of Families

That any far-reaching decisions of economists and politicians may protect the family as one of the treasures of humanity.

SEPTEMBER 2018
Universal: Young People in Africa

That young people in Africa may have access to education and work in their own countries.

OCTOBER 2018
Evangelization: The Mission of Religious

That consecrated religious men and women may bestir themselves, and be present among the poor, the marginalized and those who have no voice.

NOVEMBER 2018
Universal: In the Service of Peace

That the language of love and dialogue may always prevail over the language of conflict.

DECEMBER 2018
Evangelization: In the Service of the Transmission of Faith

That people, who are involved in the service and transmission of faith, may find, in their dialogue with culture, a language suited to the conditions of the present time.

YEAR B: THE GOSPEL OF MARK

With the beginning of Advent, the Church moves into a new liturgical year. In 2017-2018, we observe Year B in what is a three-year cycle, with the majority of Sunday Gospel readings taken from The Gospel of Mark.

Scholars remain divided about several aspects concerning this shortest of the Gospels, which in recent decades has enjoyed new attention because it has been perceived as the earliest Gospel brought to completion and, in many academic circles, one of the base texts for the Gospels of Matthew and Luke.

Many interpreters locate the composition of Mark just prior to, or shortly after, the fall of Jerusalem in 70 AD. Traditionally, the author has been associated with Peter's testimony, writing either for the Church in Rome or for some other community facing persecution.

Mark describes the preaching of Jesus as issuing God's demand to the Galileans of his time to change their hearts because, through Jesus' preaching, God's kingdom had arrived in their midst ("The time is fulfilled, and the kingdom of God has come near; repent, and believe in the Good News" [1.15]).

Mark follows Jesus' call to conversion with peremptory commands to four individuals – Simon [Peter] and Andrew, James and John – to leave their occupation (fishing) and family (Zebedee) in order to fish with Jesus for people to inhabit God's kingdom.

Jesus' invitation for his disciples to have a change of outlook touches them negatively and positively.

Negatively, discipleship meant leaving their way of life and former ties. Positively, it meant following Jesus. Henceforth, they would not only accompany Jesus, but he would let them share his ministry and eventually continue it.

As the gospel proceeds, we see these and other disciples called to "be with him and to be sent out to proclaim the message", even having authority to cast out demons as Jesus did (3.14-15). Jesus' disciples will be invited to an ongoing rethinking of their outlook on life – to conversion.

Well on into his narrative, Mark recounts crowd reactions to Jesus' presence: "Wherever he went, into villages or cities or farms, they laid the sick in the marketplaces, and begged him that they might touch even the fringe of his cloak; and all who touched it were healed" (6.56). [...]

In Mark 8.27–10.52, the evangelist (depicts) Jesus on a "journey" towards his passion, death and resurrection in Jerusalem. "On the way," he tells his disciples how his manner of life is to touch every aspect of their lives: marriage, divorce and the family (10.1-12), humility and service in the community (10.13-16, 35-45) and, lastly, one's attitude towards material possessions or riches.

In all of this divine catechesis, we find the disciples continually struggling with Jesus' teaching (indeed, often misunderstanding it). But we see as well his continual patience as he spells out for them the "way of the kingdom".

Mark's Gospel ends in puzzling fashion with his account of the discovery of the empty tomb. Mark says the faithful women who went to anoint Jesus' body "fled from the tomb, for terror and amazement had seized them; and they said nothing to anyone, for they were afraid" (16.8).

If, as I believe, this is how Mark's Gospel ended – without resurrection appearances – it leaves readers wondering how the gospel message of Jesus' resurrection became known. (Other endings were added later, including the canonical conclusion [16.9-20].)

Mark's abrupt ending challenges people to make a personal decision regarding the truth implied by the discovery of the empty tomb. Other explanations for the empty tomb – the disciples stole the body and perpetrated a hoax in proclaiming the resurrection, or someone else took the body of Jesus away – must yield to the Christian conviction that Jesus has risen from the dead.

Christian readers believe the Good News that Jesus rose from the dead "on the third day". They have heard, too, that the apostles proclaimed the gospel and some were martyred for the faith. Christians understand that what Jesus had promised the night before he died had truly come to pass ("after I am raised up, I will go before you to Galilee" [14.28]). Jesus reunited his followers in Galilee and sent them on mission.

Perhaps the open-ended conclusion to Mark's Gospel should be seen, then, as an invitation to readers to believe the message of the resurrection. Christians must imagine themselves being called by Christ today to put into action in their lives their belief in a Lord who is simultaneously the crucified

("you are looking for Jesus of Nazareth, who was crucified") and risen Lord ("he has been raised" [16.6]).

Christians live between the Easter proclamation
and the return of Christ in glory to bring all things to
their consummation. Mark actually gives his readers
an impression of how that is to be for them in Jesus' eschatological address (13.5-37). Because Jesus
uses biblical images about the end times, the truths
he communicates are simultaneously revealed in
generalities while remaining concealed in their
particularity.

All is really left in God's hands. As Jesus says,
"about that day or hour no one knows, neither the
angels in heaven, nor the Son, but only the Father".

Archbishop Terrence Prendergast, SJ, *Living God's Word: Re-
flections on the Sunday Readings for Year B* (Toronto: Novalis,
2011), pp.12-25.

EUCHARISTIC PRAYERS AND CREATION

The Greek word *eucharistia* (εὐχαριστία) means "thanksgiving" – not only for our own life, but also for the presence of God in the life of the community and for the life that God breathes into his Creation.

The Eucharistic liturgy is, surprisingly, a fertile source of environmental awareness. The liturgy has its roots in the ancient Greek and Semitic cultures, which saw their environment as the result of the creative work of God. This is evident in two commonly used parts of the Eucharistic Prayers: the prayer for the preparation of the gifts, and the prayer immediately following the Sanctus in Eucharistic Prayer III.

PRAYER FOR THE PREPARATION OF THE GIFTS

Blessed are you, Lord God of all creation,
for through your goodness we have received
*   the bread we offer you;*
fruit of the earth and work of human hands,
it will become for us the bread of life.

Blessed are you, Lord God of all creation,
for through your goodness we have received
*   the wine we offer you;*
fruit of the vine and work of human hands,
it will become our spiritual drink.

These two prayers stem from the Jewish prayer of blessing for the bread that has been sung for centuries during the Sabbath and the Passover supper: "Blessed are You, Lord our God, King of the universe, who brings forth bread from the earth." That this ritual meal is organized every year in spring, when nature is reborn, makes the need to give thanks to God even more meaningful. If God no longer provided for us, we could not eat bread, "fruit of the earth," and drink wine, "fruit of the vine." Both are also the result of human labour, a sign that human beings are co-creators with God. Holding the bread in our hands, we marvel that humankind is able to care for the earth and make it even more bountiful.

Knowing that this blessing is so essential, can we just turn our backs and not be mindful of the ecological crisis? God can give us bread and wine, provided there is an ecological balance. But if the soil is impoverished and climate change threatens the harvest, soon nothing will grow and the responsibility will be ours.

BREAD

For the apostles sitting around the table with Jesus at the Last Supper, bread was the product of the land (wheat), the result of human labour and their daily food. Jesus added another level of meaning to the bread: his body given for us.

Can we, as Christians, allow the bread of which we partake, the body of Christ, to be made of wheat grown with the use of pesticides and chemical fertilizers? Pesticides can cause cancer, and the run-off from chemical fertilizers upsets the chemical balance in many lakes, causing blue-green algae, for example. But there is good news: more and more parishes and dioceses insist that the hosts they use are made from organically grown wheat. In 2012, the Sisters of Saint Clare in Valleyfield, Quebec, agreed to use only organic flour in the making of altar breads, a first in Canada!

WINE

For the apostles sitting around the table with Jesus, the wine made from grapes was the product of the vine, the result of human labour, and a drink for celebrations. Jesus added another level of meaning to the wine: his blood shed for us.

So, Jesus took the daily food of bread, and he took the drink reserved for special occasions: wine. This wine, in all likelihood, was produced locally or regionally. It was transported to market in a cart pulled by a donkey. Today, wine can travel great distances before arriving at our table. In eastern Canada, almost all parishes use an altar wine from California, 4,000 kilometres away. The farther it travels, the more greenhouse gases are emitted by the trucks carrying it, which traps heat in the atmosphere and leads to radical changes in climate. The place of origin of the wine we buy has an impact on the quality of life of future generations. Parishes and dioceses can consider buying wine from local or regional vineyards. The *Côtes d'Ardoise* vineyard in Durham, Quebec, for example, offers both a red and a white wine that were officially approved as sacramental wine by the bishop of Saint-Hyacinthe in May 2011.

Norman Lévesque, *Greening Your Church: A Practical Guide to Creation Care Ministry for Parishes, Dioceses and Religious Communities* (Novalis: Toronto, 2014), pp. 47-49.

HOLY COMMUNION: RECEIVED BY ALL OUR SENSES

Whether it has been a month or decades since our First Communion, it is good to remember that when we receive Christ in Communion, it should involve our whole person and all our senses.

Cyril, a fourth-century patriarch of Jerusalem, gave great advice to the newly baptized on how to receive the sacrament: "In approaching therefore, come not with your wrists extended, or your fingers spread; but make your left hand a throne for the right, so as to receive a King." He then described how we are made holy by the touch of the sacred species on our hands and by looking at it with our eyes. He also talked about receiving from the cup: "Draw near also to the cup of his Blood; not stretching forth your hands, but bending, and saying with an air of worship and reverence, Amen." The key is that Communion is something received by all of our senses.

What does this mean? First, our whole person should be focused, with an attitude of reception. When we do something repeatedly, it becomes easy to think of it as a given. Even with something as special as Communion, we need to work to ensure that Communion is not taken for granted. Here are some specific suggestions.

During the week, we should spend time preparing for Communion: praying, being reconciled – including sacramental reconciliation – and doing works of justice. We also prepare by fasting for at least an hour before receiving Communion.

During Mass, we should keep Communion in mind throughout the celebration. The Introductory Rites are there in part to prepare us for Communion. So, too, the readings, the Homily, the Creed, the intercessions and the Eucharistic Prayer. We should pay special attention to the elements of the Communion Rite. This includes everything from the Lord's Prayer to the Communion Antiphon, offering moments that encourage us to prepare both with the community and in personal prayer.

Once Communion begins, we praise God for the Eucharist by singing. The Communion Chant starts as the priest receives Communion and should last until the end of Communion. The Communion procession engages our whole person in an attitude of reception, in union with the whole Church in the great parade that will one day end in the heavenly banquet. Once we reach the altar area, some form of reverence, such as a small bow, is required. This varies from diocese to diocese.

Receiving Communion should engage our heart and mind, but also our senses. Think about what is happening. If you receive in the hand, offer both hands, with the one that will lift the host to your lips supporting the hand where the host is placed. It is important that you not wear gloves, both for practical reasons and because part of the experience of receiving the sacrament is the sense of touch. Reverently consume the sacred species. If you receive on the tongue, make sure there is no danger of the host falling. Should the host fall to the ground, the minister of Communion will know to set it aside and see that it is dealt with in an appropriate manner. Should the precious Blood fall to the floor, the floor is to be rinsed with water, which is then disposed of in an appropriate manner. To avoid this, when receiving from the chalice, take the cup in your hands. The minister of Communion may also keep hold. It is important not to let reverent fear keep us from the full experience of Communion.

Those not receiving Communion — for whatever reason — are not mentioned in the ritual. In some places they are encouraged to come forward for a blessing, indicating this by crossing their hands across their chests.

After Communion, we can of course kneel in personal prayer, but in many places people are now encouraged to stand and sing until everyone has received Communion. Being called to this assembly and to receive Communion, again, as Cyril tells us, is having been "deemed worthy by the Holy Spirit." As the holy family of chosen ones, we stand and praise God.

For the rest of Sunday and during the week, we should pause from time to time in our prayer to remember that we have been fed by Jesus, our God. Whether in adoration in church or being aware of this before we have lunch, we can better see that God is reaching out to us every day, feeding us and guiding us home.

Novalis Staff

MUSIC DURING THE LITURGY

The General Instruction of the Roman Missal (GIRM) is the set of instructions that governs the celebration of the Eucharist. It was updated in 2001, as a result of reflection on the 40 years of experience since Vatican II, and came into force in Canada with the coming of the new translation of the missal.

Perhaps one of the most interesting and least known contributions of the new GIRM is its reflection on the role of singing in the liturgy. It offers a genuine theology of music at Mass, with insights into the role of the choir, the ministry of the cantor, and the meaning of various chants in the liturgy.

The GIRM places the singing of the assembly at the very centre of its reflection. All musical choices are at the service of helping the assembly to sing. In this short article, I offer some commentary on the three major moments of singing and on the closing moments of the mass.

THE ENTRANCE CHANT

When the people are gathered, and as the Priest enters with the Deacon and ministers, the Entrance Chant begins. Its purpose is to:

1. open the celebration,

2. foster the unity of those who have been gathered,

3. introduce their thoughts to the mystery of the liturgical time or festivity, and

4. accompany the procession of the Priest and ministers.

This chant is sung

- alternately by the choir and the people or
- similarly by a cantor and the people, or
- entirely by the people,
- or by the choir alone.

In the dioceses of Canada the Entrance Chant may be chosen from among the following:

- the antiphon with its Psalm from the Graduale Romanum or the Graduale Simplex, or
- another chant that is suited to the sacred action, the day, or the time of year, and whose text has been approved by the Conference of Bishops of Canada.

The Entrance chant's most important function is to open the celebration. Thus, the singing of the assembly is the genuine beginning of the Mass (as opposed to the priest's sign of the cross) This beginning has the further ritual purpose of fostering unity and focusing attention. Only as a function of all these things does it accompany the procession.

How to foster unity and focus attention? The manner of singing proposed by the GIRM offers some significant clues: the preferred manner is call and response (i.e. dialogue) between choir/cantor and assembly. This use of dialogue singing creates a dynamic of ritual interaction that brings participants together into one body; dialogical singing is also more engaging and dramatic while being easy on the people, since they need only remember a refrain or response, which also allows them to be attentive to what is going on. This dynamic of practical community building and fostering attentiveness can also be achieved by having the entire group sing together, but then attention ought to be paid to how the musical quality of the chant awakens feelings of presence and joy. Only as a last resort ought the choir to sing alone, and even then the musical selection ought to foster unity and focus attention rather than promoting the passivity of the assembly.

The GIRM mentions here the Graduale Romanum and the Graduale Simplex; these are collections of antiphons for the Church year which are to be used with seasonal psalms. The entrance and communion antiphons we see in our missals come from the Graduale Romanum. This focus reflects the GIRM's overall concern for singing TEXTS. This can provide a helpful clue for the selection of appropriate music. The idea is to choose music not according to a unifying "theme" for the whole liturgy, but to express the various texts of the liturgy. For example:

- *when trying to find an appropriate processional chant to open the liturgy, and assuming that one is not looking to sing the antiphon with a seasonal psalm, one might ask: does this antiphon text re-*

mind me of a hymn, or are its images reminiscent of a particular song?

- *rather than think of how all the songs express the same theme, think of reproducing the way in which the collect, antiphons, scripture texts and so on "bounce off" each other with contrasting or complementary images and musical ideas.*

THE OFFERTORY CHANT

The procession bringing the gifts is accompanied by the Offertory Chant, which continues at least until the gifts have been placed on the altar. The norms on the manner of singing are the same as for the Entrance Chant. Singing may always accompany the rite at the Offertory, even when there is no procession with the gifts.

The question to ask here is: what is the mystery to which the thoughts of the assembly ought to be introduced, even as the song fosters their unity and opens a new time in the celebration? The mystery in question is that of the Eucharist about to be celebrated. So a chant or hymn that helps people focus on the mystery of the Eucharist as meal and sacrifice of thanksgiving, and opens the people up to offering themselves to God with the gifts, in light of the Word's proclamation in this liturgy, is most appropriate here.

Note that the GIRM refers back to the manner of singing outlined for the Entrance Chant: first in order of

*preference, dialogue between assembly and cantor/
choir, then people as one, and lastly choir alone.*

AT COMMUNION TIME

While the Priest is receiving the Sacrament, the
Communion Chant is begun, its purpose being

- to express the spiritual union of the communicants by means of the unity of their voices,

- to show gladness of heart, and

- to bring out more clearly the "communitarian"
  character of the procession to receive the Eucharist.

The singing is prolonged for as long as the Sacrament
is being administered to the faithful. However, if
there is to be a hymn after Communion, the Communion Chant should be ended in a timely manner.

Care should be taken that singers, too, can receive
Communion with ease.

In the dioceses of Canada singing at Communion
may be chosen from among the following: the antiphon from the Graduale Romanum, with or without
the Psalm, or the antiphon with Psalm from the
Graduale Simplex, or some other suitable liturgical
chant approved by the Conference of Bishops of
Canada. This is sung either

- by the choir alone or

- by the choir or a cantor with the people.

Notice the shift in the purpose and role of singing during the Communion procession.

Notice also that this is the only place where the choir is given preference over the assembly as the main ministers of singing, although the most important purpose is still to express the union of the communicants by the unity of their voices.

Notice, finally, that the singing is tightly linked to the procession, and should end when the procession ends. A second chant or hymn is envisaged as a possibility, but as we see below, it has a different purpose and should be clearly separated from the processional chant by a short time of silence.

When the distribution of Communion is over, if appropriate, the Priest and faithful pray quietly for some time. If desired, a Psalm or other canticle of praise or a hymn may also be sung by the whole congregation.

The psalm or canticle of praise is a time for the assembly to give thanks WITH ONE VOICE, as is indicated by the reference to the whole congregation. Keep in mind the importance given to silence in the liturgy; there needn't always be a thanksgiving after Communion, and certainly, people should have the opportunity to pray silently between the Communion processional and the thanksgiving chant.

AT THE END OF THE MASS

To the Concluding Rites belong the following:

a) brief announcements, should they be necessary;

b) the Priest's Greeting and Blessing, which on certain days and occasions is expanded and expressed by the Prayer over the People or another more solemn formula;

c) the Dismissal of the people by the Deacon or the Priest, so that each may go back to doing good works, praising and blessing God;

d) the kissing of the altar by the Priest and the Deacon, followed by a profound bow to the altar by the Priest, the Deacon, and the other ministers.

There is no rubric for a song of sending forth; in Canada, the custom has been to have such a song, and the suggestion is that this song should be in the spirit of the dismissal over the people: "going out to do good works, praising and blessing God." The song should be short and should end just as the procession leaves the Church proper. This ensures that the energy of the dismissal and sending out is not lost.

Alternatively, this would be a good time to feature an organ piece or a more complex choir piece, something that is energetic and helps people go forth in the spirit of the dismissal.

Fr. Gilles Mongeau, SJ
Contributing Editor, *Living with Christ*

TRADITIONAL PRAYERS

HAIL MARY
Hail Mary, full of grace, the Lord is with thee. Blessed art thou among women and blessed is the fruit of thy womb, Jesus.

Holy Mary, Mother of God, pray for us sinners, now and at the hour of our death. Amen.

GLORY BE TO THE FATHER
Glory be to the Father, and to the Son, and to the Holy Spirit. As it was in the beginning, is now, and ever shall be, world without end. Amen.

COME, HOLY SPIRIT
Come, Holy Spirit, fill the hearts of your faithful and kindle in them the fire of your love. Send forth your Spirit, O Lord, and renew the face of the earth. Amen.

ACT OF FAITH
O my God, I firmly believe that you are one God in three divine Persons, Father, Son, and Holy Spirit. I believe that your divine Son became man, died for our sins, and that he will come to judge the living and the dead. I believe these and all the truths which the holy Catholic Church teaches, because you have revealed them, who can neither deceive nor be deceived. Amen.

ACT OF HOPE

O my God, relying on your almighty power and infinite mercy and promises, I hope to obtain pardon of my sins, the help of your grace, and life everlasting through the merits of Jesus Christ, my Lord and Redeemer. Amen.

ACT OF LOVE

O my God, I love you above all things, with my whole heart and soul, because you are all good and worthy of all love. I love my neighbour as myself for the love of you. I forgive all who have injured me, and ask pardon of all whom I have injured. Amen.

DIVINE PRAISES

Blessed be God.
Blessed be his holy name.

Blessed be Jesus Christ, true God and true man.
Blessed be the name of Jesus.
Blessed be his most sacred heart.
Blessed be his most precious blood.
Blessed be Jesus in the sacrament of the altar.

Blessed be the Holy Spirit, the Paraclete.

Blessed be the Mother of God, Mary most holy.
Blessed be her holy and immaculate conception.
Blessed be her glorious assumption.
Blessed be the name of Mary, virgin and mother.

Blessed be Saint Joseph, her most chaste spouse.
Blessed be God in his angels and in his saints.

ANGELUS

The angel of the Lord declared unto Mary, and she conceived of the Holy Spirit. *Hail Mary...*

Behold, the handmaid of the Lord; be it done to me according to your word. *Hail Mary...*

And the word was made flesh, and dwelt among us. *Hail Mary...*

Pray for us, O holy Mother of God; that we may be made worthy of the promises of Christ.

Pour forth, we beseech you, O Lord, your grace into our hearts that we, to whom the incarnation of your Son was made known by the message of an angel, may by his passion and cross be brought to the glory of his resurrection. We ask this through the same Christ, our Lord. Amen.

REGINA CAELI

O Queen of heaven, rejoice, alleluia!
For he whom you chose to bear, alleluia!
Is risen as he said, alleluia!
Pray for us to God, alleluia!
Rejoice and be glad, O Virgin Mary, alleluia!
For the Lord is truly risen, alleluia!

O God, by the resurrection of your Son, our Lord, you were pleased to make glad the whole world. Grant, we beseech you, that through the intercession of the Virgin Mary, his mother, we may attain the joys of everlasting life, through the same Christ our Lord. Amen.

HAIL, HOLY QUEEN

Hail, holy Queen, mother of mercy, our life, our sweetness and our hope. To you we cry, poor banished children of Eve. To you we send up our sighs, mourning and weeping in this valley of tears. Turn then, most gracious advocate, your eyes of mercy upon us, and after this, our exile, show unto us the blessed fruit of your womb, Jesus. O clement, O loving, O kind Virgin Mary.

MEMORARE

Remember, O most gracious Virgin Mary, that never was it known that anyone who fled to thy protection, implored thy help or sought thy intercession, was left unaided. Inspired with this confidence, I fly unto thee, O Virgin of virgins my Mother; to thee I come, before thee I stand, sinful and sorrowful; O Mother of the Word Incarnate, despise not my petitions, but in thy mercy hear and answer me. Amen.

MAGNIFICAT

My soul proclaims the greatness of the Lord, my spirit rejoices in God my Saviour; for he has looked with favour on his lowly servant.

From this day all generations will call me blessed: the Almighty has done great things for me, and holy is his Name.

He has mercy on those who fear him in every generation. He has shown the strength of his arm, he has scattered the proud in their conceit.

He has cast down the mighty from their thrones, and has lifted up the lowly. He has filled the hungry with good things, and the rich he has sent away empty.

He has come to the help of his servant Israel for he has remembered his promise of mercy, the promise he made to our fathers, to Abraham and his children forever.

ICEL

PRAYER TO SAINT JOSEPH

O Saint Joseph, whose protection is so great, so strong, so prompt before the throne of God, I place in thee all my interests and desires. O Saint Joseph, assist me by thy powerful intercessions and obtain for me all spiritual blessings through thy foster Son, Jesus Christ Our Lord, so that, having engaged here below thy heavenly power, I may offer my thanksgiving and homage.

O Saint Joseph, I never weary contemplating thee and Jesus asleep in thine arms. I dare not approach while he reposes near thy heart. Press him in my name and kiss his fine head for me, and ask him to return the kiss when I draw my dying breath.

Saint Joseph, patron of departing souls, pray for me. Amen.

THE ROSARY

In the Rosary we focus on 20 events or mysteries in the life and death of Jesus and meditate on how we share with Mary in the redemptive work of Christ. Reading a pertinent passage from the Bible helps to deepen meditation on a particular mystery. The scriptural references given here are not exhaustive. In many instances, other biblical texts are equally suitable for meditation.

~ Begin the Rosary at the crucifix by praying the Apostles' Creed (p. 13)
~ At each large bead, pray the Lord's Prayer
~ At each small bead, pray the Hail Mary
~ At the first three beads it is customary to pray a Hail Mary for each of the gifts of faith, hope, and love
~ For each mystery, begin with the Lord's Prayer, then recite the Hail Mary ten times, and end with Glory Be to the Father.

The Five Joyful Mysteries:

The Annunciation (Luke 1.26-38)
The Visitation (Luke 1.39-56)
The Nativity (Luke 2.1-20)
The Presentation (Luke 2.22-38)
The Finding in the Temple (Luke 2.41-52)

The Five Mysteries of Light:
The Baptism in the Jordan (Matthew 3.13-17)
   The Wedding at Cana (John 2.1-12)
   The Proclamation of the Kingdom (Mark 1.15)
   The Transfiguration (Luke 9.28-36)
   The First Eucharist (Matthew 26.26-29)

The Five Sorrowful Mysteries:
The Agony in the Garden (Matthew 26.36-56)
   The Scourging at the Pillar (Matthew 27.20-26)
   The Crowning with Thorns (Matthew 27.27-30)
   The Carrying of the Cross (Matthew 27.31-33)
   The Crucifixion (Matthew 27.34-60)

The Five Glorious Mysteries:
The Resurrection (John 20.1-18)
   The Ascension (Acts 1.9-11)
   The Descent of the Holy Spirit (John 20.19-23)
   The Assumption of Mary (John 11.26)
   The Crowning of Mary (Philippians 2.1-11)

THE STATIONS OF THE CROSS
(Traditional version)

PRAYER BEFORE EACH STATION:
We adore you, O Christ, and we praise you, because by your holy cross you have redeemed the world.

1. JESUS IS CONDEMNED TO DEATH

Consider how Jesus, having been scourged and crowned with thorns, is unjustly condemned by Pilate to death on a cross.

2. JESUS TAKES UP HIS CROSS

Consider how Jesus, bearing this cross on his shoulders, offers his suffering to the Father for us.

3. JESUS FALLS FOR THE FIRST TIME

Consider this first fall. Jesus, bleeding, crowned with thorns, so weak he can hardly walk, yet forced to carry this heavy burden. The soldiers strike him and he falls.

4. JESUS MEETS HIS MOTHER

Consider this meeting between mother and son... their tender love for one another, their hearts torn asunder.

5. SIMON HELPS JESUS CARRY THE CROSS

Consider how the torturers force the bystander Simon to carry Jesus' cross. They want Jesus to stay alive long enough to die crucified.

6. VERONICA WIPES JESUS' FACE

Consider how Veronica recognizes Jesus' pain and attempts to lessen his suffering.

7. JESUS FALLS FOR THE SECOND TIME

Consider this second fall. It reopens his wounds, hurts his head, pains his whole body.

8. THE WOMEN OF JERUSALEM WEEP FOR JESUS

Consider how these compassionate women wept at the sight of the tortured Jesus.

9. JESUS FALLS FOR THE THIRD TIME

Consider this third fall. Though extremely weak, Jesus is urged on by the soldiers.

10. JESUS IS STRIPPED OF HIS GARMENTS

Consider the violence with which the soldiers tear off the bloody garments which cling to his broken skin and start the wounds bleeding again.

11. JESUS IS NAILED TO THE CROSS

Consider how Jesus, arms extended on the cross, offers to his Father the ultimate sacrifice for our salvation.

12. JESUS DIES ON THE CROSS

Consider how Jesus, after hours of agony and anguish on the cross, abandons himself to the Father and dies.

13. JESUS IS REMOVED FROM THE CROSS

Consider how two disciples take the broken body down from the cross and place Jesus in his grieving mother's arms.

14. JESUS IS PLACED IN THE TOMB

Consider how the disciples, filled with grief, carry the body to the burial place. They close the tomb and come away confused and sorrowful.

THE WAY OF THE CROSS

(Revised version: The Sacred Congregation for Divine Worship recommends that the traditional Stations be revised to emphasize that the sufferings and resurrection of Christ are one redemptive mystery.)

OPENING PRAYER

Lord Jesus, all of your life led up to the Way of the Cross. In this final journey you lay down your life for your friends.

Jesus, you consider us your friends. You walk side by side with us on the journey of life. You know its joys and hopes, its suffering and pain. Today we want to walk side by side with you on your way to the Cross. Your suffering, your death, your rising from the dead give meaning to our lives. The way of the Cross is the way of life.

Lord, as you took the bread, your body, take us, bless us, break us, give us to others, so that in you we may be instruments of salvation for the world. **Amen.**

1. THE LAST SUPPER

Jesus said to them, "I have wanted so much to eat this Passover meal with you before I suffer! For I tell you, I will never eat it until it is given its full meaning in the Kingdom of God."

Then Jesus took a cup, gave thanks to God, and said, "Take this and share it among yourselves. I tell you that from now on I will not drink this wine until the Kingdom of God comes."

Then he took a loaf of bread, gave thanks to God, broke it, and gave it to them, saying, "This is my body, which is given for you. Do this in memory of me." In the same way, he gave them the cup after supper, saying, "This cup is God's new covenant sealed with my blood, which is poured out for you." *(Luke 22.15-20)*

Jesus, you love us. Make us realize we are a covenant people, make our Eucharists moments when we feel your friendship, so that we may live this out for all humankind.

2. IN THE GARDEN OF GETHSEMANE

Then Jesus went with his disciples to a place called Gethsemane, and said to them, "Sit here while I go over there and pray." He took with him Peter and the two sons of Zebedee. Grief and anguish came over him, and he said to them, "The sorrow in my heart is so great that it almost crushes me. Stay here and keep watch with me." *(Matthew 26.36-38)*

Jesus, you love us. Comfort us in times of distress. Help us to see beyond ourselves; help us to overcome the feeling of senseless chaos; help us to see the joy and hope of those who truly suffer and who truly believe. Remind us of your covenant of friendship with us.

3. BEFORE THE SANHEDRIN

Jesus was taken to the High Priest's house, where the chief priests, the elders, and the teachers of the Law were gathering. Peter followed at a distance and went into the courtyard, where he sat down with the guards, keeping himself warm by the fire. The chief priests and the whole Council tried to find some evidence against Jesus in order to put him to death, but they could not find any. *(Mark 14.53-55)*

Jesus, you love us. Help us live out your covenant of friendship; give us strength to stand against authorities who exercise power for evil. Make us nonviolent, but strong in this struggle for humankind. Jesus, strengthen us.

4. BEFORE PONTIUS PILATE

Early in the morning Jesus was taken from Caiaphas' house to the governor's palace. The Jewish authorities did not go inside the palace, for they wanted to keep themselves ritually clean in order to be able to eat the Passover meal. So Pilate went outside to them and asked, "What do you accuse this man of?" Their answer was, "We would not have brought him to you if he had not committed a crime." *(John 18.28-30)*

Jesus, you love us. You stand with the victims in this world. Is that one meaning of the covenant for us: that we too should side with the oppressed against the oppressor? Lord, this is hard for us, teach us how to side with the oppressed, with the victims.

5. THE WHIPPING AND CROWNING WITH THORNS

Then Pilate took Jesus and had him whipped. The soldiers made a crown of thorny branches, put it on his head, then put a purple robe on him. They came to him and said, "Long live the King of the Jews!" and slapped him. *(John 19.1-3)*

Jesus, you love us. Turn our sympathies to the poor victims of desperate soldiers all over the world. Empower us to stop the sale of arms to ruthless armies. Show us the way to curb senseless attacks by states against their own people. Jesus, teach us how to resist evil.

6. THE CARRYING OF THE CROSS

So they took charge of Jesus. He went out, carrying his cross, and came to the 'Place of the Skull,' as it is called. (In Hebrew it is called 'Golgotha.') *(John 19.16-17)*

Jesus, you love us. Your love for us affirms the goodness of our humanity. We are the friends for whom you suffered. Teach us to respect others, not to dismiss or diminish them as less human.

7. SIMON OF CYRENE

On the way they met a man named Simon, who was coming into the city from the country. The soldiers forced him to carry Jesus' cross. *(Mark 15.21)*

Jesus, you love us. We don't like carrying crosses, but many times our cross is of our own making. It is a self-centred cross. Help us find the true cross in the lives of the poor. Help us to help carry their burden. Jesus, help us!

8. THE WOMEN OF JERUSALEM

A large crowd of people followed him; among them were some women who were weeping and wailing for him. Jesus turned to them and said, "Women of Jerusalem! Do not cry for me, but for yourselves and your children. For the days are coming when people will say, 'How lucky are the women who never had children, who never bore babies, who never nursed them!' " *(Luke 23.27-31)*

Jesus, you love us. Allow us to comfort the grieving women of our time. But even more, enable us to prevent their grief, which so often could be avoided. Help us to break down the human systems which starve and kill. Jesus, make us angry about this unnecessary grief and suffering. Teach us to weep, knowing all the time that tears are never enough.

9. THE STRIPPING AND CRUCIFIXION

They came to a place called Golgotha, which means 'Place of the Skull.' There they offered Jesus wine mixed with a bitter substance; but after tasting it, he would not drink it.

They crucified him and then divided his clothes among them by throwing dice. *(Matthew 27.33-35)*

Jesus, you love us. Stripped naked, nailed to the cross, you have given your all for us. Jesus, help us break the bonds of our selfishness and materialism. Show us how we can give our life for others, in your covenant.

10. THE SECOND THIEF

One of the criminals hanging there hurled insults at him: "Aren't you the Messiah? Save yourself and us!"

The other one, however, rebuked him, saying, "Don't you fear God? You received the same sentence he did. Ours, however, is only right because we are getting what we deserve; but he has done no wrong." And he said to Jesus, "Remember me, Jesus, when you come as King!"

Jesus said to him, "I promise you that today you will be in Paradise with me." *(Luke 23.39-43)*

Jesus, you love us. Impress on us that the lives we live, the work we do, have consequences for others. Awaken our awareness to real evil and real faith. Help us honour your covenant of friendship in our lives.

11. MARY AND JOHN

Standing close to Jesus' cross were his mother, his mother's sister, Mary the wife of Clopas, and Mary Magdalene. Jesus saw his mother and the disciple he loved standing there; so he said to his mother, "He is your son."

Then he said to the disciple, "She is your mother." From that time the disciple took her to live in his home. *(John 19.25-27)*

Jesus, you love us. You gave us your mother Mary as our own mother. Touch our hearts with her sorrow at your death. Lift our eyes so we may see in her the beauty of your covenant; the beauty of her gift of herself to you and to us.

12. DEATH ON THE CROSS

But when they came to Jesus, they saw that he was already dead, so they did not break his legs. One of the soldiers, however, plunged his spear into Jesus' side, and at once blood and water poured out. *(John 19.33-34)*

Jesus, you love us. Teach us your way. Give us the wisdom to recognize evil. Give us the courage to confront it, to struggle against it, so that we may truly be your friends.

13. THE NEW SEPULCHRE

When it was evening, a rich man from Arimathea arrived; his name was Joseph, and he also was a disciple of Jesus. He went to Pilate and asked for the body of Jesus. Pilate gave orders for the body to be given to Joseph. So Joseph took it, wrapped it in a new linen sheet, and placed it in his own tomb which he had just recently dug out of solid rock. Then he rolled a large stone across the entrance to the tomb and went away. *(Matthew 27.57-60)*

Jesus, you love us. Help us to distinguish justice and charity. Sometimes it is easier to do charity than to do justice. Let us know which should be our response and when, in our lives. Give us the grace to act charitably and justly.

14. THE RESURRECTION

Very early on Sunday morning the women went to the tomb, carrying the spices they had prepared. They found the stone rolled away from the entrance to the tomb, so they went in; but they did not find the body of the Lord Jesus. *(Luke 24.1-3)*

Jesus, you love us. You have returned from the dead to be with us. Be our promise, our hope that all evil will be overcome. Bless us with full life for all humankind, under your covenant.

FINAL PRAYER

We know that Christ has been raised from death and will never die again — death will no longer rule over him. And so, because he died, sin has no power over him; and now he lives his life in fellowship with God. In the same way, you are to think of yourselves as dead, so far as sin is concerned, but living in fellowship with God through Christ Jesus. *(Romans 6.9-11)*

Father, your only Son gave up his life for us, his friends. Help us understand the meaning of that friendship. Help us grow in that friendship.

We are a weak and distracted people. Often we neglect you, but you never abandon us. You love us. Make us a less selfish and a more caring people. Help us to share the crosses of others, as Simon did. Show us how to live your covenant of friendship day by day with the victims and the poor of this world. Father, we depend on you.

We pray this through Jesus, the Christ, your Son who has risen from the dead. Amen.

PRAYING WITH THE EUCHARIST

ANIMA CHRISTI *(Soul of Christ)*

Soul of Christ, sanctify me.
Body of Christ, heal me.
Blood of Christ, drench me.
Water from the side of Christ, wash me.
Passion of Christ, strengthen me.
Good Jesus, hear me.
In your wounds shelter me.
From turning away keep me.
From the evil one protect me.
At the hour of death call me.
Into your presence lead me,
to praise you with all your saints
for ever and ever. Amen.

* * *

My Lord, I offer Thee myself in turn as a sacrifice of thanksgiving. Thou hast died for me, and I in turn make myself over to Thee. I am not my own. Thou hast bought me; I will by my own act and deed complete the purchase. My wish is to be separated from everything of this world; to cleanse myself simply from sin; to put away from me even what is innocent, if used for its own sake, and not for Thine. I put away reputation and honour, and influence, and power, for my praise and strength shall be in Thee. Enable me to carry on what I profess. Amen.

Blessed John Henry Newman

I believe Thou art present in the Blessed Sacrament, O Jesus. I love Thee and desire Thee. Come into my heart. I embrace Thee, O never leave me. I beseech Thee, O Lord Jesus, may the burning and most sweet power of Thy love absorb my mind, that I may die through love of Thy love, Who wast graciously pleased to die through love of my love.

Saint Francis of Assisi

***

Lord Jesus, Who in the Eucharist make your dwelling among us and become our traveling companion, sustain our Christian communities so that they may be ever more open to listening and accepting your Word. May they draw from the Eucharist a renewed commitment to spreading in society, by the proclamation of your Gospel, the signs and deeds of an attentive and active charity.

Saint John Paul II

AN ACT OF SPIRITUAL COMMUNION

My Jesus, I believe that you are present in the most Blessed Sacrament. I love You above all things and I desire to receive You into my soul. Since I cannot now receive You sacramentally, come at least spiritually into my heart. I embrace You as if You have already come, and unite myself wholly to You. Never permit me to be separated from You. Amen.

Saint Alphonsus Liguori

INSPIRATION FROM THE SAINTS

LIVING HOPE

Consult not your fears but your hopes and your dreams. Think not about your frustrations, but about your unfulfilled potential. Concern yourself not with what you tried and failed in, but with what it is still possible for you to do.

Saint John XXIII

SEEKING JESUS

It is Jesus that you seek when you dream of happiness; He is waiting for you when nothing else you find satisfies you; He is the beauty to which you are so attracted; it is He who provoked you with that thirst for fullness that will not let you settle for compromise; it is He who urges you to shed the masks of a false life; it is He who reads in your heart your most genuine choices, the choices that others try to stifle.

It is Jesus who stirs in you the desire to do something great with your lives, the will to follow an ideal, the refusal to allow yourselves to be ground down by mediocrity, the courage to commit yourselves humbly and patiently to improving yourselves and society, making the world more human.

Saint John Paul II, World Youth Day, August 19, 2000

GOD'S HANDIWORK

It is with the smallest brushes that the artist paints the most exquisitely beautiful pictures.

Saint André Bessette

PRAYER OF ST. THOMAS AQUINAS

Grant me, O Lord my God,
a mind to know you,
a heart to seek you,
wisdom to find you,
conduct pleasing to you,
faithful perseverance in waiting for you,
and a hope of finally embracing you.

Saint Thomas Aquinas

DOING GOD'S WILL

Lord Jesus, teach me to be generous;
teach me to serve you as you deserve;
to give and not count the cost,
to fight and not heed the wounds,
to toil and not seek for rest,
to labour and not to seek reward,
except that of knowing that I do your will.

Saint Ignatius Loyola

* * *

Give me, Lord, a full faith, a firm hope and a fervent love, a love for you incomparably above the love of myself. These things, good Lord, that I pray for, give me your grace also to labour for.

Saint Thomas More

THE PEACE PRAYER OF ST. FRANCIS

Lord, make me an instrument of your peace.
Where there is hatred let me sow love;
where there is injury, pardon;
where there is doubt, faith;
where there is despair, hope;
where there is darkness, light;
and where there is sadness, joy.

Divine Master,
grant that I may not so much seek
to be consoled as to console,
to be understood as to understand,
to be loved as to love.

For it is in giving that we receive,
in pardoning that we are pardoned,
and in dying that we are brought to eternal life.

Unknown, ca. 1915

IN SERVICE TO GOD

Govern everything by your wisdom, O Lord,
so that my soul may always be serving you
in the way you will
and not as I choose.
Let me die to myself so that I may serve you;
let me live to you who are life itself.

Saint Teresa of Avila

God doesn't ask for the impossible, but wants everyone to offer their good intentions, their day's work, and some prayers: that will help them a lot. The best Way of the Cross is when people accept willingly the crosses that are sent to them.

Saint André Bessette

The lover gives her life gladly for the beloved. She does not know her own interests or even her own needs. Sickness and health, prosperity and adversity, life and death, consolation and desolation are alike to her.

Saint Marguerite Bourgeoys

Give something, however small, to the one in need. For it is not small to one who has nothing. Neither is it small to God, if we have given what we could.

Saint Gregory Nazianzen

The Eucharist is the heart of the Christian religion. It is an ineffable mystery that embraces the untold depths of divine love, and in which God bestows upon us all blessings and graces.

Saint Francis de Sales

PRAYERS FOR CEMETERY VISITS

PSALM 23 — THE DIVINE SHEPHERD
The Lord is my shepherd, I shall not want.
He makes me lie down in green pastures;
he leads me beside still waters;
he restores my soul.
He leads me in right paths
for his name's sake.

Even though I walk through the darkest valley,
I fear no evil;
for you are with me;
your rod and your staff —
they comfort me.

You prepare a table before me
in the presence of my enemies;
you anoint my head with oil;
my cup overflows.

Surely goodness and mercy shall follow me
all the days of my life,
and I shall dwell in the house of the Lord
my whole life long.

ETERNAL REST
Eternal rest grant unto them, O Lord,
and let perpetual light shine upon them.
May the souls of the faithful departed,
through the mercy of God,
rest in peace. Amen.

DE PROFUNDIS *(Psalm 130)*

Out of the depths I cry to You, O Lord;
Lord, hear my voice.
Let Your ears be attentive
to my voice in supplication.
If You, O Lord, mark iniquities,
Lord, who can stand?
But with You is forgiveness,
that You may be revered.

I trust in the Lord;
my soul trusts in His word.
My soul waits for the Lord
more than sentinels wait for the dawn.
More than sentinels wait for the dawn,
let Israel wait for the Lord,

For with the Lord is kindness
and with Him is plenteous redemption;
And He will redeem Israel
from all their iniquities.

* * *

Lord, support us all the day long,
until the shadows lengthen
    and the evening comes,
and the busy world is hushed
and the fever of life is over
and our work is done.
Then in thy mercy grant us
a safe lodging,
and a holy rest,
and peace at the last.

Blessed John Henry Newman

ENCOUNTERING GRIEF AND LOSS

We cannot protect ourselves or our children from loss. It is part of the human experience, be it the death of a loved one, the erosion of health or the devastation of divorce. The way to deal with it, and eventually find healing, is through grieving. Over the centuries, humans have devised a number of rituals to move through and past the stages of mourning. Over time, they restore a sense of peace, even if the hole in our lives is never completely filled again.

At such times prayer can either flow freely out of the depth of our pain or remain stilted and stifled due to anger or depression. Praying our way through grief, loss or disappointment sharpens our recognition of God's presence in even the most distressing aspects of life.

The people of the Bible understood that all prayers can and should be brought to God – even those of anger, grief and disappointment. Thus, more than a third of the Book of Psalms are laments. In addition, an entire book in the Old Testament – the Book of Lamentations – is devoted to these sorrowful prayers. At times they are full of complaints and self-pity. Other times they are full of devastation and despair, as those offering them deal with death, exile and the fear of abandonment. God hears them all.

Biblical prayers of lament are comprised of five components. Each one can be adapted within the family as a way to express the grief, disappointment, heartache or hopelessness that we experience personally or that we see happening in the world around us.

1. INVOKING GOD'S PRESENCE.

To invoke means to "call upon" and is a form of supplication. We address God in a way that represents our understanding of God in the midst of our distress. While any form of prayer can include an invocation, prayers of lament use those that express desperation or longing, such as "My God, my God, why have you forsaken me?" (Psalm 22.1), the psalm that Jesus prayed while dying on the cross.

2. NAMING THE GRIEF, LOSS OR DISAPPOINTMENT WE ARE SUFFERING.

Imagine what it would be like to have your city, your home and everything you cherish destroyed. This is the agonizing situation of the Hebrew people during the destruction of Jerusalem and its temple in the sixth century BC. *"Look and see our disgrace!...We have become orphans, fatherless; our mothers are like widows"* (Lamentations 5.1, 3). The familial images in this cry of mourning are especially touching. They speak of loss, abandonment and the surrender of all hope. Many of us were taught "polite" prayers that were devoid of any complaints or expressions of anger or disappointment. Prayers of lament aren't polite; they're *real*. Encouraging children and adolescents to bring all of their hurts, fears, disillusionment, anger and concerns to God fosters deeper intimacy and uncovers the meaning of true faith.

3. EXPRESSING CONFIDENCE OR TRUST IN GOD'S RESPONSIVE LOVE.

I am fond of calling the Psalms a book of mixed emotions. Take Psalm 139. It's my favourite psalm, one that extols God for his wonderful works, including the intricacies of the human person. Without warning, it takes off on a rant about *"hating those who hate you..."* (verse 21). Then it turns round again with the plea, *"Search me, O God, and know my heart; test me and know my thoughts"* (verse 23). Troubled prayers often end up a jumble of emotions. While they may run the gamut from despair to delight, God's constancy remains intact. This does not mean we will reach this stage of lament in a single prayer. It comes with time and attentiveness as we hold onto hope in God's unconditional love.

4. REQUESTING EXPLICIT HELP FOR OUR TROUBLES.

Biblical writers didn't beat around the bush. They knew what they needed and asked God for it in no uncertain terms, even if it sounds horribly cruel and vengeful. Psalm 139 asks God to *"kill the wicked,"* and the writer of Lamentations asks for *"anguish of heart"* (3.65) as payback for those who wrought such destruction on Jerusalem. As parents, we're understandably wary of encouraging our children to pray in such violent terms. Nevertheless, there is a human need to give voice to our hurts and frustration without smothering them in platitudes. The help we request might be the cultivation of compassion, understanding, tolerance or hope. Doing so expands our capacity for empathy. It also offers a way to cope with injustice without denying it, nor of excusing abusive behaviour on the part of others.

5. PRAISING GOD FOR BRINGING US THROUGH OUR LAMENT.

One of the most mysterious aspects of the Christian faith is our belief in resurrection – of life coming out of death, light emanating from darkness. Anyone who has found "grace in the wound" knows that we stand to learn much from the suffering in our lives. This last component of lamentation has to come in its own time and cannot be rushed or forced. This is especially important to remember when we are tempted to press a child beyond a hurtful situation before he or she is ready. [...] Helping children move through the stages of lament provides a way to both name their feelings about what is wrong with the world, as well as to imagine how things could be better.

Kathy Hendricks, *Prayers and Rituals for the Home: Celebrating the Life and Times of Your Family* (Toronto: Novalis, 2013), pp. 92-95.

PRAYER IN THE MORNING

INVITATION TO PRAYER
Lord, open our lips.
And we shall proclaim your praise.
Glory to God in the highest.
And peace to God's people on earth.

HYMN OF PRAISE *(Optional)*

PSALM OF PRAISE
Psalm 63 and/or another psalm of praise, followed by a moment of silence.

My soul thirsts for you, O Lord my God.

R. My soul thirsts for you, O Lord my God.

O God, you are my God, I · **seek_you**,
my soul · **thirsts_for_you;**
my flesh · **faints_for_you,**
as in a dry and weary land
    where there · **is** no water. **R.**

So I have looked upon you in the · **sanctuary,**
beholding your power and · **glory.**
Because your steadfast love is better than · **life,**
my · **lips** will praise_you. **R.**

So I will bless you as long as I · **live;**
I will lift up my hands and call on your · **name.**
My soul is satisfied as with a rich · **feast,**
and my mouth praises you
    with · **joy**-ful lips. R.

For you have been my · **help,**
and in the shadow of your wings I sing for · **joy.**
My soul · **clings_to_you;**
your right · **hand** up-holds_me. R.

Glory to the Father, and to the · **Son,**
and to the Holy · **Spirit.**
As it was in the be-·**ginning,**
is now and will be for · **ever.** A-men. R.

©2009 Gordon Johnston/Novalis

PSALM PRAYER (Optional)

Lord our God, Fountain of refreshing love, in morning light we seek your presence and strength, for your love is better than life itself. Accept our prayers with uplifted hands as we proclaim your praise in songs of joy. Satisfy our longing hearts and renew our thirsting spirits that our worship may give you glory and our lives be poured out in loving service.

Glory and praise to you, loving God, through our Lord Jesus Christ, your Son, who lives and reigns with you in the unity of the Holy Spirit, God for ever and ever. **Amen.**

WORD OF GOD

Appropriate verse(s) selected beforehand from the readings of the day, followed by a moment of silence.

CANTICLE OF ZECHARIAH

1. Blessed be the God of Israel,
   Who comes to set us free,
   Who visits and redeems us,
   And grants us liberty.
   The prophets spoke of mercy,
   Of freedom and release;
   God shall fulfill the promise
   To bring our people peace.

2. Now from the house of David
   A child of grace is giv'n;
   A Saviour comes among us
   To raise us up to heaven.
   Before him goes the herald,
   Forerunner in the way:
   The prophet of salvation,
   The messenger of Day.

3. Where once were fear and darkness
   The sun begins to rise,
   The dawning of forgiveness
   Upon the sinners' eyes,
   To guide the feet of pilgrims
   Along the paths of peace:
   O bless our God and Saviour
   With songs that never cease!

Text: Michael Perry, ©*1973 Hope Publishing Co.*
Tune: MERLE'S TUNE, *76.76.D.;* ©*1983 Hope Publishing Co.* Used by per mission. All rights reserved. **Music:** *CBW III* 13E

PETITIONS

These reflect the needs of the Church, the world, the suffering, and the local community. Weekly suggestions are available at www.livingwithchrist.ca

OUR FATHER...

CONCLUDING PRAYER

God of glory and compassion, at your touch the wilderness blossoms, broken lives are made whole, and fearful hearts grow strong in faith. Open our eyes to your presence and awaken our hearts to sing your praise. To all who long for your Son's return grant perseverance and patience, that we may announce in word and deed the good news of the kingdom.

We ask this through our Lord Jesus Christ, your Son, who lives and reigns with you in the unity of the Holy Spirit, God for ever and ever. **Amen.**

BLESSING

May the Lord almighty order our days and our deeds in lasting peace. **Amen.**

Let us offer each other a sign of Christ's peace.

The celebration ends with the exchange of peace.

* * *

For a fuller version of the Liturgy of the Hours, consult the Living with Christ *missalette.*

PRAYER IN THE EVENING

The paschal candle is lit and carried in procession. During Advent, the Advent wreath may be lit instead. If you plan to use Psalm 141, prepare the thurible beforehand so that incense may be burned during the singing of the psalm.

INVITATION TO PRAYER

God, come to our assistance.
Lord, make haste to help us.
Glory to the Father, and to the Son,
and to the Holy Spirit.
**As it was in the beginning, is now,
and will be forever. Amen.**

HYMN OF PRAISE *(Optional)*

PSALM OF PRAISE

Psalm 141 and/or another psalm of praise, followed by a moment of silence.

Let my prayer a - rise like   in-cense be-fore you.

R̸. **Let my prayer arise like incense before you.**

I call upon you, O Lord: come quickly to · **me;**
give ear to my voice when I call to · **you.**
Let my prayer be counted as incense be-·**fore_you.**
and the lifting up of my hands as
    an eve-·**ning** sacrifice. R̸.

Set a guard over my mouth, O · **Lord;**
keep watch over the door of my · **lips.**
But my eyes are turned toward you,
 O God, my · **Lord;**
in you I seek refuge; do not leave me
 · **de-**fenceless. ℞.

Glory to the Father, and to the · **Son,**
and to the Holy · **Spirit.**
As it was in the be-·**ginning,**
is now and will be for ever. · **A-men.** ℞.

©2008 Gordon Johnston/Novalis

PSALM PRAYER *(Optional)*
Loving God, creator of light and life, may our prayers
ascend to you like the fragrance of incense. Purify
our hearts to sing your praise in the company of your
saints in glory.
 We ask this through Christ our Lord. **Amen.**

WORD OF GOD
*Appropriate verse(s) selected beforehand from the readings of
the day, followed by a moment of silence.*

CANTICLE OF MARY
1. My soul proclaims the Lord my God.
 My spirit sings God's praise,
 Who looks on me and lifts me up,
 That gladness fill my days.

2. All nations now will share my joy,
   For gifts God has outpoured.
   This lowly one has been made great
   I magnify the Lord.

3. For those who fear the Holy One,
   God's mercy will not die,
   Whose strong right arm puts down the proud,
   And lifts the lowly high.

4. God fills the hungry with good things,
   And sends the rich away.
   The promise made to Abraham,
   Is filled to endless day.

5. Then let all nations praise our God,
   The Father and the Son,
   The Spirit blest who lives in us,
   While endless ages run.

Text: Anne Carter, ©*1988 Religious of the Sacred Heart.*
Tune: HEATHER DEW **Music:** *CBW III* 592, 617; *CBW II 74,* 589

PETITIONS
These reflect the needs of the Church, the world, the suffering, and the local community. Weekly suggestions are available at www.livingwithchrist.ca

OUR FATHER...

CONCLUDING PRAYER

Creator of the universe, watch over us and keep us in the light of your presence. May our praise continually blend with that of all creation, until we come together to the eternal joys which you promise in your love.

We ask this through our Lord Jesus Christ, your Son, who lives and reigns with you in the unity of the Holy Spirit, God for ever and ever. **Amen.**

BLESSING

May God the Father almighty bless and keep us. **Amen.**

May Jesus Christ, his only Son, our Lord, graciously smile upon us. **Amen.**

May the Holy Spirit, the Lord and giver of life, grant us peace. **Amen.**

Let us offer each other a sign of Christ's peace.

The celebration ends with the exchange of peace.

* * *

For a fuller version of the Liturgy of the Hours, consult the Living with Christ *missalette.*

CELEBRATING THE SACRAMENT OF RECONCILIATION

When ready to celebrate the sacrament of Reconciliation (Confession), the following steps are involved.

BEFOREHAND

Examination of Conscience (p. 640):

Pray to the Holy Spirit for light and strength, examine your conscience in the light of the Scriptures and the Commandments since your last confession and become truly sorry for your sins.

GOING TO CONFESSION

Welcome:

The priest welcomes you, the penitent. It is helpful if you indicate the time of your last Confession and anything else that will help the priest hearing your confession.

Scripture:

A short passage of Scripture may be read.

Confession:

Confess your sins and listen to the advice of the priest.

Penance:

The priest proposes a good action or prayer to help make up for sin and deepen virtue.

Prayer of Sorrow (Act of Contrition – p. 642):

Pray expressing personal sorrow and asking for forgiveness.

Absolution:
The priest grants absolution in the name of God and the Church.

Praise of God and Dismissal:
The priest invites you to praise God and dismisses you with the command to go in peace.

AFTERWARD
Spend some time in thanking God for forgiving us and restoring us to full life in Christ.

EXAMINATION OF CONSCIENCE

Do I centre my life on God, on fidelity to the Gospel and the Commandments? Do I set aside time for personal prayer?

Do I keep Sunday by participating in the Eucharist?

Is Sunday a day of prayer and rest? Do I observe the penitential practices of the Church? Do I keep Lent as a time of prayer and sacrifice?

Do I behave as a Christian in daily and public life? Is my faith reflected in my employment?

Have I taken property of others including my employer?

Am I envious of what others have? Do I share my goods and time with those in need? Do I respect the reputation of others?

Do I care for my family? Do I model Christian life for my family: parents, wife, husband, children?

Do I exercise authority with genuine concern and responsibility? Do I give others the same respect that I expect for myself?

Have I dishonoured my body by thoughts or actions incompatible with Christian life? Am I faithful to my marriage? Do I set an example of committed single living?

Do I live out my commitments to my spouse and my children to the best of my ability and reflect God's love and faithfulness?

How do I deal with the difficulties, failures and disappointments of life?

Do I tend to the spiritual, physical and medical needs of my body? Can others see the grace of Baptism at work in my life?

ACT OF CONTRITION

My God,
I am sorry for my sins with all my heart.
In choosing to do wrong
and failing to do good,
I have sinned against you
whom I should love above all things.
I firmly intend, with your help,
to do penance,
to sin no more,
and to avoid whatever leads me to sin.
Our Saviour Jesus Christ
suffered and died for us.
In his name, my God, have mercy.

Excerpted from *Celebrating Reconciliation*
(Ottawa: Concacan Inc., 2006).

EUCHARISTIC ADORATION

Adoration is an act of faith and a gesture of love. Adoration is a "heart to heart" with God, a period of time presented with utter gratuity. By offering up my presence, I participate in the great offering of Jesus, that is, his life handed over "for the glory of God and the salvation of the world."

I SALUTE WITH A GESTURE OF RESPECT

I bow slowly or I genuflect as a sign of respect in front of the tabernacle or before the Blessed Sacrament exposed on the altar.

I DISPOSE MY BEING

To put myself in a state of recollection, I choose to sit or kneel. I close my eyes or I look at the host, a tangible sign of the presence of Christ.

In order to make a prayer of adoration I must be silent within myself; I must remove any sources of distractions which bother me or prevent me from letting God take over. I stop thinking of my tasks, my uncertainties, my fears, my goals of any sort.

I let go of all the concerns of the present moment to let God fill me with his love.

I am here, present, simply, freely, before the holy Eucharistic presence; I expect nothing in return and make no particular request for anything.

I am here, happy to be here, in the name of love and in the name of the Church.

I SPEND TIME

To completely enter an attitude of offering, openness, adoration, forgetting oneself is not the work of just a few minutes; so I take the time to experience this heart-to-heart in a spirit of recollection for 20, 30 or even 60 minutes.

Nathalie Dumas. Reproduced from *Saint Joseph's Oratory Prayer Book* (Toronto: Novalis, 2017). © Novalis / Saint Joseph's Oratory of Mount Royal.

PRAYERS FOR ADORATION

Loving Jesus,

I am filled with gratitude for the privilege of this
   quiet time in your Presence.

Grant me strength to go out from this place of
   sacred silence into the busy world.

May my experience of your Presence here
help me to see your Presence there –

in the faces of the lonely and seeking souls I meet,
in the outstretched hands of the poor and needy,
in the hearts of my family and my dearest friends,
in the eyes of those who are most difficult
   and hard for me to bear.

As I experience your Presence in your beloved ones,
may I act with love and generosity so that they may
   also experience it in me. Amen.

Christine Way Skinner

Dear Jesus,

here present in the Blessed Sacrament,
I know you are always with me throughout the day
and night,
but in this special time, help me to turn my mind
and heart to you.

As I pray, first of all I want to offer you praise and
glory
for inviting me to be a member of your family
through Baptism
and for enabling me to grow in your love
by receiving your Body and Blood in the Holy
Eucharist.

Secondly, I wish to thank you for watching over me
and guiding me
as I go about my daily activities.

Thirdly, I ask for forgiveness for the many times
when I fail to accept and follow your guidance —
the times when my weak human nature yields
to temptation.

Fourthly, I petition and ask for your special help
in the numerous difficult situations and problems
that I seem to encounter so often.

Without you I can do nothing.
I'm sure that not long after I leave you
here in this Eucharistic presence,
I will be calling on your special help again.
Please listen to my petitions

and grant those which will help me become more
  pleasing in your sight.

I offer this prayer to you, Our Lord Jesus,
who live and reign with the Father and the Holy
  Spirit forever and ever.

Amen.

Norbert Oberle

Excerpted from *Prayers and Devotions for Eucharistic
Adoration* (Toronto: Novalis, 2016), pp. 66, 69-70.

KYRIE – PENITENTIAL ACT, FORM 1

Presider/Cantor *Assembly*

Ky-ri-e, e-le-i-son. Ky-ri-e, e-le-i-son.

Presider/Cantor *Assembly*

Chris-te, e-le-i-son. Chris-te, e-le-i-son.

Presider/Cantor *Assembly*

Ky-ri-e, e-le-i-son. Ky-ri-e, e-le-i-son.

Assembly

Ky-ri-e, e-le-i-son.

or

Presider/Cantor *Assembly*

Lord, have mer-cy. Lord, have mer-cy.

Presider/Cantor *Assembly*

Christ, have mer-cy. Christ, have mer-cy.

Presider/Cantor *Assembly*

Lord, have mer-cy. Lord, have mer-cy.

Text and setting: *Excerpts from Chants of the Roman Missal
© 2010 ICEL. Used with permission.*

KYRIE – PENITENTIAL ACT, FORM 2

Presider/Cantor

Have mercy on us, O Lord.

Assembly

For we have sinned a-gainst you.

Presider/Cantor

Show us, O Lord, your mer - cy.

Assembly

And grant us your sal - va - tion.

Text and setting: *Excerpts from Chants of the Roman Missal* © 2010 ICEL. Used with permission.

KYRIE – PENITENTIAL ACT, FORM 3

Presider/Cantor

You were sent to heal the contrite of heart:

Assembly

Lord, have mer-cy. Lord, have mer-cy.

or

Kyrie, e - le - i - son. Kyrie, e - le - i - son.

Presider/Cantor

You came to call sin - ners:

Assembly

Christ, have mer-cy. Christ, have mer-cy.

or

Christe, e - le - i - son. Christe, e - le - i - son.

Presider/Cantor

You are seated at the right hand of the Father
to inter - cede for us:

Assembly

Lord, have mer-cy. Lord, have mer-cy.

or

Kyrie, e - le - i - son. Kyrie, e - le - i - son.

Text and setting: *Excerpts from Chants of the Roman Missal*
© 2010 ICEL. Used with permission.

GLORIA

Glory to God in the high - est,

and on earth peace to people of good will.

We praise you, we bless you, we a - dore you,

we glo - ri - fy you,

we give you thanks for your great glo - ry,

Lord God, heav - en - ly King,

O God, al - might - y Fa - ther.

Lord Je - sus Christ, Only Be - got - ten Son,

Lord God, Lamb of God, Son of the Fa - ther,

you take away the sins of the world,

have mer - cy on us;

GLORIA *(continue)*

you take away the sins of the world,

re - ceive our prayer;

you are seated at the right hand of the Fa-ther,

have mer - cy on us.

For you alone are the Ho - ly One,

you a - lone are the Lord,

you alone are the Most High, Je - sus Christ,

with the Ho - ly Spir - it,

in the glory of God the Fa-ther. A - men.

Music: *Anonymous.* **Text:** *Excerpts from Chants of the Roman Missal © 2010 ICEL. Used with permission.*

HOLY, HOLY, HOLY

Ho-ly, Ho-ly, Ho-ly Lord God of hosts.

Heav-en and earth are full of your glo-ry.

Ho-san-na in the high-est. Bless-ed is he

who comes in the name of the Lord.

Ho - san - na in the high - est.

Text and setting: *Excerpts from Chants of the Roman Missal*
© 2010 ICEL. Used with permission.

MEMORIAL ACCLAMATIONS

We pro-claim your Death, O Lord,

and pro-fess your Res-ur-rec-tion

un-til you come a-gain.

or

When we eat this Bread and drink this Cup,

we pro-claim your Death, O Lord,

un-til you come a-gain.

or

Save us, Sav-iour of the world,

for by your Cross and Res-ur-rec-tion

you have set us free.

Text and setting: *Excerpts from Chants of the Roman Missal*
© 2010 ICEL. Used with permission.

LAMB OF GOD

Lamb of God,

you take a - way the sins of the world,

have mer - cy on us.

Lamb of God,

you take a - way the sins of the world,

have mer - cy on us.

Lamb of God,

you take a - way the sins of the world,

Grant us peace.

Text and setting: *Excerpts from Chants of the Roman Missal* © 2010, ICEL. Used with permission.

Hymns

ON JORDAN'S BANK

1. On Jordan's bank the Baptist's cry
   Announces that the Lord is nigh;
   Awake and hearken, for he brings
   Glad tidings of the King of kings!

2. Then cleansed be ev'ry life from sin;
   Make straight the way for God within;
   And let us all our hearts prepare
   For Christ to come and enter there.

3. We hail you as our Saviour, Lord,
   Our refuge and our great reward;
   Without your grace we waste away
   Like flow'rs that wither and decay.

4. Stretch forth your hand, our health restore,
   And make us rise to fall no more;
   O, let your face upon us shine
   And fill the world with love divine.

Text: *Jordanis oras praevis,* Charles Coffin, 1676-1749; tr. st. 1-3 John Chandler, 1806-76; st. 4 unknown; alt.
Tune: WINCHESTER NEW, LM **Music:** CBW II 443; CBW III 350

O COME, O COME EMMANUEL

1. O come, O come, Emmanuel,
   And ransom captive Israel
   That mourns in lonely exile here
   Until the Son of God appear.

Ref: Rejoice! Rejoice! Emmanuel shall come to you, O Israel.

2. O come, O Wisdom from on high,
   Who order all things mightily;
   To us the path of knowledge show,
   And teach us in your ways to go.

3. O come, O come, great Lord of might,
   Who to your tribes on Sinai's height
   In ancient times once gave the law,
   In cloud, and majesty, and awe.

4. O come, O rod of Jesse's stem,
   From ev'ry foe deliver them
   That trust your mighty pow'r to save,
   and give them vict'ry o'er the grave.

5. O come, O key of David, come
   And open wide our heav'nly home;
   Make safe the way that leads on high,
   And close the path to misery.

6. O come, O Dayspring from on high,
   And cheer us by your drawing nigh;
   Disperse the gloomy clouds of night,
   And death's dark shadow put to flight.

7. O come, Desire of nations, bind
   In one the hearts of humankind;
   O bid our sad divisions cease,
   And be for us our king of peace.

Text: *Veni, veni Emmanuel;* Latin 9th c.; tr. by John Mason
Neale, 1818-1866, alt. **Tune:** VENI, VENI EMMANUEL
Music: CBW II 440; CBW III 312

O COME, DIVINE MESSIAH!

1. O come, divine Messiah!
   The world in silence waits the day
   When hope shall sing its triumph,
   And sadness flee away.

Ref: Sweet Saviour, haste;
   Come, come to earth:
   Dispel the night, and show thy face,
   And bid us hail the dawn of grace.
   O come, divine Messiah,
   The world in silence waits the day
   When hope shall sing its triumph,
   And sadness flee away.

2. O thou, whom nations sighed for,
   Whom priests and prophets long foretold,
   Wilt break the captive fetters,
   Redeem the long-lost fold.

3. Shalt come in peace and meekness,
   And lowly will your cradle be:
   All clothed in human weakness
   Shall we thy God-head see.

Text: Abbé Pellegrin, 1663-1745; tr. Sr. Mary of St. Philip
Tune: VENEZ DIVIN MESSIE, 78.76.888 **Music:** CBW II 441; CBW III 310

WHAT CHILD IS THIS

1. What Child is this, who laid to rest,
    On Mary's lap is sleeping?
    Whom angels greet with anthems sweet,
    While shepherds watch are keeping?

Ref: This, this is Christ the King,
    Whom shepherds guard and angels sing:
    Haste, haste to bring him laud,
    The babe, the son of Mary.

2. Why lies he in such mean estate
    Where ox and ass are feeding?
    Good Christian, fear: for sinners here
    The silent Word is pleading.

3. So bring him incense, gold, and myrrh,
    Come, peasant, king to own him,
    The King of kings salvation brings,
    Let loving hearts enthrone him.

Text: William Chatterton Dix, 1837-1898 **Tune:** GREENSLEEVES,
87 87 with refrain **Music:** CBW II 461; CBW III 338

GOOD CHRISTIAN FRIENDS, REJOICE

Good Christian friends, rejoice
With heart and soul and voice;

1. O give heed to what we say:
    Jesus Christ was born today!
    Ox and ass before him bow,
    and he is in the manger now.
    Christ is born today!
    Christ is born today!

2. Now you hear of endless bliss:
Jesus Christ was born for this!
He has opened heaven's door,
And we are blest for ever more.
Christ was born for this!
Christ was born for this!

3. Now you need not fear the grave:
Jesus Christ was born to save!
Calls you one and calls you all
To gain his everlasting hall.
Christ was born to save!
Christ was born to save!

Text: *In dulci jubilo;* Latin and German, 14th c., tr. John Mason Neale, 1818-1866, alt. **Tune:** IN DULCI JUBILO; 66 77 77 55
Music: *CBW II 465; CBW III 322*

O COME, ALL YE FAITHFUL

1. O come, all ye faithful, joyful and triumphant,
O come ye, o come ye to Bethlehem;
Come and behold him, born the king of angels.

Ref: O come, let us adore him,
O come, let us adore him,
O come, let us adore him, Christ, the Lord!

2. Sing, choirs of angels, sing in exultation,
Sing, all ye citizens of heav'n above!
Glory to God in the highest.

3. Yea, Lord, we greet thee, born this happy morning,
Jesus, to thee be glory giv'n;
Word of the Father, now in flesh appearing.

Text: *Adeste, fideles;* John F. Wade, c. 1711-1786; tr. Frederick Oakley, 1802-80, alt. **Tune:** ADESTE, FIDELES, Irregular with refrain; John F. Wade, c. 1711-1786
Music: CBW II 458; CBW III 329

THE FIRST NOWELL

1. The first Nowell the angel did say
   Was to certain poor shepherds in fields as they lay;
   In fields where they lay, keeping their sheep,
   On a cold winter's night that was so deep.

Ref: Nowell, Nowell, Nowell, Nowell,
   born is the King of Israel.

2. They lookéd up and saw a star
   Shining in the east, beyond them far,
   And to the earth it gave great light
   And so it continued both day and night.

3. And by the light of that same star
   Three wise men came from country far;
   To seek for a king was their intent,
   And to follow the star wherever it went.

4. This star drew nigh to the northwest,
   O'er Bethlehem it took its rest,
   And there it did both stop and stay
   Right over the place where Jesus lay.

5. Then entered in those wise men three,
   Full reverently upon their knee,
   And offered there in his presence,
   Their gold and myrrh and frankincense.

6. Then let us all with one accord
   Sing praises to our heav'nly Lord:
   Who with the Father we adore
   And Spirit blest for evermore.

Text: English Carol, 17th c. **Tune:** THE FIRST NOWELL,
Irregular **Music:** CBW II 460; CBW III 344

TAKE UP YOUR CROSS

1. Take up your cross, the Saviour said,
   If you would my disciple be;
   Take up your cross with willing heart,
   And humbly follow after me.

2. Take up your cross, let not its weight
   Fill your weak spirit with alarm;
   His strength shall bear your spirit up,
   And brace your heart and nerve your arm.

3. Take up your cross, heed not the shame,
   And let your foolish heart be still;
   The Lord for you accepted death
   Upon a cross, on Calvary's hill.

4. Take up your cross, then, in his strength,
   And calmly every danger brave:
   It guides you to abundant life,
   And leads to vict'ry o'er the grave.

5. Take up your cross, and follow Christ,
   Nor think till death to lay it down;
   For only those who bear the cross
   May hope to wear the glorious crown.

Text: Charles W. Everest, 1814-1877, alt. **Tune:** ERHALT UNS,
HERR, LM **Music:** CBW II 481; CBW III 352

O SACRED HEAD SURROUNDED

1. O sacred head surrounded
   By crown of piercing thorn.
   O bleeding head, so wounded
   Reviled and put to scorn.
   The pow'r of death comes o'er you,
   The glow of life decays,
   Yet angel hosts adore you,
   And tremble as they gaze.

2. In this your bitter passion,
   Good Shepherd, think of me
   With your most sweet compassion,
   Unworthy though I be:
   Beneath your cross abiding
   For ever would I rest,
   In your dear love confiding,
   And with your presence blest.

3. Christ Jesus, we adore you,
   Our thorn-crowned Lord and King.
   We bow our heads before you,
   And to your cross we cling.
   Lord, give us strength to bear it
   With patience and with love,
   That we may truly merit
   A glorious crown above.

Text: Bernard of Clairvaux, v. 1, tr. Henry W. Baker, 1821-77; v. 2 & 3, tr. Arthur T. Russell, 1806-74, alt. **Tune:** PASSION CHORALE; 76 76 D; Hans Leo Hassler, 1564-1612
Music: CBW 11 491; CBW III 377

LORD, WHO THROUGHOUT THESE FORTY DAYS

1. Lord, who throughout these forty days
   For us did fast and pray,
   Teach us to overcome our sins
   And close by you to stay.

2. As you with Satan did contend
   And did the vict'ry win,
   O give us strength in you to fight,
   In you to conquer sin.

3. As you did hunger and did thirst,
   So teach us, gracious Lord,
   To die to self and so to live
   By your most holy word.

4. And through these days of penitence,
   and through your passion-tide,
   For evermore, in life and death,
   O Lord, with us abide.

5. Abide with us, that through this life
   Of doubts and hopes and pain
   An Easter of unending joy
   We may at last attain.

Text: Claudia F. Hernaman, 1838-98, in her *A Child's Book of Praise,* 1873, alt. **Tune:** ST. FLAVIAN, CM; adapted from Day's Psalter, 1562 **Music:** CBW II 482; CBW III 367

JESUS CHRIST IS RIS'N TODAY

1. Jesus Christ is ris'n today, Alleluia!
   Our triumphant holy day, Alleluia!
   Who did once upon the cross, Alleluia!
   Suffer to redeem our loss. Alleluia!

2. Hymns of praise then let us sing, Alleluia!
   Unto Christ our heav'nly king, Alleluia!
   Who endured the cross and grave, Alleluia!
   Sinners to redeem and save. Alleluia!

3. But the pains which he endured, Alleluia!
   Our salvation have procured; Alleluia!
   Now above the sky he's king, Alleluia!
   Where the angels ever sing. Alleluia!

4. Sing we to our God above, Alleluia!
   Praise eternal as his love, Alleluia!
   Praise him, now his might confess, Alleluia!
   Father, Son and Spirit bless. Alleluia!

Text: Lyra Davidica, 1708, alt. & others **Tune:** EASTER HYMN; 77
77 with Alleluias **Music:** CBW II 500; CBW III 389

O SONS AND DAUGHTERS

Ref: Alleluia, alleluia, alleluia!

1. O sons and daughters, let us sing!
   The king of heav'n, our glorious king,
   From death today rose triumphing. Alleluia!

2. That Easter morn, at break of day,
   The faithful women went their way,
   To seek the tomb where Jesus lay. Alleluia!

3. An angel clothed in white they see,
   Who sat and spoke unto the three,
   "Your Lord has gone to Galilee." Alleluia!

4. That night th'apostles met in fear;
   And Christ did in their midst appear,
   And said, "My peace be with you here." Alleluia!

5. How blest are they who have not seen,
   And yet whose faith has constant been,
   For they eternal life shall win. Alleluia!

6. On this most holy day of days,
   To God your hearts and voices raise,
   In laud and jubilee and praise. Alleluia!

Text: Jean Tisserand, †1494; tr. John Mason Neale, 1818-66, alt.
Tune: O FILII ET FILIAE 8 8 8 4 with Alleluias
Music: CBW II 506; CBW III 404

THE STRIFE IS O'ER

Ref: Alleluia, alleluia, alleluia!

1. The strife is o'er, the battle done;
   Now is the victor's triumph won;
   O let the song of praise be sung! Alleluia!

2. The pow'rs of sin have done their worst;
   But Jesus has his foes dispersed;
   Let shouts of joy and praise out-burst! Alleluia!

3. Lord, by the stripes which wounded you,
   From death's sting free your servants too,
   That we may live and sing to you. Alleluia!

4. On the third morn you rose again,
   Glorious in majesty to reign;
   O let us swell the joyful strain! Alleluia!

Text: *Finita iam sunt praelia,* Latin 12th c.; *Symphonia Sirenum Selectarum,* Cologne, 1695; tr. Francis Pott, 1832-1909, alt. **Tune:** VICTORY, 8 8 8 with Alleluias **Music:** CBW II 503; CBW III 395

THAT EASTER DAY WITH JOY WAS BRIGHT

1. That Easter day with joy was bright,
   The sun shone out with fairer light,
   Alleluia, alleluia!
   When to their longing eyes restored,
   The glad apostles saw their Lord.

Ref: Alleluia, alleluia, alleluia, alleluia, alleluia!

2. His risen flesh with radiance glowed;
   His wounded hands and feet he showed;
   Alleluia, alleluia!
   Those scars their solemn witness gave
   That Christ was risen from the grave.

3. O Jesus, in your gentleness,
   With constant love our hearts possess;
   Alleluia, alleluia!
   To you our lips will ever raise
   The tribute of our grateful praise.

4. O Lord of all, with us abide
   In this our joyful Eastertide;
   Alleluia, alleluia!
   From ev'ry weapon death can wield
   Your own redeemed for ever shield.

5. All praise to you, O risen Lord,
   Now by both heav'n and earth adored;
   Alleluia, alleluia!
   To God the Father equal praise,
   And Spirit blest our songs we raise.

Text: *Claro paschali gaudio;* Latin 5th c; tr. By John Mason Neal, 1818-1866; alt. **Tune:** LASST UNS ERFREUEN, LM with Alleluias **Music:** CBW II 507; CBW III 392

HAIL, HOLY QUEEN, ENTHRONED ABOVE

1. Hail, holy Queen, enthroned above, O Maria!
   Hail, Queen of mercy and of love, O Maria!

Ref: Triumph, all you cherubim,
   sing with us, you seraphim,
   Heav'n and earth resound the hymn:
   Salve, salve, salve, Regina!

2. Our life, our sweetness here below, O Maria!
   Our hope in sorrow and in woe, O Maria!

3. We honour you for Christ, your son, O Maria!
   Who has for us redemption won, O Maria!

Text: *Salve, Regina, mater misericordiae,* c. 1080; tr. from the
Roman Hymnal, 1884 **Tune:** SALVE, REGINA COELITUM, 84 84
with refrain **Music:** CBW II 610; CBW III 457

IMMACULATE MARY

1. Immaculate Mary, your praises we sing,
   You reign now in heaven with Jesus our king.

Ref: Ave, Ave, Ave, Maria!
   Ave, Ave, Ave, Maria!

2. In heaven, the blessed your glory proclaim;
   On earth, we your children invoke your fair name.

3. Your name is our power, your virtues our light;
   Your love is our comfort, your pleading our might.

4. We pray for our mother the Church upon earth,
   And bless, dearest lady, the land of our birth.

Text: Anon., in *Parochial Hymn Book,* Boston, 1897, rev. version of "Hail, Virgin of Virgins," by Jeremiah Cummings, 1814-
1866, in his *Songs for Catholic Schools,* 1860, alt.
Tune: LOURDES HYMN, 11 11 **Music:** CBW II 611: CBW III 463A

HOLY GOD, WE PRAISE YOUR NAME

1. Holy God, we praise your name;
   Lord of all, we bow before you.
   All on earth your sceptre claim;
   All in heav'n above adore you.
   Infinite your vast domain;
   Everlasting is your reign.

2. Hark, the glad celestial hymn
   Angel choirs above are raising:
   Cherubim and seraphim,
   In unceasing chorus praising,
   Fill the heav'ns with sweet accord:
   "Holy, holy, holy Lord!"

3. Lo, the apostolic train
   Joins your sacred name to hallow;
   Prophets swell the glad refrain,
   And the white-robed martyrs follow;
   And from morn to set of sun,
   Through the church the song goes on.

4. Holy Father, holy Son,
   Holy Spirit, three we name you,
   Though in essence only one;
   Undivided God, we claim you,
   And, adoring, bend the knee
   While we own the mystery.

Text: *Te Deum laudamus; tr.* Clarence Walworth, 1820-1900,
in *Catholic Psalmist,* 1858, alt. **Tune:** GROSSER GOTT, 7 8 7 8 77
Music: CBW II 631; CBW III 555

ALL PEOPLE THAT ON EARTH DO DWELL

1. All people that on earth do dwell,
   Sing to the Lord with cheerful voice;
   Him serve with mirth, his praise forth tell,
   Come we before him and rejoice.

2. Know that the Lord is God indeed;
   Without our aid he did us make;
   We are his folk, he does us feed,
   And for his sheep he does us take.

3. O enter then his gates with praise;
   Approach with joy his courts unto;
   Praise, laud, and bless his name always,
   For it is seemly so to do.

4. For why? The Lord our God is good:
   His mercy is for ever sure;
   His truth at all times firmly stood,
   And shall from age to age endure.

5. To Father, Son, and Holy Ghost,
   The God whom heav'n and earth adore,
   From us and from the angel host
   Be praise and glory evermore.

6. Praise God, from whom all blessings flow,
   Praise him, all creatures here below;
   Praise him above, you heav'nly host;
   Praise Father, Son, and Holy Ghost.

Text: Psalm 100; William Kethe, d. c. 1594; v. 6: Thomas Ken,
1637-1711 **Tune:** OLD HUNDREDTH, LM 8 8 8 8
Music: CBW II 621; CBW III 578

COME, HOLY SPIRIT

1. Come, Holy Spirit, Creator blest,
   And in our hearts take up your rest;
   Come with your grace and heav'nly aid
   To fill the hearts which you have made.

2. O Comforter, to you we cry,
   The heav'nly gift of God most high;
   The fount of life and fire of love,
   And sweet anointing from above.

3. To ev'ry sense your light impart,
   And shed your love in ev'ry heart.
   To our weak flesh your strength supply:
   Unfailing courage from on high.

4. O grant that we through you may come
   To know the Father and the Son,
   And hold with firm, unchanging faith
   That you are Spirit of them both.

5. Now let us praise Father and Son,
   And Holy Spirit, with them one;
   And may the Son on us bestow
   The gifts that from the Spirit flow.

Text: *Veni, Creator Spiritus,* anon., 9th c.; tr. by Edward
Caswall, 1814-1878, et al.; alt. **Tune:** LAMBILOTTE, LM
Music: CBW II 516; CBW III 416

FOR ALL THE SAINTS

1. For all the saints,
   Who from their labours rest,
   Who their great faith
   To all the world confessed,
   Your name, O Jesus,
   Be forever blest. Alleluia, alleluia.

2. You were their rock,
   Their fortress and their might,
   Their strength and solace
   In the well-fought fight,
   And in the darkness
   their unfailing light. Alleluia, alleluia.

3. O blest communion,
   Family divine,
   We live and struggle,
   You in glory shine;
   Yet all are one
   within God's great design. Alleluia, alleluia.

4. And when the strife
   Is fierce, the conflict long,
   Then from the distance
   Sounds the trumpet song,
   And hearts are bold again,
   And courage strong. Alleluia, alleluia.

Text: William How, 1823-1897 **Tune:** SINE NOMINE, 10 10 10 with Alleluias **Music:** CBW II 617; CBW III 449. SERVICE MUSIC

Music Index

SERVICE MUSIC

HYMNS